THE TULIP

BY THE SAME AUTHOR

GROWING THINGS

FOLIAGE

THE FLOWERING YEAR

GARDENING COMPANION

THE BORDER BOOK

THE NEW KITCHEN GARDEN

THE TULIP

ANNA PAVORD

BLOOMSBURY

Published by Bloomsbury Publishing, New York and London.
Distributed to the trade by St. Martin's Press

A CIP catalogue record for this book
is available from the Library of Congress

ISBN 1-58234-013-7

First published in Great Britain 1999 by Bloomsbury Publishing Plc.

First U.S. Edition 1999
10 9 8 7 6 5 4 3 2 1

Typeset in Great Britain by Selwood Systems, Midsomer Norton
Origination by Radstock Reproductions Ltd, Bath
Printed in Italy by Artegrafica S.p.A., Verona

CONTENTS

Dedicated to Valerie Finnis

INTRODUCTION

THE MOST interesting things in life often happen by accident. That is how I found myself one May sitting outside a taverna at Alikampos in the western half of Crete, with no guide book, no decent map, but an excellent collection of wild-flower books. I spoke little Greek and the village elders solemnly ranged around the table – high leather boots, thorn walking sticks, moustaches luxuriant enough to hide a family of mice – spoke even less English. Small cups of coffee, tots of lethal, white, home-made brandy and dishes of salted marrow seeds piled up around us as the books were passed around from hand to hand, all open at the picture of the same flower. It was *Tulipa bakeri*, named after the man, George Percival Baker, who first exhibited it at a Royal Horticultural Society show in 1895.

It is not a particularly showy flower, compared with the wild, seductive, flamboyant tulips of the Crimea and Central Asia. The Cretan tulip is mauve-purple, with a pronounced and well-defined yellow blotch at its base. The backs of the petals are washed over with a faintly green flush, the overlay which gives so many tulips the texture of the finest, most luscious satin. But for some reason, I'd set my heart on finding it and Crete was its only known habitat. Intermittently, the Alikampos elders set my flower books in front of me, opened at photographs of dragon arums, asphodels, and grape hyacinths. These, they indicated, they could

1

show me by the hundred. But no one knew the tulip. More brandy was brought on to compensate for the disappointment.

Then, after a rapid exchange in Greek, one of the elders and a small boy beckoned me over to the hired car that I had parked nearby. I thought that they might need a lift, so we set off down the hairpin bends of the no-through road that leads to this hill-top village. Obeying violent hand signals from the old man, we bumped down a track off the road, parked, walked further down the hill and arrived suddenly at a small whitewashed building, no more than twelve feet by ten feet, standing by a spring.

The old man unlocked the door and, with a magician's flourish, threw it open. It was a church of course, though I didn't know that until I stepped inside and saw the grave, elongated faces of a whole lexicon of saints staring out with pitted eyes from wall and ceiling. Eighth century, said the man, tracing the figures with the end of a beeswax candle. Byzantine. He lit the candle and I peered slowly round at the ancient saints, the dark ochre colours of the paintings disappearing and then coming to light again as the candle flame bent and flickered. It was a weird moment: expecting tulips and finding frescoes instead.

Indirectly, the saints led to the tulip, for the small boy, left outside sitting on a rock, had hijacked a passer-by and showed *him* the picture of the flower that I was looking for. 'Omalós,' he said triumphantly as we emerged. 'Omalós,' he said again, pointing at the picture and then somewhere to the west, way over the horizon. The next day I drove myself to Omalós, along narrow roads lined with clouds of blue scabious and heads of wild oats and barley. The backdrop was gargantuan: stony mountain peaks with thick flanks of snow.

Omalós is a bleak town set high on a pancake plain, imprisoned between walls of mountain. The plain was nibbled bare by sheep. It was so quiet that you could hear the seed pods of the wild spurges popping in the heat. I quartered the ground like a blood hound, cheered at finding anemones in all colours, the wild forebears of the florist's 'De Caen'. It seemed likely that where there were anemones, there might also be tulips.

Without realising how much ground I had covered, I found after an hour or so that I was almost halfway up the mountain. The snow-line was clearly visible. I wanted to touch the snow and the track was easy. I calculated that it would take no more than a hour of climbing to get there. When I reached the snow, I found crocus on its melting edges. Even higher were flat, rock-hugging mats of an alpine anchusa, the flowers dazzling blue amongst the leaves. But no tulips.

AD TE LEVAVI OCVLOS MEOS
QVI HABITAS IN CÆLIS ·ECCE SI
CVT OCVLI SERVORVM·IN MA
NIBVS DOMINORVM SVORVM·
SICVT OCVLI ANCILLÆ IN MA
NIBVS DOMINÆ SVÆ ET CÆT,

Tulip and Larkspur
by Joris Hoefnagel c1590

3

At the top, I threw a snowball at an eagle before beginning a descent very much more rapid than the upward climb had been. Then, as I mooched back to the car, *Tulipa bakeri* suddenly sprang into view. I thought it was a mirage, but no. While I had been flailing up the 'because-it's-there' route, they had been flowering in an area mercifully fenced off from grazing animals, on the old olive terraces of the Omalós plain. They were growing in thin, poor grassland, their shiny leaves poking out from sheaves of anemones, with orchids thrown in for good measure, as well as the strange pale-green-and-black flowers of *Hermodactylus tuberosus*. I gazed at them in respectful – no, more than that – in reverent silence. I could find nothing suitable to say. This was the first time I had seen tulips growing in the wild. I knew how Galahad must have felt when he finally caught up with the Grail.

At this moment, I happily recognised an obsession that had been creeping up on me for some time. I suppose there must be one or two people in the world who choose not to like tulips, but such an aberration is scarcely credible. Who could resist *T. eichleri* from northern Iran, with its brilliant crimson-scarlet flowers, the petals nipping in slightly at the waist to finish in sharp needle points? The backs of the outer petals are washed over in greeny-buff, so in bud it looks very sober. Then it flings open its petals and reveals itself as the wildly sexy flower that it is. Who could not fall in love with the Cottage tulip 'Magier' as it opens its buds in May? The petals are a soft milky-white splashed with purple around the edges. As the flower ages, which it does gracefully and well (a worthwhile attribute) the whole thing darkens and purple leaches out from the edges through the entire surface of the petals. It is a mesmerising performance.

But as in any love affair, after the initial *coup de foudre* you want to learn more about the object of your passion. The tulip does not disappoint. Its background is full of more mysteries, dramas, dilemmas, disasters and triumphs than any besotted *aficionado* could reasonably expect. In the wild, it is an Eastern flower, growing along a corridor which stretches either side of the line of latitude 40 degrees north. The line extends from Ankara in Turkey eastwards through Jerevan and Baku to Turkmenistan, then on past Bukhara, Samarkand and Tashkent to the mountains of the Pamir-Alai, which, with neighbouring Tien Shan is the hotbed of the tulip family.

As far as western Europe is concerned, the tulip's story began in Turkey, from where in the mid sixteenth century, European travellers brought back news of the brilliant and until then unknown *lils rouges*, so prized by the Turks. In fact they were not lilies at all but tulips. In April 1559, the Zürich physician and botanist

Bloemstuk 1644 by Hans Bollongier (1600–1675)
Frans Halsmuseum Haarlem

Conrad Gesner saw the tulip flowering for the first time in the splendid garden made by Johannis Heinrich Herwart of Augsburg, Bavaria. He described its gleaming red petals and its sensuous scent in a book published two years later, the first known report of the flower growing in western Europe. The tulip, wrote Gesner, had 'sprung from a seed which had come from Constantinople or as others say from Cappadocia'. From that flower and from its wild cousins, gathered over the next 300 years from the steppes of Siberia, from Afghanistan, Chitral, Beirut and the Marmaris peninsula, from Isfahan, the Crimea and the Caucasus, came the cultivars which have been grown in gardens ever since. More than 5,500 different tulips are listed in the *International Register* published regularly since 1929 by the Royal General Bulbgrowers' Association in the Netherlands.

Holland was the setting for one of the strangest episodes in the long, mesmerising story of the tulip. The 'Tulipomania' that raged in Holland between 1634 and 1637 has puzzled historians and economists every since. How could it have ever happened that single bulbs of certain kinds of tulips could change hands for sums that would have secured a town house in the best quarter of Amsterdam? How was it possible that at the height of the tulip fever, a bulb of 'Admiral van Enkhuijsen' weighing 215 *azen*, could sell for 5,400 guilders, the equivalent of fifteen years' wages for the average Amsterdam bricklayer?[1]

Certain facts are brought forward to support less certain theories. The setting-up of the Dutch East India Company in 1602 and Amsterdam's increasing importance as a port, marked the beginning of an era of great prosperity for the Dutch. Merchants became rich, and in their wake, lawyers, doctors, pharmacists and jewellers did too. Adriaen Pauw, Lord of Heemstede, Keeper of the Great Seal of Holland and envoy of the States General to various foreign courts, was one of the directors of the new East India Company. His house, which was just outside Haarlem, stood in magnificent gardens where tulips grew clustered around a mirrored gazebo. The mirrors gave the illusion that the hundreds of blooms were thousands, for even Adriaen Pauw could not afford to plant thousands of tulips. For rich merchants, fountains, aviaries of rare birds and temples in the Greek style were standard accoutrements of the garden. But the tulip was the ultimate status symbol, the definitive emblem of how much you were worth. In the 1980s, the City trader's Porsche performed the same function, though in a cruder way. Among the many rare tulips in Pauw's garden was the entire known stock of 'Semper Augustus', the most beautifully marked of all the red and white striped tulips of the early seventeenth century. By the 1640s, when tulipomania was officially over, there were thought to be only twelve bulbs of 'Semper Augustus' still in existence, priced at 1,200 guilders each. This was the equivalent of three times the average annual wage in mid seventeenth-century Holland, perhaps £80,000 in modern-day terms.

If you could not afford the flowers themselves, you commissioned an artist such as Ambrosius Bosschaert or Balthasar van der Ast to paint tulips for you. Even the grand master of Dutch flower painting, Jan van Huysum, could rarely command more than 5,000 guilders for a painting. But a single bulb of the tulip 'Admiral Liefkens' changed hands for 4,400 guilders at an auction in Alkmaar on 5 February 1637, while 'Admiral van Enkhuijsen' was even more expensive at 5,400 guilders. The last of the big spenders bid at this auction of tulip bulbs: ninety-nine lots which realised 90,000 guilders, perhaps as much as £6 million in today's money. Because the sale was held in February, while the bulbs were still in the ground, each was sold by its weight at planting time, the weights recorded in *azen*. Offsets carry the same characteristics as their parents. That is why they were valuable. They were the equivalent of the interest earned on the capital invested in the bulb. Tulip seed, by comparison, usually produces a wide number of variations on the theme of the parent bulb.

Selling tulip bulbs by weight seemed sensible but the system contained the germs of its own destruction. Once the concept of the *azen* had taken hold, these *azens* could be traded on their own account, without the bulbs actually changing hands at all. The *azens* took on a 'futures' life of their own and the tulip itself in Zbigniew Herbert's words, 'grew pale, lost its colours and shapes, became an abstraction, a name, a symbol interchangeable with a certain amount of money'.[2] For this, tradesmen mortgaged their houses, weavers their looms. Many were bankrupted. Innkeepers flourished, for it was in the inns that most trading took place and the *drietje* or wine money was an integral part of each tulip deal.

In the end, there is no way to explain why tulip fever affected the solid, respectable burghers of Holland in such an aberrant way. They were possessed, obsessed by this flower with its intoxicating aura of the infidels who, as recently as 1529, had been battering at the gates of Vienna. And the flower itself had a unique trick which added dangerously to its other attractions. It could change colour, seemingly at will. A plain-coloured flower such as Councillor Herwart's red tulip, might emerge the following spring in a completely different guise, the petals feathered and flamed in intricate patterns of white and deep red. Seventeenth-century tulip lovers could not know that these 'breaks' were caused by a virus which was spread by aphids for the research that provided the answer to a mystery

A plate from the Hortus Eystettensis
*(1613) a record of the collection of flowers in the garden
of the Prince-Bishop of Eichstätt*

that had intrigued and ensnared tulip growers for centuries was only carried out in the late 1920s. Connoisseurs throughout Europe (and in the Ottoman Empire) had always rated 'broken' flowers more highly than plain-coloured ones. For that reason, the broken flowers were the ones that commanded outrageous prices. But out of a batch of a hundred tulips only one or two would turn their coats each year and emerge the following season with highly desirable 'feathered' or 'flamed' flowers. As all the bulbs received exactly the same treatment, no grower could fathom the reasons for these differences. Each broken flower, each superbly complex pattern was as original as a fingerprint. The virus was the joker in the tulip bed. Since its cause was for so long not known, its effects could not be controlled. Fortunately, once a bulb had broken, it remained broken and the offsets produced by the bulb carried the same characteristics. But the virus had the effect of weakening the tulip, so offsets were not produced so freely and vigorously as might be the case with a virus-free bulb. Consequently, fine broken varieties such as 'Semper Augustus' were slow to increase, and that in turn increased their value.

The virus works by partly suppressing the laid-on colour of a tulip, its anthocyanin, leaving the underlying colour, always white or yellow, to show through. The contrasting red or purple of a broken tulip looks as though it has been painted on the petals with a fine camel-hair brush. Sometimes the feathered and flamed markings make symmetrical patterns and these were always highly prized by tulip fanciers. The contrasting colours of a broken tulip are always sharply defined, the effect quite distinct from the indeterminate flushes of different colours displayed on the backs of tulips such as 'Prinses Irene' or the pink and white species, *T. clusiana*, the Lady Tulip. The base of a broken tulip always remains pure white or yellow. The contrast between the purity of the base and the patterned petals was an important criterion of excellence among the florists who, from the middle of the seventeenth century, cultivated the tulip as one of six florists' flowers, shown in keenly contested competition.

Deeply intrigued by the process of breaking and spurred on, no doubt, by the thought of the vast sums of money to be netted from a good break, early growers noted the characteristic effects of the virus on the tulip – the mottled leaves, the smaller flower, the reduced vigour of the plant – without ever being in a position to relate effects to cause.

The very word 'virus' was not understood in the modern sense[3] until the 1880s. Only the advent of the electron microscope in the late 1920s gave researchers the necessary means to unravel its true nature. Aided just by the evidence of their own

Flower Piece
by Ambrosius Bosschaert (1573–1621)
Rijksmuseum, Amsterdam

enquiring eyes, early growers had a thousand theories about the best way to bring about the magic break. Some charlatans sold miracle recipes for the purpose at a guinea a time. Some fools bought them. Pigeon dung was a favourite catalyst, as was plaster from old walls, and water that ran from dung hills. Some growers, taking their cue from contemporary alchemists, laid the desired colours in powdered paint on their tulip beds, expecting the colours somehow miraculously to transmute the flowers. It was no stranger than the alchemists' own attempts to turn base metal into gold. Indeed it was rather better, for while the alchemists consistently failed in their endeavours, it seemed that the tulip growers occasionally succeeded. They just did not know why.

Some old tulip growers tried cutting the bulbs of red-flowered tulips in half and binding them together with halves of bulbs of white-flowered tulips, hoping that a red and white striped tulip would result. It sounds crude, laughable even, but it was exactly by this means that the process of breaking was finally unravelled. It happened in 1928 when Dorothy Cayley (1874–1955), a mycologist at the John Innes Horticultural Institution in Merton, on the outskirts of London, grafted halves of tulip bulbs known to be 'broken' on to halves of the cochineal-red, Single Late tulip 'Bartigon' which were known to be unbroken. More than a quarter of the resulting flowers broke within the first year, a far higher proportion than in the control group. Earlier experiments on tulips at the John Innes Institute had been carried out by the botanist Dr E J Collins (1877–1939), who had suspected that aphids were the vectors, the carriers of the virus from bulb to bulb. He encouraged his pet aphids to gorge first on broken bulbs and then on bulbs that were presumed to be free of virus. Unfortunately, his experiments were inconclusive because the so-called clean bulbs of the control group actually contained tulips that were already broken. But the deliberately infected bulbs did break over the next three years at twice the normal rate. The aphid in question, the most effective one at least, was *Myzus persicae*, the peach potato aphid, which flourishes in warm situations surrounded by an abundance of fruit trees. Fruit trees in abundance were an outstanding feature of seventeenth-century gardens, and peach trees were particularly prevalent in the Eastern countries in which the tulip had its home. Although those early, observant gardeners realised that shifting their tulips into fresh soil often caused them to break more abundantly, none of them made the connection between the broken flowers, the fruit tree and its helpful, virus-inducing aphid.

The virus that affects the tulip is the only known instance of a plant disease

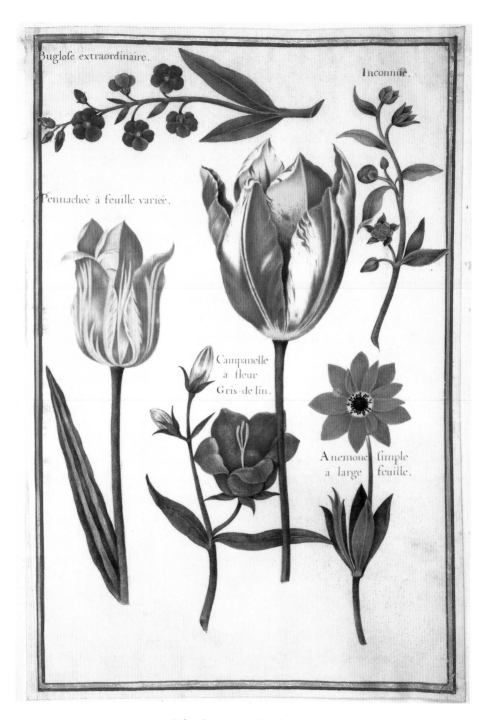

Buglofe extraordinaire.

Inconnüe.

Pennachée à feuille variée.

Campanelle
a fleur
Gris-de-lin.

Anemone fimple
a large feuille.

Tulips from Les Velins du Roi
by Nicolas Robert (1614–1685)

12

which hugely increases the value of the infected plant. Since the turn of the century, however, when the single-coloured, mass-market Darwin tulips began to dominate the scene, breeders have done all they can to prevent breaking. The tulip, prized and cherished through more than 300 years as a jewel flower, refined and exquisite, revered for its individual intricacy, was redefined as brightly coloured wallpaper. Fortunately, it knows how to rebel. The joker still lurks in the tulip bed.

History is often interpreted through the laws and the wars that helped to shape it. The greater part of the book that follows is concerned with the history of a flower, but a flower that has carried more political, social, economic, religious, intellectual and cultural baggage than any other on earth. For centuries, it has invaded people's lives, demanding – and getting – attention both in the Ottoman Empire and in most of the countries of Europe. Under the Stuarts for instance, England witnessed two civil wars, a regicide, a republic, a restoration, and a revolution in breathless succession. But what was the gardener and staunch Royalist, Sir Thomas Hanmer (1612–1678) of Bettisfield in Flintshire doing during this time? With one hand he was levying 200 supporters of the King to help him defend his patch in north Wales. With the other he was sending tulips to John Lambert (1619–1683), one of Cromwell's generals. Lambert, like Hanmer, a besotted tulip fancier, lived at Wimbledon Manor, where he had a renowned garden. Hanmer sent him 'a very great mother-root of Agate Hanmer', one of his best tulips, 'grideline [a greyish-purple], deep scarlet and pure white, commonly well parted, striped, agated and excellently placed, abiding constant to the last, with the bottom and stamens blue'.

Throughout the cataclysmic events of the seventeenth century, the comings and goings of kings and protectors, the Gunpowder Plot, the Plague, the Great Fire of London, the tulip reigned, untoppled, on its flowery throne. It was the most sought after, most precious plant of the seventeenth-century garden, the flower of the age, and like the age, intensely dramatic, prone to sudden change. This was not just in Britain. The tulip ruled all Europe, holding sway in the gardens of the Prince Bishops at Würzburg, Bavaria, and at Nymphenburg, Bavaria, the summer residence of the Electors; in the parterres at Schönbrunn, the Hapsburg palace in Vienna; in the Mirabelle Gardens originally built for Archbishop Dietrich outside the city walls of Salzburg; at Saint Cloud, Hauts-de-Seine in France where the Duc d'Orléans, brother of Louis XIV, employed the painter Nicolas Robert (1614–1685), to record his fabulous collection of tulips, variously described as *burinées, fouettées* and *pennachées*. Robert painted a striking, parti-coloured Parrot tulip of red, green and yellow; several red tulips, including the 'Jaspée de Haarlem', flared and streaked

Tulip by Jan van Huysum (1682–1749)
British Museum, London

with yellow; elegant pale creamy-white tulips, touched at the edges of their petals with pink, and a deep-pink tulip, perhaps a forerunner of the modern Lily-flowered types, pinched in very tightly at the waist and flaring out at the top, the petals tipped and streaked with green. Many of Gaston d'Orléans' treasures had been supplied by the Paris nurseryman, Pierre Morin, who had customers all over Europe.

From the late sixteenth century onwards, tulips, too, provided a map of the movements of the many people persecuted for their religious beliefs. Bulbs were valuable and they were eminently portable for refugee travellers. Like messages written in invisible ink, tulips emerged slowly in the new grounds that Flemish and French refugees were forced to seek in the wake of Philip II's Catholic crusades. In the second half of the sixteenth century, these Protestant Huguenots most probably brought the tulip into England from Flanders, for, long before the Dutch cornered the market, Flanders was the most important centre of tulip breeding in Europe. Many of the immigrants were weavers and some settled in Norwich, at that stage the third most important city in Britain. Others, such as the Flemish botanist Matthias de l'Obel (1538–1616), settled round Lime Street in the City of London. A second wave of French Huguenots, including Maximilien François Misson, arrived in England in the 1680s, escaping persecution by Louis XIV, and furthered a massive explosion of tulip growing in England between 1680 and 1710. Huguenot refugees brought the tulip into Ireland too, where the Dublin Florists' Society was founded in 1746 by Colonel Chenevix, Captain Corneille and Captain Desbrisay, officers in the Huguenot regiments that had fought for Prince William of Orange at the Battle of the Boyne.

A thin, tenuous line marked the advance of the tulip to the New World, where it was unknown in the wild. The first Dutch colonies had been established in New Netherland by the Dutch West India Company in 1624 and Adriaen van der Donck, who had settled in New Amsterdam (Manhattan) in 1642, described the European flowers that bravely colonised the settlers' gardens. They were the flowers of Dutch still lifes: crown imperials, snakeshead fritillaries, roses, carnations, and of course tulips.[4] They flourished in Pennsylvania too, where in 1698, William Penn received a report of John Tateham's 'Great and Stately Palace', its garden full of tulips. By 1760, Boston newspapers were advertising fifty different kinds of mixed tulip 'roots'. But the length of the journey between Europe and America created many difficulties. Thomas Hancock, an English settler, wrote thanking his nurseryman for the 'Plumb Tree and Tulip Roots you were pleased to make me a Present off, which are very acceptable to me'. But he had changed his tune by the following year when, on 24 June 1737, he wrote that 'The garden seeds and Flower seeds which you sold Mr Wilks for me and Charged me £16 4s 2d Sterling were not worth one farthing… The Tulip Roots you were pleased to make a present off to me are all Dead as well.'

Tulips arrived in Holland, Michigan with a later wave of early nineteenth-century Dutch immigrants, members of the Dutch Reformed Church, persecuted by King Willem I. Under their leader, the Rev. van Raalte, they quickly colonised the plains of Michigan, establishing, together with the many other Dutch settlements, such as the one at Pella, Iowa, a regular demand for European plants. The demand was bravely met by a new kind of tulip entrepreneur, the travelling salesman. The Dutchman, Hendrick van der Schoot, spent six months in 1849 travelling through the US taking orders for tulip bulbs. On 29 August he began the return journey to Holland, setting sail in the windjammer *Serapis*. 'The ship rolls violently from side to side,' he wrote in his diary. 'High seas ahead – terrifying northwesterly winds – seas that reach to the heavens.' He finally landed on 5 October 1849 at Hellevoetsluis, near Rotterdam, his order book intact.

While tulip bulbs were travelling from Europe to the States to satisfy the nostalgic longings of the first settlers, both English and Dutch, American plants were travelling in the opposite direction, often through the agency of John Bartram (1699–1777) who had established an important nursery and collecting point for American plants at Kingsessing, near Philadelphia. The new enthusiasm in England for American plants such as the red oak, the 'great laurel' (*Rhododendron maximum*), sugar maples and the beautiful *Stewartia malacodendron* was one of the reasons tulips dropped out of fashion in the gardens of the rich and famous. At this time too, there was a great change in gardening taste, which set the landscape style of Lancelot 'Capability' Brown (1716–1783) above the flower-filled parterres of the preceding age. The tulip in England was generally considered a French rather than a Dutch flower. As a result, it suffered in the rejection of all things French that followed the outbreak of the Seven Years War in the middle of the eighteenth century. For all these reasons, the tulip lost its glamorous place in the most stylish gardens of England.

It was rescued from the dung heap by a completely different class of grower, men such as the Rev. William Wood (1745–1808), a Unitarian minister at the Mill Hill Chapel, Leeds, Tom Storer of Derby, railwayman and tulip maniac, who, lacking any garden, grew his tulips along Derbyshire's railway embankments, John Slater (c1799–1883) of Cheetham Hill, Manchester, who bred the supremely elegant

SAMUEL BARLOW.

Samuel Barlow (1825–1893)
Florist of Stakehill, Manchester

17

feathered red and white tulip 'Julia Farnese' and Sam Barlow (1825–1893), whose life as apprentice, manager and finally proprietor of the Stakehill Bleach Works at Castleton could have provided the entire plot of an Arnold Bennett novel. They would have all described themselves as 'florists', using the word in its original, seventeenth-century sense; men who devoted themselves, singlemindedly, to the culture of a particular flower, who developed it by their own breeding to conform to a tightly laid-down set of rules, and who showed it in sometimes viciously contested competitions. Saddlers, glaziers, barbers and weavers were members of the Norwich Florists' Society in the 1750s. Shoemakers seemed to predominate in the Wakefield Tulip Society, founded in 1835.

The tulip, along with the auricula and the ranunculus was one of the six flowers cultivated as florists' flowers and in the careful, patient hands of the florists, the tulip reached its apogee. Hanmer and his like had bought their tulips at great expense, usually from European nurserymen. The florists, lacking the means to do that, grew their own tulips from seed, waiting seven years for a flowering bulb to develop from the initial sowing. Gradually, three clearly delineated groups of tulips emerged from the florists' breeding programmes: 'Bizarres' which showed red or dark purplish-brown markings on a yellow ground, 'Roses' which were white tulips feathered and flamed with pink or red and 'Bybloemens', white flowers marked with mauve, purple or black. The types had existed before, but the constraints of competitive showing put clearer markers between the groups and gave a little firm ground for judges to stand on. Frequent barbs in the *Midland Florist* and *Gossip from the Garden,* magazines founded specifically to cater to the needs of the florists, make it clear that judging was a dangerous pastime.

The uncompromising search for perfection in the English florists' tulip produced elegant beauties such as 'Miss Fanny Kemble', a Bybloemen with purple, almost black markings etched around the edges of the petals. The tulip had been raised in the 1820s by a Dulwich florist, William Clark (*c*1763–1831), praised in his obituary as 'an honourable and upright man'. Purity was an obsession with tulip fanciers and both the base and the filaments of 'Miss Fanny Kemble' were extremely white and pure. It produced the famous 'stud' tulip 'Polyphemus' raised in 1826 by another southern grower, Lawrence of Hampton. 'Polly' as it was more familiarly called by the Lancashire growers who finally got their hands on it, was a Bizarre, highly rated for the pale lemon ground colour of the petals, against which the dark markings, feathers and flames, showed up dramatically.

Of the hundreds of tulip societies that once existed, only the Wakefield and

*The Bybloemen tulip 'Miss Fanny Kemble', a great sensation when
it first appeared in the 1820s, bred by the amateur florist,
William Clark of Croydon. The nurseryman, Thomas Davey, of the
King's Rd, Chelsea, paid £100 for a single bulb.
From Joseph Harrison's* Floricultural Cabinet *published 1833*

'Lawrence's Polyphemus' from The Florist's Guide *(1827)*
A Bizarre tulip raised by William Clark of Croydon and broken by
Mr Lawrence of Hampton Court

North of England Tulip Society in Yorkshire now remains. Its dedicated members represent the last of the long line of amateur florists who have played such an important part in the development of the flower. In the petals of the exquisite, rare tulips still exhibited in competition each year by the Wakefield florists, runs the blood of flowers first grown by John Evelyn and John Rea in the middle of the seventeenth century.

English florists, though, were no less compromising than Turkish ones. In Turkey, tulips were such an obsession that an entire historical period, spanning the reign of Sultan Ahmed III (1703–1730) has been labelled the *Lale Devri*, the 'Tulip Era'. Three hundred years before the Royal Horticultural Society in England and the Dutch bulbgrowers in the Netherlands got together to prepare the first Classified List of tulip names, Turkish florists-in-chief were already setting up councils to judge new cultivars of tulips and give them official names. Whereas English florists favoured round, wide-petalled tulips, as close to half spheres as possible, the Turks only rated the dagger-shaped tulips made up of needle-pointed petals that feature so prominently in the decorative arts of the Ottoman period. *T. acuminata* was the species name given to this spidery, mad tulip, its tall, thin bud opening to creamy flowers, sometimes streaked and flecked with red. But although it is given species status, it is unknown in the wild, either in Turkey or elsewhere.

Fourteen different species of tulip can be found growing wild in Turkey, but probably only four of them, including the brilliant red *T. armena* and *T. julia* are truly indigenous. The rest may have been introduced from similar habitats further east and became naturalised, particularly along old trade routes. Not long ago, I was in Eastern Turkey with my husband and two friends, looking for *T. armena* and *T. julia* in the areas around Erzerum, Hosap and Van, where the lake gleamed turquoise under mountains still covered in snow. It was May, and we ricocheted along roads and through snow-drifts that would have tested the toughest four-wheel-drive vehicle. We had a small, hired Renault saloon, but against all the odds, it survived, and carried us deep into the bare hills and rocky screes where pockets of bright red tulips grew among small geraniums and eremurus just coming up into flower.

T. armena or *T. julia*? It was a question we debated endlessly with almost every colony of red tulips we found. They seemed indifferent to the rules of nomenclature set down by taxonomists. On the road between Askale and Tercan, for instance, we came across an isolated group of tulips, with at least two dozen flowers in full bloom. Not one of them could be twinned with another. If you found two

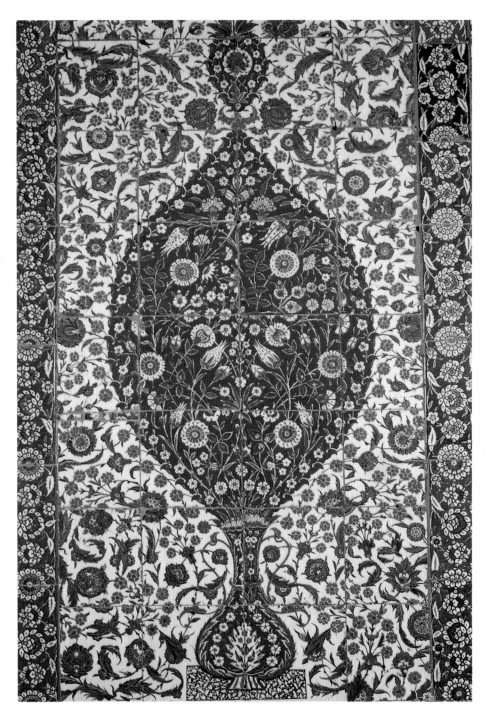

Underglazed Iznik tile panel c1560
Mausoleum of Eyup Sultan, Istanbul

flowers that seemed the same, you would soon discover that their leaves were different. If sets of leaves seemed similar, then the flowers cocked a snook at you as they flaunted yellow feathering on their red petals, or showed that they could do without their black basal blotches altogether. We excavated one bulb and, before reburying it, established that it, at least, must have been *T. armena*, for it did not have much wool under its tunic. *T. julia* has a very woolly coat.[5]

The loveliest colonies of tulips we found were in a valley above Tortum, north of Erzerum where groups of *T. armena* grew in little pockets between the limestone crags. We always found something intriguing there, sometimes a draba, sometimes an iris, once a wolf. That day, I was spread-eagled with my eyes closed, on a flat piece of rock in the sun. The *T. julia/T. armena* conundrum was rolling round my head like a riddle. I opened my eyes − who knows why − to find a wolf silhouetted against the sun. It sat upright, facing me on a neighbouring rock, its tail neatly curled around its front legs. Only inches from my eyes were the tulips, brilliant red blazes in the foreground. Behind them was the wolf, stark against the sky. When I sat up, it bolted away, disappearing into a low cave under a neighbouring rock crag. The conjunction of the two was as enigmatic in its way as the saints had been in Crete. As I lay on in the sun above Tortum, I thought still of these tulips, slashes of brilliant blood welling from the bare, brown, shale-strewn slopes of the mountain. Wolves were nothing to them. Saints were nothing to them. Millennia had passed by on this slope, while the tulip, wild as the wolf, slowly, joyously had evolved and regenerated itself. Even now, in their dark underground grottoes beneath the rocks, the tulips were plotting new feats, re-inventing themselves in ways that we could never dream of.

PART I

CHAPTER I

A FLOWER OF THE EAST

BURIED DEEP in the make-up of the flamboyant, cultivated tulips that fill flower shops in spring, must be the ghostly genes of their wild cousins. Garden tulips did not leap, fully formed onto the horticultural scene. They can only have been bred from, or selected from the species scattered through Central Asia and the Caucasus. And a malleable species, such as *T. schrenkii*, is likely to have been a more useful building block than a species, such as *T. butkovii*, which shows relatively little variation in the wild. *T. schrenkii* grows in the steppes and semi-desert areas of the Crimea, the Lower Don, in the Caucasus and Kurdistan. Its narrow buds open into cup-shaped flowers that may be claret-red, or perhaps yellow, pink, or white. Sometimes different colours merge imperceptibly in the same flower, the red drifting into pink so subtly that no ordinary eye could ever distinguish where the one colour began and the other ended. The fusion between the two is cloaked and softened by the glaucous bloom that covers the backs of so many of the wild species tulips. Or is it perhaps the spectre of *T. praecox* that haunts the flowers produced now in tens of millions by the tulip growers of the Netherlands? *T. praecox* is an altogether bigger, beefier thing than the elegant *T. schrenkii*. It has thick, stout stems topped by orangey-red flowers. The inner petals are shorter and narrower than the pointed outer ones, and they are flamed with yellow up the midribs. It was first described (in 1811) by the Italian botanist

Michele Tenore from flowers that he had found growing around Bologna in northern Italy. It is known in other places in southern Europe too: Provence, the Languedoc, the Rhône valley. But was it always here? Or was it, as seems more likely, since none of the early, busy botanisers of Europe wrote about it, brought here by travellers and traders from places further east? Turkey perhaps, or even Iraq. In Turkey this particular tulip was well known enough to have acquired the common name *kaba lale*. Or is *T. praecox* perhaps not a true species at all, but the result of some early tulip lover's interest in improving the strains of wild flowers that he found growing about him? In genetic terms, the majority of wild tulips are diploids, with twenty-four chromosomes marching in harmony. But scientific investigation in the 1920s demonstrated that *T. praecox* is a triploid, with thirty-six chromosomes. Polyploidy of this kind is often a clue that, in nature's time scale at least, the plant is a relatively recent arrival. The one form arises out of the other.

The questions cannot be answered because the tulip, more than any other flowering bulb, continually slips out from under the careful parameters laid down by botanists and taxonomists. The taxonomist's job is to pin labels on plants, each bearing a description that will enable anyone, from China to Czechoslovakia, to recognise how and why it is different from other members of its family. Often, taxonomists work from dried specimens, pressed and preserved on the dark, dusty shelves of a herbarium. But anyone who has seen tulips growing in the wild, notes the extraordinary diversity of flowers, even in a single colony of what must be a single species. Flowers of the Central Asian species *T. borszczowii*, for instance, growing along the banks of the Syr-Dar'ya river near Tashkent may be yellow, orange or vermilion. *T. armena*, widely spread in Turkey and northwest Iran, would be described by a taxonomist as a medium-sized, bright red tulip with a rather small black blotch at the base of its petals. But a group growing on the side of the road between Aşkale and Tercan, in eastern Turkey, includes flowers that are striped with yellow on the red ground. Some that are all red have no basal blotches at all. What is a taxonomist to do with such an unruly genus? The splitters among them elevated variants to the rank of yet more species. A strong-growing yellow form of *T. armena* found in the Transcaucasus and the mountains of Armenia was christened *T. mucronata*. A pale yellow form, tinged with olive on the backs of its petals became *T. galatica*. Another yellow-flowered type growing around Amasya in northern Anatolia, with a bluish, rather than a blackish blotch at its base, was dubbed *T. lutea* by the Bohemian botanist and engineer Josef Freyn (1845–1903).

Poor Freyn! In the long-drawn-out game of leap-frog between tulip and taxono-

Detail of sixteenth-century earthenware tile from Syria
Fitzwilliam Museum, Cambridge

mist, the tulip was always going to win. Its extraordinary diversity, its desire always to be trying on new clothes, is precisely what made it a source of wonder and delight to the gardeners who over hundreds of years gradually nursed it into shapes and shades that even the tulips themselves had not thought of. The family is still in a state of flux, but about 120 different species are thought to be spread over the Old World, three-quarters of them concentrated in Central Asia. In the New World, they did not exist until man took them there. From their hotbed, bounded by the Tien Shan and the Pamir-Alai mountain ranges, tulips spread northwards through mountains and steppes to the regions of Pribalkhash and Altai, halted eventually by the extreme cold of the Arctic. To the south, they moved in the direction of the Himalayas and Kashmir. Most extensive was their migration west-wards, where they were no doubt helped on by merchants on the well-travelled trade routes which led from Central Asia into Europe. Tulips spread towards Syr-Dar'ya, the steppes of Karakum, the Hindu Kush and Turkmenistan, to Iranian Khorasan and then through northwest Iran to the Caucasus. From the Caucasus, migration continued westwards into the Balkans and from there to Italy, France, Spain and the Atlas Mountains of northwest Africa.

As the tulip march had been halted to the north by cold, here it was stopped by the inhospitable heat of the desert. Desert met them too in Israel, where tulips had moved south from the Caucasus through Syria, Iraq and the Lebanon. Nineteenth-century travellers in Kashgaria and Dzungaria, the areas east of the heartland, reported seeing the same species here as in the Tien Shan. Some species also have been found in the Kiangsi, Hupeh and Shantung provinces of China. About four-teen different species grow in the mountains of Turkey, though only four of these, *T. armena*, *T. biflora*, *T. humilis* and *T. julia* are thought to be indigenous. When it had subjugated the Turks, the tulip jumped the Bosphorus and continued its slow journey to the west, travelling with traders, explorers, even in the diplomatic baggage of envoys such as Ogier Ghislain de Busbecq, to reach gardens in Italy, Austria, Germany and Flanders by the middle of the sixteenth century.

Before that, it seems to have been unknown outside its natural habitat. No tulips appear in the flower-strewn borders of the medieval manuscripts of Europe. When Hugo van der Goes (*c*1440–1482) painted his Portinari altarpiece, dark aquilegias, bright red lilies, blue and white iris and a scatter of violas were prominently dis-played in the foreground, but there were no tulips. The botanist Conrad Gesner, describing in 1559 a red tulip growing in Councillor Herwart's Augsburg garden, made clear that this was a grand event – as far as he was concerned, a first. But as far back as the thirteenth century, the tulip was being celebrated by Persian poets such as Musharrifu'd-din Sa'adi. In *Gulistan* he described his visionary garden where 'The murmur of a cool stream / bird song, ripe fruit in plenty / bright multicoloured tulips and fragrant roses…' created a paradise on earth for its fortunate owner. 'O cup bearer, serve us the wine soon, before the tulips wither,' wrote another poet. 'The flames in our fireplaces are the tulip gardens of winter.' Tulips are commemorated in Turkish place names such as Laleli (place of the tulips) near Erzerum, and Laleli gecidi (tulip pass) between Kayseri and Sivas. There were grimmer references too. On St Vitus' Day, 15 June 1389, the Ottoman Turks under Sultan Murad I fought the Serbian ruler Prince Lazar and his Bosnian allies at Kossovo Field, a high plateau sixty miles north of Skopje. A Turkish chronicler compared the battlefield, strewn with heads and turbans to a huge bed of tulips, the vivid yellow and red head-dresses mirroring the equally vivid and varied colours of the flowers.

The tulip flourished spectacularly in the later Ottoman Empire, appearing as a motif on tiles, textiles, illuminated manuscripts, miniatures, headstones, prayer rugs and murals. But it does not appear at all on artefacts of the earlier Byzantine era. This is more likely to be because they did not value the tulip than because they were unfamiliar with it, though the anonymous writer of the *Defter-i Lalezar-i Istanbul*, the 'Book of Tulip Gardens in Istanbul', does say that before the Seljuk invasion of Baghdad in 1055 only one kind of tulip, the *Sahra-i Lale*, or meadow tulip, was known in Istanbul. They were certainly known to the Seljuks who from the eleventh century onwards migrated west from their tribal lands in Central and Northeast Asia through Iran, Mesopotamia, and Syria. In 1096, they captured Konya in Inner Anatolia and tiles decorated with tulips, made by Anatolian Seljuks, have been excavated from the Palace of Alaeddin Keykubad I on the shores of Lake Beyşehir.

In the relatively settled period following the Ottoman conquest of Constantinople, tulips flourished in the gardens laid out by Sultan Mehmed II (1451–1481), who remade great tracts of the city. He built himself a palace, the Topkapi Saray, on one of Constantinople's seven hills, and laid out pleasure gardens inside the city's courtyards. Surplus flowers from the Sultan's twelve gardens were regularly sold in the flower markets and eventually a staff of 920 gardeners was needed to maintain his orchards, kitchen gardens and vast pleasure grounds. In his *Treatise on Husbandry*[1], Qasim ibn Yuruf Abu Nasri Haravi gave precise instructions for laying out such gardens. Water channels and pavilions, he wrote, should

Detail from Iznik tile panel
second half of the sixteenth century
Mausoleum of Eyup Ensari, Istanbul

be enclosed within lines of poplars. For each bed in the pleasure garden, Qasim suggested different flowers: colchicums with violets, roses with narcissus and saffron crocus, Persian lilac with tulips and mauve stocks. The beds nearest the house were often filled with roses, sacred in Islam as the flower which sprang from Mohammed's sweat.

In this culture, only particular flowers were valued: hyacinths, roses, jonquils, irises, carnations, and of course, tulips. Derived from the Persian, the Turkish word for tulip – *lale* – was written with the same Arabic letters as were used for the name of Allah, so the flower was often used as a religious symbol. Carved as a decorative device on buildings or fountains, it was the immediately recognisable emblem of the ruling House of Osman. Early manuscripts make it clear though that the different types of tulips in gardens 'occurred' rather than being specifically bred, as happened under later Ottoman emperors. As Victorian fern fans enthusiastically collected from the wild strangely aberrant forms of hart's-tongues and lady ferns with crinkled edges and tasselled ends, so curiosities in the enormous family of tulips must have been collected from the wild and brought into cultivation in Ottoman gardens. The historian Hodja Hasan Efendi, who accompanied Sultan Murad IV on his Eastern expedition, brought seven kinds of tulip back from Persia to raise in his garden in Istanbul.

Under Süleyman the Magnificent (c1495–1566), the Ottoman Empire reached its apogee, the zenith of its political and military power. It stretched from the Crimea to Egypt and covered a large part of the Balkans. Ottoman dynasties ruled in Bukhara and Samarkand and the warrior-gardener Mohammed Babur took control of Afghanistan and India. Wherever Babur went on his restless pilgrimage through Asia, he made gardens linked by a common Islamic tradition, derived ultimately from Persia. This tradition determined the kinds of plants he put in his gardens and Babur's own journal[2] lists the trees and flowers he particularly favoured. He liked fruit trees of all kinds, poplar, willow, jasmine, narcissus, violets and tulips. Before he died in 1530, he visited the tulip fields around Samarkand, having already planted tulips in all the gardens he had made in Turkey and India. Miniatures painted in the *Beyan-i Menazil-i Sefer-i Irakeyn* by Matrakci Nasuh[3] illustrate the places that his victorious armies passed through on their campaigns. One reveals tulips, growing in the wild near Konya. Another shows the tulip growing as a cultivated flower in a convent garden at Seyitgazi near Eskişehir.

From the sixteenth century onwards, the tulip became an integral part of Ottoman culture, universally employed as an ornamental motif. They were embroi-

33

Tulips and cherry blossom
on an Iznik dish c1550

34

dered in rows on Süleyman the Magnificent's gowns of cream satin brocade. Even his armoured champron bears the emblem of a tulip, embossed on the gilded metal. Tulips also featured prominently on the pottery and particularly the tiles of the period, which are such a spectacular feature of the Topkapi Palace in Istanbul and the upper galleries of the city's mosques. The designs reflected the way that these tiles were often used in Ottoman buildings to cover entire walls[4] and were often built up from groups of four tiles, each with a quarter of the central motif printed in one corner. Tulips first appeared on Iznik ceramics between about 1535 and 1540; sometimes the flowers were shown as though they were growing in a garden, sometimes as single blooms displayed in small vases. European travellers had already noted this particularly Turkish custom: to present a single, perfect bloom in a narrow-necked container or *laledan*. The earliest tiles were decorated with simple blue and turquoise glazes, but later, sage green, an opaque yellow and violet were added to the palette. The superb, singing red that could have been created especially for the tulip, appears around 1560, but lasted only until the end of the century.[5]

The *nakkasan* (designers, painters, decorators, illuminators) of the imperial studios had a great influence on the work of other artists and craftsmen in the capital. As their designs spread, a new national style was established, different and separate from Persian-based art. Tulips bloomed everywhere, painted with the same three confident brush strokes to create an elegant, waisted flower with petals that flipped out at the top. These tulips are altogether more comfortable, rounded creatures than the etiolated, starved flowers preferred under the later reign of Sultan Ahmed III. Sometimes they are painted in the entirely appropriate bole-red colour that distinguishes pottery of this period. But just as often, they appear bright blue, one of the few stunts that the real tulip cannot perform. A similar, strange blue was used by European artists such as Joris Hoefnagel, who produced the first paintings of the tulip in Europe at much the same time as the Iznik ware was being made. The tulips that appear on Iznik plates and tiles, tankards and jugs are most often underglazed in a single colour. Sometimes though, the potters painted the petals with stippled designs in contrasting colours. Were they perhaps copying the broken tulips that florists came to admire so extravagantly?

The French traveller and botanist, Pierre Belon, who was in Turkey and the Levant for three years from 1546, wrote admiringly of Turkish gardens, saying that there were 'no people who delight more to ornament themselves with beautiful flowers, nor who praise them more than the Turks'. The English traveller, George

Sandys (1578–1644), youngest son of the Archbishop of York, was more dyspeptic. 'You cannot stirre abroad,' he wrote of his Turkish adventures, 'but you shall be presented by the Dervishes and Janizaries with tulips and trifles'[6]. Seyhulislam Ebusuud (1490–1573) was one of the first of the Ottoman florists to specialise in tulips, introducing one of the great favourites of contemporary gardens, the Nur-i Adn, or 'Light of Paradise'[7]. The different tulips available in Turkey in the sixteenth century were illustrated in a painted mural decorating the walls of the fine Tulip Kiosk, which once overhung the Bosphorus at Anadolu Hissar. It was built, not by the Sultan himself, but by one of his Grand Viziers, desperate to curry favour with his master. Sultan Selim II was a besotted gardener. In 1574, he ordered the Sheriff of Aziz (now Azez in Syria, 7km south of the Turkish frontier) to send him 50,000 tulip bulbs for the imperial gardens at Constantinople. These must have been species tulips, gathered from the wild to be used in mass plantings. Another 300,000 bulbs were despatched for the palace gardens from Kefe (now Feodosiya in the Ukraine).[8] Needless to say, the Sultan never had to put his hand in his own pocket to pay for his passions. However, high prices were paid for particular kinds of unusual tulip. In Turkey (and later in Holland) laws had to be enforced to bring speculation under control. The Sultan ordered the Mayor of Istanbul to publish fixed prices for the most sought-after tulips; anyone who tried to sell bulbs at a higher price was expelled from the city. Transgressors were lucky to get off so lightly. The Sultan's high-ranking head gardener was also his chief executioner.

Later Sultans continued to demand equally vast quantities of bulbs from their subordinates in the provinces. 'Orders to the Administrator of Maras' wrote Sultan Murad III, who ruled from 1574–1595. 'Since there are no hyacinth bulbs in the palace gardens, you are ordered to collect 50,000 white hyacinths and 50,000 sky-blue hyacinths from the hyacinth colonies growing in the mountains and high-lands of Maras. And because of the urgency of the matter, you are ordered to do the following:

'Dispatch youths who are knowledgeable of flowers into the region and send them out with people who can be trusted to gather the above amount of hyacinth bulbs with all haste. Once obtained, hand them to ones dispatched under my orders and bring the bulbs to the castle gate of the town. Also write to inform me how many bulbs you could obtain. Those who brought bulbs can demand payment according to the numbers brought. The foregoing is of extreme impor-tance. Strive to make efforts and be careful. Avoid sloth or carelessness. Emperor's Order, the year 1001 of the Islamic calendar, the 7th day of the month of Sa'ban

Stylised tulips and peonies
underglazed Iznik tile, second half of the sixteenth century
Tomb of Hurrem Sultan, Istanbul

37

[9 May 1593].' Similar orders had already gone out to the Governor of Uzeyr in Aleppo. But how did the poor collectors tell the flowers apart when they were out of bloom and ready to dig up? The whisk of the executioner's axe must have been echoing very loud in their ears as they packed up the bulbs for their long journey to the capital from the wilds of southern Anatolia.

A miniature of 1582 from the *Surname* by the Ottoman artist, Osman, celebrates the circumcision of Sultan Murad III's heir, Prince Mehmed, when, according to contemporary accounts, the feasting went on for fifty-two days. The *Surname* miniatures indicate how sophisticated the cultivation of tulips must have been in Turkey at this time. One shows a procession of turbaned Turks carrying towering pagodas (like huge tulip vases), each one sprouting a cargo of red tulips. In another illustration, bands of gardeners carry entire miniature gardens, about nine feet square, built on flat platforms. They are decorated with clipped evergreens and miniature garden buildings. Cages of canaries hang from the fruit trees and long, thin-flowered tulips are planted formally in the borders. Contemporary accounts suggest that the gardens may have been made entirely from wax or marzipan.[9]

This devotion to tulips was not confined to the rulers in Constantinople. Sir Thomas Herbert, who travelled in Iran between 1627 and 1628, described one of many gardens made by Shah 'Abbas, this one in a desert near Isfahan. Between stone pools lined with marble, flourished peaches, pomegranates, plums and pears, all underplanted with damask roses, tulips and other flowers.[10] A similar scene is captured in an Indian miniature of *c*1685, where a garden pavilion overlooks a central water canal. Either side figs, pomegranates and mangos are planted in a geometric grid, the grass underneath them lit up with narcissi and tulips. Throughout the whole of the Mogul period in India, following the great Babur's victory at Panipat in 1526, gardens flourished. Babur's own favourite garden was at Kabul. His great-grandson, the Emperor Jahangir, an equally obsessive and gifted maker of gardens, favoured Kashmir. 'In the soul enchanting spring', he noted on a visit to Kashmir in 1620, 'the hills and plains are filled with blossoms; the gates, the walls, the courts, the roofs are lighted up by the torches of banquet-adorning tulips.' Jahangir engaged the artist Ustad Mansur to paint a hundred of his favourite flowers, including some superb red tulips which look like the wild species *T. lanata*.[11] *T. lanata* is a Central Asian tulip, probably introduced into Kashmir by the Moguls during the sixteenth century and much planted on the roofs of mosques. Mansur's painting shows four of the tulips, each at a different stage of development, from bud to full-blown flower, contained within an intricate double border.

Underglazed Iznik tiles c1560
Mausoleum of Eyup Sultan, Istanbul

39

The Three Sons of Shah Jehan
Mogul miniature by Balchand c1635
Victoria and Albert Museum, London

40

He noted the characteristic pale midrib that often runs from tip to base of tulip petals, usually more prominent on the outer surface than the inner. The image, superbly detailed, must have been painted from life, but it was not always so. Some Indian miniatures show tulips that seem to have been copied from the illustrations in early European books such as those published by Rembert Dodoens in 1569 and Clusius in 1576. One, painted c1635 by the Mogul artist, Balchand, shows the three sons of Shah Jehan riding out together, the whole scene contained in a rich border of flowers. The stocky red tulip in the top right-hand corner of the border is extraordinarily like the tulip illustrated by Conrad Gesner in his Appendix to Cordus's *Annotationes* of 1561.[12] Another miniature of the same period centres on a splendid turkey, the brilliant red of his wattles echoed in the colour of the delicate tulip to his left. Was the painter, like Mansur, painting from life? Or was he copying a strikingly similar tulip illustrated in Clusius's *Rariorum aliquot Stirpium* of 1583.[13] Later, in China and Japan, ceramicists also plundered European originals for motifs. Tulips in rigid bouquets copied from the flower paintings of artists such as Jan Brueghel and Jacques de Gheyn began to appear in the early eighteenth century as motifs on the export porcelain known as *Chine de Commande*. Tulips glittered in gold with pink carnations, roses and botanically impossible daffodils.

By the 1630s, the traveller, Evliya Celebi, estimated that there were at least 300 florists based in and around Istanbul as well as about eighty flower shops. He also noted how richly the gardens along the Bosphorus were planted with tulips, many of them popular destinations for visitors making excursions by boat from the capital. The meadows at Kâğithane, where two streams ran into the Golden Horn, were particularly famous for their display of tulips, 'intoxicating', Celebi said, in their season. He also mentions 'Kefe' tulips, that is, tulips from Kefe (Feodosiya) a name that was known in western Europe too. Clusius (Charles de l'Ecluse 1526–1609), the first director of the botanic garden at Leiden in Holland, also talked of the *Cafe lale* and the same tulip appeared in the 1630 list of flowers grown by Sultan Murad IV (1609–1640). He had fifty-six different kinds of tulip; some were so scarce that even the Sultan himself could not get hold of more than one bulb. But during this period, there was a marked increase in the number of different varieties available and Turkish florists-in-chief were already setting up councils (*encumen-i danis-i sukufe*) to judge the new tulips being bred by the country's florists. In a system adopted later by early European florists, only the best flowers were given distinguishing and official names. Sari Abdullah Efendi was florist-in-

A Turkey Amongst Flowers
Mogul miniature of the period of Shah Jehan (1627–1658)
Fitzwilliam Museum, Cambridge

chief (*ser sukufeci*) to the Sultan Ibrahim who ruled from 1640 to 1648, but it was Sultan Mehmed IV, ruler for the next forty years, who brought the system to perfection. Only the most flawless cultivars were entered into the official tulip list, each appearing with a description and the name of the grower who had bred the flower. The Council even had its own research laboratory, where new cultivars could be assessed in a more leisurely way.

Once Turkish florists started to breed their own tulips, rather than select the best of what nature offered in the wild (and this was now happening in the West as well as the East), the flower was shaped in a very particular way. In western Europe, tulip lovers favoured a rounded, cup-shaped flower, well marked with contrasting colours. The Turkish florists' standards were equally uncompromising, but they favoured tall thin tulips, narrowly contoured and made up of dagger-shaped petals. The petals themselves had to be of good texture – stiff yet smooth – and of one colour. Each of the six petals had to be the same size and length. In a perfect flower, the petals would conceal the stamens, with no gaps between them, but the pistil would just be visible. The flower had to stand erect on its stem, thin and well balanced. The shape of the petals was the cause of most concern. Tulip breeders always selected strains with narrow, pointed petals. Daggers and needles were what they wanted. 'If the tulip has not these petal characters' wrote an early pundit, 'it is a cheap flower. The tulip with the needle end is the better of the two; if it has both the dagger shape and the needle point, it is priceless'.[14] There was an equally rigid list of defects in a flower. A flawed tulip was one with a soft stalk and scattered, dull, loose, irregular petals. Sometimes – a characteristic inherited from many wild tulips – the inner petals were broader and shorter than the outer ones. This was a fault too. Evaluating the new cultivars was a long and difficult job. But if a tulip did manage to get onto the magic list, it was universally fêted. Poets wrote couplets to the debutante flowers, celebrating their beauty and form. Prizes were given for the best verses, as well as to the breeders of the best flowers. Even the most resourceful poet might be stumped by the prosaic names – 'Goudstuk', 'Hit Parade', 'Mickey Mouse' – of some modern tulip cultivars but Turkish tulips were given wonderfully evocative names – 'Those that Burn the Heart', 'Matchless Pearl'. That helped. So did the fact that *lale*, the Turkish word for tulip, happened to rhyme with *piyale*, a wine glass. The wine metaphor was squeezed to the last drop. The names themselves were often Arabic or Persian – *Nize-i rummani* (Pomegranate lance), *Peymane-i Gulgun* (Rose-coloured Glass), *Ferah-efza* (Increaser of Joy), only occasionally Turkish – *Buyuk al* (Big Scarlet), *Ikbal Yildizi* (Star of Felicity). The

43

*A Turkish tulip with fashionably etiolated petals
from a tulip book c1725*

44

wonderfully extravagant tags – 'Delicate Coquette', 'Slim One of the Rose Garden', 'Light of the Mind', 'Diamond's Envy', 'Beloved's Face' – were a testament to the esteem in which the tulips themselves were held.

But how did this almond-shaped, dagger-petalled tulip arise? What wild species contributed to its singular conformation? In shape it is closest to the spidery-petalled *T. acuminata*. But that tulip, although given species status, is actually unknown in the wild and is generally supposed to be itself a garden tulip. The needle-pointed Turkish tulip did not necessarily come from any of the fourteen wild-species tulips to be found in the country for, by the mid-seventeenth century, the tide of the tulip trade had turned. The first tulips seen in western Europe had arrived there from Turkey, but in 1651 the Austrian Ambassador, Schmid von Schwarzenhorn, brought forty tulips of ten different varieties from Europe into Istanbul as a gift for the Emperor Mehmed IV. They continued to be grown in Turkey under their Austrian names and Mehmed Efendi, the author of the *Lalezar-i Ibrahim* (1726) said that the whole development of what became known as the Istanbul tulip with its thin dagger-petalled flowers, originated with those ten varieties. Others, too, believed that the Turkish tulip had been created with the *gubari tali* – literally fertilisation powder or more prosaically pollen – from the European bulbs. Tulips also arrived in Turkey from Crete (probably the mauve-flowered *T. saxatilis*) and were noted by an Italian traveller, Dr Bennetti, in his diary of 1680: 'In the garden of the house at which a dinner was given to me at Eyoub on the Golden Horn, were magnificent tulips growing three or four on a stem. They are imported from Crete'. M H Hoog, a Dutch authority on tulips, has argued that the long thin-petalled species *T. schrenkii* from the steppe regions of the Crimea, brought to Istanbul under the name 'Kefe tulip', must have played a part in the breeding of the Istanbul tulip. It was from Kefe in the Ukraine that Sultan Selim II had ordered 300,000 tulips to be despatched for the palace gardens. And sixty years later, the historian Hodja Hasan Efendi, who in 1638 was with Sultan Murad IV on his expedition to Baghdad, brought back seven different kinds of tulip to grow in his Istanbul garden. Out of this great melting pot of species and their variants, the Istanbul tulip somehow emerged.

Other travellers, besides Belon and Busbecq, commented on the overwhelming passion that the Turks had for tulips. In 1673, Antoine Galland, a diplomat from the French embassy, passed along the same road between Edirne and Istanbul that Busbecq had taken more than a hundred years earlier. 'Had a wonderful time today,' he wrote in his diary on Monday 15 May 1673. 'This was because of the fine weather and the large fields of tulips and peonies along the road to Burgaz.' Sir John Chardin, the seventeenth-century author of *Travels in Persia* made it clear that the flower was no less extravagantly regarded over the border in Iran. 'When a young man presents a tulip to his mistress he gives her to understand by the general colour of the flower, that he is on fire with her beauty, and by the black base, that his heart is burned to coal'.[15] Mehmed bin Ahmed-ul Ubeydi's *Netayicu'l-ezhar* [The Achievement of Flowers] published in 1699, was only the first of a long series of Turkish manuscripts celebrating the beauty of the tulip and the skills of those who bred them. Ubeydi was the Imam of the Cerrahpasa Mosque and his work names 202 of the most outstanding tulip breeders of the age. They seem mostly to have been people of rank – pashas, mullahs, captains in the Janissary Guard. He also included descriptions of the tulips – and narcissi – grown by these specialists. 'The Juge', he wrote, was the colour of the buds of the Judas tree. 'The stripes are white or nearly so. The tips of each petal are pointed acutely. Sometimes this same tulip has no stripe. It was first exhibited by Juge Chelebi at Scutari. Some pretend that this bulb comes from Europe.' It could have. The description fits the celebrated Dutch tulip 'Viceroy'.

The most important florist in Istanbul at the beginning of the eighteenth century was Seyh Mehmed Lalezari, head gardener to Grand Vizier Damad Ibrahim Pasa. His book *Mizanu 'l-Ezhar* [The Manual of Flowers], published in Istanbul, gives a thorough account of the properties of the etiolated Istanbul tulip, peculiar to this time and place. In Part 1, Mehmed lists the twenty points to which a good tulip should conform. The six petals should be long and equal in length. They should close together neatly, with no gaps between them. The pollen should not be allowed to stain the flower. The stem should be long and strong. The leaves should also be long, but not so long that they overshadow the flower. The flower itself should be held erect on the stem and its colour pure and clear. In 'broken' or bi-coloured tulips, a white ground colour was preferred to yellow (French and English florists shared this preference for white grounds). The petals should be smooth-edged rather than jagged. Double flowers were completely beyond the pale. One of the most valuable tulips of the time was 'Luluu Ezrak' (Blue Pearl) which grew in the palace gardens at Ciragan with a flower as big as an ostrich egg. Sometimes, as with 'Luluu Ezrak', the name of a tulip reflected the colour of its flower; sometimes it commemorated the person who had bred it, as in 'The Deep Red of Ibrahim Bey'. Mostly the epithets were purely fanciful, 'One that Confuses Reason', 'One that Burns the Heart'.

نازنده آل

Nazende al (Flattering Red)
from The Book of Tulips c1725

47

The Turkish code was even tighter than the one which ruled fanciers of the English florist's tulip, though in many ways the two bodies shared similar prejudices in their definitions of the perfect tulip. The chief difference between the two concerned the shape of the flower. English florists alternately boxed and coaxed the tulip into the shape they considered the zenith of perfection – the half sphere. Turkish growers selected tulips that had long, thin pointed petals, aiming at a flower that was as spidery as they could make it. After setting out these criteria for the perfect tulip, Mehmed devotes the second part of his book to ways of achieving them. The third part deals with narcissus.[16]

Ahmed's reign, which lasted from 1703–1730, is generally designated by historians as the *lale devri*, the Tulip Era. The Sultan was completely ruled by the vagaries of his favourite flower and it was at this stage that the tide turned in the bulb trade between East and West, for Ahmed III imported millions of tulip bulbs from Holland to decorate his gardens. By this time, no one in Europe could match the Dutch growers in the production and marketing of flower bulbs. According to a contemporary manuscript, Turkish tulip traders 'increased from day to day' and 'exchanged amongst themselves different kinds of tulip bulbs which gave rise to different and most beautiful varieties'.[17] But Ahmed's passion for tulips led to his downfall. His subjects rose in revolt against him, because of the vast amount of money he spent each year on extravagantly staged tulip festivals. The Dutch, with their own tulipomania of the 1630s firmly behind them, had no compunction in encouraging others down the same prodigal route.

Tulips filled the imperial gardens. They also appeared on carvings, fountains, tombs and murals. Even the Fruit Room at Ahmed III's Topkapi Palace was decorated with tulips: bunches of flowers in vases which contained hyacinths and carnations as well as the immensely long dagger-like tulips favoured in the Ottoman Empire. The bulbs that filled the Palace garden were now western ones, and the style of decoration in the Fruit Room also suggests a western influence. The Turkish custom had been to display flowers, whether real or painted, as single specimens; now they were shown in mixed bunches. Trade with the West was increasing and early European travellers, such as Belon, were followed by a wave of incomers, many of them diplomats like William Sherard (1659–1728), British Consul at Smyrna from 1703–1716. Sherard was an accomplished botanist and, after taking his degree at Oxford in 1683, studied with Tournefort in Paris between 1686 and 1688, and with Hermann in Leiden from 1688 to 1689. It was he who was responsible for bringing to England the brilliant German botanist, Johann Jacob

An un-named bloom from
The Book of Tulips c*1725*

Dillenius (1684–1747). In 1732, Sherard's brother James persuaded Dillenius to compile the *Hortus Elthamensis*, an important survey of the plants growing in Sherard's Eltham garden. James Sherard was an apothecary and his garden at Eltham was noted for its rare plants; some of them, including tulips, may have been supplied by his brother in Smyrna.

Under Sultan Ahmed III, Turkey became a hotbed of floriculture. High in the summer pastures of the Sipylus mountains above Manisa were the Sultan's tulip fields, where bulbs were propagated to fill the palace gardens at Ciragan, Sa'd Abad and Nesat Abad. At tulip time, the Grand Vizier provided his father-in-law, the Sultan, with nightly entertainment in the Ciragan gardens. (The name Ciragan was derived from the word for the mirrored lanterns that were used in their thousands to light the gardens.) Music filled the grounds where the Sultan's five wives took the air. One of the courtyards of the Grand Seraglio was turned into an open-air theatre; thousands of tulip flowers were mounted on pyramids and towers, with lanterns and cages of singing birds hung between them. Tulips filled the flower beds, each variety marked with a label of filigree silver. At the signal from a cannon, the doors of the harem were opened and the Sultan's mistresses were led out into the garden by eunuchs carrying torches. Guests had to dress in clothes that matched the tulips (and avoid setting themselves on fire by brushing against candles carried on the backs of hundreds of tortoises that ambled around the grounds). One of these tulip extravaganzas was described by Monsieur d'Andresel, the French Ambassador to Constantinople in the early eighteenth century. 'The Grand Vizier [Ahmed III's son-in-law, Damat Ibrahim Pasha] and others of the Court have a great taste for flowers, above all for Tulips,' he wrote in a letter dated 24 April 1726. 'There are 500,000 bulbs in the Grand Vizier's garden. When the Tulips are in flower and the Grand Vizier wants to show them off to the Grand Seigneur, they take care to fill in any spaces with Tulips picked from other gardens and put in bottles. At every fourth flower, candles are set into the ground at the same height as the tulips, and the pathways are decorated with cages of all sorts of birds. All the trellis-work is bordered with flowers in vases, and lit up by a vast number of crystal lamps of various colours. Greenery is brought in from the woods roundabout and used as a background behind the trellises. The colours and reflections of the lights in mirrors makes a marvellous effect. The illuminations are accompanied by noisy music and Turkish music lasts through all the nights that the tulips are in flower. All this is at the expense of the Grand Vizier, who during the whole of tulip time, lodges and feeds the Grand Seigneur and his suite.' And doubtless found a way to reimburse himself later for the expense.[18]

Izzet Ali Pasa and other poets of the period celebrated tulips in chronograms, poems which gave clues as to their date in the letters of their last verses. The fabulous tulip 'Nize-i-Rummani' (variously translated as 'Pomegranate-coloured Lance' or 'The Roman's Spear') was endlessly chronogrammed. But, unlike the situation in Holland, where many tulip books were made, either to commemorate the collections of tulips built up by rich owners, or to advertise the bulbs for sale at specialist dealers, only one illustrated book of Turkish tulips is known to exist. This is a fine, leather-bound volume measuring 22cm × 31cm and containing illustrations of forty-nine different varieties of Istanbul tulip. It is not dated, but by comparing the names of the tulips with those in other published and dated manuscripts and the frames painted around them on the pages with similar decorations in other sources, the Turkish historian Ekrem Hakki Ayverdi concluded that it must have been produced in the reign of Sultan Ahmed III, most probably around 1725. Ayverdi owned the book for a time, but sold it in the 1960s to raise funds to publish his four-volume work on the history of the Ottoman Empire.[19]

Ayverdi pointed out that in all the Turkish literature on tulips, this is the only book to contain illustrations.[20] The paintings are done on thick, coated, wheat-coloured Indian paper. Forty-four tulips are named, seven of them painted more than once. Most of the tulips are shown contained in frames, painted round them on the page. The book starts with the valuable 'The Roman's Spear' tulip, painted in three different styles. One of the paintings seems to show its narrow petals tied round with a thin thread. This is a trick that tulip fanciers used later in England to stop their blooms opening out wider than the much-to-be-desired half sphere, the little corset of cotton thread being whipped away just before the judges approached the show bench. Turkish growers also followed English growers in believing that they could change the colour of their tulips, or persuade them to 'break' into multi-coloured stripes, by mixing the required colour into the earth in which the bulbs were to be planted. The writer of the *Revnak'i Bostan* suggested in 1660 that growers could turn flowers purple by mixing a little grape juice into the soil.

'The Roman's Spear' is followed by paintings of 'One That Scatters and Blooms' and 'One That Changes Owners' both of them red finely streaked with yellow. It may have been that the order in which the tulips appeared in the book reflected their relative value. The colour range is wide, reproducing the equally wide range found in wild populations of *T. schrenkii*, the species from which these Istanbul tulips may have been derived. Reds predominate, in every shade from the palest

'Furuzende' (One that Gives Light)
from The Book of Tulips c1725

pink of 'One That Flatters' to the deep, saturated red of 'Huseyni'. 'One That Increases Joy', a pale creamy-yellow tulip streaked with pinkish red, is very like the form of *T. acuminata* that grows in the National Collection of tulips at the Cambridge Botanic Garden, England. There is one pure white tulip, 'Spring Morning', and three clear yellows, 'The Vizier's Finger', 'Turuncu Sheyhi' and 'One That Gives Light'. One of the most unusual is 'Cucemoru', deep purple, grey and cream, the colours of the gris-de-lin that Sir Thomas Hanmer had valued so highly in his Welsh garden a hundred years earlier. But no one in Britain grew tulips so strangely etiolated as these Istanbul tulips. All the flowers shown in the manuscript are of the same type, most of them accompanied by a single, undulating leaf. Some of the paintings are signed by Rekame Mehmed and E H Ayverdi believed that all the paintings were by the same artist. Most of the tulips appear as single specimens, most often shown facing to the left. Just one of the tulips, the fabulous 'The Roman's Spear', appears in a rich blue *laledan*, the special glass vase with a bulbous base and a long, thin neck, developed by the Turks to show off single, precious blooms. Almost 200 years earlier, the French traveller, Pierre Belon, had noted how important these vases were in the Turks' ritualistic devotion to the tulip. The *laledan* were usually about 20cm high and could be made of silver or other highly polished metals, as well as glass. *Sukufedan* were larger vases and were used for all kinds of flowers, not just tulips. They were wider at the neck than the *laledan* and swelled out to a bulb in the middle, narrowing to a pedestal or foot at the bottom.

Mehmed described himself as a *bendegan* or servant of the ruler, so it is most likely that he worked as a member of the *nakassan* in the imperial studios and that these paintings of rare and expensive tulips may have been made as a record of flowers in the collection of the Sultan, or at the very least, one of the Viziers.[21] *The Book of Tulips* was made when the passion for Istanbul tulips was at its height and huge prices were being paid for particular types; Turkey was indulging in its own form of tulipomania. The book contains little by way of words, apart from the name of each tulip, usually inscribed in red ink (more rarely in black) in a flowing Talik script. Only the strange purplish-grey 'Cucemoru' has a description of its characteristics, written in a slanting block of text arranged to the left of the flower. But *The Book of Tulips* appeared at almost the same time as the official price lists that the government had decreed should be published as an attempt to keep soaring prices under control. By comparing the two, it is possible to build up an idea of the value of the bulbs. In the catalogue of prices, issued on 28 June 1726, *Nize-i Rummani*, the fabled 'The Roman's Spear', is the most expensive of the 239 tulips registered. It was priced at fifty kurus or seven gold coins. That same rich red flower also headed the list of 306 tulips published in August of the following year, but in that short time, the price had increased fourfold to 200 kurus. 'The Roman's Spear' was followed in value by 'One That Changes Owners', a sumptuous red tulip, intricately streaked and edged with chrome-yellow. That cost 150 kurus. Third in value was another red and yellow tulip, 'One That Scatters and Flowers', priced at 100 kurus. Tulip sales generally took place behind the New Mosque (Eminonu) in Istanbul, where there is still a flower market.

The official list named only the most expensive varieties available, the ones most likely to tempt speculators, and represented only about a fifth of the total number of Istanbul tulips known to exist in the Tulip Era. Mehmed Ucambarli's manuscript of 1726, *Lalezar-i Ibrahim* (Notes of Ibrahim, a Tulip Grower) lists 850 varieties. In the same year, Ali Emiri Efendi Kutuphanesi brought out his *Defter-i Lalezale-i Istanbul* (Notes of a Tulip Grower in Istanbul) which gave the names and characteristics of 1,108 tulips grown in Istanbul between 1681 and 1726. Kutuphsanesi includes all the information that a keen tulip grower of today might hope to find in a specialist nursery catalogue. Writing of the variety 'Vala-san', he says, 'The colour is a deep red, like the red of a pomegranate flower. The petals are almond shaped. The size of the petals are equal, with thin pointed tips – tips as delicate and flexible as *sulsani* [a type of written script]. It is a perennial and grows well outdoors. The anthers are yellow and longer than the ovarium. It is a plant with filaments, and is delicate. The flower, as a whole, is extremely beautiful. The flower has been named 'Vala-san' after Ali-san.' Sheik Mohammed, official *lalizari* or chief tulip grower in the last two years of Ahmed III's reign, produced two tulip manuscripts while in office. One of them lists 1,323 varieties of Istanbul tulip and names, unusually, two women growers: Azize Kadin who in 1728 raised 'The Gem of the Shah' and 'Grey Swallow' and Fatma Hatun who raised 'The Seeker of Hearts'.

With the end of Ahmed III's reign in 1730, the tulip abruptly lost its status as an imperial flower. A few private displays were arranged at court for Ahmed's successor, Mahmud I, but the secretive courtyards of the Topkapi Palace never again glittered with the lanterns and fiery torches that had lit up the priceless collection of tulips gathered by Ahmed, tulips that had been almost as valuable as the jewels in his strong-room. The cascade of manuscripts celebrating the Istanbul tulip's beauty dried to a trickle. Members of the court's high-ranking Council for Screening Flowers diplomatically drifted away into the shadows of the labyrinthine palace. In the summer pastures, high in the Sipylus mountains above Manisa only shepherds and their vast herds of sheep and goats gazed at the swathes of tulips once grown for the Sultan's garden in Istanbul. But the tulip was not entirely forgotten. Up until the end of the eighteenth century at least, craftsmen working in textiles and in stone continued to use the flower as a motif. A headstone of 1746 in the graveyard of the Hadim Ibrahim Pasha Mosque, Silivrikapi in Istanbul shows superb, long, thin dagger-petalled tulips displayed in typical thin-necked *laledan*. And, just occasionally, the Istanbul tulip returns to haunt twentieth-century gardeners. Sometimes a bulb, especially a bulb of a Parrot tulip, will revert to a form which the Dutch growers used to call *Tulipa dief* or tulip thieves. These tulips have strange, tall, spectral flowers with pointed, dagger-shaped petals. Not thieves, but benefactors, ones that increase joy.

CHAPTER II

THE TULIP IN NORTHERN EUROPE

IT IS ENTIRELY possible that the tulip reached Europe, unchronicled, before Ogier Ghiselin de Busbecq, Ferdinand I's ambassador to the court of Süleyman the Magnificent in Constantinople, claimed the honour of introducing it. After all, Süleyman had annexed much of the Balkan peninsula and Hungary early in his reign and, although he failed to take Vienna in 1529, he maintained trade throughout his reign with the Habsburg Empire. Nevertheless, no tulips appear in European paintings of the fifteenth or early sixteenth centuries. No mention is made of them before the mid sixteenth century by the busy botanists, herbalists and physicians who at the great centres of learning in Europe – Wittenburg, Montpellier, Padua, Vienna – were beginning to describe and list the plants growing around them. The first botanic gardens in Europe were established at Pisa and Padua between 1543 and 1545.

Busbecq (1522–1591) was one of a long series of Flemish ambassadors who represented the Habsburg emperors in Constantinople and sent plants and other curiosities back to their patrons. Accompanied by the physician Willem Quackelbeen, Busbecq set off for Turkey on 3 November 1554. 'Having delayed at Adrianople one day', he wrote in a letter describing his journey, 'we were going on towards Constantinople, now near, for we were almost accomplishing the end of our journey, and as we were passing through the district an abundance of flowers

56

Ogier Ghiselin de Busbecq

was everywhere offered to us – Narcissus, Hyacinths, and those which the Turks call *tulipam*, much to our wonderment, because of the time of year, it being almost the middle of winter, so unfriendly to flowers. Greece abounds in Narcissus and Hyacinths remarkable for their fragrance. Scent in tulips is wanting or very slight; they are admired for the variety and beauty of their colours. The Turks cultivate flowers with extreme zeal, and though they are careful people, do not hesitate to pay a considerable sum for an exceptional flower.'

So started the muddle over the tulip's proper name. The Turks did not call tulips *tulipam*. They called them *lale*, the name coming with the flower from its Iranian heartland. Busbecq evidently confused his interpreter's description of the flower, made in the shape of a turban (*tulband* in Turkish) with the flower itself. But his letter clearly shows that he was unfamiliar with tulips. He knew the narcissus and the hyacinth well enough, but he had to ask the name of the *tulipam*. As oddities, novelties, they were amongst the seeds and bulbs that he later sent back for Ferdinand I's gardens in Vienna and Prague, but tulip bulbs also turned up in cargoes at other European harbours, including Venice.

Busbecq's role in introducing the name of the tulip to Europe rests on the date he wrote his four famous letters. Until recently, it was generally supposed that these *Legationis Turcicae Epistolae Quator* had been composed during or shortly after his seven years (1555–1562) in the Ottoman Empire. But new research suggests that they were in fact written and published twenty years later, between 1581 and 1589 when Busbecq was back in Europe.[1] Perhaps the honours for the tulip's introduction should belong not to this Fleming but to the intrepid French explorer, Pierre Belon.

Belon (1517–1564) started his garden at Touvoie near Le Mans in 1540 and, helped by his patron, René du Bellay, Bishop of Le Mans, made an important collection of foreign trees and shrubs, which included cedar of Lebanon and the first tobacco plants that France had ever seen. His aim was to increase the range of plants available to French gardeners and, to that end, he went in 1546 to the Levant where he spent the next three years travelling and collecting. He described his adventures in an important book, *Les Observations de Plusieurs Singularités*, published in Paris in 1553, the year before Busbecq began his journey to Constantinople. It was a huge success, with three reprints in Paris and another, two years later, in Antwerp. In the third part of his *Observations* he writes: 'Il n'y a gents qui se délectent de porter de belles fleurettes, ne qui les prisent plus que font les Turcs: car quand ils trouvent quelque belle girofflée, ou autre élégante fleurette,

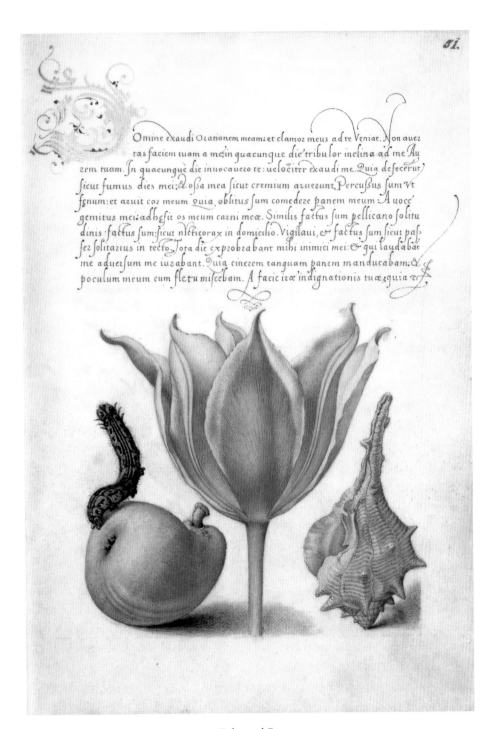

Omine exaudi Orationem meam: et clamor meus ad te veniat. Non auertas faciem tuam a me:in quacunque die tribulor inclina ad me Aurem tuam. In quacunque die inuocauero te: uelociter exaudi me. Quia defecerut sicut fumus dies mei: & ossa mea sicut cremium aruerunt. Percussus sum vt fenum: et aruit cor meum Quia, oblitus sum comedere panem meum. A uoce gemitus mei: adhesit os meum carni meae. Similis factus sum pellicano solitudinis: factus sum: sicut nicticorax in domicilio. Vigilaui, & factus sum sicut passer solitarius in tecto. Tota die exprobrabant mihi inimici mei: & qui laudabat me aduersum me iurabant. Quia cinerem tanquam panem manducabam: & poculum meum cum fletu miscebam. A facie irae indignationis tuae: quia rc.

Tulip and Pear
by Joris Hoefnagel c1590

59

encore qu'elle soit sans odeur, néantmoins elle ne perdra point son pris. Nous aymons les bouquets de plusieurs fleurs et petites herbettes odoriférentes meslées ensemble: mais les Turcs ne se soucient que de la vue, and ne veulent porter qu'une fleur à la fois: et encore qu'ils en peussent avoir de plusieurs sortes, toutes fois suivant le common usage, ils en portent plusieurs seule à seule dedans le reply de leurs turbans. Les artisans ont communément plusieurs fleurs de diverses couleurs devant eux, dedans quelque vaisseau plein d'eau, pour les tenir frâichement en leur beauté.'

He goes on to describe flowers – 'Lils rouges' – which are without doubt tulips, so common, he says that 'il n'y a celuy qui n'en ait des plantes en son jardin. Tels Lils rouges sont différents à ceux que nous avons par deça, desquels la fleur ressemble aux lils blancs: mais la feuille des Lils Turquois est faite comme de la canne nommée Elégia, et sa racine comme celle du chiendent, sinon qu'elle est beaucoup plus grosse. Parquoy plusieurs estrangers qui viennent à Constantinople sur navires de divers pays apportent les racines des plantes qui sont belles fleurs, et ainsi les vont vendant par les marchés, et de toutes choses qu'ils apportent sont argent'.[2]

Like Busbecq, Belon notes the Turkish passion for flowers, celebrated in painted miniatures, embroidery, poetry and ceramics. He remarks that the lack of scent in these 'Lils rouges' (red tulips are rarely scented) did not make them less precious in the eyes of the Turks. He compared the European taste for mixed posies of flowers with the Turks' manner of displaying just one bloom on its own, either in 'quelque vaisseau plein d'eau', the *laledans* of pottery or metal designed especially to show off single specimens of tulips, or in the folds of their turbans. Surely this is how the *tulipam* muddle began? Busbecq pointed to an unfamiliar flower worn in a Turkish turban, wanting to know its name. His translator, thinking he meant the turban itself, gave him the name for that, rather than for the flower that was being worn in it.

The 'Lils rouges' cannot have been true lilies, for few are native to Turkey and none of them are red. In Turkey, these red flowers were so common, wrote Belon, that they appeared in everyone's gardens. Although widespread, they were evidently as unfamiliar to him as they were to Busbecq, but Belon attempts to relate them to other flowers known in Europe ('la canne', 'la chiendent'), in order to conjure them up more plainly to his readers. He also makes it clear that merchants coming by sea into Constantinople had already built up an export trade in Turkish bulbs. In 1562, some of those bulbs came into the port of Antwerp in northern Belgium where, as Clusius later wrote, a merchant was sent tulips along with bales

Carolus Clusius (Charles de l'Ecluse), one of the most important of the sixteenth-century botanists who helped to spread the tulip through Europe

of cloth from Constantinople. He thought they were onions, had them roasted over the embers of his fire and ate them with oil and vinegar. 'Others he dug into his garden amongst the cabbages and other vegetables where, by neglect, they all perished in a short time, except for a few which George Rye, a merchant of Mechlin, keen about garden matters, gathered up, and to his wise diligence and industry we give the credit that it has afterwards been permitted to us to see the flowers which bring so much pleasure to our eyes by their charming variety.' Like the Antwerp merchant, Clusius experimented with eating tulip bulbs and asked a Frankfurt apothecary, J Muler, to preserve some in sugar, as orchid roots sometimes were. He ate them as sweetmeats and pronounced them far superior to orchids.

Carolus Clusius, or Charles de L'Ecluse, plays a seminal part in the early history of the tulip in Europe. He was particularly interested in bulbs and was responsible for distributing many new ones: crown imperials, irises, hyacinths, anemones, ranunculus, narcissi and lilies as well as tulips. Single-handed, he transformed the appearance of gardens in northern Europe, introducing many of the most precious delights of Renaissance flower beds. Perhaps more than any other figure, he embodies the cosmopolitan ethos of the time. Born in Arras, France, he was educated at Louvain until, at the age of twenty-three, he went to study under the great Protestant reformer, Philipp Melanchthon in Wittenberg. From there he moved on to Montpellier where he became a student of Guillaume Rondelet's. After that he began a two-year journey, plant-collecting in Spain and Portugal. In 1573 at the invitation of the Holy Roman Emperor, Maximilian II, he went to Vienna to establish and direct the Imperial Botanic Garden. By the time the Emperor died three years later, Clusius had already published his pioneering work on the flora of the Iberian Peninsula, *Rariorum aliquot Stirpium...* The book included an important Appendix (starting at page 509) which had nothing to do with Spain, but contained a detailed list of the plants that Clusius had up to that time received *"ex Thracia"*: anemones, ranunculus and, above all, tulips. He was also in touch with Busbecq who had sent him seeds and bulbs (including tulips) for the Vienna garden, although Busbecq was only part of a flourishing Turkish export trade which during the reigns of Sultan Selim I and Sultan Murad I, maintained strong links between Turkey, Austria and the Netherlands.

Clusius also corresponded with gardeners in England and visited the country twice, meeting Philip Sidney and Sir Francis Drake. Between 1587 and 1593 he was based in Frankfurt and advised Wilhelm IV, Landgrave of Hesse, on the botanical garden that Camerarius had founded there. But another correspondent, Joest Lips

(1547–1606) eventually persuaded Clusius to leave Frankfurt and come to Leiden to a new job as Horti Praefectus at Leiden's new university. He arrived on 19 October 1593 with a commission to lay out a physic garden, bringing the bulbs he had been growing in his garden at Frankfurt.

Clusius was already sixty-seven when he arrived in Leiden, but continued to maintain a vast network of international contacts (he was fluent in seven languages). With his letters, his bulbs too spread out over Europe. Three years after he had settled at Leiden, a young Norwegian physician, Henrik Hoyer, arrived there to take a degree in medicine. When Hoyer returned to Bergen, he had some of Clusius's bulbs in his luggage, and more were sent to him the following year. The pivotal role that Clusius played in spreading the tulip through Europe is told by his friend, Joachim Camerarius (1534–1598) in his *Hortus Medicus* of 1588. The two had first met as students at Wittenburg and their friendship is documented in 195 letters which Clusius wrote to Camerarius over the next thirty years.[3] In the course of the correspondence, Clusius compliments Camerarius on the number and variety of tulips in his garden (many of which he had provided). He sends Camerarius seeds of a plant newly arrived from Turkey, mentioning a Turkish pasha in Budapest who often provided him with specimens. He lists various bulbs from Constantinople which he sent to Camerarius (often in the hands of itinerant booksellers) with detailed instructions on the best way to look after them.

By the time Clusius went to Leiden, tulips were already being grown in the city by an enthusiast called John Hogeland. He had got his bulbs from George Rye, the Mechlin merchant who had rescued them from the garden of the unappreciative Antwerp trader. Clusius, though, was so possessive of his rarities 'that no one could procure them, not even for money. Plans were made by which the best and most of his plants were stolen by night whereupon he lost courage and the desire to continue their cultivation; but those who had stolen the tulips lost no time in increasing them by sowing the seeds, and by this means the seventeen provinces were well stocked'.[4] Tulips were in Amsterdam too, before Clusius arrived at Leiden. Nicolas Wassenaer wrote that the first tulip seen in Amsterdam grew in the garden of the apothecary Wallich Zieuwertsz, 'to the great astonishment of all the florists'.[5]

Although Clusius was so closely involved in bringing the tulip into Europe, he was not the first to describe it in print. That honour belongs to the Zürich physician and botanist Conrad Gesner (1516–1565), who saw the first tulips to be noted in Europe flowering in April 1559 'in horto magnifici viri Johannis Heinrichi Herwarti'. He described its red petals and its scent and said that it had 'sprung from

Conrad Gesner (1516–1565) author of
Caspari Collino Pharmocopoeo, *which*
contained the first description and the first illustration
of the tulip in Europe

a seed which had come from Constantinople or as others say from Cappadocia. It was flowering with a single beautifully red flower, large, like a red lily formed of eight petals of which four were outside and the rest within. It had a very sweet, soft and subtle scent which soon disappeared'.[6]

Councillor Herwart's garden was at Augsburg in Bavaria, a centre for silversmithing, a rich town and an important one. It is not a surprising place for Gesner to have seen his first tulips, but where had Councillor Herwart got his tulips from? Did they come from Antwerp or Vienna? Were they given to him by Busbecq or Belon? And was Gesner correct in describing the flower as having eight petals instead of six? There may, indeed, have been eight of them, as tulips occasionally produce sports, not true doubles, with seven or eight petals. One of the tulips illustrated in the 1565 *Codex* made by Leonhart Fuchs (1501–1566) has eight petals, but the illustration accompanying Gesner's description of the Augsburg tulip shows it with six. And he describes it as being scented, whereas both Busbecq and Belon had noted the tulip's lack of scent – scent being then an even more desirable characteristic in a flower than it is now.

Gesner called this tulip *T. turcarum*. It may possibly have been a Turkish species, such as *T. armena*, widespread in the country. But by the time the first tulip bulbs started leaving Constantinople for Europe, huge parts of the Balkans and the country round the Black Sea had been conquered by the Turks. The 'Turkey' implied in the *T. turcarum* tag embraced a far vaster area than the country as it is now defined. *T. turcarum* could be a Russian species as easily as a Turkish one. Constantinople traders were known to offer two kinds of tulip: the 'Cafe Lale' and the 'Cavala Lale'.[7] Clusius used the same terms in his *Rariorum plantarum Historia* (1601), but by then it was too late for *lale*, the correct Turkish word for tulip, to replace the mistaken 'tulipam'. The 'Cafe Lale' was an early-flowering tulip from Kefe (now Feodosyia in the Ukraine). The late-flowering 'Cavala Lale' probably came from Kavalla in the Macedonian region of the Balkans and may have been the variable *T. schrenkii*, native to the steppes and low mountains of Crimea and Transcaucasia.

Gesner also published the first European illustration of a tulip, the Augsburg one, shown in a vigorous woodcut, copied from a painting made either by him or one of his team of assistants. Scribbled around it are notes about the tulip: its provenance, its foliage and other *aides-mémoire*. The painting shows a fat, low-growing flower as wide as it is high, with six pointed petals that first close in, then flip out insouciantly at the top. Gesner noted that the tulip originated in 'Byzantium' and

Councillor Herwart's Tulip (1557)
as described by Conrad Gesner
University Library, Erlangen

says that he had already been sent a picture of this tulip by Johan Kentmann (1518–1574), a German naturalist and painter who was in Italy between 1549 and 1551. Gesner's original watercolours[8] included not only the Augsburg tulip, dated 1557, but also a yellow tulip, a series of three blooms, shown from the front, the back and in profile. Although it is labelled 'Narcissi lutei odorati' it is obviously the species now called *T. sylvestris*, which appeared in many of the early treatises on tulips. They are beautifully arranged on the page, with bulbs and a seed capsule, as well as the three flowers. Two of them have seven petals. The middle one has eight, but *T. sylvestris* does show a greater tendency than any other species to produce flowers with extra petals. The description notes the tulip's scent, another relatively unusual trait in this tribe.[9]

After Gesner, tulips appeared in a tumult of books, though not always under the right name. When in 1565, the Italian physician and botanist, Pier Andrea Mattioli (1501–1577) published his *Commentarii in sex libros Pedacii Dioscoridis*, the tulip again masqueraded under the label 'Narcissus', though the fine illustration (the woodcuts were by Giorgio Liberale of Udine and the German, Wolfgang Meyerpeck) shows that it is undoubtedly a tulip, the leaves, broad and undulate, climbing up the stem in a way that is more typical than the foliage shown in Gesner's illustration. Mattioli was followed into print by the Mechelen physician and botanist, Rembert Dodoens (1517–1585). A beautiful tulip was one of the seven woodcuts contributed to his book by Pieter van der Borcht, but stepping uncertainly in the minefield of nomenclature, Dodoens mostly opted for the wide-embracing tag of 'Lilionarcissus' for his tulips, saying they came from Thrace and Cappadocia.[10] Eight years later, one of the tulips illustrated in Dodoens's book appeared as 'Lilionarcissus chalcedonicus' in a herbal called *Plantarum seu Stirpium Historia*, written by Matthias de L'Obel (or Lobelius). It describes thirty-seven tulips, including the beautiful red and white Lady Tulip, *T. clusiana*. He also showed what seems to be a yellow form of the variable, multi-flowered *T. praestans*, a less formidable tongue twister than Lobelius's name, 'Lilionarcissus luteus Bononiensis'. Lobelius noted the fact that this tulip could have two or three flowers on a stem and that it smelt of yellow wallflowers. The English physician John Gerard later used the same illustration in his *Herball* of 1597, but called the flower *T. narbonensis*. This was typical of the taxonomic mess that existed before Carl Linnaeus (1707–1778), the Swedish botanist, brought order to the naming of plants.

Like Clusius, Lobelius (1538–1616) had studied under Rondelet at Montpellier, and on Rondelet's death, inherited all his manuscripts. He practised as a physician

Tulip from Pier Andrea Matthioli's
I Discorsi *(1565)*

in Antwerp and Delft before departing for England around 1566. There, he settled temporarily among fellow Flemings such as James Garrett in London but returned to the Netherlands to become physician to William the Silent. After William's murder, he settled permanently in England as James I's official botanist. That position gave him prestige, but was nowhere near as important as his job superintending Lord Zouche's garden at Hackney. Until the botanic garden at Oxford was set up in 1621, Britain had no equivalent to the great European centres of learning at Padua, Vienna or Leiden. Plant collections were put together by rich aristocrats and, among these, Zouche was paramount. His Hackney garden was a gathering point for all the best British botanists; Lobelius provided an important intellectual link between Britain and mainland Europe.

Lobelius, born at Lille in Flanders, wrote that a taste for plants had existed among the Flemish as far back as the time of the crusades and had flourished particularly under the Duke of Burgundy. He claimed that they had been the first to bring back plants from the Levant and that Flemish gardens contained more rare plants than could be found in the whole of the rest of Europe put together. Most of the gardens had been destroyed in the civil wars of the sixteenth century, but Lobelius mentions several Flemish tulip growers: Carolus de Croy, Prince of Chymay, Joannes de Brancion (who later lent his name to a particular kind of feathered tulip, the 'Testament Brancion'), Joannes van der Dilf, George Rye, Johannes Mutonus and Maria de Brimeu, wife of Conrardi Scetz.[11]

Tulips appeared of course in the first plant picture book,[12] traditionally attributed to Lobelius, but now thought to have been compiled by Gobelius, physician to the Duke of Prussia.[13] This was an entirely opportunistic venture by the Flemish printer, Christophe Plantin (c1520–1589), a way of getting yet another return from some very tired woodblocks. Tulips, twenty-three different kinds of them, took up ten pages of the book, several of them, including *T. praecox alba*, *T. praecox lutea*, and *T. praecox rubra*, then being used by Plantin yet again in Clusius's study *Rariorum aliquot Stirpium...* published in the same year.

Because the earliest illustrations of tulips were printed in monochrome (and because names varied so wildly), identifying them by their present names is a chancy business. Written descriptions rarely give information that is detailed enough to distinguish between one species and another. Early descriptive names often mention flowering period – 'praecox' (early) or 'media' (mid-season) and colour – typically 'luteus' or 'coccineus'. Sometimes there are phrases such as 'rubris striatis' or 'candore et rubore confusus' which suggest that tulips with broken

REMBERTI
DODONÆI
ÆTA. XXXV.

VIRTVTE
AMBI.

Rembert Dodoens aged thirty-five
from Trium priorum de stirpium historia
printed in Antwerp 1553

Tulipa minor (possibly T. celsiana*)*
From Florum et Coronarium *by Rembert Dodoens*
published in Antwerp in 1568

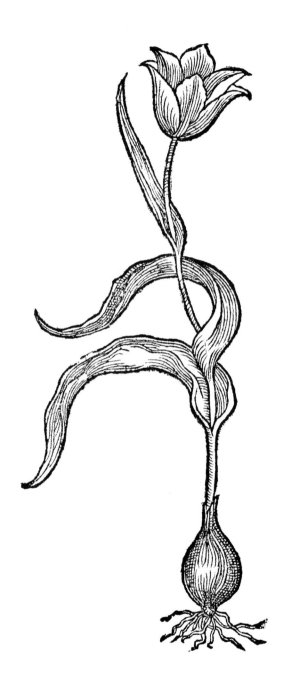

Tulipa praecox flava *one of the many*
early woodcuts prepared for Clusius's books

colour had arrived on the scene. The books in which tulips first appeared were primarily herbals, used to identify plants and note their usefulness in terms of food or medicine. Even tulips had a practical application: the bulbs could curdle milk. The herbals were used by physicians who were necessarily also gardeners; they were not made for gardeners *per se*. Their needs were met by the florilegiums which began to appear in the early seventeenth century, when covetousness started to play a greater part in gardening. 'Broken' tulips had been enthusiastically collected since 1585, after Gesner, Mattioli and Lobelius had published their various works. Clusius talks of enthusiasts such as Joanne de Hogelande, who in 1590 had sent him news of a tulip 'cujus flos omnia folia mucronata habet'.[14]

Long before Linnaeus, Clusius tried hard in this last book to bring order into the confused nomenclature of the time; as the new name of the genus became established, the 'Lilionarcissi' of previous books gave way to 'Tulipa'. Clusius sorted them into several groups: eight different 'praecox' (the early-flowering kinds), followed by 'serotinas' (late-flowering) and 'dubias' (in between). The illustrations were the familiar ones originally commissioned by Plantin, possibly the hardest-working woodblocks in the history of printing. The names of course were different. The 'Lilio-narcissus alba' of the 1581 *Icones* became 'Tulipa praecox flava'. 'Lilionarcissus luteus phoenico' from the same book became 'T. dubia major'. One of the *Icones* tulips, 'Lilionarcissus rubellus nitidus, candidis oris' appears (reversed out) on the fancy title page of Clusius's book, the centrepiece of the design, with Theophrastus and Dioscorides reclining in anguished attitudes either side of it. A few of the woodcuts ('T. serotina minor', 'T. pumilio altera') were new, suggesting that these tulips were more recent arrivals on the garden scene.

By the time this last work of Clusius's was published, painters had begun to overtake illustrators. Joris Hoefnagel (1542–1600), court painter to the Emperor Rudolph II, bridged the hazy division between the illuminators of manuscripts and the painters of still lifes. His tulips are fat, waisted flowers with pointed petals that flip out at the top, more sophisticated than Gesner's red tulip, and in a wider range of colours. He shows a beautiful yellow tulip, finely feathered in red, an elegant pink one surveyed by an *Alice in Wonderland* caterpillar rearing from a pear alongside, and, on another folio, two tulips emblematically and symmetrically arranged with entwined stems. The leaves are undulate, the flowers pear-shaped with petals that finish in the characteristic pointed flourish; Hoefnagel emphasises the broad midrib running up the back of the tulips' petals. One of his flowers is red, the other a curious and not entirely convincing combination of red, blue and green. The

Tulips and an ichneumon fly
from the Mira Calligraphiae Monumenta
decorated by Joris Hoefnagel c1590

green flare up the back of the petals is, though, typical of the type of tulips known as 'viridifloras', and it may be that the pigment he used on the parts that are now blue was originally a colour more typical of the tulip.[15] Oddly, exactly the same colour appears in a later flower study by Jan Brueghel the Elder (1568–1625).[16]

This was an age of overwhelming interest in plants: in Vienna and throughout Germany, in the Low Countries and in England, those with time and money spent it on laying out gardens and filling them with the treasures that explorers and botanists such as Belon, Gesner and Rauwolf brought back from their travels. Leonhardt Rauwolf was a German physician who corresponded with both Clusius and Gesner and was part of the great network or information exchange that linked scholars in western Europe. In 1573, he had left his home in Augsburg with the purpose of gaining 'a clear and distinct knowledge' of plants by seeking them out in their native habitats. His plant-collecting took him to the Near East, from where he brought back more than 800 different plants, some still preserved in the herbarium at Leiden. He saw the original cedars on Mount Lebanon, found wild rhubarb, collected 'a pretty sort of tulip' with yellow stripes, and, like Belon, noted the Turks' delight in flowers of all kinds. Like Belon, too, he described their habit of wearing flowers in their turbans, useful to him, as he could 'see the fine plants that blow one after another daily'.[17]

Once introduced, the tulip spread rapidly. It had been first noted in Europe at Augsburg in 1559. It was in Antwerp by 1562, in other parts of Belgium by 1583, in Leiden (thanks to Clusius) by 1590, in Middleburg and Lucerne by 1596, in Montpellier by 1598. Double tulips were already being described by the beginning of the seventeenth century. The flowers fitted admirably with the spirit of the age and the prevailing craze for 'curiosities' to be displayed in horticultural *Wunderkammer*, with each rare and cherished flower exhibited like a jewel. Scholars such as Clusius and Lobelius collected these curiosities to further their scientific work. Princes and power brokers wanted them as status symbols, for only the wealthy could afford to garden for pleasure. The painter Crispyn de Passe showed the kind of gardens they made: small, enclosed spaces, divided into a grid of rectangular beds, sparsely planted by modern standards, but containing fabulous treasures such as crown imperials, *Iris susiana* newly introduced from Turkey, hyacinths and, of course, tulips, the most sought after, costly and prestigious flowers that a seventeenth-century gardener could possess.

With this new interest in growing plants for show, the emphasis of plant books

Tulips from the Hortus Eystettensis *(1613)*
a record of the flowers growing in the garden of the
Prince-Bishop of Eichstätt in Germany

published in the early seventeenth century gradually changed. Emmanuel Sweert's superb hand-coloured *Florilegium* published in Frankfurt in 1612, and the *Hortus Eystettensis* which came out the following year are books for gardeners, catalogues, records of collections. Magnificent 'garden' tulips appear, feathered and flamed in gorgeous colours, obviously much more highly developed than the tulip species illustrated in earlier books. Technology helped too, for engravings on copper plates, which gradually replaced woodblocks as a source of illustration, allowed much more detail to be captured on the pages of early seventeenth-century books.

The *Hortus Eystettensis* was made for Johann Conrad von Gemmingen, the Prince-Bishop of Eichstätt in Germany, who had one of the finest gardens of the early seventeenth century, planted with nearly all the shrubs and flowering plants known at the time. Tulips were there in quantity of course, as were shrubs just imported from America. When the garden was finished, the Bishop commissioned the botanist-apothecary Basilius Besler, who had helped develop the garden, to produce a record of it. It was published in 1613 with 367 plates illustrating more than a thousand of the Bishop's plants.

Writing to Wilhelm V, Duke of Bavaria, the Bishop explained that 'the garden plants were brought back, through the offices of local merchants, above all from the Netherlands, for example from Antwerp, Brussels, Amsterdam and other places...' Wilhelm's agent visited the garden on 17 May 1611 and described eight different areas, each of which 'contained flowers from a different country; they varied in the beds and flowers, especially in the beautiful roses, lilies, tulips.' Each week, one or two boxes of flowers were sent to Nuremberg to be drawn by artists working on the great book, which the Bishop estimated would cost him upwards of 3,000 florins. Among the tulips sumptuously illustrated is a short-stemmed *T. praecox* with hyacinths and an unmistakeable *T. sylvestris* (still labelled as 'Lilionarcissus bononiensis') alongside leucojum. Most of the tulips, though, were showy striped, edged and flamed garden varieties rather than species. Some look remarkably modern. The Parrot tulip 'Fantasy' is a twentieth-century creation, but here in the Bishop's book is its twin, a mad raspberry-pink tulip, feathered in green. His 'Tulipa nivea oris purpurascente' shows a strange aberration, the colour of the petals repeated on a quasi-leaf further down the stem, just the same oddity that characterises the double late tulip 'Blue Flag' that flowers in my own garden.

The *Hortus Eystettensis* was part of an early-seventeenth-century explosion of books which followed on from the pioneering works of Gesner and Mattioli.[18] The Bishop's book was a record of a collection. Emmanuel Sweert's 1612 *Florilegium* was

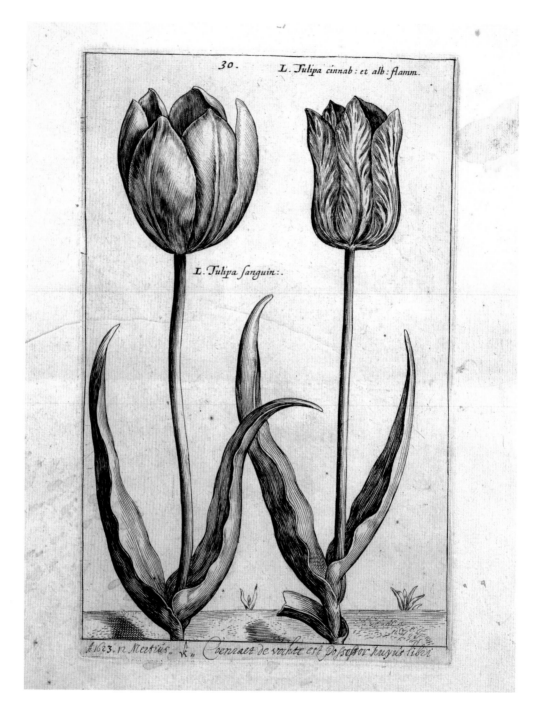

Tulips from the Hortus Floridus *(1614)*
by Crispyn de Passe

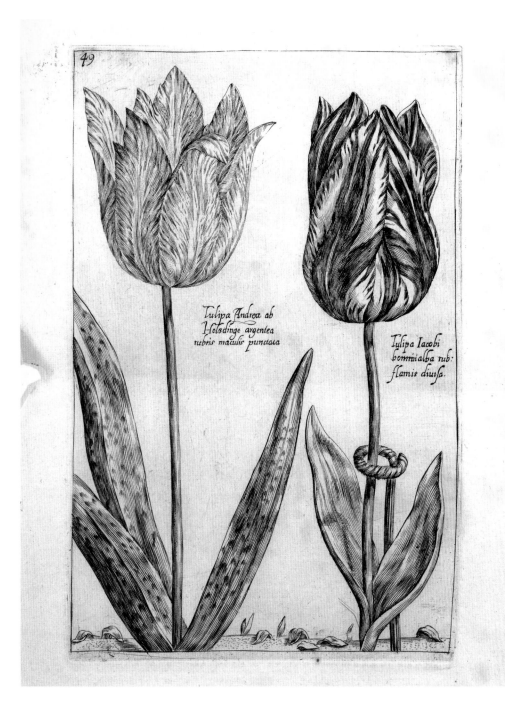

Tulips from the Hortus Floridus *(1614) by*
Crispyn de Passe

a nursery sales catalogue, the first Europe had seen. It had no text, but the plants were helpfully arranged in family groups on the pages. Unlike earlier herbals, many of Sweert's plants were described in purely ornamental terms and he included pages of ravishing tulips, intricately patterned in an extraordinarily diverse range of colours.

The Margrave of Baden-Durlach was a model customer, ordering thousands of bulbs each year from Holland. He spent more than a thousand florins each season on bulbs, fifty times as much as a nurse or a washerwoman could earn in an entire year. By 1636, his garden inventory listed 4,796 tulips. Some of the rarest were represented by a single precious bulb; other more common varieties grew in their thousands. The Margraves never lost their taste for tulips. In 1715 the new Margrave, Karl Wilhelm (1679–1738), rebuilt fabulous gardens at Karlsruhe, Baden-Württemberg, the two wings of the new castle enclosing a pleasure garden with complex parterres. Hand-written catalogues of the plant collections still exist and the list for 1730 shows 2,329 tulips. By 1733 the collection had grown to 3,868 different varieties, with nearly another thousand added over the next three years. The Margrave bought his tulip bulbs from seventeen different Dutch firms, fifteen of them in Haarlem. Like the Prince-Bishop before him, he commissioned paintings of his most precious plants. The watercolours made by Georg Ehret (1708–1770) alone filled twenty volumes and he painted 5,000 tulips.

Johann Jakob Walther (c1600–1679) made a similar florilegium for Count Johann of Nassau at Idstein. The castle, near Frankfurt am Main, had been rebuilt at the beginning of the seventeenth century, but by the end of the Thirty Years War was once again in ruins. On his return from exile, Count Johann set repair work in hand, laying out a fine formal garden with a summerhouse and grotto. Walther came to paint the rare flowers in the garden and showed the place in all its glory: neat parterres planted with crown imperials and tulips, carefully clipped box edgings, tubs of evergreens, statues and garden buildings, the proud owner with his wife and daughter, posed in the garden, portraits of peonies, irises, roses, carnations and of course tulips, many of them gorgeously striped in contrasting colours. The pointed, waisted tulip that Hoefnagel had portrayed a hundred years earlier has already changed into a wider flower, the petals more softly rounded at their tips. The three types that would later be designated as Bizarres, Roses and Bybloemens are clearly distinguished, the Bizarres streaked with red on a yellow ground, the Roses feathered and flamed with red on a white ground and the

*Tulips and other rare flowers in a formal garden of the early
seventeenth century, from the* Hortus Floridus *by Crispyn de Passe*

Bybloemens marked with rich purple on a white ground. The leaves are decidedly waved.[19]

The seventeenth-century Margrave of Baden-Durlach and the Count of Nassau were not alone in their passion. In Italy, the Duke of Sermoneta boasted of 15,000 tulips in the flower parterre of his garden at Cisterna. Tulips had been known in Italy since at least the middle of the sixteenth century when the Venetian, Pietro Michiel (1510–1566) left the important Botanical Garden at Padua, which he had been looking after, and returned to his own garden in Venice to produce a fine herbal, *I Cinque Libri di Piante,* with drawings of *T. sylvestris*, and *T. praecox*. The Spanish painter Juan van der Hamen y Leon's grand flower pieces of the 1620s show that the flower was a favourite in the Iberian peninsula too. His stiff heraldic tulips, predominantly reds and yellows, appear with sunflowers, irises and gladioli in several important still lifes, the flowers often arranged in the same ornate glass vase with fittings of scrolled gold.

Sweert's and de Passe's catalogues helped to broaden the potential market for tulips and, slowly, the fancy moved out from court circles to embrace a wider circle of *aficionados*, especially in the Dutch and German towns of the lower Rhine. By the 1620s the tulip was the *sine qua non* of fashionable gardens in the Netherlands, the western parts of Germany and Flanders, where a great deal of breeding was already going on. The work of the Flemish artist, Jan Brueghel, shows how much the tulips had developed since the first striped kinds had been noted by Clusius. Paintings such as the fabulous *Vase of Flowers* at the Fitzwilliam Museum, Cambridge, show tulips intricately feathered in contrasting colours, red on white, red on yellow, yellow on red (though there are none of the dark purple and white types that were later to become fashionable; that 'break' does not yet seem to have occurred). Brueghel's *Allegory of Spring*,[20] painted in 1616, shows similar tulips growing in a garden border. There is just one of each kind, including a showy bi-colour splayed open to show the regular markings of red round the edges of the white petals. Fleurs-de-lys, tree peonies, anemones, a grand *Fritillaria imperialis* and aquilegias are the tulips' companions.

By the beginning of the seventeenth century, the tulip was well established in France, reaching the Provençal garden of M Peiresc by 1611. The country subsequently entered into a period of tulip madness even more extravagant than the better-known tulipomania which later engulfed Holland. A thriving brewery, worth 30,000 francs, was handed over to one grower as the price for a single bulb of the modish variety 'Tulipe Brasserie'. In 1608, a miller exchanged his mill for a

Detail from Allegory of Spring *(1616)*
by Jan Brueghel the Elder (1568–1625)

Frontispiece from Florilegium Amplissimum et selectissimum
*by Emanuel Sweerts, Amsterdam 1647
(first published in Frankfurt 1612)*

Tulips from the Florilegium
Johann Jakob Walther (c1600–1679)

bulb of 'Mère Brune'. Later, a groom was overjoyed when his father-in-law gave him, as a dowry for his daughter, the entire stock (one bulb) of a fine double red and white striped tulip that he had bred and christened, appropriately, 'Mariage de ma Fille'. No woman of fashion stepped on to the street without a posy of rare tulips, the flowers worn like jewels in her *décolletage*. They were scarcely less expensive. Cashing in on the craze, Pierre Vallet (1575–1635), described as 'embroiderer' to Henry IV of France, published a book of engravings of flowers, including tulips, taken from specimens growing in the extensive collection at Pierre Robin's nursery garden in Paris. In well-to-do households, flowers began to be used inside houses, as well as in gardens. They filled empty fireplaces, they were strewn over the table-cloths brought out for important banquets. At a French wedding of 1680, the table was decorated with nineteen baskets of flowers, with anemones, hyacinths, jasmine and orange blossom as well as tulips.[21] A beautiful florilegium made in 1610 by Jean Le Roy de la Boissière of Poitiers[22] shows many of the garden flowers popular at the time and includes more than forty tulips. The gorgeous paintings made by Nicolas Robert (1614–1685) for Louis XIV's brother, Gaston d'Orléans, also show the flowers that French tulip fanciers prized at the time. Already, tulips had attracted a particular French vocabulary, which was adopted wholesale by both Dutch and English growers. The French terms remained common currency in England at least until the middle of the eighteenth century when the fashion for all things French waned in the wake of England's war with France.

Born in Langres, the son of an innkeeper, Robert had made his name with a small book of flower etchings, *Diversi Fiori*, published in Rome in 1640, but his major work was done for his influential patron, Gaston d'Orléans. Using watercolour on vellum, Robert painstakingly recorded the extraordinary collection of animals and plants that the Duc d'Orléans had in his garden and menagerie at Blois: a striking, parti-coloured Parrot tulip of red, green and yellow, several red tulips, including the 'Jaspée de Haarlem', flared and streaked with yellow, elegant pale creamy-white tulips, touched at the edges of their petals with pink, a deep pink tulip, perhaps a forerunner of the modern Lily-flowered types, pinched in very tightly at the waist and flaring out at the top, the petals tipped and streaked with green. The tulips are variously described as *burinées, fouettées, pennachées*, all terms that characterise the feathering and flaming or 'breaking' of the colour that was the distinguishing mark of the most highly sought-after tulips of the time. They are charmingly arranged on each sheet, the tulips mixed with other treasures of the Blois garden: anemones, hepaticas, hyacinths, pansies, campanulas.

Tulips from Les Velins du Roi
by Nicolas Robert (1614–1685)

87

Many of these treasures had been supplied by the Paris nurseryman, Pierre Morin, who had customers all over Europe. The English diarist, John Evelyn (1620–1706), more of a tree-man than a bulb-man himself, mentions in his *Memoirs* Morin's collection of rare shells and flowers, which included 10,000 tulips. Evelyn visited him in 1651, the year Pierre Morin and his brother René published their first trade catalogue and reported seeing thousands of tulips, as well as 'books painted with all his flowers'. The Morins also sold bulbs to John Tradescant for the grand Cecil garden at Hatfield in England.

Commanding huge prices in France, the tulip was indeed 'l'Impératrice des Fleurs et la plus belle Production de la Nature', as Charles de la Chesnée-Monstereul described it.[23] Given the French obsession with the flower, it was not surprising that specialist monographs such as this proliferated through the century. Most of them stemmed from the *Traité compendieux et abrégé des Tulippes et de leurs diverses sortes et espèces* – snappy titles were a seventeenth-century speciality – published anonymously in Paris in 1617 and mercilessly plagiarised for the next hundred years. The tulip's value gave it a special aura, surrounding it with mystique and the language of alchemy. Growers wanted it to seem strange, unattainable and difficult because that increased its worth. The tulip, said Monstereul, ranked as high among flowers as man among other animals and the diamond among precious stones. Much of its mystique, its charisma, had to do with the mysterious process of 'breaking', whereby a plain tulip could change into a fabulous multi-coloured one, feathered and flamed in contrasting colours. In seventeenth-century terms, this was nothing less than magic and Monstereul's response was typical: 'J'ai pensé que c'étoit quelque Puissance Souveraine, qui me le defendoit, ne voulant pas que les secrets de la divinité fussent connus que des sages, afin de n'être pas profanes du vulgaire…& suivant ce dessein je dirai aux curieux Floristes:

'Si tu multiplie la vertu de ta mère, la nourissant de la cendre de ses os, & de la substance de son père, alors tu possédera la terre de promission, en laquelle sera un étang de lait, au vers duquel passera des fleuves de vin & autres liqueurs de diverses couleurs, plusieurs rochers d'or seront espars en lui, son fond sera rempli de ces huitres, qui vomissant leur rouge cramoisy sur le sable, produiront le beau pourpre, & si tu veux suivre la mode le lait de l'étang se changera en liqueur de safran qui te donnera du souci.'

The riddle was not difficult to decipher, but the smoke-screens that seventeenth-century writers puffed around the tulip compared badly with the clarity, the thirst to explain and teach, that had characterised the work of the earliest writers on

Tulips from Les Velins du Roi
by Nicolas Robert (1614–1685)

plants. But among the mumbo-jumbo there was also practical advice. Monstereul explained that white, yellow and red tulips were the most common but the least esteemed. 'There are likewise speckled Tulips, which have more and more different Colours; yet not separated from one another, but mixed together like a Jaspar.'[24] He mentions double tulips with twenty or more petals. Like Clusius earlier, he distinguishes three different sorts: early, mid-season and late-flowering. He looks at the properties of a good tulip: the need for a good shape and a good bottom. The most highly favoured tulips of the time had bases of the finest sky-blue, like the present-day Cottage tulip 'Shirley'. Colour on the flower had to be evenly distributed and glossy, as good on the insides of the petals as out. Any stripe or flame ought to begin at the bottom of the petal and travel all the way up it. Beauty consisted not just in certain colours being there, but in their being distinct. He recommended that the petals themselves should turn on the outside like a bell. This was purely a matter of fashion. English florists equally adamantly expressed a preference for tulips shaped as half-spheres.

The best of the striped tulips were called Crowns and they could be either red and yellow or white and red. The Paltodys were finer and more neatly striped than the Crowns. The Agats were striped with two colours, the more desirable Agatines with three. The Marquatines or Marquetrines might have four, five and sometimes even more colours. 'These are the most esteemed of any by the Curious, who look upon them as the End and Highest Reward of their Art and Labour,' said Monstereul. He also mentioned 'another Sort of Tulip of an uncommon Shape, of several Colours and frightful to look upon; for which Reason they are called "Monsters"'. Were these the first Parrot tulips?

On the matter of tulip seed producing flowers that were different from either of their parents, Monstereul pronounced himself frankly 'in the Dark'. He concluded that those seeds that had most air would produce blue tulips, those that had most weather would be white and those that had most sun would be red. It was a kind of doctrine of signatures. He supported the charming notion that 'Tulips receive their colours at the Moment of their Birth from the Principles which the predominant Elements infuse into them'. Like other good gardeners since, he urged the 'Curious' to mark the best of their Tulips so that offsets of the most highly prized kinds would not be lost.

As to planting, Monstereul advised it to be done in October, 'laissant le commencement de Novembre pour les paresseux, et sa fin aux nonchalents'. The bulbs had to be stored during the summer in tulip boxes, laid out in the order in which

Tulips 'Noons Wyt', 'S. Pietter' and 'Admiral Pottenbacker'
from a tulip book by Jacob Marrell (1614–1681)
Rijksmuseum, Amsterdam

91

they were to be replanted in the beds. Like other keen tulip fanciers, Monstereul noticed that the longed-for striping was often associated with a weakening of the tulip. A plain-flowered tulip that turned into a Paragon usually had a smaller flower. ('Paragon' was a term indiscriminately attached by growers to a striped tulip that was better than any other of its kind). The leaves were closer together, the stalk thinner. But he put effect before cause. He supposed that the striped flower was not strong enough to draw all its colour up to the tops of its petals. Infuriatingly too, striped flowers produced fewer offsets than plain-flowered tulips. All enthusiasts had worked out that offsets, the small bulblets produced alongside the mother bulb, differed from seed in that they always showed the same characteristics as the parent. They were the only means by which stock of a prized flower could be increased. This was a particular problem with the Marquetrines, 'the only Tulips upon which the most curious Florists chiefly employ their time and thoughts, and spare no expense to increase the Beauty of them'.

Among his favourite tulips were 'Cedanulle' (from the Latin *cede nulli*) 'a fair Violet very distinct from the Purple', 'Dorille' and 'Passe Zablon' which were both mixtures of purple, violet and white. He liked the tawny tulips, 'Roman Agate', 'Galate' and 'Widdow' and speckled flowers such as 'Tuder' and 'Harlon'. The Marquetrines had a great deal of white in their petals. The Fantasticks had yellow petals striped with brown, sometimes threaded with purple, a combination much favoured later by the English florists who called them Bizarres. Despite the fact that they were slightly muddy in appearance, Monstereul noted that florists were particularly fond of the Fantasticks, not only because they were rare, but because they were inconstant. The inconstancy gave an extra edge to their growing, an extra prospect of producing a 'Fantastickissimo' to beat all other Fantasticks. 'The inconstancy of Man always runs after Novelty,' he wrote wearily.

He noted that yellow tulips were most likely to 'retain the smell of the Plant from whence they came' and that striped tulips usually came from flowers that in bud 'have the shape of two small horns or Cock-spurs'. In breeding, the secret lay in understanding the bottoms of the flowers. Tulips with white or blue bottoms were far more likely to produce desirable breaks than those with black or yellow bottoms, though the Fantasticks came from yellow-bottomed flowers. 'We finish by Art things which Nature has only projected.' On the matter of breaking, Monstereul was 'in the Dark' again, though he did not want to admit it. Hence the conundrum, with its enigmatic, almost masonic overtones. In his opinion 'none but Understanding and knowing Florists, ought to be taught the Mystery of bringing

Tulips to Perfection'. He had, he wrote, been forbidden to throw light on the puzzle 'to any but the knowing, that it might not be defiled by the Profane and Vulgar'. Perhaps he took his cue from Bacon who considered that a man who 'discovers Secrets, diminishes and lowers their Value'. 'Those that have Eyes and Ears will understand,' he finishes, after all his mumbo-jumbo about bones, rocks and rivers of wine. As was later to happen in England, the tulip, which had reigned as the supreme flower of fashion among the rich, was later captured by a clique of growers whose self-interest demanded that they keep amateurs at arms' length. Monstereul held up to his readers the terrible example of a florist at Rouen who had ruined his entire stock of tulips by treating the beds with pigeon's dung, which he supposed would make them break. 'I will not therefore throw Pearl before Swine, since this Treasure ought to be made known only to the skilful by Communication in Writing, and not by Printed Books,' he said severely.

In his opinion, the difference between a true Florist and an ignorant pretender was that the pretenders, like swine, 'love to scuffle through our Flower-Gardens, to carry off their Riches by their Greatness and Impudence... To hear them speak of Tulips is a murdering Noise.' He credited the Flemish with introducing the taste for tulips to the French who consequently 'devinrent les adorateurs de ces divinités terrestres' and puts forward another contender for the honour of introducing the tulip into Europe – Lopez Sampayo. The Portuguese navigator, Édouard Barberose, author of a book about his voyage to the Indies, wrote that Sampayo, a sea captain, had brought tulips into Portugal in 1530. Sampayo presented the flowers to the King of Portugal who gave them 'plus valoir que les excréments de la terre'. The tulips multiplied – as they would in that country of hot, bulb-baking summers – and their reputation quickly spread into the other countries of Europe.[25]

According to this account, Flemish traders 'épris de la beauté & majesté de cette belle fleur', were responsible for bringing the tulip out of Portugal and into the Low Countries 'en changèrent à des précieuses marchandises, & l'ayant apportée en Flandre, la plantèrent & cultivèrent si curieusement, qu'en peu d'années les cayeux [the French term for the bulb's offsets] & la graine leur donnèrent lieu d'en orner notre France, & ensuite tous les pays voisins'. From Flanders they arrived in Paris, possibly in the hands of M Cambier de l'Isle, around 1546. 'Avant celles-là , il n'avoit rien paru en ce genre', but having seen them, Paris went wild about them.[26] The first Frenchman to raise good tulips from seed was a M. Lombard, who had begged a bulb, not a very good one, from a fellow grower called Laure. The flower that grew from Lombard's bulb was 'huilée', dull and sombre, rather than striped in the

Tulip 'Agate Maurine'
by Maria Sibylla Merian (1647–1717)
Rijksmuseum, Amsterdam

94

vibrant, zinging colours that tulip growers so admired. From this unpromising stock, Lombard raised seedlings more splendid than anyone had ever seen in France. He guarded his tulips as jealously as M Laure had, but *c*1670, towards the end of his life, was persuaded to sell some of his bulbs to three other fanciers, de Valnay himself, M Desgranges and a lawyer called Caboud. They paid through the nose for them, but their judgement was sound; from Lombard's seedlings rose the strong race of Flemish 'breeders' that later provided the building blocks for present-day Darwin tulips. Monstereul had dismissed the simple bordered tulips which 'le sieur Bachelier' (that is, Busbecq), brought out of Turkey as suitable only for decorating dishes of food. These early-flowering tulips, as growers soon discovered, were not capable of 'breaking'.

There were sound commercial reasons for the nurseryman Pierre Morin to add his own bit of trumpet-blowing to the general clamour surrounding the tulip. His *Remarques Nécessaires pour la Culture des Fleurs*, published by the unscrupulous Charles de Sercy in Paris in 1678, was a nursery list very lightly disguised as a book. Morin's *Catalogue of Flowers* makes up a large part of the volume and lists 100 tulips, plenty enough, he wrote, to 'remplir un carreau' or fill 'une planche de médiocre grandeur'. His two favourites were the yellow and brown 'Amidor' and 'Erimante'. John Rea, the English nurseryman who had published his *Flora* only a few years before, also knew 'Amidor', describing it as among the 'pretty flowers which arose from good self colours which the French call "Bizars" and we "French modes"'.[27] Morin justified the list by saying that it was 'pour faire connoitre aux Curieux, qui (estant éloignez d'ici et n'en pouvant avoir les portraits) sont désireux de savoir qui sont celles que nous estimons à Paris'. His list includes the first mention of a tulip with varie-gated foliage, the white-flowered 'Ondée' with leaves that were also 'godronnées et environées' in white. Most of his tulips are late-flowering kinds such as 'Paragon d'Acosta', a white flower 'panachée' with purple and gris-de-lin. As far as tulip fanciers were concerned, this combination represented the height of chic; purple and white breaks, which do not feature in the earliest illustrations of tulips, became the *sine qua non* of tulip style. Morin's 'Brabanconne' was made in the same mould: purple, milky-white with just the faintest smudge of red. The Dutch, said Morin, called their tulips after admirals and generals. In Paris, the fashion was to call them after kings, or some-times after provinces or towns, as 'La Florentine', 'La Lucoise' or 'La Turinoise'. One breeder gave all her tulips Roman names, another favoured painters. Cardinal Richelieu (1585–1642) was more random; no particular theme seems to link the tulips he bred and named 'Jean Scime', 'Gagnepain' and 'Chancelière'.

Where tulipomania reigned, the satirist was never far behind. Dutch fanciers were mercilessly ridiculed in cartoons such as *The Fool's Cap* by Cornelis Danckerts and Jan Brueghel's *Allegory on the Tulip Mania*, which showed monkeys dealing in bulbs. English florists were lampooned by Steele in the *Spectator*. French *tulipistes* had La Bruyère to contend with. The idle and the rich, he said, had to have their fads and fashions to ease the boredom of their lives. The tulip lover 'at sunrise, hurries out to his garden in the suburbs, and does not come back till bedtime; you see him standing in the middle of his tulips as if rooted to the spot. There is "La Solitaire"; he rubs his hands with delight; he bends down to kiss her; he has never seen anything so beautiful. He goes over to "La Veuve", to "Drap d'Or" and "Agathe" but he comes back to "La Solitaire"; he will not part with her, no, not for a thousand crowns. Yet he is a person of good sense; he has a heart, he goes to church'.[28]

La Bruyère's scorn did not deter Louis XIV from filling the Grand Trianon at Versailles with tulips. A planting plan of 1693 shows tulips, white narcissus and hyacinths planted in borders in a strict ABABAC rotation, where A equals tulips, B equals narcissus and C equals hyacinths. By this time, hyacinths had outstripped all but the rarest tulips in price and consequently had to be used more sparingly, but there was a vast collection of tulip cultivars in this Grand Trianon *plate-bande*. They made an appropriate backdrop to Louis XIV's escapist entertainments: the Plaisirs de l'Isle Enchantée of 1664 or the Grand Divertissement Royal of 1668. They were *the* parties to be seen at, if you had any pretension to a place in smart society. By the giving or the withholding of invitations to these Arcadian extravaganzas, Louis XIV gradually reduced the French nobility to a state of quivering dependence on his good favour. But his successor Louis XV was the greater plantsman and the showy florimania that had characterised Louis XIV's tenure of Versailles gave way to a more serious collection of plants, especially exotics, and tulips lost their pre-eminent place in the display.

A thriving export business in tulips was built up in France at the beginning of the eighteenth century. Buyers in England, Holland and Germany sought out Agats such as the bi-coloured, short-stemmed 'Agat Fenis da Costa', 'Agat Royal' and 'Agat Oriental'. The Agat family got their name from their resemblance to the semi-precious stone, a variegated, usually banded chalcedony. They snapped up the new Violettes, which were marked with purple or lilac on a white ground. They paid through the nose for Baguettes, flamed with red or purple which made a sharp contrast against the white background of the flower. The petals of the Baguettes were large and rounded, and the flowers often had thick and particularly long stems,

Flower painting
by Jean Michel Picart (1600–1682)
Fitzwilliam Museum, Cambridge

97

sometimes more than 80cm in length. Developed first by Flemish breeders, these were amongst the most sought-after tulips of the late seventeenth and early eighteenth century. The Fantasques held their ground with those who appreciated the featherings of red, purple or brown on the saturated yellow petals. The fabulous late-flowering Marquetrines, so loved by Monstereul, commanded extraordinary prices and remained for a long period the most fashionable tulip to be found in French gardens. The Flemish growers though, particularly those around Lille, were still considered pre-eminent in breeding and in producing flowers that would give good breaks. The secret seemed to be that they always worked with tulips that had either white bases bounded with blue, or blue bases, bounded in white.[29]

Antoine-Joseph Dezallier-d'Argenville (1680–1765), the Russell Page of his day, recommended tulips in many of the garden plans and planting schemes he prepared for his clients. His schemes were formal – box-edged beds in geometric patterns – and Dezallier's plans often show tulips set in double rows close to the box edging of these parterres. The inner rows were made up of hyacinths and narcissus planted alternately. The general effect, he said, should be a 'mélange émaillé de toutes sortes de couleurs'. The planting was formal, grid-like, an arrangement carried on to the present day in the tulip beds of English florists. Dezallier recommended planting a variety of early tulips for the spring garden and 'Tulippes tardives', or late tulips, for the summer garden, though gardeners would be lucky to have many tulips that lasted beyond the end of May.[30]

Trade in tulips gradually drifted away from the French to the Dutch. (Karl Wilhem, the eighteenth-century Margrave of Baden-Durlach, bought his bulbs from Holland rather than France.) However, the predominance of French culture and the general use of the French language in polite society – at least until the middle of the eighteenth century – ensured that France for a long time retained its pre-eminence as the fount of all knowledge on tulips. This is reflected in many of the names given to tulips of the period such as 'La Couronne Imperiale', a showy double, white striped with bright red like 'Mariage de ma Fille'. It is also borne out by the extraordinary succession of treatises on tulips that were published in France after the first anonymous *Traité compendieux* of 1617. Le Père d'Ardène's *Traité des Tulipes*, published at Avignon in 1760, marked the end of the flood and, as it turned out, the end of the tulip's dizzy reign at the court of the French kings.

As befitted his calling, d'Ardène made many pious remarks about the original nature of his work, comparing it favourably with the wicked plagiarisms that had preceded it. But his own work also drew heavily on Monstereul. The difference was that he acknowledged the fact. Little seemed to have materially changed in the hundred or so years that separated the two books, except that tulips, in France as in England, were now securely in the hands of florists, specialist growers, much like the dedicated chrysanthemum and leek growers of northern England who still show their magnificent creations in competitive shows as arcane as anything in Monstereul's writings. Competition was the new element that had entered the game. Not entirely free of the deadly sins, d'Ardène noted the secret thrill of possessing a tulip that aroused jealousy in all who saw it.

Although mostly concerned with the tulip as a florists' flower, d'Ardène notes the appearance of seemingly wild (though more probably naturalised) tulips in France, both around Boulogne and in the mountains of the Auvergne. Other botanists, he says, had noted them near the towns of Montpellier (shades of Rondellet and his pupils?) and at Aix. Le Père d'Ardène says that he himself had seen wild tulips in several places 'assez jolies dans la petitesse de leur taille'. These were yellow, stippled with red, yellow stippled with grey, sometimes yellow edged with red. They were probably either *T. agenensis*, *T. australis* or *T. didieri*. Tulips also grew abundantly in the mountains of the Gappençois.

Tulips, said d'Ardène, provided 'quelques douceurs' in the midst of man's penitence and 'certaines consolations' in the midst of his work. The 'douceurs' and the 'consolations' however were not likely to be to the fore in dealings with other florists, where 'tromperies odieuses' were more the order of the day. The glossary which d'Ardène includes in his book shows how highly developed and specialised the language of the French tulip fanciers had become. Tulips might be *glacées* (that is, washed over on the backs of their petals with a colour paler than the ground colour) or *huilée*, stained, without lustre. *Jaspée* was a term applied to a particular type of tulip, like Robert's 'Jaspée de Haarlem' in which the colours were not separated, but mingled together, rather as in the red, yellow or brown semi-precious quartz known as jasper. *Rectifier* was the longed-for state that came about when a tulip 'broke' and stabilised its newly broken colours in a feathered or flamed pattern acceptable to the highly critical eyes of the florists' fraternity. The same term 'rectified' is still used by the Wakefield florists in Yorkshire, the last remaining group of English tulip fanciers to retain the traditions and the flowers of two centuries past.

Bizarres (yellow tulips striped with black, brown or red) had now become highly prized, said d'Ardène, but the further the markings moved away from red towards black, the better. The complicated Marquetrines marked with four or five differ-

Tulips *by G D Ehret*
Signed and dated 1744

100

ent colours were not now so highly esteemed. With increasing sophistication, French florists realised that 'c'est moins la multiplicité des couleurs que leur éclat et leur vivacité qui rend la Tulipe considérable'. Lowest of the low were the plain yellow tulips, but they would do in parterres, said d'Ardène or 'sur le théâtre'.[31] Whites were better than yellows, but the best were 'cramoisie, pourpre, violet obscur, incarnadin vif'. The late varieties were much preferred to the earlies, because they were so much more diverse. But, said d'Ardène, some of his earlies bloomed before the end of February and were much in demand 'à parer l'Autel'.

Whichever varieties you planted, it was important, as d'Ardène emphasised, to arrange them well. This not only gave the grower satisfaction but had the added benefit of earning the admiration of fellow florists on their ritual visits. Broken tulips should be planted next to plain ones, so that nothing could distract from the complexity of their markings. Like Dezallier, d'Ardène recommended planting in a strict grid formation, the bulbs set five inches apart each way. When all the bulbs were set in their correct positions on the bed, then you began to plant. The flowers were generally thought to be too big and unwieldy for the delicate mixed posies fashionable at the time, so they were rarely picked. A hundred years earlier, they had been worn like jewels. Now, in their formal beds, the tulips continued to capture florists with 'les entrelassements de leurs panachès; le lustre satiné de leurs feuilles; l'éclat brillant de l'or'. But d'Ardène's book marked the end of French dominance in the tulip world. By the time France had emerged on the far side of its Revolution, the Dutch had taken over the show.

CHAPTER III

EARLY BRITISH GROWERS

'THERE IS LATELY a *Flower* (shall I call it so? in courtesie I will term it so, though it deserve not the appelation), a *Toolip*, which hath ingrafted the love and affections of most people unto it; and what is this *Toolip*? A well complexion'd stink, an ill favour wrapt up in pleasant colours: As for the use thereof in *Physick*, no *Physitian* hath honoured it yet with the mention, nor with a *Greek* or *Latin* name, so inconsiderable hath it hitherto been accompted; and yet this is that which filleth all Gardens, hundreds of pounds being given for the root thereof...'[1] So you would not expect to find tulips in Thomas Fuller's London garden, but his stand was as hopeless as a twentieth-century gardener railing against petunias. Flailing, contemptuous, dismissive, he was still a man swimming against the prevailing tide. Tulips had quickly swept through mainland Europe after their introduction from the East, and they also became the instant darlings of seventeenth-century gardeners in England. The speed and suddenness of the tulip's conquest is borne out by the fact that, everywhere, it was known by the same (false) Turkish name. The flower that English gardeners and botanists called the tulip was known to the French as *tulipe*, to the Italians as *tulipano*, to the Spanish (and the Danish) as *tulipan*, to the Portuguese as *tulipa*, to the Dutch and Germans as *tulpe* and to the Swiss as *tulpan*. Fuller minded that the flower had never acquired a 'proper' Greek or Latin tag, but it had never acquired any common names either.

N.º 1202.

T. sylvestris
from Curtis's Botanical Magazine *(1809)*

Even though some species, such as *T. sylvestris* became naturalised in England and the rest of Europe, etymology suggests the tulip's heart must be buried elsewhere.

It probably slipped into England during the early part of Elizabeth I's reign (1558–1602), though it may have come earlier, arriving with the Flemish, Walloon and French refugees who from the 1540s onwards had been driven out of their own country by the depredations of Philip II. It may have been brought over by the Flemish botanist, Matthias de l'Obel (generally known as Lobelius), who came to London in 1570 and settled temporarily in a part of the city where Protestant refugees from France and the Low Countries had already been living for some time. His house was in Lime Street, where one of his neighbours was the apothecary James Garrett, also a Fleming (contemporaries described him as from 'Belga'). Both men were early associates of John Gerard (1545–1612), physician, gardener and curator of the physic garden belonging to the College of Physicians. He also looked after Lord Burghley's garden in the Strand and the garden at Burghley's proto-palace, Theobalds in Hertfordshire. A contemporary portrait, painted when Gerard was forty-one, shows a wary, weasel-faced opportunist, the countenance made all the sharper by a neat, pointed beard. The slashed pantaloons and crazy, long-toed shoes suggest a dandy, as does the posy of pinks that Gerard is holding.

The first published mention of tulips in English crops up in Henry Lyte's *Nievve Herball or Historie of Plantes*[2] but he only repeated Dodoens's vague belief that the tulip had been 'brought from Greece and the countrie about Constantinople'. Twenty years later, Gerard was more specific. He says he got his tulips from Aleppo in Syria as did 'Master Garth, a worshipful gentleman'. He also says that 'his loving friend Master James Garrett…a curious searcher after simples and learned Apothecarie in London' had been cultivating tulips for twenty years.[3] This suggests that Garrett had been growing them since at least 1577, but how did he get hold of them? Did he get them from Lobelius when he arrived in London? Or had he been growing them even earlier, corresponding with and receiving seeds from Lobelius while he was still in Flanders? Being Flemish himself, language would have been no barrier to Garrett in the exchange of information. Latin, anyway, was the *lingua franca* of the time, particularly among botanists, who consequently could talk to each other more easily in the seventeenth century than they can in the twentieth.

Lobelius, while in the Low Countries, must have had news of the dramatic flowering of the tulip in Johannes Heinrich Herwart's garden in Augsburg in 1559 and perhaps passed the news on to Garrett. Gerard writes that Garrett had 'undertaken to find out, if it were possible, the infinite sorts [of tulip] by diligent sowing of their seeds, and by planting those of his own propagation and others received from his friends beyond the seas for the space of twenty years, not being yet able to attain to the end of his travail, for that each new year brought forth new plants of sundry colours not before seen, all which to describe particularly were to "Roule Sisiphus Stone" or number the sands'.

Since a tulip usually takes seven years to grow from seed to flowering bulb, this was long-drawn-out work, but Gerard considered Garrett one of the earliest and most successful growers of the tulip in the country. In his garden at London Wall, Garrett grew yellow, white, light purple and red (the most common) tulips. Gerard mentions specifically a tulip that was 'a greater sort than the rest…a stalke a foot high or something higher, upon which standeth only one flower bolt upright'. The inference is that most of the tulips being grown at the time were less than a foot tall which suggests that, while perhaps not truly wild species, these Elizabethan tulips had not strayed very far from their low-growing wild parents. Garrett was collecting and sowing his own seed, but there is nothing in Gerard that specifically says that he was cross-pollinating different kinds.

Gerard's *Herball*, now so well known, was very nearly Priest's *Herball*, for John Norton, the printer, had originally commissioned it from the botanist Robert Priest, not as an original work, but a translation of another Dodoens's book, *Pemptades*. Priest died before he finished the job and Gerard took over, adapting the Dodoensesque translation to something more closely modelled on the works of his friend Lobelius, who kindly and quietly corrected some of the worst howlers before publication. Gerard was a good publicist, but not a scholar. The first edition contained 1,800 woodcut illustrations, most of them lifted from an earlier Dutch herbal by Tabernaemontanus (later editions had familiar Plantin woodcuts). Six tulips were shown, and another eight described in the text, but as Gerard acknowledged, the family was a difficult one to pin down. 'The chives or threads in the middle of the flowers, be sometime yellow, other whiles blackish or purplish, but commonly of one overworne colour or other, Nature seeming to plaie more with this flower, than any other that I do know.'

He portrayed the tulip as 'a strange and forraine flower, one of the number of the bulbed flowers, whereof there be sundrie sorts, some greater, some lesser with which all studious and painefull herbarists desire to be better acquainted, because of that excellent diversitie of most brave flowers which it beareth'. Following the prevailing mode, he divided tulips into three different groups – early, late and mid-

Matthias de l'Obel (Lobelius) 1538–1616
in an engraving by François Dellarame 1615

season – describing them as 'Italian', 'French', 'timely-flowering', 'late-flowering' or 'blush-coloured'. One, cumbersomely titled 'Tulipa media sanguinea albis oris', Gerard calls the 'Appleblossom Tulip'. His description brings to mind *T. clusiana* but the illustration shows a tulip of different outline to the narrow, chaste form of the Lady tulip. He talks about tulips being 'striped confusedly' which suggests that fancy feathered and flamed types were already well known. He talks too of a tulip 'in our London gardens of a snow white colour, the edges slightly washed over with a little of that we call blush colour'.

As in mainland Europe, the early history of the tulip in England has to be interpreted as much by its absence as its presence. No tulips occur in the beautifully detailed portraits of flowers that decorate early manuscripts, nor do they appear in English pictures of the fifteenth and early sixteenth centuries. If they had been available, you would expect to see them for instance in the portrait of Sir Thomas More and his family painted in 1526 by Hans Holbein the Younger (1497–1543). All the totemic (and expensive) flowers of the period are there, arranged in three vases behind the family group. There are huge and showy irises, some beautiful pinks, aquilegias, lilies, but no tulips. But tulips do appear in a strange miniature, watercolour on vellum, showing *A Young Daughter of the Picts*, painted, probably towards the end of his life, by Jacques Le Moyne de Morgues (*c*1533–1588). The girl stands chillily naked except for a sword slung round her waist on a chain. The landscape around her is barren, but symmetrically arranged like tattoos all over her body are flowers: single and double peonies, hollyhock, heartsease, double columbines, lilies, tazetta narcissus, cornflowers, rose campions, yellow horned poppies and splendidly anachronistic *Iris susiana* and tulips, only recently introduced into England. Two plain red tulips decorate her knees, two plain yellow ones curve round the contours of her thighs. Is this the first picture (as distinct from illustration) of tulips to have appeared in England? Tantalisingly, it bears no date.

A contemporary of the Flemish painter, Joris Hoefnagel, de Morgues was born in Dieppe, a centre renowned for its cartographers and illuminators. When he was about thirty years old, he set sail from Le Havre as cartographer and artist/recorder on René de Laudonniere's exploratory expedition to Florida. In September 1565 Spaniards overran the Huguenot colony in Florida, but de Morgues escaped and returned to France. By about 1580 he had settled amongst other Huguenots in the parish of St Anne's, Blackfriars, London, and was granted letters of denization on 12 May 1581. A return of aliens living in Blackfriars, dated 28 April 1583, describes him as 'James le Moyne, alias Morgan, paynter, borne under the obezance of the

Tulips on A Young Daughter of the Picts
by the Huguenot artist
Jacques le Moyne de Morgues (c1533–1588)

Frenche kinge, and his wife, came for religion, and are of the French church, denison ij years'.[4] Like Joris Hoefnagel, de Morgues occupied the shifting ground where illustration turned into something more like art. While he was living in Blackfriars he produced *La clef du champs* (1586), a little pattern book of woodcut illustrations of plants, possibly using the press of a fellow Huguenot, the scholar-printer Thomas Vautrollier. De Morgues had some powerful patrons: Sir Walter Raleigh and Lady Mary Sidney whose son, Sir Philip, had been in touch with Clusius on his journeys to England. An impressive picture emerges of an extensive intellectual network of plant lovers in the second half of the sixteenth century which embraced Flemings, Huguenots, Englishmen – Clusius, Dodoens, Gerard, Gesner, Hoefnagel, de Morgues, Lobelius – in places as far flung as Antwerp, Leiden, London, Prague, Strasbourg and Vienna. The tulips that de Morgues painted may have been familiar to him before he arrived in England. More likely, he saw them in James Garrett's garden at London Wall, or Lobelius's at Lime Street, both within a short walk of Blackfriars. Garrett was a friend of Clusius's too, who mentioned him at least nine times – always in terms of commendation and esteem – in his last book *Rariorum plantarum Historia* (1601). Perhaps it was he, rather than Lobelius, who sent Garrett his first tulips.

By the time Garrett, the first of the English tulip fanciers, died in 1610, the tulip was well established as a favourite flower of Jacobean gardens, though it was ignored by William Shakespeare (1564–1616), who managed to cram a herbaceous border full of other flowers into his poems and plays. But at Hatfield House in Hertfordshire, the 1st Earl of Salisbury was only one of the rich landowners of seventeenth-century England to plant tulips in his parterres. You had to be rich to take part in this particular fancy. On 3 January 1611, the Earl's gardener, John Tradescant, sent in his bill for 'Routes, flowers, Seedes, trees and plants by him bought for my Lo: in Holland'.[5] His list includes roses, anemones, quince, two Naples medlar trees, *Iris susiana* and – from Haarlem – 800 tulip bulbs at ten shillings the hundred. The cost of the tulips alone was equal to a gardeners' half-yearly wage. The expenditure was not quite as extravagant as the Margrave of Baden-Durlach's, but it was still a remarkable sum to part with for plants that were so prone to attack by mice and slugs, so ready to rot in England's wet and clammy soil. But novelty prevailed. Tradescant may also have brought back Russian tulips for Hatfield, for he was in Archangel in 1618 and was well aware that 'thear groweth in the land both tulipes and narsisus'.

Thirty years or so after Gerard had brought out his *Herball*, the apothecary John Parkinson published his huge compendium of plants *Paradisi in Sole Paradisus*

109

Terrestris. The book with its punning title stood with the *Herball* as one of the great pillars of seventeenth-century botany. In the intervening years, Gerard's fourteen tulips had swelled tenfold. Gerard had loosely grouped them by their flowering times, but Parkinson could not get off so lightly. By the time he came into print, gardeners and nurserymen had begun to give tulips varietal names. Given its brilliantly anarchic character, its ability to bounce up one spring wearing an entirely different coat from the year before, this was a hopeless enterprise. But Parkinson tried, listing among others a 'Gingeline', a 'Testament Brancion, a 'Red Flambant', a 'Purple Holias', a 'Crimson Foole's Coate', a 'Greene Swisser', a 'Goliah', a 'Stamell, dark or light', a 'Prince or Bracklar'. 'These doe flower' he says, 'some earlier, some later, for three whole moneths together at the least, therein adorning out a garden most gloriously, in that being but one kinde of flower, it is so full of variety as no other…doe the like besides.'

Purity of form, the one great over-riding criterion of later English tulip fanciers, was not so important to the early growers as distinct colour breaks and unusual markings. Parkinson noted the tulip's 'stately aspect' but the 'admirable varietie of colours' was its chief asset in the cabinets of horticultural curiosities that seventeenth-century gardeners marvelled at. By the rigorous standards of nineteenth-century florists, these tulips were fatally flawed: long-petalled, loose in shape, often showing gaps between the petals, the whole flower rarely forming the neat cupped shape that was later deemed to be the acme of perfection of the English florists' tulip. But the early tulips were rare, therefore precious.

Parkinson had the edge on Gerard. Not only was *Paradisi in Sole* a better-informed book, it was also better illustrated. Tulips appeared prominently on the illustrated title page, one sitting in the centre of the Garden of Eden, another flanking a pineapple. It is evident from Parkinson's engravings that the 'broken' tulips, feathered and flamed in patterns as diverse as fingerprints, were the types that were chiefly admired and that in the thirty years between Parkinson and Gerard, the flower had developed enormously. Even Parkinson, who tried so hard to pin labels onto the errant tulip, had to admit defeat in the end. 'But as to tell you of all the sorts of Tulipas (which are the pride of delight)…doth both passe my ability, and as I beleeve the skill of any other,' he said. 'Besides this glory of variety in colors that these flowers have, they carry so stately and delightful a forme, and do abide so long in their bravery…that there is no Lady or Gentleman of any worth, that is not caught with this delight, or not delighted with these flowers' – except Thomas Fuller.

Title page
from Paradisi in Sole Paradisus Terrestris *(1629) by John Parkinson*

Parkinson suggested that tulips should be planted so that their colours resembled a piece of curious needlework or a painting. The Stoke Edith tapestries at Montacute House in Somerset show the prevailing style: tulips planted in narrow borders around the edge of lozenge-shaped beds, each with a fountain in the centre. They make double rows, as do the carnations that are lined out in another narrow strip bed alongside grass. Neatly clipped balls and cones of evergreen box or yew are planted at regular intervals along the walks and fan-trained fruit trees are spread-eagled against the red brick wall that forms the boundary of this tapestry garden. The same formality is evident in the group portrait of the Capel family (Arthur Capel, 1st Baron of Hadham 1604–1649, Elizabeth, Lady Capel and their five children) painted by Cornelius Johnson c1640. The Capels are posed in the formal garden at Little Hadham, Hertfordshire, which lies behind them. There are broad gravel sweeps with fountains in the centre of curved quadrants. Urns decorate the balustrades. The two urns behind Elizabeth's head are filled with tulips, blue (unlikely), white, yellow and orange.[6]

When Parkinson published his *Paradisus*, the word 'florist' was already being used to describe the cultivators and admirers of a certain group of flowers.[7] The group included the anemone, auricula, carnation, polyanthus and ranunculus, as well as the tulip. Later, pinks and pansies were added to the collection. Four of these flowers, the anemone, the carnation, the ranunculus and the tulip, were already being eagerly collected and bred by the middle of the seventeenth century. All florists' flowers had blooms that were best admired at close quarters; all were capable of being developed and diversified by patient cross-breeding. Although in *Paradisus* Parkinson addressed his remarks about the culture of tulips to 'gentlewomen for their delight', the florists' societies in existence from the middle of the seventeenth century were almost exclusively male preserves. Nevertheless, several women such as Mary Capel (holding roses in Johnson's group portrait) became distinguished horticulturists. After her marriage to the Duke of Beaufort, Mary Somerset, as she became, made botanic gardens at Badminton and Chelsea which were praised everywhere for the excellence of their plants, drawn from all quarters of the earth. The garden at Beaufort House, Chelsea had its 'Bedd of Tulips with Bedd of Batchelers Buttons'. There was also a raised walk, the Mount Walk, leading to a banqueting house which had a border of tulips on either side. Many named auriculas and tulips appear in the *Hortus Siccus* made from flowers grown by the Duchess of Beaufort and she also commissioned an important series of flower drawings to document her collection.[8]

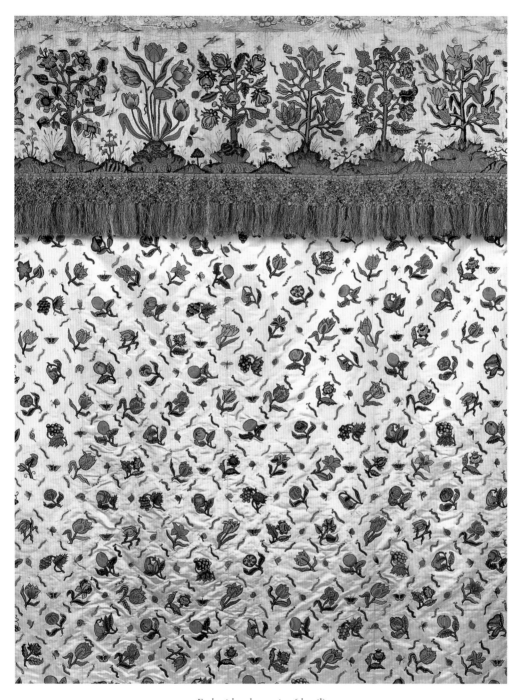

Embroidered curtains (detail)
satin with silk embroidery English mid seventeenth century
Victoria and Albert Museum, London

113

Alexander Marshall (c1625–1682) was rich enough to be able to paint for his own amusement, rather than on commission. His flower album, collated from c1659 onwards, was one of the wonders of the age, the English equivalent of Nicolas Robert's work for the Duc d'Orléans. John Evelyn saw it on 1 August 1682 when Marshall was staying with Bishop Compton at Fulham Palace, London. From his garden in Wimbledon, Lambert, the mutinous Roundhead general, sent a Guernsey Lily for him to paint. The royal gardener John Tradescant begged him to 'limn in vellum' some of the plants in his Lambeth garden. Three fine red and white tulips, accredited by Marshall to The Widow Lancsel are set on a page with heartsease, leucojum and a double pink anemone. The name sounds Dutch or perhaps Flemish, but most of the tulips Marshall painted had French names, like his delicate 'Prunelle', finely feathered with red on a white ground, or the more randomly marked 'Agatte Robin' named perhaps after the French nurseryman, Pierre Robin. A yellow tulip finely striped in red is called 'Chamelotte' by Marshall, the name perhaps coming from an Arab term used to describe the pile on velvet. The texture of a tulip's petal was an important part of its charm.

The bulbs, though, were still unfamiliar enough at this time to be misused. Parkinson had written that 'divers have had them sent by their friends from beyond the sea, and mistaking them to be onions, have used them as onions in their pottage or broth, and never found any cause of mislike, or any sense of evil quality produced by them, but accounted them sweet onions'. Like Clusius, Parkinson also tried eating them; he preserved the bulbs in sugar and thought them pleasant, though hardly worth the trouble. They would not have made this mistake in Norfolk, where there had been Flemish refugees, well versed in the culture of bulbs, since the mid sixteenth century. They had brought gillyflowers, Provence roses and carnations with them, as well as tulips. Many of them were weavers and some settled in Norwich, where later, in the early seventeenth century, the first florists' feasts were held. The light, free-draining soil of East Anglia (which Dutch engineers had helped rescue from the Wash) was well suited to growing bulbs such as the tulip. Ruth Duthie's pioneering work[9] into the history of the florists' societies indicates that the first florists' feast was held at Norwich on 3 May 1631, where guests were entertained by Ralph Knevet's play *Rhodon and Iris*.[10] The play was dedicated to Nicholas Bacon of Gillingham, who was said to be 'fervently addicted to a speculation of the virtues and beauties of all flowers'. There is no specific mention of tulips, though the date (equal to 14 May in the present calendar) would have caught the peak of their flowering. Knevet addressed the preface of his play to 'his much respected friends the Society of Florists', and referred to the 'feast celebrated by such a conflux of Gentlemen of birth and quality in whose presence and commerce (I thinke) your cities welfare partly consists'. The Feast got the florists into trouble with the Norwich Puritans, who disapproved of such carousings, in part because they were dedicated to the pagan goddess Flora. William Strode, chaplain to the Bishop of Norwich in 1632, tried to put things right in *A Prologue crown'd with Flowers on the Florists' Feast at Norwich*,[11] but these were hard times for those who worshipped at the altar of beauty rather than utility. Parkinson's celebratory *Paradisus* had been published in the very same year that Parliament first rose up against the King.

Strode's *Prologue* mentioned tulips. So did Matthew Stevenson in *At the Florists' Feast in Norwich. Flora Wearing a Crown,* which commemorated the same society of florists fourteen years later.[12] 'Had yee but met when Tulops were in towne,' he wrote, 'She then had given you every one a crowne.' The Norwich florists did not appear to be cowed by the Puritans, but while the Commonwealth was in place, many Royalists escaped abroad or slid quietly away to their country estates, kept their heads below their hedges and, like Sir Thomas Hanmer of Bettisfield, Flintshire, cultivated their gardens. But even some flower-loving Puritans fell foul of their master. One of Cromwell's commanders, General Lambert, who had refused in 1657 to take an oath of allegiance to the Roundhead leader, was forced to retire to his manor in Wimbledon where he occupied himself growing tulips and gillyflowers. He is commemorated satirically in a pack of Royalist playing cards as 'Lambert, Kt of ye Golden Tulip'. Lord Capel of Little Theobalds was actually a member of the Long Parliament, but was so shocked by the violence of the opinions expressed there, that he became a loyal supporter of the King. He escorted Queen Henrietta Maria to France in 1646 and helped Charles escape briefly in 1647, but he was taken prisoner at Colchester in 1648 and imprisoned in the Tower.

Some Royalists lost their estates. Theobalds, the Cecil's great house in Hertfordshire, where forty years earlier John Gerard had gardened, was one of the great houses taken over (as Lambert's Wimbledon Manor had been) by the Parliamentarians. Raphe Baldwyn surveyed Theobalds in April 1650, finding among other things 'a quicksett hedge wch goeth round ye Garden, with a square knott in ye middle of ye Garden turned into a compleate fashion and shape, with 3 ascents, boorded and planted with Tulipps, Lillies, Piannies, and divers other sorts of flowers'.

Sir Thomas Hanmer took a few prudent trips abroad in the 1640s but in 1646, at

A set of four wriggle-work engraved plates by Daniel Barton of London, c1700.
Each plate is decorated with a tulip, the owner's initials HsA appearing on the rim

the end of the Civil War, retired to his estate at Bettisfield, Flintshire which (unlike Wimbledon Manor and Theobalds) was too far from the centre of things to be of interest to the Parliamentarians. Hanmer was an almost exact contemporary of the French court painter Nicolas Robert. While Robert was painting glorious tulips such as 'Jaspée de Haarlem' and 'Perroquet de trois couleurs' for Gaston d'Orléans, brother of King Louis XIV, Hanmer was growing them in Flintshire. By the time of the Restoration, Hanmer was acknowledged as one of the most accomplished gardeners in the country, an expert, particularly, on tulips. And unlike his counterparts in the Netherlands, he had not been ruined by them. Between 1634 and 1637 tulipomania had reached a fever pitch in the Netherlands that is difficult to understand now. The Civil War brought one benefit: Roundheads and Cavaliers alike had been too preoccupied to gamble with bulbs. Hanmer's love of gardening transcended politics. In June 1655, as he noted in his pocket book, he sent to General Lambert at Wimbledon 'a very great mother-root of Agate Hanmer'. This was one of his best tulips, described by John Rea, a nurseryman of Kinlet in Shropshire, as 'grideline [a greyish-purple], deep scarlet and pure white. This gallant tulip,' wrote Rea, 'hath its name from that ingenious lover of these rarities, Sir Thomas Hanmer, who first brought it into England, from whose free community myself and others partake the delight of this noble flower.' John Evelyn had 'Agate Hanmer' too, sent by Hanmer on 21 August 1671 for his garden at Sayes Court, Deptford.

Hanmer's *Garden Book* (completed in manuscript by 1659, but not published until 1933) paints a clear picture of the typical gentleman's garden of the mid seventeenth century: parterres with the alleys between filled with coloured gravels, compartments and borders for flowers, trimmed evergreens, and perhaps for flower-lovers such as Hanmer himself a 'little private seminary, to keep such treasures as are not be exposed to every one's view'. Hanmer grew bear's ears (auriculas), anemones, primroses, cowslips and gillyflower but his greatest favourite was the tulip, 'the Queen of bulbous plants, whose flower is beautiful in its figure, and most rich and admirable in colour, and wonderful in variety of markings'.

Tulips grew in thirteen ranks of four in one of Hanmer's flower beds on the right next to his house. Another thirteen ranks of four tulips were set in the boarded bed furthest from the house on the left. In the border under the west wall by the door leading through to his courtyard he planted offsets of a wide variety of tulips and anemones. A catalogue of the contents of the flower garden at Bettisfield in 1660 seems chiefly concerned with tulips. Each bed is mentioned and every row of bulbs is taken separately with each bulb named: 'Peruchot', 'Admiral

Enchuysen', 'Angelica', 'Comisetta', 'Omen', 'Diana', some of the 'very good bearing rootes' that in 1654 Hanmer had sent to his friend, Sir John Trevor.

He also left detailed notes on the way that tulips should be grown, recommending that they be set in the ground about the time of the full moon in September, planted four inches deep and the same distance apart. Already keen tulip growers, such as he, had identified the best kinds of tulips to propagate from seed, the kinds that would be most likely to 'parrach' or break. 'Keep old strong roots for seed,' he wrote, 'such kinds as have blue cup and purple chives and are striped with pure white and carnations, or gridelines or murreys. The single colours with blue cups or bottoms and purple chives will most of them parrach or stripe and will stand two years unremoved when the roots are old.' He may have picked up this information on his journeys into France and Flanders, where, at this stage, tulip-growing was more advanced than it was in England. The single-coloured tulips with the blue bottoms that Hanmer mentioned were later used as 'breeders' by English florists of the late eighteenth century, who 'broke' from them the beautiful feathered and flamed Bybloemen and Rose tulips that were shown in competitive classes throughout the country. Good breaks changed hands for remarkably high prices.

Tulips – 190 different kinds – featured prominently in Rea's own book, *Flora, seu de Florum Cultura*, published in 1665. Broken tulips were already known, but now Rea described jagged-petalled Parrot tulips too, 'very strange in fashion and colours from all others'. Rea dedicated his book to his friend, the 'truly noble and perfect lover of ingenuity', Sir Thomas Hanmer. The goddesses Flora, Ceres and Pomona (who provide the alternative title of the book) decorate the title page, Flora in the central position, holding a bunch of flowers which includes a tulip and a rose. Tulips are arranged in the fancy urns either side of her, along with peonies and crown imperials (*Fritillaria imperialis*).

One of Rea's patrons was Baron Gerard, of Gerrard's Bromley, Staffordshire, for whose wife he had laid out the garden there. Rea evidently deemed it politic to include her in the dedication too. This he did in the form of a long, laudatory poem, which together with another preliminary poem, *Flora to the Ladies*, is full of coded references to flowers, especially tulips. 'Agate Hanmer' is there of course, 'the Queen of all delights', who

> Wears Graydeline, Scarlet and White
> So interwoven and so plac'd
> That all the other are disgrac'd.

The poem makes clear that tulips of 'Tyrian purple and fine white' were far more highly prized than the red and yellow kinds:

> The meanest here you can behold
> Is cloth'd in Scarlet, lac'd with Gold.

Rea suggests a design for a relatively modest garden with about forty square yards set aside for fruit and twenty square yards for flower beds. He recommended the building of a brick boundary wall at least nine feet high all round the garden, and another wall of about five feet to divide the fruit garden from the flower garden. He talks of bounding the square beds with painted wooden rails, or else with box trees or palisades for dwarf fruit trees. In the corners of the flower beds, he advised planting crown imperials, martagon lilies and peonies. 'The streight beds are fit for the best tulips, where account may be kept of them. Ranunculus and Anemonies also require particular beds – the rest may be set all over with the more ordinary sorts of Tulips…' He also thought the ideal flower garden should have 'a handsom octangular somer-house roofed everyway and finely painted with landskips and other conceits furnished with seats about and a table in the middle which serveth not only for delight and entertainment but for many other necessary purposes as to put the roots of Tulips and other flowers in, as they are taken up upon papers'.

Rea's descriptions show what great attention was paid at this time to the culture of bulbs, especially tulips, even in relatively small gardens. Just over a hundred years after the first tulip had been seen at Augsburg, the number of varieties available had increased to 190. A distinction had already arisen between the best sorts and more ordinary kinds. Despite the political upheaval that had characterised the century, in mainland Europe as well as Britain, the flower was well known and widely cultivated. Tulips though were still thought of as foreign flowers – 'French flowers' Rea called them in his introductory paragraph on 'The Flower Garden'. At this time, French and Flemish florists, growers and breeders played a more important part than the Dutch in bringing the tulip on and developing its potential, increasing its market value all the while. The flower garden, wrote Rea, should be fashioned 'in the form of a Cabinet, with several Boxes fit to receive, and securely to keep, Nature's choicest jewels'. Chief among these were the tulips, variously 'Mixed, edged, striped, feathered, garded, agotted, marbled, flaked, or specled'. Descriptive vocabulary was stretched to keep up with the number of new tricks the tulip performed with the lazy, laid-back grace of a natural superstar.

Table from Warwick Castle
English, 1675
Victoria and Albert Museum, London

Rea describes several of the tulips that had caused havoc among the Dutch at the height of tulipomania. The most notorious were 'Viceroy' and 'Semper Augustus'. 'Viceroy', he wrote, 'is an old flower of a violet purple colour, edged, feathered and striped with white, the bottom and Tamis [stamens] of a greenish yellow colour; to the name of this flower Paragon is often added, as if it were a distinct kind, when it is but the same, better marked than usual.' 'Semper Augustus' flowered mid-season. 'Heretofore' said Rea, this tulip had been 'of much esteem', the inference being that it had already been superseded by better types. The bloom itself was not very big, but it was beautifully veined and striped with deep crimson and pale yellow, set off against a base and stamens of dark violet-purple.

Rea followed Gerard in grouping tulips into three classes, early, mid and late-flowering. Among the thirty-one early-flowering (Praecox) tulips he mentioned, Rea considered 'The Superintendant' one of the best. 'It riseth higher than ordinarily others do; the flower is fair and large, excellently marked with violet purple and good white, the bottom and Tamis pale yellow.' Only nine late-flowering kinds (Serotinas) are listed. By far the biggest group are the mid-flowering kinds (Media) and their names suggest that they are mostly of foreign rather than English origin. Rea was particularly keen though on a tulip called 'Paragon Blackburn', a tall-growing type with 'a fair Flower with broad leaves [petals] yet sharp pointed, of light carnation colour, with some marks of deeper red, flamed and striped with white; the bottom and Tamis blue. This was raised by Mr Humphrey Blackburn, late keeper of the garden at York House in the Strand, from the seeds of the "Pass Oudinard", as he told me when he gave me the root.' Rea also recommended 'Rickets Fine Agot', a beautiful flower, 'striped, agotted and variously marked with rose colour, deep crimson and fine white'. Presumably, this had been raised by George Ricketts (*fl.* 1660s–1706), a nurseryman of Hoxton, Shoreditch, London, whom Rea called 'the best and most faithful florist now about London'.

He was not always so complimentary. 'It is a trick much used by those who sell flowers about London', he grumbled, 'to add Paragon to the name of any common flower when it comes well marked and then impose a treble price'. Rea's tulips cost between a penny and five pounds each. 'Edgers', that is the early-flowering kinds, were not as esteemed as the striped, feathered and flamed varieties, but 'Winter Duke' was deemed useful because it flowered before 10 March. The Dukes, Ducs, or Ducks (the spelling varied depending on which language the writer thought he was copying) were a distinct type of tulip which is still available as 'Duc van Thol' or other such Single Early tulips. They were low-growing, often distinguished by a clear, neat rim of contrasting colour around the edges of the petals. The most common types were red with yellow margins.

As a nurseryman, it is not surprising that Rea had such a keen eye for detail in the flowers he described. Like later florists, he was much concerned with the beauty of the inside of the tulip, the differences between the size, shape and colour of the basal blotch, the various colours of the stamens, the distinctions in texture between the inside and the outside of the petal, the inner surface often being much more highly glossed than the outer. He noticed the tendency of the separate colours of some feathered and flamed flowers to run together in the sun. This was a problem that bothered later florists just as much. But he noticed, too, that the sun would sometimes bleach a pale yellow ground colour into a much more desirable (more highly regarded and therefore more expensive) white. His notes on tulips such as 'Paragon Blackburn' make it clear that organised breeding of tulips was now more common in England and that the beginnings of a tulip stud book were being put together, as growers kept records of the parentage of their new seedling varieties. Some new tulips were chance breaks from other, more established varieties, but a number of seedlings were also being raised, bred as 'Paragon Blackburn' had been, from tulips that were judged to be the best of their particular group. Rea put his finger on another reason for the flower being taken up so enthusiastically by commercial nurserymen. It was 'aptly conveyable (the season considered) many miles distant'.

By the time a new edition of Rea's work was published in 1676, the taste for tulips and other florists' flowers had trickled down from the aristocracy and gentry to capture gardeners of all kinds. The best bulbs may have been expensive, but the seeds could be free, and not difficult to get hold of if you had a friend who was a gardener at one of the big houses in the district. Few didn't, when communities were small and garden workers rather thick on the ground. Those who were not rich had to be patient and wait the seven years that it took to raise flowering-size bulbs from a pod of tulip seed. The number of tulips listed in the second edition of Rea's book increased to 300, mirroring the increasing demand for the flowers, which peaked in popularity between 1680 and 1710. Rea died in 1677, followed only a year later by Sir Thomas Hanmer. With their deaths, the first pioneering chapter of tulip-growing in England came to an end, just as the flower itself began to explode into general favour.

Rea left his plants to Samuel Gilbert, who had married his daughter, Minerva.

A tulip charger of English delftware
London, 1661

123

Gilbert was rector of Quatt in Shropshire and also chaplain to Jane, wife of Charles, the fourth Baron Gerard, celebrated in the preface to Rea's book. Gilbert was better placed than his father-in-law to exploit the new craze and his *Florist's Vade mecum* (1682) was wildly successful. He recommended a tulip garden with beds divided into squares, each division to be planted with a separate variety. He was the only author of the time to recommend plants (amaranthus, marvel of Peru and nasturtiums) to fill the gaps left when tulips had finished flowering. Seventeenth-century gardens peaked in spring and early summer; there were relatively few plants available that flowered later in the season.

Andrew Marvell, the poet, was one of many who lamented the settled times before the Civil War. 'Shall we never more / That sweet militia restore,' he asked,

> When gardens only had their towers
> And all the garrisons were flowers?
> Tulips in several colours barred
> Were then the Switzers of our guard[13]

With the restoration of Charles II, the settled times briefly returned (until the Jacobite rebellion) and nurserymen benefited mightily. Roger Looker, who had started his career as a gardener at Hatfield House, later found it more profitable to set up a nursery at St Martin's in the Fields, London. In September 1684, he supplied the Marquis of Bath at Longleat with 4,000 crocus roots for £2, 1,000 best mixed tulips for £5 and 1,000 second-best mixed for £2 10s. George Ricketts, the Hoxton nurseryman who had bred 'Rickets Fine Agot', was busy too. In 1689, he sent mulberries and apples, spruce and cypress to Levens in Westmorland. Included in the order were '100 lilys (white) of Constantinople, 50 Campernello, 200 Good Tulipps mixt, 100 Ranunculus'. The lilies were 12s., Campernello 4s., Tulips £1 4s., Ranunculus £1. At this stage, lilies and tulips were roughly equal in price, while ranunculus, a very popular florists' flower, were more expensive. Thirty black cherry trees in the same order cost only 10s. Ricketts, one of three nurserymen based in Hoxton at the time,[14] offered a very wide variety of plants. His 1688 Catalogue was divided into several sections: 'Greens that are Housed in the Winter'; 'Flower Bearing Trees'; 'Winter Greens'; 'Other Ornamental Trees'; 'Flowers and Choice Plants' under which are listed 'Tulips great variety'. Florists were flourishing too. It was around this time that the London Floral Feasts started, set up by Thomas Wrench (*c*1630–1728), auricula grower and nurseryman of Fulham.

The Stoke Edith tapestry (now at Montacute in Somerset) shows tulips planted in the typically formal fashion of the late seventeenth century

Nurserymen prospered. Some of them, such as George London, became rather grand. London teamed up with Roger Looker and others to start the famous Brompton Park Nursery, Kensington in the 1680s, but by 1694 had bought out the others and established himself with Henry Wise as his sole partner. His daughter, Henrietta, contributed some of the drawings of plants in the Duchess of Beaufort's collection. George London was involved in designing and creating many of the best gardens of the time, including the Beauforts' garden at Badminton and the Duke of Devonshire's place at Chatsworth. Tulips in their borders were planted according to the same formal, grid-like arrangement that Dezallier-d'Argenville was advocating in France.

London and Wise recommended that the gardener 'ought first of all to draw Rills upon his Borders, four inches distant from one another longways and crossways, so that the Borders being thus laid out may form a sort of Grate'.[15] The system, though rigid, had practical advantages. The grid provided an easy way of recording what was growing where. At lifting time (all tulip bulbs were lifted and dried off when they had finished flowering ready for replanting the following autumn), one bulb looked exactly like another, yet it was vital that the bulbs should be distinguished, for there was a vast difference in price between the stars and the also-rans. Offsets – the small bulblets – of very expensive tulips were carefully hoarded, for they provided the only reliable way to bulk up stock of named tulips. The virtuoso John Evelyn went one step further in grid planting. In his unpublished manuscript, *Elysium Britannicum*, an illustration shows a ready-made lattice which, pressed on the earth, made a planting grid for tulips and other bulbs. Evelyn credited the bulb-crazy French with inventing the device, which was six feet long and three feet wide (1.8m × 0.9m), each square 'at competent distance for bulbous rootes'. Using this, the gardener could 'avoide the frequent removing of the line'.

By the time the essayist and dramatist Sir Richard Steele (1672–1729) contributed his teasing piece about tulips to the *Tatler* (31 August 1710), the hyacinth was already beginning to outstrip the tulip in popularity. But Steele knew his readers would understand the tulip jokes, even if they were at their expense. The flower had become a nation-wide phenomenon, appearing on furniture and fabrics, silver and all kinds of ceramics from lead-glazed Staffordshire posset pots to tin-glazed Southwark dishes. 'I asked them to let me be one of their company,' wrote Steele. 'The gentleman of the house told me, if I delighted in flowers, it would be worth my while; for that he believed he could show me such a blow of tulips, as was not to be matched in the whole country. I accepted the offer and found that they had been talking in terms of gardening, and that the Kings and Generals they had mentioned were only so many tulips, to which the gardeners, according to their usual custom, had given such high titles and appellations of honour... I accidentally praised a tulip as one of the finest I ever saw; upon which they told me, it was a common Fool's Coat... He told me that he valued the bed of flowers which lay before us and was not above twenty yards in length and two in breadth, more than he would the best hundred acres of land in England.' Florists and the puffed-up names that they gave to their flowers were an easy target for a satirist. Given the prices that were now being paid for tulips, growers, said Steele, must be suffering from an illness, a distemper, which affected their minds and judgement.

Undeterred, gardeners continued to plant. At the Manor of Little Crosby in southwest Lancashire, Nicholas Blundell put 'Anemonyes, Pilianthes, Geliflowers, Arenunulases, Riclasses and Tulops', each in its own bed in the knot garden which he had started to make in front of the dining-room window of the manor. Blundell succeeded to the Lordship of the Manor in 1702, when he was thirty-two, starting at the same time a diary, his *Great Diurnal,* which he kept for the next twenty-five years. He mentions 'Ordinary Tulops', by which he probably means the cheaper, early-flowering kinds and also 'Forrain and York' tulips. By this time, York had established itself as an important centre of supply for northern growers, and there were good nurserymen there such as Samuel Smith, who, on 7 and 14 April 1730, advertised in the *York Courant* the fact that at his flower garden without Micklegate Bar was to be seen 'a choice Collection of Auriculas, Animonies, Renunculos, Tulops and other Flowers' all available for sale at reasonable rates.

The 'Forrain' tulips came from Flanders, familiar ground to Blundell, who had been a pupil at the Jesuit College at St Omer. In the wake of the Jacobite rebellion he fled back to Flanders in 1716, and visited Ghent, Bruges, Brussels and Liège. From 1717 onwards, he made frequent visits to Flanders as his daughters were also being educated there. In his diary he records the various bulbs he brought back from his travels. On 21 October 1717 he planted the 'Anemonys, Renunculus and Tulops which I brought out of Flanders'. On 28 April 1720 he noted that he had thirty-three different sorts of tulip in bloom and in July of that year set 1,500 tulip bulbs and their offsets in his Nursery of Flowers. Planting and lifting times mostly correspond with today's dates, although on 22 July 1715 he 'set two beds in the Knot...tis too early by some months'. In 1727, he planted more correctly on 30 October putting 'Tulops in the four hearts [of the knot] & in the New Flower Pots at the Side of the Canall'.[16]

FLORA

The Dutch
GARDENER
or the Curious
Florift
&c.

Frontispiece from The Dutch Gardener
by Henry van Oosten
published in London, 1703

The next thirty years saw the beginning of a slow divorce between the tulip and the garden. The problem was not the craze for hyacinths, because these were used in much the same way as the tulip had been, planted in formal rows or to decorate knots and parterres. The real problem, especially from the 1730s onwards, was the changing taste in garden design, which both reflected and encouraged a different kind of planting. Glasshouses became an increasing obsession, along with the tender plants that could be grown in them. Trees and shrubs from America began to be imported in vast quantities. Above all, the flower-filled parterre and the knot were banished in favour of 'Capability' Brown's green swards which lapped right up to the walls of houses such as Petworth and Burghley. The ha-ha arrived to make the smoothest of transitions between the garden and the landscape which it imitated. 'Landskips', such as those that Rea had suggested in 1665 be painted on the walls of the garden 'somer-house' that was to provide a summer store for tulip bulbs, now replaced the garden itself. The great arboriculturist Francis Bacon (1561–1626) had prophesised the sea change a hundred years before; the poet Milton (1608–1674) had been its herald and now the poetry of Alexander Pope (1688–1744) and the work of the architect, painter and garden designer William Kent (c1685–1748) glorified a style that had very little to do with flowers such as tulips and everything to do with images of a classical past. It was exemplified in the new gardens laid out at Claremont in Surrey, Chiswick House on the western outskirts of London, Stowe in Buckinghamshire and Badminton in Gloucestershire, where in the late seventeenth century the Duchess of Beaufort had built up such a fine collection of flowers.

Not all the old gardens were swept away. Levens Hall in Cumbria kept its topiary, a feature now universally reviled by those who threw in their lot with the landscape movement, and some gardeners, such as Henry Ellison of Gateshead Park near Newcastle-upon-Tyne, went on planting tulips. On 18 October 1729, he had from Henry Woodman, Nurseryman of Strand-on-the-Green, Middlesex, cherries and apricots, damask roses and Persian jasmines, '100 Ranunculus Common (5s.) and 100 good Mixt tulips (7s.6d.)', so by this time, tulips had become *more* expensive than ranunculus. Forty striped lilies could be had for £2.[17] At Goodwood in 1735, flowers for the border under the southeast wall included tulips in the third row of flowers with jonquils, sweet williams, rocket and columbines. Sir Thomas Parker, 1st Earl of Macclesfield (c1666–1732) was not afraid to proclaim himself a tulip man either, though he was buying earlier in the century than Ellison, when bulbs were not so much out of fashion. Parker, who was made Lord Chief Justice in 1710, acquired many of his bulbs from the nurseryman and gardener Thomas Greening, whose base was at Brentford in Middlesex. Parker paid Greening £20 for a small bed of tulips which he wanted for the garden he was making at Shirburn Castle in Oxfordshire. The transaction is noted, not by Parker (or Greening) but by the Rev. George Harbin, first chaplain, then librarian to the 1st Viscount Weymouth at Longleat where his manuscript 'Memoirs of Gardening' covering the years 1716–1723 is housed.

'Mr Cranke, The Parish Clark of Kensington, is very curious in his cultivation of carnations, Tulips and Ranunculus', he noted on 2 November 1716. 'He told me one Mr Greenhill [a slip – Harbin named Greening correctly later in the manuscript] had a share in ye same Garden with him, who delighted chiefly in Tulips in cultivating of wch. he had spent above 30 years and had at length arrived to that perfection that he had certainly the best collection in England and wd. not take under £10 for some single Roots… About ye beginning of November, he makes his beds for Tulips and setts them. The beds are composed of a mixture of sea-sand (whose Saltnesse is very beneficial) and also of Rich fresh loam or earth… When a Tulip breaks (i.e. wn. from a plain Breeder it first appears striped) it is not valued if it does not hold its colours at least three years.' The finest tulips, wrote Harbin, were those raised from Dutch 'breeders', the 'breeders' being the plain-coloured flowers which occasionally produced the 'breaks', the fine feathered and flamed varieties that tulip fanciers so admired. 'Those wch. Mr Greening most esteem'd are raised from the plain Buff-colour. The plain Peach-colour'd ones are called by ye Dutch Baquette primo. Our Gardiners now sell as good Breeders of their own raising, as we used to send to Holland for formerly. The Tulips with pointed leaves [petals] at top, as ye mourning Widow and Fools-Coats, are not now esteemed. Those whose leaves are broad and round at top are most valued and whose cups open well and wch. are white in ye bottom (within side) of the Purplish sort.'

Harbin's memoir shows how firmly the flower was now in the hands of the florists, who were boxing and coaxing it to fit an increasingly rigid set of rules. The pointed petals which had been a marked characteristic of the tulips originally brought in from the East were now less desirable than petals with a rounded outline, the product of nearly 200 years' patient breeding and selection. White bases were much more to be encouraged than yellow or black ones, a tenet that still holds good among the few discerning florists who have continued to cultivate the English florists' tulip to the end of the twentieth century. When Harbin was writing, florists included a great many nurserymen. Increasingly, the tulip was seen as a specimen, like a moth or a sea shell, a single entity, which could be grown and displayed for its own sake, not necessarily in a garden setting. Previously, tulips had not been dissociated in this way, but had been grown as one of a series of jewel flowers to be displayed in well-designed cabinet-gardens. Now, too, the tulip lost its foreignness. The accession of the Dutch King William and his Stuart Queen Mary to the English throne had of course facilitated trade between the Netherlands and Britain, but during the wars with the Dutch, English tulip breeders, as Harbin noted, became increasingly bullish about the value of their home-bred flowers – as good, they believed, as anything to be seen abroad.

The growth and popularity of florists' societies were helped greatly by the growth and popularity of newspapers. From the early years of the eighteenth century onwards, societies advertised their meetings and shows in newspapers and newspapers carried reports of society proceedings. Norwich was one of the first provincial towns in England to have its own paper, the *Norwich Gazette*, which on 28 June and 5 July 1707, carried details of 'The Florists Feast, or Entertainment for Lovers of Flowers and Gardens' which was to be held at 'Mr Thomas Riggs in St Swithin's Lane on Tuesday the 8th day of July next'. Tickets cost half a crown, so Mr Riggs was evidently expecting some well-heeled florists. On the 29 June 1724, the *Gloucester Journal* advertised a General Meeting of the Society of Florists and Gardeners the following week 'at Ten in the Forenoon at William Ball's at the Spread Eagle in Ross'.

The age was defined by a huge thirst for knowledge, particularly scientific knowledge, and this showed itself in an explosion of clubs and societies whose members met to discuss anything from the movement of the heavenly bodies to the circulation of the blood. Slowly, people were trying to sort, order and under-stand the natural world. Some societies were rather grand, like the Botanical Society of London which met every week at the Rainbow Coffee House, Watling Street. It had some illustrious members: Johann Jacob Dillenius, the first Sherardian Professor of Botany at Oxford and Philip Miller, curator of the Physic Garden at Chelsea, who was the society's President. Miller was also a fellow of the Royal Society, where he published a paper 'On the Early Flowering of Tulips and Other Bulbous Plants When Placed in Bottles filled with Water'. He discovered what we now take for granted, namely that the system worked better with hyacinths and narcissus than it did with tulips. But this kind of activity was not confined to London. Societies, like newspapers, sprang up in provincial towns all over the country. In Lincolnshire, the Spalding Gentleman's Society was founded in 1710. It was not specifically a florists' society, but tulips, anemones, ranunculus and carnations were among the curiosities exhibited at their gatherings. The meetings began soberly enough with tea or coffee, but later a quart tankard of ale was provided, along with clean pipes, a chamber pot and a Latin dictionary.[18]

The prevailing ethos – scientific, enquiring – had an effect on the way that flowers such as tulips were perceived at this time. They were still objects of beauty of course, and appreciated as such, but the way people wrote about them reflected a widespread and growing interest in the practical details of their culture and propagation. Increasingly gardeners, nurserymen, florists, began to ask the question 'Why?'. Why did the tulip grow in some positions better than it did in others? Why did bulbs have to be lifted each year? And, the biggest question of all, why did tulips sometimes break into colours and sometimes not?

Philip Miller exemplified the new, enquiring approach in his *Gardener's and Florist's Dictionary*. This came out in 1724, a forerunner of the great *Gardener's Dictionary*, the first edition of which appeared seven years later. Dropping florists from the latter title was a smart move by Miller's publishers, who would not want a hint of anything out-of-date to cling to this expensive and, they hoped, lucrative project. With easy familiarity, Miller passed on to his readers tips gleaned from the best tulip growers in Europe: François Beulinx, a florist of Brussels 'who has raised many extraordinary fine Bisard tulips from seeds', a 'Gentleman of my acquaintance' in Holland who knew more than most about the breaking of tulips. The emphasis was no longer on how tulips should be used in the garden. It was on how they should be cultivated. John Rea had grouped his tulips into three classes: early, mid and late-flowering, categories useful to the gardener. Miller used three different classifications, arising from the new status of the tulip as a florist's specimen. He mentions 'Bisards' such as 'Aigle Noir', 'Hippolyte', 'Iphigénie', 'La Belle Columbine', 'Lucifer', 'Semiramis', which would all have been yellow tulips, feathered or flamed with red, brown or – if you were lucky – near-black. 'Bisards', or 'Bizarres', as they later became, formed one of the three classes of tulips to which florists' flowers had to conform. The other two were Roses, white flowers feathered and flamed with pink and red and Bybloemens, white flowers marked with mauve, purple or black.

The classifications and the rules that governed them were an inevitable result of the way that florists' societies gradually developed. At the beginning, the feast seemed to be the chief *raison-d'être* of the florists' gatherings, but then a competitive edge developed. Instead of bringing their flowers simply for other members to

THE NATURALIST'S VISIT TO THE FLORIST.

A Gentleman who was remarkably fond of raising fine Tulips, shewing his Collection to a Friend who was equally curious in Butterflies, a scarce Fly called the Emperor of Morocco presenting itself to our Naturalist on one of the Tulips, He without any hesitation made his way over the whole Bed to seize the prize, crying out regardless of his Friends entreaties, an Emperor! an Emperor! an Emperor! by all that's lucky.

Published 24th May 1798, by LAURIE & WHITTLE, 53 Fleet Street, London.

Conflicting interests, as shown in the naturalist's visit to the florist, a cartoon of 1798

admire, florists began to vie against each other for prizes which were awarded to the best flower in each of the three classes. This could not have happened before the tulip and other florists' flowers had reached the highly developed state they were in by the 1720s. *The Craftsman* for 16 April 1729 reported 'a great Feast of Gardiners call'd Florists' which was held at the Dog on Richmond Hill, near London for about 130 florists. After dinner, 'several shew'd their Flowers (most of them Auriculas) and five ancient and judicious Gardiners were judges to determine whose flowers excell'd'. By 1738, the *York Courant* was offering the prize of a gold ring to the 'best blown Carnation' at a forthcoming feast. At this stage, auriculas and carnations were more commonly shown in competition than tulips, though advertisements for tulip shows appeared later, such as the one advertised in the *Ipswich Journal* on 7 and 14 May 1748, advertising a meeting on 17 May at the Rising Sun, Bury St Edmunds and the next day at the Swan in Needham Market. The event was billed as a show rather than a feast.[19]

English florists, though increasingly breeding their own flowers, still modelled themselves to a great extent on their French and Flemish counterparts. But could it really have been true, as Cowell's French correspondent, P Belandine, said, that the prevailing fashion in France was to encode the colours of a tulip in the name that it was given, 'Bonne Veuve' being white (*blanc*) and violet? The nurseryman John Cowell (*fl.* 1690s–1730), famed for the huge aloe he grew at his nursery in Hoxton, London, thought so. The tulips Cowell liked best were either 'Grideline colour' (one of the colours of Sir Thomas Hanmer's prize tulip 'Agate Hanmer'), purple, violet or flesh-coloured. From these, he said, came the best breeders.

Like his fellow nurseryman, John Rea, Cowell looked at flowers with intelligent curiosity. He noted that tulips with thin petals were more likely to break than others. He also grappled with the problems of cross-pollination. A friend of his had sowed seed of a 'Baguet Primo', a notable tall flower of a purplish colour, 'from which', wrote Cowell, 'many a valuable Flower has been broke into Colours, or brought to stripe, even so valuable, as to be sold for a Thousand Guilders, Dutch money, one of them… The same seed produced Flowers of several Makes and different Colours when they first open'd. But according to the Philosophy of our Times, with regard to the Generation of Plants by coupling with one another, it might probably happen from that Cause, that the several Seedlings were so diversify'd…I wish some curious Gentleman would try the Parrot Tulips the next year, by planting the yellow and the red sorts together and save the Seeds from them, and sow them…these Couplings might bring a number of Rarities, if a little Care was taken to put them forward'.[20]

Like all growers of the time, Cowell's chief concern was with the 'breaking' of tulips. Already growers were aware that some types seemed more prone to break than others and that particular colours gave particularly good breaks. Samuel Trowell, Steward of the Estates of Benchers at the Inner Temple, London, had raised some promising tulips from seed of 'Triumph of Europe', a purple and white flower, finely feathered and recognised as one of the most constant in its markings and colours of any tulip around at the time. Cowell thought its constancy was due to the fact that its purple stripes were on the outside rather than the inside of the petals.

The nurseryman James Maddock's grand catalogue of 1742 finally stamped the tulip as a flower for specialist growers, perceived in much the same way as the show chrysanthemum is today. It listed 665 different kinds of tulip, the most expensive costing seventy-five florins a bulb. Maddock's Walworth nursery, established after he moved south from Warrington, Lancashire c1770, later became a mecca for tulip lovers. The tulip, which in the sixteenth century had first intrigued botanists and apothecaries with its strangeness and novelty had then been enthusiastically taken up by the aristocracy and gentry, who paid huge sums for new kinds to display in their borders and parterres. Now it had evolved into a hobby flower, but not before James Justice (1698–1763), Principal Clerk to the Court of Sessions in Edinburgh (and tulip maniac), had bankrupted himself in regular seventeenth-century style for the sake of his passion.

Justice, with Philip Miller a fellow member of the Royal Society, was splenetic, opinionated, reckless with money, boastful, but in the end an endearing man. He made his first garden at Crichton, Midlothian, about three miles outside Edinburgh, and was there for more than thirty years. At the time it was considered one of the best gardens in Scotland. He was the first to fruit the pineapple in Scotland (perhaps the most expensive pineapple ever grown), went several times to Holland to study the culture of bulbs, was familiar with the Flemish grower, François Beulinx, whom Cowell had quoted as an authority on tulips, and spent a fortune at the Haarlem nurseries of Voorhelms and Van Zompell. They 'always dealt very honestly by me' said Justice unrepentantly, even though he sometimes paid fifty pounds for a single tulip bulb. He grew fabulous Bybloemen tulips such as 'Rex Indiarum', 'Incomparable Brunon', 'Grand Roy de France', 'Reine de Congo', 'Triumphe de Lille', 'Parroquet Rouge', and 'Konig van Siam'. He was also mad about the once fashionable French Baguet Rigauds, rosy-purple on a white ground. 'Fine large Flowers, very strong, and some of them so large, as when they are in Perfection of Bloom, they will contain an English Pint of Wine within their Petals or Flower Leaves'.[21]

Practical experiments played an important part in the way Justice gardened. The impetus for these may have been competitive rather than altruistic, but whatever the motive, the experiments yielded results. He spent a long time devising a good compost for his beloved bulbs. 'To make a soil…equal in goodness to this, for Hyacinths, Tulips, Ranunculus, and Anemonies and to make them blow and increase in the same way they do in Holland, is to most of our British Gardeners, a thing unknown.' For his own compost, Justice gave directions as precise as a recipe for a fine fruit cake. The ingredients included one third of rotted leaves of trees, until then unthought-of as an element of mulches or composts. Like everyone else, he also worried away at the question of tulip breaking, deciding that here, too, the soil must be the answer. His solution, an expensive one, was to import not only his tulip bulbs from Holland, but a shipload of Dutch soil as well.[22]

James Justice's financial problems were already acute when, in June 1757, he was ousted from the Royal Society for not paying his annual subscription. Undeterred, he continued to use the magic FRS after his name and jauntily kept up a voluminous correspondence with a network of fellow plant enthusiasts. In 1758 he promised Lord Milton some tulips and ranunculus, adding in his letter detailed instructions about the proper way to prepare beds for them. 'Amongst your Tulips you will have some Kings, Queens and other Great Personages and I hope you will give suitable Entertainment to these Great Folk.'[23] By the time he died, five years later, he had lost his house and the fortune that had never been equal to the level of his spending on the garden. On Friday 9 September 1763 at ten o'clock in the morning, the flowers that had ruined James Justice were put up for auction: 'all the finest kinds of Auriculas…hyacinths, bulbous iris and tulips, that are in either the English or foreign Catalogues, are to be exposed to sale, in Mrs Justice's garden at Leith, in large or small parcels, as purchasers incline.' Most of the flowers were bought by the local seed merchant, Drummond & Co, who had a shop opposite Libberton's Wynd, Lawnmarket in Edinburgh. A month later, the *Caledonian Mercury* carried an advertisement for Justice's flowers, available now from Drummond's, and they were still being advertised by the same firm four years on: 'Tulips, Double Italian polyanthus, narcissus…' But the last of the great tulip growers of the old style had gone down in uncompromising fashion. If anything was worth bankrupting yourself for, tulips were.

CHAPTER IV

THE DUTCH AND TULIPOMANIA

T HOUGH HOLLAND and tulips now seem as synonymous as America and hamburgers, the Dutch cannot claim any of the firsts in the story of the tulip in Europe. The first bulbs were probably introduced by a Frenchman. Cargoes of bulbs arrived in Antwerp from Constantinople in 1562 long before they were shipped into Amsterdam. The first known flower bloomed in the garden of a merchant in Augsburg, Bavaria and was recorded by the Swiss botanist and physician, Conrad Gesner. But, once introduced, tulips spread quickly through the Seventeen Provinces of the Spanish Netherlands, in spite of the Civil War that shortly afterwards broke out. The war led to the setting-up of the Dutch Republic in the Seven Provinces of the north, where, around Haarlem, the first cultivation of tulips in The Netherlands began. By this time, Flemish breeders had already coaxed the flower to a level far removed from Councillor Herwart's plain red species. Flemish flowers had fed the tulip mania in France, which was flourishing twenty years before the Dutch crashed under their own tulip madness. But the Dutch were stayers. By their industry and application in growing and selling bulbs, they ensured that they were the last, triumphant survivors in the tulip trade.

The first tulip growers established their nurseries at the beginning of the seventeenth century along the Wagenweg and the Kleine Houtweg, south of Haarlem. For the first two decades of the century, tulips were mostly sold in large units.

Self-portrait
by Crispyn de Passe the Younger (1594–1670)

Whole beds, planted in formal ranks, would pass expensively into the hands of estate owners and their gardeners. As the initial stock bulked up, the market expanded, so that during the 1620s, customers could buy the cheaper, single-coloured varieties for twelve florins a pound, or even by the basket. But new 'breaks', bi-colours delicately feathered and flamed, commanded from the beginning the most extraordinary prices. The Dutch tulipomania of the mid 1630s was only the culmination of a process that had been going on ever since the first tulips were stolen from Clusius's garden at Leiden.

Emmanuel Sweert (c1552–1612) was only one of those who had businesses in Amsterdam selling curiosities – shells and stuffed birds as well as seeds and tulip bulbs. Already Dutch traders were trying to corner the market in tulips, by buying in bulbs from Flanders and France to pass on to well-heeled customers. Sweert described himself as gardener to Rudolph II and supplied plants to the courts at both Vienna and Prague as well as to Dutch gardeners. His nursery catalogue, the *Florilegium* of 1612, followed the early herbals in giving each tulip a long Latin tag; Latin confirmed status, reinforced respectability. His red and yellow striped tulips labelled 'Tulipa lutea rubris flamulis latis' and the like would soon acquire more comfortable varietal names – 'Lak van Rhijn' or 'Admiral van Hoorn'. Tulips were the first flowers to acquire such names and in The Netherlands, where royalty had gone out of favour, they were more generally christened as admirals and generals than the kings and queens of French-born tulips. The names did not commemorate real admirals and generals: 'General Bol' was named after the tulip grower Pieter Bol of Haarlem and 'Admiral Pottebacker' glorified plain Henrik Pottebacker of Gouda. New seedling varieties were often called 'conquests', as in 'Conquest van Royen'.

As early as 1614, writers were making fun of those who spent extravagant amounts of money on the tulip bulbs offered by traders such as Sweert. 'A fool and his money are soon parted' is the motto above a Claes Jansz engraving of two tulips in Roemer Visscher's *Sinnepoppen* published in Amsterdam that year. But catalogues of expensive novelties continued to be produced, countered by yet more moralising tracts railing against the dangers of worldly indulgence. Indulgence was the prime concern of Crispyn de Passe the Younger's (1594–1670) *Hortus Floridus* of 1614, an anthology of engravings of common garden plants that nurserymen could use to whet customers' appetites for their wares. In effect, these were classy advertisements, point-of-sale materials as marketing men call them now. In the dark days of October and November, when bulbs went on sale, potential customers needed a vision of what was packed inside these implausible, foreign bulb-bundles

Jacob Bomm's tulip from
Crispyn de Passe's Hortus Floridus *1614*

and de Passe gave it to them. The compilation was a best-seller – in seventeenth-century terms – and around 1617, a twelve-page supplement was added to the original anthology, with twenty tulips illustrated in magnificent detail. One species tulip, *T. saxatilis*, appears among the illustrations, which mostly show striped and mottled tulips, still with the sharply pointed petals characteristic of the first imports from Turkey. De Passe included the double tulip 'Iacobi Bommii'; a device remarkably like a modern Link-Stake holds the bloom upright, and braces it against attack by a stripy bee which is homing in on it with all the concentrated attention of a kamikaze pilot. In his work, de Passe included names of *liefhebbers* or tulip growers throughout northern Europe: Abraham de Goyer, Volckert Cornhert and nine more in Amsterdam, together with others from Delft, Rotterdam, The Hague (where the painter and draughtsman Jacques de Gheyn appears on de Passe's list), Gouda, Utrecht and Haarlem. The biggest group of growers is listed at Brussels, with further growers at Antwerp, Frankfurt (home of the engraver and publisher Johannes de Bry), Valenciennes, Prague and Strasbourg where the Comte de Rapstijn was one of de Passe's contacts.

Heavy-footed tracts were no match against the jewel-like beauties de Passe laid out so temptingly, but the moralists thundered on:

> All these fools want is tulip bulbs
> Heads and hearts have but one wish
> Let's try and eat them; it will make us laugh
> To taste how bitter is that dish.[1]

That was the kind of thing that the congregation at Terneuzen in Zeeland could expect to hear from the pulpit, where Petrus Hondius (1578–1621) was pastor. Only the most devoted of the pastor's flock, though, could have been expected to struggle through to the end of his poem, 16,000 verses in all.

Despite such denunciations, tulip prices continued to rise inexorably. By 1623 the fabled flower 'Semper Augustus' was already selling for 1,000 florins a bulb (the average annual income was about 150 florins). The stock of it was jealously guarded by the Grand Pensionary of Amsterdam, Dr Adriaen Pauw, who grew nothing but 'Semper Augustus' on his estate in Heemstede. 'Among the many Precious examples of these Flowers' wrote the chronicler Nicolas Wassenaer, '…one that for its beauty is named Semper Augustus is the foremost of this Year. The colour is white, with Carmine on a blue base, and with an unbroken flame right

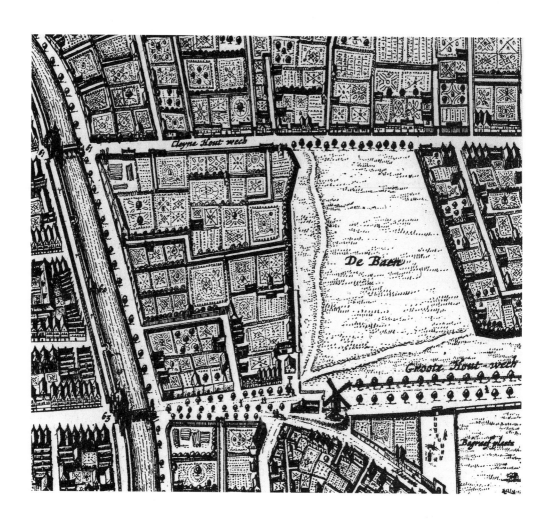

The Haarlem tulip fields
from J Wil's map of Haarlem (1646)

to the top. Never did a Florist see one more beautiful than this...'[2] 'Semper Augustus' held its price over a long period, so it must have been a break that was slow to produce offsets. In 1624 only twelve bulbs of the variety were known to exist, valued at 1,200 florins each; by 1625 the asking price had more than doubled. By 1633 though, estimates of 5,500 florins were floating round each bulb, almost doubling to 10,000 florins at the height of the tulipomania. The highest price ever asked for 'Semper Augustus' was noted in the *Nederlandsch Magazijn* of 1838 where the writer quoted a price of 13,000 florins for a single bulb, more than the cost of the most expensive houses on the canals at the centre of Amsterdam. In the mid seventeenth century you could have picked up such a house, complete with gardens and coach house for about 10,000 florins.

From the early seventeenth century onwards, tulips flourished not only in gardens but on furniture, embroideries, and especially tiles. In a low-lying country like Holland where damp was a permanent problem, lime plaster deteriorated fast and tiles made more practical wall coverings. The technique of tile-making, first developed by Ottoman manufacturers at Iznik in the second half of the fifteenth century, had gradually travelled west, through Spain and Italy, into The Netherlands and a whole pattern book of Ottoman motifs, stylised fruit such as pomegranates and grapes, equally stylised flowers (most commonly carnations and tulips) travelled west too.[3]

Delft was only one of the cities of the northern Netherlands where tile-making flourished; Amsterdam, Gouda, Harlingen, Hoorn, Makkum, Middelburg, Rotterdam and Utrecht all produced their own tiles, though similar patterns and designs were used in all the centres. The first tulips appeared on tiles around 1610, the flowers often accompanied by fruit such as pomegranates and grapes. By 1620, the tulip was being used as a motif on its own, the tile-makers influenced perhaps by illustrations in books such as Crispyn de Passe's *Hortus Floridus*. Gradually, a standard three-tulip design emerged which was used until well into the nineteenth century. Sometimes tulips are shown in cross-section, with a stylised stamen and pistil, another trick borrowed from the illustrators of botanical books. In terms of colour, the tile-makers were more limited than the illustrators. They did not have such a wide palette to use in the first place and the colours changed when the tiles were fired. Despite this, wonderfully subtle effects were achieved, the tile-makers sometimes producing multi-coloured, life-sized tulips that stretched over two tiles. The flowers mirrored the most desirable colour combinations of the time: brown and white, mustard with brown and white, purple with brown and white, dark red

Tulip planting in Spring *by Abel Grimmer (1570–1619)*

and white and yellow with brown and white.[4] Gradually these polychrome tiles gave way to simpler blue and white versions, imitating the Chinese porcelain that was being imported by companies such as the Verenigde Oostindische Compagnie. A gallery of Chinese motifs was added to the tulips and carnations that still featured heavily on these blue and white tile panels. Flamed and feathered tulips were way beyond the means of ordinary people; tulips on tiles were a cheaper option.

So were tulips painted in flower pieces by such masters as Ambrosius Bosschaert, Jan Brueghel and Roelandt Savery. Any flower piece worthy of the name had at least three tulips in the arrangement, surrounded by rare columbines, iris, jonquils and fritillaries. Even if you paid top prices for the best artist, you could still, in the 1630s, get a bunch of painted flowers for a fraction of what it would cost to put together the same arrangement of real flowers in your garden. Dutch and Flemish painters flourished in the seventeenth century because prosperous citizens and merchants could afford to buy their work. For the rich, this was a golden time in The Netherlands, like Athens in the time of Pericles, or Italy under the Medicis. Art blossomed under the patronage of those whom trade had enriched. 'Paintings were everywhere: in the town hall and other public places, in orphanages and offices, in the houses of patricians and burghers alike.'[5] The popularity of flower-painting mirrored a growing interest in botany; the flourishing trade in tulips stimulated it further. Never have flowers figured more prominently in the lives of ordinary people than they did in Holland in the first decades of the seventeenth century.

Dr Paul Taylor, an authority on Dutch flower-painting of this period, charts four distinct periods in the development of the flower piece. The first age (1600–1620) encompasses artists such as Jacques de Gheyn, Ambrosius Bosschaert, Jan Brueghel and Roelandt Savery. Their bouquets are centrally placed in the frame. The paintings are symmetrical, detailed, accurate, almost scientific. The flowers are perfect, each blossom clearly displayed. These are records, early seventeenth-century mementos, of highly prized possessions. The second epoch (1620–1650) includes artists such as Bosschaert's brother-in-law, Balthasar van der Ast, Jacob Marrell and Anthony Claesz. After the trauma of tulipomania, flowers were increasingly used as symbols of human *vanitas* and the transience of all earthly delights. This transitional period led to the era (1650–1720) of Simon Verelst, Rachel Ruysch and Jan Davidsz de Heem, who specialised in arrangements of flowers set against dramatically dark backgrounds. Finally (1720–1750) came Jan van Huysum whose elaborate compositions brought flower paintings of the Golden Age to a peak of perfection.[6]

Tulip in a Kendi
by Dirck van Delen (1604/5–1671)
painted 1637
Museum Boymans van Beuningen, Rotterdam

That is the art historian's analysis, but tulip fanciers can chart a different pro-gression as the tulip, often a pivotal element in these flower pieces, began itself to change. Paintings by Ambrosius Bosschaert (1573–1621) such as *Flowers in a Rummer*,[7] *Glass Vase with Four Tulips*[8] and *Flower Piece*[9] show neat, bulbous-shaped tulips with pointed petals, like the flowers of Sweert's *Florilegium*, though more believable. The petals flip out at the top from a narrow waist and show a tendency to curl in on themselves. The inside of the flower, so important later to the English florists, is rarely shown. The markings of the petals are minutely recorded. Each is different: bright yellow, streaked with red, white delicately feathered in red, and in the foreground of the *Glass Vase with Four Tulips*, a superb tulip of red and white stripes. Occasionally among these gaudy varieties, a much simpler tulip appears, as in the *Vase of Flowers*[10] by Jan Brueghel (1568–1625). Under the extraordinary tri-colour double tulip with a butterfly perched on it is a modest little apricot flower, very like *T. batalinii* 'Apricot Jewel'.

In *Still Life with Tulips*,[11] Ambrosius Bosschaert's son, Johannes (c1605–c1629), shows tulips with more rounded petals. Red and white varieties are more favoured than red and yellow ones, and the picture shows the results of some of the first attempts to breed purple and white tulips, later to become the florists' Bybloemens. Jacob Marrell (1614–1681) painted these too, as in *Flower Still Life*[12], which shows an elegant tulip, brownish-purple flamed on white, balanced precariously on a ledge with pink roses, lilies of the valley and heartsease. Where just one tulip is shown in a composition, it was most probably a spectacularly rare one such as the 'Generael der Generaelen van Gouda' shown in Dirck van Delen's painting of 1637.[13] The General of Generals stands on its own, militarily to attention, in a bulbous blue and white vase, its only companions some curious shells, arranged to the left of the vase.

In his *Still Life of Flowers and Fruit*[14] painted around 1626, Johannes Bosschaert showed two different tulips of the kind now classified as Viridifloras and Parrots. The thin-petalled tulip at the top of the composition shows a distinct overlay of green on the red and white colouring. The flower on the left is of a stubbier, chunkier, more muddled form, the red and cream petals showing the ragged edges typical of the Parrot tulips that the French called Monstreuses. Ambrosius Bosschaert's young brother-in-law Balthasar van der Ast (1593/4–1657) shows one unusually modest tulip in his *Basket of Flowers*[15] painted in the 1620s. It appears on the right of the picture, a short, blunt flower of purple, edged with white. Emmanuel Sweert offered the same type (no. 32) in his catalogue, labelling it

Flower Still Life
by Ambrosius Bosschaert (1573–1621)
painted c1620
Mauritshuis, The Hague

'Tulipa purpurea rub. saturata albis oris'. The 'Edgers' were not as highly valued as the striped tulips and breeders spent less time improving them. Van der Ast's little purple tulip is almost half the size of the showy red and white beauty that dominates the composition. The 'Dukes', or 'Ducs' as they were generally known (named after Adrian Duyck of Oud-Karspel), remained remarkably stable in their conformation and colouring. Violet Ducs, just like van der Ast's tulip, still grow in the Hortus Bulborum, the collection of historic bulbs maintained at Limmen. Van der Ast seemed to have a penchant for oddities in the tulip field. The Violet Duc appears to be a five- rather than the more normal six-petalled flower. So does the exquisite white tulip, delicately feathered in red, which lies in the foreground of *Still Life with Fruit and Shells*,[16] painted in 1620. The work is in van der Ast's best doomed manner, the fruit crawling with insects. He painted other curiosities too, tulips with more petals than the norm. His *Vase of Flowers with Shells*[17] shows two white tulips feathered and flamed with red. They may have been especially prized as one has seven petals, the other eight. The petals are notched and untidy (another effect of the virus) but the lower flower is splayed open, to show the intriguing complexity of the stamens and anthers. The exquisite red and white tulip lying on a ledge in *Tulip and Forget-me-not*[18] has an odd little horn of petal protruding from the flower. Van der Ast shows the same tulip (same horn, same markings) again on its own in his *Tulip in a Gilt-Mounted Glass Vase*.[19] At this period of course, the tulip was an extraordinarily costly flower, often worn like a jewel, as in France, by women of fashion. The anonymous portrait of Amalia van Solms[20] shows the style, tulips with lilies of the valley caught up to fasten the sitter's hair at the back. But professional tulip growers, such as Abraham Catoleyn in Amsterdam, Pieter Bol and Jan Quackel in Haarlem, established reputations which at the time were at least as great as those of Bosschaert or van der Ast.

De Heem and Daniel Seghers show tulips that are larger in relation to the rest of the flowers in the arrangements than those of Ambrosius Bosschaert. The distribution of the colour on the petals becomes ever more subtle, the flower itself becomes looser in shape. In works such as Jan van Huysum's famous *Flowers in a Terracotta Vase*[21] or *Vase of Flowers in a Niche*[22] the transformation is complete. These are big, blowsy, familiar tulips with rounded petals. What has been lost in finesse of form has been gained in the refinement of the markings. Though the petals are longer and looser, they are exquisitely marked and van Huysum shows that the long, patient process of breeding Bybloemens, as close to black and white as nature would allow, was now almost complete. The markings on these tulips are

Still Life with Fruit and Shells
by Balthasar van der Ast (1593–1657)
Mauritshuis, The Hague

150

very much lighter, more symmetrically arranged, than on the early flowers when nature's own breaks (caused by virus) had been indiscriminately seized on and exploited. Standards of excellence had been set and in Roses and Bybloemens florists in Flanders and Holland, as in England, were looking for flowers with only the finest pencilling of red or dark purple on a predominantly white ground. Van Huysum's beautiful purple and white tulip, shown in the *Vase of Flowers in a Niche*, was brought to perfection in 'Louis XVI', the quintessential Bybloemen of the eighteenth-century tulip fancy. This was introduced into The Netherlands from Flanders and offered for the first time (at 250 guilders a bulb) in 1789, forty years after van Huysum's death, by the Dutch florist, M van Nieuwkerk.

The first phase of the tulip craze, dominated by connoisseurs and scholars, was followed, from the late 1620s onwards, by a second phase, distinguished by the increasing professionalism of the growers. As the tulip became a commercial commodity, the nursery trade became more entrepreneurial and many new businesses were set up. Contemporary registers of property owners in Haarlem record Claes Verwers's garden of seventy-six rods in the Eerste Laen. Hendrick Swalmius had seventeen rods in the Boll's Laen. Hendrick Vestens cultivated forty-eight rods in the Coninx Laen. Pieter van Dorp, Davidt de Milt and Guillaume de Milt were all in the Dorpen Laen. Jan de Smet, François van Engelant (an English incomer, surely?), Bartel Harmans, Pieter Maertsz and four others were on the east side of the Kleine Houtweg. Jan Jacobsz, Hendrick Joosten, Claes Hendricxz, Frans Markus and thirteen other nurserymen were on the west side. Jan Casteleijn, who raised the 'Amerael Katelijn' and the 'Parragon Kateleyn' sold at the 1637 Alkmaar bulb auction, traded from the south side of the Campenslaen[23]. Some of the new generation of nurserymen had worked as apprentices in the older-established companies. Barent Cardoes, for instance, whose name crops up regularly in the papers dealing with the estate of another florist, Davidt de Milt, had been Pieter Bol's head man but left in his thirties to set up his own nursery near Haarlem. The rich alluvial soil around Haarlem was ideal for bulb production, and along the Houtweg, growers such as Jan van Damme started trading directly with buyers. Shortage of available land was a constant problem for growers. Contracts drawn up between buyers and sellers at the height of the Dutch tulipomania show that bulbs were often grown on plots belonging to a third party, who doubtless took a cut from the proceeds of any sale. Van Damme rented land from a local almshouse to keep up with the ever increasing demand for tulip bulbs. The majority of the growers were

'Speramondi' from a tulip book of c1640
made by Ambrosius Bosschaert the Younger (1609–1645)

of course Dutch, but foreigners, such as the Portuguese Jew Francisco Gomez da Costa, also flourished. He had a nursery at Vianen and specialised in growing the brilliant yellow and red striped Bizarden.

Growers supplied a huge range of tulips from astronomically expensive striped varieties to the much cheaper single-coloured Switsers and Yellow Crowns that sold for only a few *stuivers* an *azen*. Growers traded directly from their nurseries, but they also employed itinerant salesmen who hawked the cheaper bulbs around fairs and markets far away from the centres of production in Haarlem and Utrecht. Rotgans were popular, white tulips striped in rose. So were Brabansons with deeper crimson stripes on a white ground. The Anvers with violet stripes on a white ground became popular later. Nurserymen were also familiar with the best ways of preserving and sending bulbs and roots to foreign countries, to ensure that they arrived in good condition.[24] Dutch dominance in the tulip trade had begun.

In the wake of the pioneering flower paintings produced by artists such as Ambrosius Bosschaert and Jan Brueghel came more specialised tulip books, produced by Pieter van Kouwenhoorn, Judith Leyster (c1610–1660), Jacob Marrell, Anthony Claesz and Pieter Holsteyn the Younger. In about 1640, Ambrosius Bosschaert the Younger (1609–1645) produced such a book, now at the Fitzwilliam Museum, Cambridge, which shows many of the current beauties of the day, including the fine pink and white striped tulip 'Olinda', worth 400 guilders a bulb. The books served several purposes. Some were like the *Hortus Eystettensis*, records of collections held by tulip lovers; the flower book made at Leeuwarden by P F de Geest c1650 is thought to show the flowers growing in the garden laid out by Willem Frederik van Naussau at Leeuwarden two years previously. At a time when Dutch growers were becoming nurserymen to the whole of Europe, other tulip books acted as very superior sales catalogues to tempt buyers into further extravagances. Bulbs changed hands when they were dormant and growers evidently felt it worthwhile to pay artists to show potential customers the delights packed inside the unprepossessing dry brown 'roots' on offer. Even after the great crash that signalled the end of tulipomania, tulips remained expensive items, expensive enough for the commissioning of these sumptuous inventories to continue. The tulip book which appeared at the Christie's sale of Dutch and Flemish Old Master Drawings in Amsterdam on 13 November 1995 was used to advertise the bulb auction at Alkmaar in 1637. The album is made up of 168 watercolours: 124 of tulips, the others of lilies, narcissus, anemones and carnations. At the Alkmaar auction, 180 were sold for a total of 90,000 guilders, the equivalent of about £6 million today.

'Schoon Solffer'
Bartholomeus Assteyn (1607–1667)
Historisch Museum, Amsterdam

Like Bosschaert, the painter Jacob Marrell produced catalogues as well as his flower pieces, the one perhaps feeding the other. The red and white tulip in the foreground of his 1635 painting, *Still Life of Tulips, Roses and Other Flowers* can easily be matched with a bloom in his tulip book of about 1640.[25] But if he copied himself, that was better than being plagiarised by others. Several subsequent catalogues were copies, by other hands, of Marrell's originals. Tile-makers plundered the tulip books too. The flowers on the ten-tile panel of lifesize tulips[26] seem to have been copied from a tulip book made by Judith Leyster.

The illustrations in Dutch tulip books were done in watercolour or gouache, the flowers sometimes outlined with fine black lead pencil, or silver point to give the impression of gloss on the petal. Cross hatching was added with pen and ink, or extra shine given to a flower with a layer of gum arabic or egg white. As portrait painters often left assistants to fill in the backgrounds of their paintings, flower painters sometimes set less competent assistants to paint tulip stems and foliage. Tulips in dealers' catalogues are often numbered and annotated with names, weights (in *azen*) and prices. Sometimes they are painted in pairs or groups, each flower showing a similar pattern of feathering or flaming. These were probably either sister seedlings, or different breaks from similar 'breeder' bulbs. Some of the tulips in the Jacob Marrell book are arranged in this way, one page showing a Rose heavily feathered with strawberry pink on a white ground next to a far more finely marked example of the same type, where the pink is applied with the finest brush and the yellow of the base drawn up the central midrib of each of the five petals.[27]

The tulip books mostly show the expensive novelties bred by tulip growers. Just occasionally, as in the *Verzameling van Bloemen*, made by Pieter van Kouwenhoorn *c*1630,[28] a species such as *T. sylvestris* appears, dwarfed by the highly bred cultivars alongside it. And is it the dazzling *T. vvedenskyii* that appears in the bottom right-hand corner of Folio 40? Kouwenhoorn would not have known it under that name of course; the species, from central Asia, was not named until the twentieth century. Kouwenhoorn shows many of the most fashionable tulips of the period: the highly developed kinds striped in red and white, two tall, long-petalled tulips, roughly marked in an unbalanced combination of purple and white (breeding of these Bybloemens still had a long way to go before they equalled the red and white tulips in finesse), Viridifloras, plain white, yellow and red Crowns and the purple tulip, edged with white, which Balthasar van der Ast had included in his *Basket of Flowers*, painted in the 1620s.

By the winter of 1635 the tulip trade had been invaded by speculators from all backgrounds:

Florilegium made by Pieter van Kouwenhoorn
in the first half of the seventeenth century (Lindley Library, London)

156

Bricklayers, carpenters, woodcutters,
    Plumbers, glassblowers, gardeners,
Ushers, farmers, tradesmen,
    Commoners, pedlars, charcuterers,
Second-hand dealers, confectioners, smiths, cobblers,
    Coffee grinders, guards and vintners.

Dry shavers, furriers, tanners,
    Coppersmiths, clergymen,
Book binders, printers, type setters,
    Lawyers, clerks, prosecutors,
Schoolmasters, millers, glass engravers,
    Seniors, demolition men, swineherds.[29]

Tulipomania, the most cataclysmic phenomenon in the tulip's long and complex history, spread like a fever through the land. Nobody in the select band invited by Councillor Herwart in 1559 to admire his latest acquisition, his stubby red flower on its short stem, could have imagined that in less than a hundred years this flower, this tulip, would bankrupt many of the most solid burghers of The Netherlands. But in the first half of the seventeenth century, the tulip was still young, irresponsible and fancy-free. It could capture hearts and it could break them.

As it stood, Councillor Herwart's plain, dumpy flower could hardly have induced the frenzied trading that tulip fanciers in Holland hurled themselves into between 1634 and 1637. The driving force was the element of chance in the game, the possibility that a plain, relatively valueless bulb might emerge one season miraculously feathered and flamed in contrasting colours. 'Breaking' was a mystery that was only unravelled in the twentieth century (*see* Introduction) but in seventeenth-century Holland it provided an irresistible element of the lottery for players in the wildest game that any flower has ever provoked. If the players had all been growers, then perhaps tulipomania would never have happened. But they weren't. Wherever demand outstrips supply (and since no grower understood how to make the flower break, this was certainly the case with the tulip), get-rich-quick merchants will smell an opportunity. It happened in England in the great house-buying boom of the 1980s when the buying and selling of houses was enthusiastically undertaken by people who had no intention of ever living in them. It was the same with tulips in the early seventeenth century. And, like some unlucky buyers who

Beste Bruyne
by Pieter Holsteyn the Younger

threw themselves blindly into the house-mania, the purchasers of tulips too, found themselves stuck with negative equity. The painter Jan van Goyen was one of them. On 27 January 1637, at the height of the tulipomania, van Goyen put his name to a sale note prepared by the dealer Albert Claesz van Ravesteijn. 'I have sold to Master Jan van Goyen one tulip called "Hagenaer" for 18 guilders and four tulips called "Rijnwijcker" at nine guilders each. Ravesteijn shall enjoy for four of these "Rijnwijckers" a painting called Picture of Judas, worth 36 guilders and also 32 guilders in money. Also one tulip "Macx" with an offset of 50 azen weight in exchange for a painting of Ruijsdael's, worth £60.' The money expended on that deal alone, let alone the paintings, represented more than a month's wages for an Amsterdam bricklayer. On 4 February 1637 van Goyen committed himself to even more extravagant purchases: two 'Kamelotten' (the red and yellow tulip that Alexander Marshall painted in his flower album) at four pounds each, one 'Parel' at eighteen pounds, one 'Jan Gerijts' for the astonishing sum of sixty pounds, four 'Maerzen' also at sixty pounds each and quarter shares in a host of other tulips. The sale note was ominously headed 'Obligation on Jan van Goyen...£858'. He died insolvent, still haunted on his death bed by the spectres of 'Jan Gerijts', 'Switser', 'Root en Geel Gevlamt', and all the other tulips that he had bought so dearly on the eve of the crash that brought tulipomania to an end.[30]

But why did tulipomania happen in Holland? Partly of course because in 1593, forty years or so before tulipomania broke out like another plague, Clusius had arrived in Leiden with the job of laying out a new botanic garden. He brought with him the best collection of tulips owned by anyone in western Europe. So the stock was in the right place at the right time. Then a great plague, a real one, had swept through Holland between 1633 and 1635. Did the subsequent shortage of labour perhaps improve wages so dramatically that, for the first time in their lives, bricklayers, carpenters, woodcutters and plumbers had money to lose?

America played a role too, in a roundabout way. During the first part of the six-teenth century, Europe's great trading ports were still centred on the Mediterranean, but the New World which had loomed up over the bows of Amerigo Vespucci's fleet in 1500 gradually changed the pattern of trade. Ports such as Lisbon and Antwerp, on Europe's west coast, gradually became more important than Mediterranean Genoa. When, in 1576, Spanish soldiers sacked Antwerp, Amsterdam profited. Between 1585 and 1650 it boomed and became the hub of commercial activity in northwest Europe. Paintings such as Willem van de Velde the Younger's (1633–1707) show Amsterdam's harbour crammed with craft of all

Tooneel van FLORA.

Vertonende:

Grondelijcke Redens-ondersoekinge,

vanden

HANDEL DER FLORISTEN.

Ghespeeld/ op de spreucke van Anthonius de Guevara:
Een voorsichtich eerlijck man; sal altijt meer ghedulden,
dan straffen.

T'samen gesteld; mits/datter dagelijx:

Uyt haat: spruyt smaad.

Noch is hier by-gevoegt de Lijste van eenige *Tulpaen* vercocht aende meest-
biedende tot Alcmaer op den 15 Februarij 1637. Item 't Lof-dicht
van *Calliope*, over de Goddinne FLORA, &c.

t'AMSTERDAM,

Ghedzuckt by Ioost Broersz. Boeck-dzucker inde Gzaeve-straet/
inde Dzuckerpe/ Anno 1637.

*One of the many satirical pamphlets attacking the tulip trade
Published in Amsterdam 1637*

kinds. The city became the world's warehouse: silks and other textiles, spices, wood, wine, dried fish, metals, all found a market here. Amsterdam also became the most important centre in Europe for the trading of grain, which led to another innovation – a commodities market. A stock exchange was set up, and a bank, the Wisselbank, to oversee exchanges of currency. Once this technical framework was in place, it was only a short step from trading in commodities that you could physically hold in your hand to trading in dreams.

In Holland too, seed of the tulips stolen from Clusius's Leiden garden fell on fertile soil. It takes seven years for tulips to grow from seed to flowering-size bulbs, so in the years between 1593 and 1634, six harvests would have taken place, increasing hugely the number of bulbs available. The centre of cultivation was Haarlem, but as demand grew, the bulb fields grew too, taking in Delft, Alkmaar, Gouda, Hoorn, Rotterdam and Utrecht. The Dutch were already making a name for themselves as nurserymen to the gardeners of Europe. They were careful, industrious growers and clever at selling plants. In their hands, tulip bulbs bulked up fast; fast, but not too fast. That was important. If the flower was to command vast prices, it had to retain a certain aura. The virus that caused flowers to 'break' ensured it kept its mystery.

From a twentieth-century perspective, of course, tulipomania seems scarcely credible. We see a flower that is widely available. We can give a name to it and set it in its appropriate place at the great table of botanical families, or *taxa*. We are familiar with a huge range of plants: bananas, pineapples, orchids, plants that eat insects, plants that live on other plants, plants that glow in the dark. We know how they grow, about photosynthesis and pollination. We know how plants reproduce themselves and how to breed them for our own ends. But it was not like that in the seventeenth century. The naming of names had scarcely begun. The natural world was a source of endless wonder, fascination and debate. The flowers, insects, shells and minerals painted in minute detail by artists such as Jacques de Gheyn II and Ambrosius Bosschaert were considered as rare and precious as the jewels and pieces of silver displayed in the *Wunderkammer* or display cabinets of the time. John Rea, the English nurseryman, writing only a little time after the period of tulipomania, said the perfect flower garden should be fashioned 'in the form of a Cabinet, with several Boxes fit to receive, and securely to keep, Nature's choicest jewels'.[31] Those who could not afford such jewels commissioned paintings of them. Even Ambrosius Bosschaert or Jan Davidsz de Heem could rarely command more than 20,000 *stuivers* for a still life; most cost half of that.[32] But in a sale of tulip

Semperaugustus.

*'Semper Augustus', the quintessential flower of the Dutch tulipomania,
in a painting by Pieter Holsteyn the Younger*

bulbs that took place on 5 February 1637 at Alkmaar, the *average* price per bulb was 16,000 *stuivers*. Exceptional varieties such as the red and white 'Semper Augustus' could command prices up 260,000 stuivers. It was in this heady atmosphere that the germ of tulipomania took hold. The infection turned malignant when those that had glorified the tulip now began to exploit it.

The drama of tulipomania is told in a satirical dialogue, the *Samenspraecken* published in Haarlem by Adrian Roman in 1637, the year the bubble burst. It takes place between two weavers Waermondt (Truemouth) and Gaergoedt (Greedygoods), with Gaergoedt trying to persuade Waermondt to join him in the speculative hysteria. Though manic, the tulip trade was still governed by ritual. First, says Gaergoedt, Waermondt must join one of the collegiums or clubs, the companies of florists (flower growers, not flower sellers) who based themselves in various inns. They existed in all the main centres of bulb-growing: Haarlem, Delft, Enkhuizen, Alkmaar, Leiden, Utrecht, Rotterdam. 'Because you are a newcomer, some will squeak like a duck. Some will say "A new whore in the brothel" and so on, but don't take any notice. That's all part of the initiation. Your name will be put down on a slate.' (The closest modern parallel to these rites of passage are perhaps the Masons' lodges.) Once accepted in the company, says Gaergoedt, Waermondt could choose one of two ways to sell his tulips, either *met de Borden* or *in het Ootjen*. The former was effectively sale by arbitration, the *borden* being two slates or tablets. On one the buyer wrote down what he would offer for a particular tulip; on the other the seller wrote what he would accept. The slates were handed over to two arbitrators or proxies, one nominated by each party to the transaction. They adjusted the prices to a sum which they considered fair and returned the slates to the buyer and seller. If they accepted it, the price remained. If they didn't, they rubbed it out and started again.

The process called *in het ootjen* was more like a public auction. The *ootje* was a circle in which the auctioneer wrote the highest bid made for a bulb. It was part of a quick diagrammatic sketch showing the progress of the bidding and recorded the amounts, in hundreds and thousands of guilders, that buyers were prepared to pay. After an auction *in het ootjen*, the seller decided whether he would accept the price offered by the highest bidder. Under both systems, some contribution (a kind of agent's percentage, usually about half a *stuiver* on each guilder) was deducted for the collegium's funds. This was known as the wine money and besides paying for the light and fuel used at the meeting place, it kept the members of the club or collegium well supplied with tobacco and beer. It was the buyer, rather than the

Flower piece
by Jan Brueghel (1568–1625)
from the Rijksmuseum, Amsterdam

seller who paid. Gaergoedt tells Waermondt 'I have been on several journeys, when I brought home more money than I brought to the Inn. And then I had eaten and drunk wine, beer, tobacco, cooked or roast fish, meat, even fowls and rabbits and sweets to finish, and that from the morning till three or four at night.' 'It is very pleasant to be treated like that' observes Waermondt mildly.

A system such as this, though, was wide open to abuse and the crowds of free-loaders in the inns must have tested the generous capacity of the *drietjen* or wine money to its limit. Gaergoedt himself said there were nights when the wine money 'fell like drops off the thatch when it has rained.' But imagine the temptations. As Gaergoedt points out, Waermondt is earning barely ten per cent on the profits of his present business. 'With Flora,' he says, 'it is cent for cent. Yes, ten for one, a hundred for one, and sometimes a thousand.' Before tulipomania took hold, a bulb of the finely striped red and yellow tulip 'Gheel ende Root van Leyden' weighing 515 *azen* sold for 46 guilders. Within a month, the price had risen to 515 guilders. Pale yellow Switzers elegantly feathered in red leapt in price from 60 guilders a pound to 1,800 guilders. As van Goyen's accounts show, payments were not always made in cash. One seller exchanged a single bulb of the fine purple and white tulip 'Viceroy', for a suit with a coat, which could be as costly as he wanted. Sensibly, he had the material for the coat cut at once. The cuffs were edged with gold lace, the tails with green velvet and the coat entirely lined. 'Even the stuff which used to be weeded and thrown in basketfuls on the dung-heap has been sold for heavy money' says Gaergoedt, who had mortgaged his house to buy bulbs. Other weavers mort-gaged their looms. But the much-quoted deal involving two loads of wheat, four loads of rye, four fat oxen, eight fat pigs, twelve fat sheep, two hogsheads of wine, four barrels of beer, two barrels of butter, 1,000 pounds of cheese, a bed complete with bedlinen, a suit of clothes and a silver beaker never took place. That list was compiled by one of the many pamphleteers campaigning against the evils of tulipo-mania. He compared the price paid for a single 'Viceroy' tulip (2,500 florins) with the cost of a rather more useful list of goods. But with such huge prices being paid for tulips, tulip growers had to make elaborate arrangements to protect their crops. One nurseryman at Hoorn in the north of Holland, rigged up a trip wire round his bulb beds. The wire was connected to a bell which rang if intruders crept into his nursery at night.

The last of the big spenders bid in the auction of ninety-nine lots of tulip bulbs, held at the Nieuwe Schutters Doelen, Alkmaar on 5 February 1637. This was arranged by the Governors of the local orphanage, under whose care were the

De drie t'Zamenspraeken

Tusschen

WAERMONDT

En

GAERGOEDT,

over de Op- en Ondergang van

FLORA;

Als mede FLORAES Zotte-Bollen, Troost-
brief, en een Register der tegenwoor-
dige meest geächte

HYACINTEN,

met der zelver Prysen.

Verçiert met een curieuse Prent.

𝕯𝖊𝖟𝖊 𝖙𝖜𝖊𝖉𝖊𝖓 𝕯𝖗𝖚𝖈𝖐 𝖛𝖊𝖗𝖒𝖊𝖊𝖗𝖉𝖊𝖗𝖙 𝖊𝖓 𝖛𝖆𝖓
𝖛𝖊𝖊𝖑𝖊 𝖋𝖆𝖚𝖙𝖊𝖓 𝖌𝖊𝖟𝖚𝖞𝖛𝖊𝖗𝖙.

TOT HAERLEM,

𝕭𝖊𝖉𝖗𝖚𝖈𝖐𝖙 𝖇𝖞 Johannes Marshoorn, 𝕭𝖔𝖊𝖈𝖐𝖉𝖗𝖚𝖈𝖐𝖊𝖗
𝖔𝖕 𝖉𝖊 𝕸𝖆𝖗𝖈𝖐𝖙. 𝕬𝖓𝖓𝖔 1734.

Title page from the Samenspraecken
first published in Haarlem 1637 and reissued at the beginning of the hyacinth boom in 1734

children of Wouter Bartelmiesz, lately innkeeper of the Oude Schutters Doelen at Alkmaar. The average price per bulb paid at this auction represented about two years' pay for a master carpenter in Leiden. It realised 90,000 guilders, perhaps £6 million in today's money. Prices depended on the weight of a bulb (measured in *azen*) as well as its name. Selling by weight was supposed to regularise the tulip trade, but it actually had the opposite effect. Bulbs were weighed and planted in early winter, each weight carefully noted by the grower. But trading took place while the bulbs were still in the ground. The weight at planting time might or might not have increased by lifting time in midsummer. It might, or might not, have produced an offset. Nobody could dig the bulb up before buying, to see how it was getting on. Or could they?

One of the many law suits brought forward at the time concerned a bulb of the tulip 'Admiral Lieffkens' bought by a fifty-year-old baker, Jeuriaen Jansz, at a price of six guilders, or twelve *stuivers* an *azen*. At the time the deal was made, the tulip, a handsome variety with pointed petals, crimson stripes on white, was growing in the garden of a neighbour, Sr Cresser. But, wrote the lawyer, 'the witness coming to the house of Cornelis Arentsz. Kettingman, innkeeper here, at the college and in the society of several tulipists overheard, from remarks freely made in other conversation, that they knew for certain that the aforesaid tulip "Admiral Lieffkens" had been looked at, and taken out of the ground, and the earth scraped off. Because once the exact weight of the offset of the aforesaid tulip was known, no one would desire to buy for so high a price as he, the plaintiff, had paid previously', the deal was legally cancelled.[33] Lawyers, as well as speculators, got rich during the tulip boom.

Jeuriaen Jansz's action was brought on 1 August 1636, when silly money was still being paid for tulip bulbs, or rather tulip futures. Once the flower became a trader's notion rather than a gardener's joy, it attracted more and more middle men, each intent on taking his cut. From spring 1636, when selling by *azen* was first introduced, these fees alone pushed up tulip prices dramatically. Only the finest tulips, 'piece-goods' such as 'Viceroy' and 'Semper Augustus', were sold by the *azen*. The most highly prized tulips were, like those, 'breaks' of red and white or purple and white. Breaks of red and yellow were the next most valuable, with good 'Lacs' of red or purple, bordered with whites coming a bad third. Single-coloured tulips were least highly valued, unless they were varieties known to be good 'breeders', likely to break into expensive stripes. Cheaper tulips were sold by the pound, or even by the basket.

Lijste van eenighe Tulpaen /

Verkocht aende meest-biedende / op den 5. Februarij 1637. Op de Sael vande Nieuwe Schutters-Doelen / int bywesen vande E. Heeren Wees-Meesteren / ende Voochden / ghecoomen van Wouter Bartelmiesz. Winckel / in sijn Leven Castelepn vande Oude Schutters Doelen tot Alckmaer.

Inden eersten.

Een veranderde Botter-man van 563. Asen gheplant.	263.
De Schipio, van 82. Asen gheplant.	400.
Een Parragon van Delft of Mols-wijck, van 354. Asen gheplant.	605.
Een Bruyne Purper, van 320. Asen gheplant.	2025.
Een Viseroy, van 410. Asen geplant.	3000.
De Monassier, van 510. Asen geplant.	830.
Een vroeghe Blijenburgher, van 443. Asen gheplant.	1300.
Een Gouda, van 187. Asen gheplant.	1330.
Een Iulius Ceser, van 82. Asen gheplant.	650.
De Tulpa Kos, van 477. Asen gheplant.	300.
Een Botterman, van 400. Asen geplant.	405.
Een Schapesteyn, van 246. Asen gheplant.	375.
Een Bellaart, van 399. Asen gheplant.	1520.
Een Parragon van Delft of Mols-wijck, van 294. Asen gheplant.	650.
Een Ameraal Liefkens, van 59. Asen gheplant.	1015.
Een Viseroy, van 658. Asen gheplant.	4200.
De Monassier, van 542. Asen gheplant.	920.
Een vroeghe Blijen-burgher, van 171. Asen gheplant.	900.
Een Gouda, van 244. Asen gheplant.	1500.
Een Tulpa Kos, van 485. Asen gheplant.	305.
Een Butterman (schoon) van 246. Asen gheplant.	250.
Een wit Purper Ieroen, van 148. Asen gheplant.	475.
Een Parragon van Delft of Mols-wijck, van 123. Asen gheplant.	510.
Een Aanvers Vestus, van 52. Asen geplant.	510.
Een Sjery Katelijn, vande beste soozt / van 619. Asen gheplant.	2610.
Een Ameraal van der Eyk , van 446. Asen gheplant.	1620.
Een Grebber, van 95. Asen geplant.	615.
Een Gouda, van 156. Asen geplant.	1165.
Een Tulpa Kos, van 117. Asen geplant.	205.
Een Parragon Schilder, van 106. Asen gheplant.	1615.
Een Laroy, van 306. Asen geplant.	510.
Een Sjery na by, van 129. Asen geplant.	755.
Een Fama, van 158. Asen geplant.	700.
Een Fama, van 130. Asen geplant.	605.
Een Of-zet van Sjery Katelijn, van 206. Asen gheplant.	1280.
Een Somer-Schoon, van 368. Asen geplant.	1010.
Een Amerael vander Eyk, van 214. Asen gheplant.	1045.
Een Parragon Kasteleyn, van 100. Asen gheplant.	450.
Een Gouda, van 125. Asen geplant.	1015.
Een Ameral Katelijn, van 181. Asen gheplant.	225.
Een ghevlamde Iacot, van 100. Asen gheplant.	94.
Een Wit-Purper van Buscher, van 134. Asen gheplant.	110.
Een Wit-Purper van Buscher, van 315. Asen gheplant.	245.
Een Wit-Purper van Buscher, van 481. Asen gheplant.	295.
Een Parragon Liefjes , van 348. Asen gheplant.	730.
Een Parragon Liefjes , van 300. Asen gheplant.	705.
Een Parragon Liefjes , van 200. Asen gheplant.	500.
Een Troyaen, van 470. Asen geplant.	720.
Een Troyaen, van 252. Asen geplant.	500.
Een Troyaen, van 165. Asen geplant.	400.
Een IanGerriefz. van 263. Asen geplant.	210.

Een swymende Ian Gerritsz. van 925. Asen geplant.	210.
Een swymende Ian Gerritsz. van 80. Asen geplant.	51.
Een Bruyne Blaeuwe Purper van Kouper, van 790. Asen geplant.	220.
Een Lantmeter, van 277. Asen geplant.	365.
Een Lantmeter, van 71. Asen geplant.	175.
Een Parragon de Man , van 148. Asen geplant.	260.
Een Bruyne Lack vander Meer, van 365. Asen gheplant.	215.
Een Amerael vander Eyck, van 92. Asen gheplant.	710.
Een Fama, van 104. Asen geplant.	440.
Een Brabanson Bol, van 524. Asen geplant.	975.
Een Grebber, van 523. Asen gheplant.	1485.
Een Brabanson, van 542. Asen geplant.	1010.
Een Brabanson, van 346. Asen geplant.	835.
Een Schapesteyn, van 95. Asen geplant.	235.
Een Gouda, van 160. Asen geplant.	1165.
Een Gouda, van 82. Asen geplant.	765.
Een Gouda, van 63. Asen geplant.	635.

Dese naevolghende Perceelen zijn by de Aes verkocht / ende te leveren als de Bollen acht daghen upt der Aerden sijn gheweest.

Inden eersten 1000. Asen Groote Gepluymezeerde.	280.
Noch 1000. Asen Legrandes.	780.
Noch 1000. Asen Vyolette Gevlamde Rottganfen.	805.
Noch 1000. Asen Aenversen, vande ghemeene soozt.	930.
Noch 1000. Asen Aenversen.	905.
Noch 1000. Asen Lanoijs.	500.
Noch 1000. Asen Zay-Blommen vande Kasteleyn, vande beste soozt.	1000.
Noch 500. Asen Lak van Rijn.	160.
Noch 1000. Asen Saij-Blommen, vande gemeene soozt	495.
Noch 1000. Asen Nieu-Burgers	430.
Noch 500. Asen Nieu-Burgers	235.
Noch 1000. Asen Ian Symonsz.	140.
Noch 500. Asen Ian Symonsz.	70.
Noch 1000. Asen Mackx	300.
Noch 1000. Asen Mackx	300.
Noch 1000. Asen Recktors	310.
Noch 1000. Asen Vyolette ghevlamde Rotganfen.	725.
Noch 500. Asen Vyolette ghevlamde Rotganfen.	375.
Noch 1000. Asen Late Blyen-Burgers.	570.
Noch 1000. Asen Ducke-winckel.	210.
Noch 1000. Asen Petters.	730.
Noch 1000. Asen Wt-roep.	705.
Noch 1000. Asen Wt-roep.	725.
Noch 1000. Asen Petters.	705.
Noch 1000. Asen Tornay Kasteleyn.	705.
Noch 1000. Asen Tornay Rijkers.	345.
Noch 500. Asen gevlamde Bransons de Nou vijl.	130.
Noch 1000. Asen Senekoets.	105.
Noch 1000. Asen Aanvers.	900.
Noch 1000. Asen Oudenaarders.	530.
Noch 1000. Asen Oudenaarders.	510.

Dese bovenghemelde Bloemen of Tulpaas / sijn verkocht ten profijte vande kinderen van Wouter Bartholmiesz. voozschzeven / bedzaecht de Somme van 68553.

Noch te voozen Mondelingh vercocht / een Admirael van Enckhupsen / met een clepne Affetjen vande selve / t'samen vooz 5200. Guldens.

Twee Bzabansons / t'samen vooz 3800. Guldens.

Noch aen verschepden Planten en Point goet / tsamen vooz 12467. Guldens.

Somma int gheheel 90000. Guldens.

A list of prices realised for the bulbs sold at the Alkmaar tulip auction held on 5 February 1637

As one of the crusading pamphleteers had predicted, once there were more sellers than buyers in the market (and given the number of people that could easily happen), the collapse of tulipomania would be inevitable. It was. Trade in 1637 began briskly enough. On 16 January 1637 Pieter Willemsen van Rosven paid ninety florins for one 'Legrant' tulip, which had weighed 122 *azen* at planting time. The tulip grew in the garden of the local *predicant* or priest, Henricus Swalmus. Walmius, as his name was more usually written, looked after the parish of the Nederlands Hervormde Gemeente church at Haarlem from 16 October 1625 to 12 January 1649 and had his garden in the Bollslaen (Bulb lane), near the Kleine Houtweg, Haarlem. The previous day, the same van Rosven had sold (for 230 florins) a 'Jan Gerrits' tulip growing in Cornelis Verwer's garden and weighing 288 *azen* when planted. The wine money amounted to twelve *stuivers*. Over the next two weeks, van Rosven traded like a maniac, making – on paper at least – nearly 3,000 guilders on tulips.[34] Despite the sky-high prices realised at the Alkmaar sale on 5 February 1637 (or perhaps even precipitated by it), rumours were eating away at the flimsy foundations of the tulip boom. At the end of these fabulously long chains of traded *azen*, somebody, somewhere had to want the flower itself. If nobody did, the whole edifice would fold, as it did, spectacularly, when all dealing in tulip bulbs was suspended in the middle of February 1637.

On 23 February florists (that is, the growers) from Alkmaar, Delft, Enkhuizen, Gouda, Haarlem, Hoorn, Leiden, Medemblik, Rotterdam, de Streek, Utrecht and Vianen met at Amsterdam to 'deliberate on the actions of Flora and to abolish the misunderstandings which have arisen recently between them owing to the high auctions of the tulips'. The delegates included Francisco Gomez da Costa from Vianen, Barent Kardoes from Haarlem, Jacques Baelde from Leiden, Cornelis Rotteval from Gouda and François Sweert from Utrecht. The following day they issued a statement (Amsterdam dissenting) setting out their solution. Any sales made up until the end of the previous planting season (November 1636) were to be treated as binding. Transactions made after that date could be cancelled by the buyer, by paying ten per cent of the agreed price to the seller.[35] But as Gaergoedt complained to Waermondt, the buyers were 'nowhere to be found'. The law courts were packed out with dealers seeking to claim their percentages from buyers reluctant to pay them.

Then a counter-petition drawn up by improvident buyers was handed to the Governors of Holland and West Friesland at The Hague, asking for *all* transactions entered into over the previous winter to be cancelled. On 27 April 1637 the States

'De Vroege Brabantsson'
from the Judith Leyster tulip book (1643)
Frans Halsmuseum, Haarlem

of Holland and West Friesland, who seemed to be more on the side of the buyers than the sellers, decreed that sellers should get what they could for tulips promised to buyers who refused to pay up, and make the original buyer answerable for any difference in price. Further trading was suspended. But the States should have foreseen that such legislation would be unworkable. On 1 May the Burgomasters and Governors of Haarlem told the town's solicitors and notaries not to bring forward any more cases relating to the tulip trade. On 20 June, E van Bosvelt, a Haarlem solicitor, declared that 'only a few honest people have compromised by paying one, two, three, four, yes, even five, which was the utmost, out of a hundred. They, the witnesses [Haarlem florists], understand that such has happened in the same way at Amsterdam, Gouda, Hoorn, Enchuizen and Alkmaar. There are also a great number of persons unwilling to pay or come to a compromise. No justice has been administered.'[36]

There the matter rested until, on 30 January 1638, an arbitration council, with five members, was set up in Haarlem to mediate between dissatisfied sellers and buyers. The aim was to reconcile the two parties, but later, on 28 May, sufficient power was given to the council to make its judgments binding. Whether reconciled or not, buyers and sellers had to accept the council's decision. Outstanding contracts could be liquidated at 3.5% of the original price, the bulbs remaining with the seller. The commission in Haarlem was kept busy during the whole of 1638 and there were penalties for those (usually buyers) who did not appear at a hearing when summoned. Other towns adopted similar measures, so it was brave of the Dutch artist, Jacob Gerritsz Cuyp to paint in 1638 a picture of a tulip bed gay with extravagantly flamed flowers.[37] After this wild fling, moderation, prudence and discretion returned to the burghers of The Netherlands. They nearly lost control again in 1734 when a passion for hyacinths threatened to equal the earlier mania for tulips, but a hasty reissue of the *Samenspraecken* brought the eighteenth-century speculators to their senses.

As the Dutch economist, N W Posthumus has pointed out, all the conditions generally associated with the first period of a boom were present in The Netherlands of the 1630s. 'An increasing currency, new economic and colonial possibilities, and a keen and energetic class of merchants, together had created the optimistic atmosphere in which booms are said to grow'.[38] All that was needed was the right commodity, and the tulip obligingly presented itself at the right time and in the right place. Less prosaically, Zbigniew Herbert ascribed the cause to 'the old myth of humanity about miraculous multiplication',[39] setting the tulip in the same

Two 'Semper Augustus'
from a tulip book by Brandemandus
Municipal archives, Delft

172

context as loaves and dragon's teeth. Or was this uncharacteristic rush of blood to Dutchmen's heads a symptom of relief after the twin evils of the plague and the Thirty Years War? In 1630, the prospects for the Dutch Republic had been gloomy, for the armies of the Catholic Emperor dominated Central Europe from Bohemia to the Baltic Coast. The Dutch were completely hemmed in on the south and east; their only escape lay on their seaward side. When, in 1632, the victories of Gustavus Adolphus, the Protestant King of Sweden, ensured that the Protestant religion would survive, this must have seemed like a miraculous delivery. The war was not over, but the deliverance, perhaps, was expressed in wild speculation.

In the *Samenspraecken*, Waermondt asks how tulips got so many names. 'If a change in a tulip is effected' explains Gaergoedt, 'one goes to a florist and tells him and it soon gets talked about. Everyone is anxious to see it. If it is a new flower each one gives his opinion; one compares it to this, another to that flower. If it looks like an "Admiral", you call it a "General" or any name you fancy, and stand a bottle of wine to your friends that they may remember to talk about it.' Tulips, with carnations, were the first flowers to be given special names, what would now be called cultivar names: purple and white 'Viceroy', scarlet and white 'Admiral van der Eyck', 'Bruin Purpur' which was purplish-brown on a white ground. For traders, the baptism was important, because it created and distinguished particular components of a general commodity. Then, as now, it was partly a matter of whim that some colour combinations were more highly prized than others. But it was also a fact that red and white breaks such as 'Semper Augustus' were more difficult to produce than red and yellow ones and consequently could command higher prices. Pieter Holsteyn the Younger's painting of 'Semper Augustus' shows, though, that this was a very unusual break. Most often, the two colours of broken tulips ran in long, continuous stripes down the petals. But in 'Semper Augustus' the red colour breaks into flakes, symmetrically set round the outsides of the petals. Long before tulipomania raged, it was considered a masterpiece. But neither of the lists of fine tulips published in the *Samenspraecken* include 'Semper Augustus'. Nor was it offered for sale in the great Alkmaar auction of 1637. In the *Samenspraecken*, Waermondt makes clear that although he has heard of the fabled flower, he has never seen it. He could see it at the homes of only two people, replies Gaergoedt, 'one in Amsterdam from which it comes, and also here at the home of one who will not sell for any money; so they are in close hands'. The one bulb that had changed hands for 2,000 guilders at the beginning of the tulipomania had done so with the restriction that the buyer could not pass the tulip on to anyone else

Flora's Fools-Cap
engraved by Cornelis Danckerts after a painting by Pieter Nolpe
British Museum, Department of Prints and Drawings

174

without the consent of the original seller (Adriaen Pauw of Heemstede). One of the last of the great English Florists, the Rev. Francis Horner, who died in 1912, took a jaundiced view of the legendary 'Semper Augustus', describing it as a 'rough bizarre of spattery flame and with skips in feather, long in the cup and thin in petal, foul in stamen and perhaps base in base – in fact with a touch of all the faults and blemishes from which we have led the tulip through to purity and beauty'. But English florists only had eyes for English florists' tulips. Call it patriotism. Or xenophobia.

It was inevitable that tulipomania would be followed by an equally intense hatred of the flower. The professor of botany at Leiden grew so to loathe them that he attacked them savagely wherever they stood, thwacking them with his cane. Artists turned out some pungent cartoons and caricatures. *Floraes Gecks-kap* (Flora's Fool's Cap) shows an inn made in the shape of a fool's cap, the tulip fanciers huddled inside, weighing tulips with a set of goldsmith's scales. The name of the inn, written on a banner is 'At the Sign of the Fools' Bulbs' and it shows two fools fighting. To the right of the inn is Flora, seated on a donkey, a symbol of stupidity, being beaten by disappointed florists. In the foreground, separated from the mayhem, are a group of three tulip growers holding the tools of their trade – a rake and a wicker basket. To the left of the inn is a smiling speculator, a rich one too, by the look of his hat and cloak. Behind him is the Devil with a rod and line, fishing for tulip sale notes. In his right hand he carries an hour glass, suggesting that the speculators' time is up. In front of him, other speculators are already tipping their bulbs on the rubbish heap. The engraving's sub-title tells the full story: 'A Picture of the wonderful year 1637 when one Fool hatched another, the Idle Rich lost their Wealth and the Wise lost their Senses.'[40]

In *Flora's Malle-wagen* (Flora's Chariot of Fools) three florists called Sweet Beard, Eager for Wealth and Travelling Light are riding in a chariot with Flora who is clasping a cornucopia of tulips. In her other hand she holds a trio of hopelessly expensive tulips, 'Semper Augustus', 'General Bol' and 'Admiral van Horn'. Her companions in the chariot are Hoard-it-all and Vain hope, who has just released a bird. 'Vain hope has flown the coop' runs the legend above its head. A great crowd of weavers runs after the chariot shouting 'We will all sail with you', trampling their looms in the process. The chariot is rolling over a carpet of single precious tulips (added by the engraver Crispyn de Passe to the original painting by Hendrik Pot). 'Gouda' is here and the fabulously expensive 'Viceroy'. De Passe also included four vignettes in each of the four corners of the engraving, showing the various

Flora's Chariot of Fools,
the original painting by Hendrik Pot

stages of the tulipomania. In the top left is a view of Pottebacker's nursery at Haarlem. In the bottom left, tulip fanciers meet in their club room at Haarlem. The vignette in the top right shows a similar company of florists at Hoorn. In the bottom right, a florist tenders a sale note.[41] To a seventeenth-century Dutch audience, the meaning of the cartoons would have been as clear as Vicky's political cartoons were to a newspaper-reading English audience of the twentieth century. They would immediately have seen the point of Jan Brueghel's satirical painting of monkeys enthusiastically engaged in the tulip trade.[42] But though Dutch speculators may have been disenchanted by the tulip after the savage upsets of 1637, the true lovers of the flower were not. Slowly, gently, quietly, the tulip continued to re-invent itself. The best was yet to come.

CHAPTER V

DUTCH DOMINANCE

TULIPOMANIA WAS a chastening experience for the Dutch. The gay paintings of tulips accompanied by vividly plumaged parrots and strange shells which had mirrored the early seventeenth-century fascination with all things exotic, gave way to more gloomy groupings of tulips with skulls, hourglasses and other reminders of the transitoriness of things. But even after the crash of spring 1637, tulip bulbs still had value. An anonymous Dutch painting *c*1640[1] shows Flora with a pair of scales, a jewel on one side, a tulip bulb on the other; the bulb weighs more heavily. A malevolent-looking Pan surveys the scene while supporting Cupid who is clutching a tulip flower in his hand. And documents of 1643 relating to the estate of the nurseryman Jan van Damme of the Kleine Houtweg, Haarlem, show that, even after the end of tulipomania, the average yearly wage of a Haarlemer would still not be enough to buy one of van Damme's best tulips. Salomon Seijs paid him 180 guilders for one 'Gouda' and 315 guilders for a 'Manassier'. Dirck Janss parted with 300 guilders for a single bulb of the variety 'Bellaert'. The widow Ruth van Berckhoff paid 325 guilders for an English 'Admiral', evidently a highly prized tulip as another buyer, Willem Willemss handed over 402 guilders for the same variety. 'Paragon Lieffkens' commanded high prices too, Anthony Gerrit paying van Damme 300 guilders for his bulb. But bulbs from the Lieffkens stable were always among the most expensive available; at the Alkmaar

A Vase of Flowers
Jan Brueghel I (1568–1625)
Fitzwilliam Museum, Cambridge

tulip auction of 1637, an offset of an 'Admiral Lieffkens' bulb, weighing only 59 *azen*, had sold for 1,015 guilders.

The continuing demand for flower paintings, too, showed that the tulip was not universally reviled, even though it had been responsible for bankrupting so many who had traded in tulip futures. From 1650–1720 Jan Davidsz de Heem, Daniel Seghers, Abraham Mignon, Simon Verelst, Rachel Ruysch all included tulips in their work, often setting them in the top right-hand corner of the mixed arrangements they painted. None of the later artists, though, plagiarised themselves as gaily as Jan Brueghel had done at the beginning of the seventeenth century. His flower piece in the Rijksmuseum, Amsterdam is virtually identical to his panel in the Kunsthistorisches Museum, Vienna. His son Jan Brueghel II continued the process, making another copy of the painting, which is now in the Alte Pinakothek, Munich. The elder Brueghel had done much the same with his *Vase of Flowers*[2] which has a virtual twin in *Flowers in a Stoneware Jar*.[3] The *Vase of Flowers* painting has the more interesting foreground, with jewels lying carelessly to the right of the vase and in the *Flowers in a Stoneware Jar*, the tulip at the top of the *Vase of Flowers* painting is replaced by an iris, another favourite of covetous collectors.

In the decorative arts, tulips bloomed, especially on painted and inlaid furniture. They appear on a money chest decorated with panels of painted flowers[4] and on the front of an ebony and cedarwood Kunstkabinet made in the third quarter of the seventeenth century and inlaid with tulips in mother of pearl. The doors of the cabinet open to show drawers and four small cupboards, each cupboard front painted with a tulip.[5] The versatile Jacob Marrell turned his hand to stained glass, using enamel paint and grisaille to produce a wonderful orange and red flamed tulip in a coat of arms possibly from the Oosterkerk in Hoorn.[6] Tulips appeared too on bed hangings, tapestries and curtains. Embroidered curtains from the second half of the seventeenth century show bunches of characteristically waisted tulips, worked in satin stitch, knot stitch and stem stitch.[7] Tulips were woven into the borders of Flemish tapestries, the flowers arranged in bouquets which often seem to have been copied from contemporary flower paintings.[8]

Fifty years after the end of tulipomania, the first of the so-called tulip vases began to appear, strange tall pagoda-like creations with spouts jutting out at the top and sides. For a long time it was assumed that the vases were used either for displaying tulip flowers or for growing tulips indoors, the bulbs placed over water in the spouts, much as hyacinths are grown today. But as the English botanist, Philip Miller had discovered, tulips do not grow well like this; at a time when bulbs were

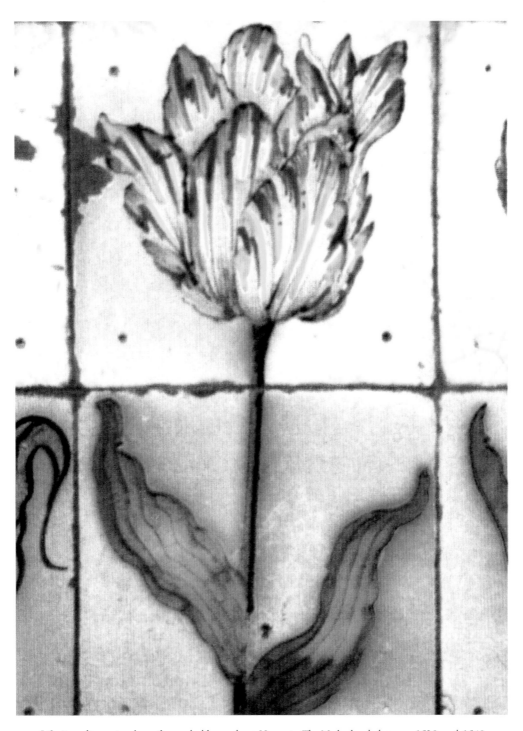

Life-size tulips painted on tiles, probably made at Hoorn in The Netherlands between 1630 and 1640

still expensive, it seems odd that anyone would have chosen such a risky way of flowering them.[9] The vases may have been used to grow hyacinths and were described as such ('portebouquets, avec huite tubes pour jacinthes') in 1877 by the French expert Henry Havard in his *Catalogue des Faiences de Delft*. Hyacinths would certainly be happier than tulips growing in this way, and the period when these strange vases were made (1680–1720) is closer to the time of the Dutch hyacinth craze than it is the earlier tulip mania. But their use remains a puzzle. None of the hundreds of flower paintings of the Golden Age shows flowers in a Delftware holder. None of the paintings in the *Hortus Regius Honselaersdicensis*, a record of the fresh cut flowers delivered weekly to Honselaersdijk, William and Mary's summer house, around 1688, show flowers in a Delft flower holder. Embroidered chair covers at Croft Castle in Herefordshire feature them, but they mostly show mixed bouquets of flowers coming from the spouts; only one embroidery shows a tulip.

Blue and white chinoiserie-style Delft ware was avidly collected in the late seventeenth century, mixed with genuine Chinese porcelain in special display cabinets. One was made in 1663 at Oranienburg near Berlin for Louise Henriette, the wife of the elector of Brandenburg. Louis XIV had one too, the Trianon de Porcelaine, full of chinoiserie ware ordered from the potteries at Delft. The style setter of the time was Daniel Marot, a Huguenot who, after the repeal of the Edict of Nantes, had fled from France to The Netherlands. He quickly found his feet for in 1686, only a year after he had arrived in the country, he was employed by William and Mary to bring a touch of French glamour to the Dutch court. He carried out work for them too at their hunting lodge, Het Loo, near Apeldoorn, considered at the time to be the last word in modernity and style. Marot tackled architecture, interior design and garden-making all with equal verve and created splendid settings for Mary's impressive collection of ceramics, though none of the contemporary engravings of his interiors show a Delft flower holder. The influence worked the other way. The swags, garlands, shell motifs and diamond patterns of Marot's interior decor began to appear as decorations on the flower vases themselves, particularly the ones coming from the De Grieksche A factory belonging to Adriaen Kocks. As well as the popular pagoda design, Delft flower pots also appeared in the shape of busts of Turkish sultans[10]. Marot may have had a hand in this too, for he had a passion for all things Turkish. But whether in the shape of pyramids, sultans or other guises, there is little evidence that these flower pots were ever used for growing tulips. Only since the beginning of this century have they assumed the name (and by extension the function) of tulip vases.[11]

Delft tulip vase
Het Loo, Apeldoorn

Regular advertisements in the *Haerlemse Courant*, the Haarlem newspaper, confirm that at the end of the seventeenth century and beginning of the eighteenth, trade in tulip bulbs was still buoyant, though the advertisements (as in that of the Widow van Severijn Oosterwijk who advertised 'Anjelieren, droge Tulpen-Bollen, Hyacinthen, Narcissen and Dubbelde Jonquilles' on 17 July 1694) touted tulips in general rather than named tulips in particular. A clear distinction was beginning to emerge between nurserymen and what in England would be called florists, tulip-fanciers, or in Dutch, *liefhebbers*. In his preface to *The Dutch Gardener*, the Leyden gardener, Henry van Oosten, sniffily pointed out that his book (published in 1700) was aimed at 'the true Sons and Lovers of Flora' rather than 'those who trade and deal in Flowers'. Van Oosten's treatise, like Monstereul's *Le Floriste Français* published in Caen in 1654 and Samuel Gilbert's *Florist's Vade Mecum* published in London in 1682, was an opportunistic and very successful piece of publishing.[12]

Tulip seed, said van Oosten, should be sown in September. He recommended collecting seed from dark flowers 'for when the White comes to play through these heavy Colours, it gives immediately to them a fine lustre and Beauty'. Flowers of black, purple, red or brown, were equally good for the purpose. Yellow flowers were to be avoided for 'the Yellowness gives a Faintness to the Tulip that dulls the gloss of the Colours'. Van Oosten spells out the preference for tulips with petals that are 'round above' and do not 'turn much about' that is evident in the flower paintings of Jan van Huysum. Seed was best collected from flowers with white or yellow bases, 'experience having taught us, that the Tulips that have such Bottoms sooner change from one to two colours, than those whose Bottoms are black'. This suggests, as one would expect, that the tulips still close to black-based wild species were less likely to 'break' than selected cultivars. 'The Bottom is Master of the Colours which they seem to be willing to receive,' as van Oosten put it. It was better also to take seed from single-coloured 'breeders' rather than from striped tulips. This was a useful observation, as it ran counter to what horticulturists of the time might have expected. The virus which produced the stripes (though nobody then knew that) also weakened the tulip, whose seed would not anyway produce flowers that matched the parent. The seed, wrote van Oosten, would come up 'like leeks' but gardeners had to wait between five and seven years before bulbs grew to flower-bearing size. Florists were becoming more rigid and uncompromising in their interpretation of the perfect tulip. 'The parrot greens' that had so delighted early painters such as Ambrosius Bosschaert 'must go without Distinction to the Dunghil'.

Three Tulips *(c1640)*
by Jacob Marrell (1614–1681)
Teylers Museum, Haarlem

185

Like other authors of the time, van Oosten was puzzled by the business of 'breaking'. The whole shaky edifice of tulipomania had been built on the tulip's sudden ability to burst into stripes and multi-coloured patterns. Van Oosten was more honest than other so-called experts. Many skilful florists, he wrote, had 'puzzled their Heads in search of this Secret… Some pretend they have had good Success in it, but whether by Art or by Chance is yet uncertain'. Whereas in the early seventeenth century, there had been general agreement among tulip fanciers that 'Semper Augustus' was the best flower of its age, florists in the early eighteenth century found it more difficult to reach a consensus. 'Some esteem the Violets striped with white, whose Colours as well within as without, are clean and distinct from one another, without any Mixture. Others prize the Bissarts; yet both are to be valu'd and a Florist ought to be provided with both of them. The Bissarts are duller than the Violets and more inclined to Inconstancy; for when they have bloomed one Year exceedingly beautifully, they sometimes appear the next as if they had never had any Beauty in them.' There is no mention of the red and white tulips, the Roses such as 'Semper Augustus' which had so delighted an earlier generation of tulip fanciers. Judging tulips, wrote the sensible van Oosten, would be made very much easier 'if many things were not despised because they are common, and if we did not always covet that which is seldom seen'. He had little time for those who complained that tulips had no scent. 'They may supply themselves with Perfumes, and not upbraid this Queen of Flowers for want of that Quality.'

Van Oosten noted how, in full sun, the separate colours on a petal tended to run together. This was a problem that English florists fretted about too and it led to the construction of very complicated tulip beds with covers of canvas or rattan that could be used to shade the flowers when necessary. Van Oosten thought it was honeydew (the sticky secretion of aphids) that caused the colours to run. He was halfway to the truth. The sun was actually the cause, but the honeydew was deposited by the aphids who carried the virus that caused the tulips to break in the first place. In *Le Floriste Français*, the French author Monstereul had surrounded the business of tulip-growing with all kinds of ritualistic mumbo-jumbo. Van Oosten was evidently an observant grower and his treatise is more practical. He noticed for instance how ground could become tulip sick and that bulbs were best moved onto fresh beds every few years. He observed that only fat, full-grown bulbs would generally produce flowers. This was why the weight of a bulb played such an important part in the transactions between tulip growers and their customers.

ACCURATE DESCRIPTION
of the Whole Collection of FINE
HYACINTHS,
T U L I P S
AND
RANONCULUSES;

That are Collected from the different
Dutch Flowrift's, and to gether
to be found in the Large
dutch Flowergarden from

VOORHELM and SCHNEEVOOGT,

Flowrifts and feedsmen at Haerlem in Holland,
Which Direction was formerly V o o R-
H E L M and van Z o M P E L.

H A E R L E M,

Printed for the Authors, by whom it is to be
had *Gratis* to Every Curious Man.

The English language catalogue produced by the
Dutch nurseryman Voorhelm in Haarlem c1770

Weighing bulbs after lifting them in summer was also a good way of checking growing conditions. If the bulb had not bulked up, the grower was not giving it what it needed.

Van Oosten describes the process by which the mad trading, usually in public houses, of the Dutch tulipomania gave way to florists' fraternities, the forerunners of the florists' societies which flourished in England from the early eighteenth century onwards. 'Tulips have always been greatly esteemed and chiefly by the Dutch, who in the Year 1637 intended to Traffick with them, as with Pearls and Diamonds: But the States forbad it for a Political Reason of State, and when the publick buying and selling of Tulips was thus prohibited, they fell to trucking and private selling; but because this could not be done without Animosities, thereupon the Flemish Florists erected a Fraternity in the Cities and took St Dorothea to be their Patroness and the Syndicus to be Judge of the Differences, that might arise by their trucking; and he to add Authority to it, called in four of the chief of the Brother-hood and this was the occasion of the sweet Conversation of the Brothers, and brought them into great Esteem. The *Dutch* keep in this matter another rule; they meet together on a certain Day, when Tulips are in their full Bloom, and choose, after having seen the chief Gardens of the Florists, and taken a friendly and frugal Dinner together, one of the Company to be Judge of the Differences that might arise about Flowers in that Year.' These were the first competitive events surrounding the tulip. It was a short way then to the process of *picking* the tulips and bringing them to a central place – usually an inn – for competition. In the hands of the English florists, the frugal dinner became a rather more debauched feast. Their shows were always based around local inns.

From the beginning of the eighteenth century onwards then, there was an increasing divergence between the nurserymen and the true 'sons of Flora'. Often the one fed the other, the nurseryman buying from the amateur florist new breaks of a tulip that would subsequently appear at a vast price in his catalogue. *His* customers were the rich landowners too busy, too impatient, to spend years breeding these beauties themselves. But they could not do without them. On 17 May 1707 the Hague lawyer, Bartholomeus van Leeuwen sold his collection at auction, 230 lots that realised 3,858 guilders. The highest price (321 guilders) was paid for the Baguet 'Fieldmarshal Averquercq', with the Haarlem florist, Voorhelm, paying 195 guilders for another Baguet, 'Schoon Aethiopica'. Not all the lots were of single bulbs. A bed of 120 seedling tulips sold in the same auction for 358 guilders. The

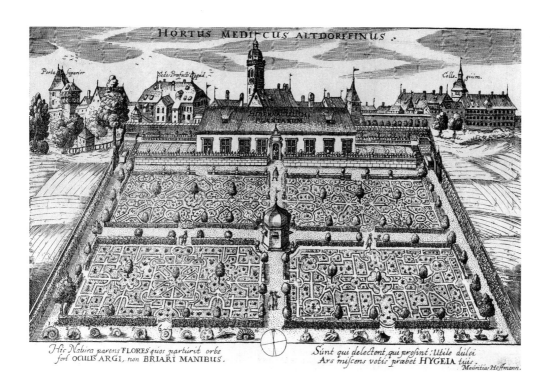

A seventeenth-century botanic garden,
the Hortus Medicus at Altdorff,
from Florae Altdorffinae, *published in Altdorff 1662*

bed was made up of twenty rows each containing six bulbs and each row was sold off separately.

May was the prime time for auctions of private collections; the flowers were in full bloom and buyers could clearly see the worth of the tulips they were bidding for. The sale the following year of the Rotterdam merchant Henricus van der Heym's collection of tulips was also set for May: 16 May 1708. For twenty-one years van der Heym had owned a garden close to the outskirts of the town, where he had built up a noted collection of flowers. The catalogue of the sale listed tulips by number, name and weight. They were arranged in two beds – 240 bulbs in all – and the sale realised 8,662 guilders. Once again, the Baguets commanded the highest prices, particularly the four lots of the Baguet 'L'Imperiale' which sold for 140, 204, 276, and 336 guilders each (about £65,000 in late twentieth-century terms).[13]

The Baguets, wide-cupped, round-petalled flowers, capable the Scottish grower James Justice had said, of holding 'a pint of wine' in their blooms, were a Flemish speciality and it is noticeable how many of the flowers, both in the van Leeuwen and the van der Heym sales, bore French rather than Dutch names. Some of van der Heym's flowers were dated (Number two in the first bed the Baguet 'Queva' 1696, Number twelve in the first bed the Baguet Number two, 1696), which suggests that they might have been flowers of van der Heym's own raising. But many of the rest – 'Nouvelle de St Omer', the Baguets 'Potteau', 'Buisson Ardant' and 'Duchesse de Baviere' suggest a French or Flemish origin. There were certainly close links between the two, the Flemish growers perhaps content to rely on the Dutch to get them prices for their tulips which they could not realise locally.

Bulbs as valuable as 'Fieldmarshal Averquercq' and 'L'Imperiale' were often owned by several people in partnership, which made buying and selling complicated – especially when the bulb was grown in ground belonging to a person who may or may not have been one of the syndicate. On 26 June 1709, the bulb dealer Jacob Bart wrote to Bartholomeus van Leeuwen at The Hague reporting from Utrecht on the condition of 'our' tulips. Bart had a third share in three Baguets, 'Perel van der Hooge', 'La Torre' and 'Grand Mogol' which together were valued at 720 guilders (about £49,000). He and his two partners, Jan Eutewael and Cornelis van Luchtenburgh had bought the bulbs from Philips van Borselle van der Hooge in Zeeland in May 1708. A 'Conqueste de Zeelande' had been in the van Leeuwen sale in 1707, raised perhaps by van der Hooge. Both Bart's partners lived in Utrecht and Bart, who later sold half of his share in the tulips to van Leeuwen, reported favourably on the state of the bulbs after lifting. 'La Torre', which had been growing in van Luchtenburgh's garden, had produced a large offset. The other two bulbs grew in Jan Eutewael's garden. The 'Perel van der Hooge' had produced two offsets, one weighing forty *azen*. 'Grand Mogol' had not done so well. Bart subsequently sold his share in the bulbs to van Leeuwen for 120 guilders, rather less than the book price. Van Leeuwen's auction had perhaps revealed that the prices of certain varieties had to be revised downwards.

Bart's letter shows that he was the middle man in several tulip deals. He had been trying to sell 400 self-coloured tulips on van Leeuwen's behalf and had, he wrote, already got one bid of fifteen guilders a hundred for them. Perhaps these were wild Turkish or Russian species which had come into van Leeuwen's hands at The Hague. He was looking for an offset of the renowned 'Premier Noble' and was also hoping to get his hands on 'Juweel van Utrecht'; a very small offset, he said, was on offer for thirty guilders. But Bart's partner, Bartholomeus van Leeuwen, died in 1710 and all his bulbs were auctioned off for the benefit of his children. They raised 1,100 guilders, about £75,000 in late twentieth-century terms.

In France and England in the middle of the eighteenth century, a passion for all things classical and antique was sparked off by the archaeological excavations that were going on at Paestum and Herculaneum. Neo-classicism blossomed which was one of the reasons the tulip fell out of fashion. But in Holland, tulips continued to be advertised right through to the beginning of the nineteenth century. On 14 May 1711 the Flemish grower Thomas de Cafmeyer of the Guldeulies brewery at Brussels announced to the 'Liefhebbers van Flora' that he had raised from seed two or three hundred new flamed Bybloemens and Bizarres, better than anything that had ever been seen before. Abraham de Haes and Alexander de Vos both advertised tulips regularly, offering Haarlem customers Primo Baguets (the Primo prefix first crops up around 1712), Seconde Baguets which presumably were not quite so good, Grand Violetten and Bizarren. In a sale that took place in Henricus van der Heym's Rotterdam garden, buyers could bid for 'Curieuse Liefhebberij Tulpaen'.[14] Here, as in England, the florists and their tulips were drawing further apart from the mainstream trade in bulbs, and tulips were advertised using the florists' definitions: Bizarres (red, brown or black on yellow) and Violets, later to be called Bybloemens (violet or purple on a white ground).

Sales were highly organised; Heer Hodenpijl of Schiedam, who advertised a sale for the 20 May 1717, had catalogues available for interested customers not only in Schiedam, but in Dordrecht, Delft, Rotterdam and 's'Gravenhage as well. English customers were drawn in too, particularly by the well-known firms of Voorhelm and van Kampen. Voorhelm had been founded in the seventeenth century by Dirk Jansz Voorhelm who came from Westphalia to set up bulb gardens in the Kleine Houtweg, Haarlem. His son Pieter, who died in 1728, bred many fine hyacinths, for by the late 1720s, hyacinths were overtaking tulips in popularity. At about the time the Voorhelms went into partnership with Seger van Zompel, George Voorhelm (1711–1787) wrote a treatise on cultivating hyacinths, published in French in 1752. He was not popular with his fellow nurserymen for giving away what they considered to be trade secrets, which may be why the book, translated into English in 1753, never appeared in Dutch. Robert Hales, an English enthusiast, called at the nursery of Voorhelm, 'the famous Flowerist at Haarlem', and wrote to a friend that his stock was good, 'but so mighty deer yt I did not venture to buy any'.

The Haarlem nurseryman, Nicolaas van Kampen, reflected the prevailing taste by opening his 1739 catalogue with hyacinths – nearly 500 of them. But he still offered masses of tulips too, including almost a hundred early varieties. They were followed in the list by various kinds of late tulip: 123 'Veranderde Primo Baguetten', that is breeders that had broken into feathers and flames, eighty-two different yellow and red Bizarres, and 176 additional late tulips. Selling bulbs by their weight in *azen* was no longer the norm. Bulbs of the first division were sold only at flowering size, with prices quoted for a single bulb. By this stage tulips – even the fine ones – were not such rare commodities and prices had dropped dramatically. Where previously prices had been quoted in hundreds, even thousands of guilders, van Kampen now asked more modest sums: eight guilders for a 'Juweel van Haarlem', eight guilders for a 'Rigaut Admiraal'. Those were the most expensive. The average price was closer to one guilder per bulb. Smaller bulbs were sold by the hundred and van Kampen's catalogue suggests that nurserymen were by this stage using bulb griddles of various gauges to grade bulbs by size. Bulbs of the first sorting cost twenty-five guilders a hundred. The bulbs left after the sixth sorting could be had for only four guilders a hundred, but tulip fanciers had to be patient and grow them on to flowering size. By this stage it really was cheaper to plant your garden with real flowers rather than get van Huysum, the artist of the day, to paint them for you.

Like George Voorhelm before him, Nicolaas van Kampen also supposed that a book would be good for business; like Voorhelm too, he published it in French. The French had been the first to single the tulip out for special attention, distinguishing it as a flower that was not just there to decorate a garden, but was worth

TRAITÉ

DES

FLEURS

A OIGNONS:

Contenant tout ce qui eſt néceſſaire
pour les bien cultiver,
fondé ſur une

EXPÉRIENCE

de pluſieurs Années, .

P A R

NICOLAS van KAMPEN et FILS,

FLEURISTES

de HARLEM en HOLLANDE.

à HARLEM
imprimé chez C. H. BOHN.
MDCCLX.

*The title page of Nicolaas van Kampen's
book on bulbs published in Haarlem in 1760*

cultivating for its own sake. Van Kampen's English translator piously hoped 'that the following Translation will be an acceptable present to the English Florists, as it teaches the whole art of raising, cultivating and treating all kinds of Bulbous Rooted Flowers, according to the method practised by the most experienced Florists in Holland and Flanders, whose industry and skill in this respect have been such, that they have for above a century enjoyed the reputation of being alone possessed of some secret in this Business unknown to the rest of the world, and by that means secured to themselves a very gainful monopoly... Our countrymen that love and delight in Gardening have it now in their power, by pursuing this certain method, to reap the same profit, as well as to enjoy the in-felt satisfaction of seeing their parterres adorned with native beauties, propagated by their own pains, without squandering away English money upon Foreigners'.[15]

Van Kampen dealt with the hyacinth first, then the tulip, followed by the ranunculus and anemone, the order reflecting quite accurately the relative importance of these flowers at the time (and also the order in which van Kampen listed the flowers in his own catalogue). In terms of cultivation, van Kampen had little to say that van Oosten had not already made clear in *The Dutch Gardener*, but the English translation makes some nice distinctions between the tulip fanciers of Europe. 'The florists of different countries have very different methods of distinguishing their flowers. The English bestow upon them the titles of the British nobility etc. and hence it is that several sorts have the name... They sometimes indeed add to their names that of the person who raised them, which is a tolerable good method to prevent the confusion arising from the scarcity of their names.

'The French distinguish their flowers by numbers only, or at the most by the name of the principal colour, but this method occasions too much confusion, because a great number of different flowers may have the same denomination.

'The method practised by the Hollanders is preferable. They not only denominate their flowers from the principal colours, but also add the names of the bravest generals, the gods, goddesses, nymphs, illustrious persons... They also bestow some names on them that denote their value.'

Van Kampen recommends Tournefort as the authority for anyone who wants botanical names. He evidently doesn't, and divides tulips into four main classes: early or spring tulips, double-flowered tulips, late expectant tulips and late striped tulips, with yellow or white bottoms. He talks of the fashion for forcing early-flowering tulips: 'Duc van Thol', a scarlet tulip edged with yellow could be brought into flower by December.[16] He named just two doubles, 'La Couronne Imperiale' and 'Mariage de ma Fille' both white, striped with red, rather like the modern variety 'Carnaval de Nice'.

Late expectant tulips were so called because tulip growers expected to raise fine new flowers from them. These were the plain-coloured flowers that English florists called 'breeders' and German florists called 'Mutter Tulpen'. There were two sorts of late expectant tulips: Bizarres and Violettes. The tulips that produced the best striped Bizarres were plain brownish copper or dark fawn with a yellow-black basal blotch. The Violettes could be purplish-violet, pale violet, gridelin (a greyish colour), cherry-crimson, red, with a basal blotch of white or grey-blue mixed with white. The Violettes would later be broken into two separate classes, one covering the purple/violet end of the spectrum, the other the pinkish-red colours.

The 'breeders' were not valued for themselves, but for their ability to 'break' into variegated feathers and flames. Van Kampen had as little idea as van Oosten about the cause of the breaking. Some florists tried to induce the process by cutting various bulbs in half and then binding different halves together. Van Kampen had noticed that broken flowers were not as vigorous as plain-coloured ones and so supposed that the breaking was caused by the weakness, although in fact it was the other way around. Planting in poor soil was one of his solutions. He also recommended that growers should vary the soil the bulbs were grown in, either by changing the soil itself, or by planting the bulbs in different parts of the garden. He even suggested that growers in other countries should import soil from Holland 'which is the best way of all for foreigners', advice followed to the letter by James Justice in Scotland.

Van Kampen's fourth group of tulips, 'the variegated late blowers' were, he said, 'the most diversified, beautiful and perfect of all'. The Baguet Primo and the Baguet Rigaut tulips both had white flowers, striped with brown, the bases pure white. He places great emphasis on the tulip's height, which he says should be between three and four feet (0.9m x 1.2m). The most highly valued and most sought-after tulips of the day were black, golden yellow, purple-violet, rose and vermilion. But, he says, 'it sometimes happens that a flower of very great price degenerates and becomes of no value. There is no way to prevent this shocking metamorphosis for which nature alone is answerable; nor can the dealers in flowers, whatever care they take, prevent these grievous changes, on account of which they undergo so much vexation, and receive so many reproaches from the lovers of flowers, who not knowing what may happen, complain that the dealers have sent them roots which had degenerated the year before.'

Detail of a marquetry cabinet (c1690–1710)
attributed to Jan van Mekeren
Rijksmuseum, Amsterdam

This seems a transparent case of special pleading but van Kampen goes on to describe 'a very critical affair of this kind' which had happened to himself. A florist had written to order tulips from him at a ducat a bulb. Van Kampen packed them up and sent them, but his customer complained bitterly when, at flowering time, his tulips came up and were far inferior to those he had been promised. He sent petals of the flowers to van Kampen, who agreed they were not as ordered and replaced them. 'We concluded that the parcel must have been opened and the roots changed.' The second time he sent each bulb wrapped in paper sealed with his own seal.

Many of the best tulips were raised not in The Netherlands but in Flanders, especially around the towns of Gent, Valenciennes and Lille, where in 1538 one of the first of the tulip fanciers, Matthias de l'Obel (Lobelius) had been born. From these Flemish growers came mouth-watering beauties such as 'La Somptueuse' raised in 1772 by a florist called Boncomerre. His collection later passed into the hands of the Galliez family at Lille, whose ground was renowned for causing tulips to 'break' quickly. 'Louis XVI', the most celebrated tulip of the age, was also probably Flemish, raised in 1776 by an unknown amateur. He sold it to a commercial florist who in turn passed his collection to a Dunkirk innkeeper called Delezelles. It was offered for sale in Holland for the first time in 1789, appearing in the catalogue of the nurseryman M van Nieuwkerk at the astonishing price of 250 guilders a bulb.[17]

The following spring, van Nieuwkerk invited his colleagues to come and admire the tulip in his garden. Even Schneevoogt and Kreps, who had the best collections in Holland, had to admit they were outgunned. Van Nieuwkerk told them he had got the bulb from his son who worked as a gardener at Bagatelle, the Duc d'Orléans's garden near Paris. Despite this, Schneevoogt thought the tulip must originally have been Flemish rather than Parisian because growers in the two centres had different tastes in tulips. To his eyes, this was a tulip made in the Flemish mould, so he got in touch with two of his contacts in Flanders and asked them to look out for a 'Louis XVI' for his own collection. Again the innkeeper Delezelles was the source of supply. Schneevoogt's Flemish friends bought one bulb for him (paying 600 francs) and another for their own stock. From this one 'Louis XVI', they raised enough bulbs to supply all the other florists in Flanders. Just after Schneevogt had secured his own 'Louis XVI' tulip, the innkeeper Delezelles called on him, saying he had another 'Louis XVI' for sale. He had already offered it to the nurseryman van Nieuwkerk, who had turned it down, saying he hadn't enough money to pay for it. Schneevoogt, though, knew that several florists in London

Three Tulips by Herman Henstenburg (1667–1726)
Teylers Museum, Haarlem

were longing to get hold of this tulip, so he bought the bulb. Then, when van Nieuwkerk was forced to sell his entire stock, Schneevoogt bought his 'Louis XVI' too. He paid 150 guilders for it, rather less than the catalogue price, and then sold it on to the famous Walworth Nursery in south London, by then in the hands of Samuel Curtis. The tulip appeared in the nursery's catalogue of 1800, priced at twenty guineas.

The price was high, because the bulb was slow to make offsets and so remained rare, but for a long time 'Louis XVI' remained the best of the Bybloemens. Later, it was generally offered in three grades – fine, superfine and rectified. In the 'rectified' state, the markings of the flower were supposed to be stable, the pure white of the petals edged with a regular, delicate feathering of violet. Although tulip growers in France, Flanders and England all had their ideas about what made a good tulip, 'Louis XVI' was a favourite in all three countries. The flower was regular in shape, both stalk and petals had plenty of substance and the colours on the petals were clearly defined.

Though by 1821, the pre-eminence of the Flemish tulips was beginning to fade, 'Louis XVI', even fifty years after its introduction, was still admired by florists and nurserymen alike. The English nurseryman John Slater remembered seeing a small stock of 'Louis XVI' breeders in Voorhelm's Dutch nursery, and in the garden of an amateur florist, who around 1838, had bought at auction a large part of the Voorhelm bulb collection. At that time it was considered the finest in Europe. Then, in 1842, Slater had seen a hundred blooms of 'Louis XVI', the greater part feathered ones, flowering in the unnamed amateur's garden.[18] Perhaps it was the huge success of 'Louis XVI' that persuaded florists of the time to grow more of these purple and white Bybloemens and less of the yellow and red Bizarres which until 1800 had been such favourites in Flanders. Florists ruled now, as the number of Flemish nurserymen dwindled; between 1830 and 1860, amateur florists in Flanders far outnumbered commercial growers such as Dehove at Tournai and Galliez at Lille.

At about the same time that Dr Hardy was thundering in the *Midland Florist* over the rules governing the perfect English florist's tulip, Monsieur Tripet was doing the same for the French florist's tulip.[19] Tripet was a florist and nurseryman in Paris and in 1843, had swept the board at the spring show of the Paris Horticultural Society, winning the gold medal offered for the first time by the Duchess of Orléans. His exhibit included 800 different kinds of tulip massed together in vases in an artificial bed a metre wide and seventeen metres long. That

Three tulips in a French painting of c1700. If the relative sizes are correct, then the centre flower and the one on the left are more likely to be species than cultivars

was only a fraction of the varieties growing in Tripet's nursery, where more than 40,000 tulips bloomed in season. The collection was reputed to be worth a cool 100,000 francs.

Tripet's Paris triumph did not impress the tulip growers of Lille or Tournai whose worst flowers, they said, were better than anything that Tripet had produced for the Paris Horticultural Society. But the members of the Société d'Horticulture du Nord de la France were always tough on growers outside their own charmed circle. They were pretty tough even on those inside it. The Society's annual report for 1837 criticised so many florists and their flowers that no one would agree to serve on the Society's committee until the reports were dropped. No florist ever seemed to agree with another's judgment, particularly on the show bench, and at this time, at least a hundred amateur tulip growers were keen members of the Society.

The Flemish tulips were noted for their exceptionally strong stems and chunky, squarish flowers. Though few later varieties commanded the huge prices paid for 'Louis XVI', the florist Dehove at Tournai still sold a hundred tulips in 1837 for 8,000 francs. Bulbs of superior varieties such as 'Duchesse de Berry' fetched 150 francs each. When Dehove died, his entire stock was sold at auction, the plum of the sale being a cache of 'Triomphe de Dumortier', which had broken from the brilliant red breeder 'Meteor'. Dehove's heirs were hoping for 2,000 francs for the forty bulbs, but they were disappointed.

'Breeders' (that is, bulbs with clear-coloured flowers that might later break into feathered and flamed varieties) of a dazzling clear red were a speciality of Flemish growers of the 1830s and 1840s: Dezangre at Louvain raised the beautifully shaped 'L'Astre Fulminant', Dumortier at Tournai had raised 'Meteor'. For brilliance and vigour, the flowers outstripped by far anything that Dutch breeders were producing at the time, but the Dutch were supremely good at growing, which made bulbs big business in Holland. By the nineteenth century, bulb fields had expanded to the areas round Overveen and Bloemendaal and by the middle of that century had spread as far as Hillegom, Lisse and Noordwijk. Travelling salesmen cast the bulb firms' nets even wider. In 1849 Hendrik van der Schoot became the first travelling salesman (*bollenreisiger*) to cover the increasingly lucrative marketplace of the United States. There had been tulips in the US since about 1640 when the first Dutch settlers planted the gardens of their New Amsterdam homes, but the desultory trade between the two countries which had grown up in the eighteenth century, was now more thoroughly exploited by the Dutch.

1. *Sans Pareille*

2. *Princes van Asturien*

Tulips 'Sans Pareil' and 'Princes van Asturien'
from Nederlandsch Bloemwerk *published in Amsterdam 1794,*
'a symbol and representation of the ascendancy of the Dutch
nurseryman at the end of the 18th century'

Until at least the middle of the nineteenth century, tulip growers in Flanders and England continued to develop their own flowers, oblivious of what was going on in The Netherlands, though in both countries, the pockets of growers were dwindling. Though English and Flemish growers had the edge on the Dutch as far as breeding was concerned, they were not such good salesmen. In Flanders, where the speciality was strong, long-stemmed seedlings of dazzling colours, a 300-year-long tradition of tulip-growing ended with the sale in 1885 of Jules Lenglart's tulips. Lenglart had inherited a fine collection built up by his father-in-law, M Tripier, but he was also a celebrated tulip breeder himself, specialising in fiery red breeders, many of them seedlings from 'Princesse Aldobrandini'.

The Lenglart auction was fixed for 15 May 1885, the sale being made up of 200 different breeders and 800 different varieties of broken tulips, 10,000 bulbs in all. But no bidders were interested and eventually the entire stock was sold to the famous firm of E H Krelage, which had traded from the Kleine Houtweg, Haarlem since 1811. The fabulous striped, feathered and flamed flowers that had intrigued growers for centuries were cast aside. From the plain-coloured breeders, previously only valued for their ability to break into other colours, Krelage selected the best flowers (no yellows) and launched them in 1886, re-christened as Darwins. Patiently marketed, publicised, exhibited by Krelage's company, they became a phenomenally successful race of tulips, brash flowers for a new, brash age. In England, the other independent centre of tulip-growing, the battle for dominance was longer drawn out.

CHAPTER VI

THE ENGLISH FLORISTS' TULIP

B Y THE MIDDLE of the eighteenth century, florists' societies, devoted to the culture of a particular group of flowers (it included the auricula and the pink as well as the tulip), had been established all over England. Early newspaper advertisements for florists' 'feasts' (*see* Chapter III) were replaced by news of shows, such as the tulip show held at the White Horse, Bury St Edmunds where 'lovers of these amiable bulbs' could win a silver punch ladle for the best bloom.[1] But since it was usually pubs, such as the White Horse, the Golden Cock Inn, Kirkgate, Leeds, the Shears Inn, Lee Bridge, Halifax or the Crown Inn, Nottingham, which offered convenient meeting rooms for the tulip shows, carousing continued just the same. The arrangement suited both parties: the florists got a venue at a minimal sum and the landlord sold vast quantities of ale. Some severe florists in Newcastle pointed out that *their* show was 'a Source of Delight and not of Extravagance and Luxury, which was the only Rock former societies of this sort split upon'.[2] Fortunately, in the larger manufacturing towns, rival shows were common and Newcastle florists with a thirst would find themselves well catered for by Mr James Beech at the Rising Sun. Some publicans, such as Mr Cock of the Botanical Tavern, Ashton-under-Lyne honoured the florists' societies in the names of their inns.

In the hundred years between 1750 and 1850, scarcely any town of importance in the north of England was without its tulip show. Members of the Ancient Society of York Florists, founded in 1768, brought hyacinths, polyanthus and auriculas to their spring display, which ended with a feast. Tulips were shown separately in May. The Botanic Society of Manchester held its first tulip meeting on 20 May 1777 and the Rev. William Hanbury (1725–1778), rector of Church Langton, Leicestershire, wrote that 'the florists are now become more numerous in England than has been known in any preceding age…many clubs have been founded and feasts established, when premiums are allowed the best and fairest. These feasts are now become general, and are regularly held at towns, at proper distance almost all over England. At these exhibitions, let not the Gardeners be dejected if a weaver runs away with the prize, as is often done'.[3]

Florists' societies flourished too in Ireland where the Dublin Florists' Society had been founded in 1746 by officers in the Huguenot regiments that had fought for William III (Prince William of Orange) at the Battle of the Boyne. Many of these Huguenot soldiers, such as the Marquis of Ruvigny, were given grants of land and, as Ruvigny did at Portarlington, brought over French builders to provide houses for Huguenot soldiers and their families.[4] Tulips were a speciality among Flemish and Huguenot growers. The bulbs were valuable, but at the same time, eminently portable and ripples of tulip-growing everywhere followed Huguenot refugees fleeing religious persecution in mainland Europe. Huguenots brought tulips to meetings of the Dublin Florists' Society to be judged by fellow members; if a tulip passed their stringent scrutiny, it was given a name and toasted with drinks all round.

In Scotland, Huguenots – weavers rather than soldiers – started florists' meetings in Edinburgh, where refugees from France and Flanders had established themselves in Picardie Row in the suburbs of the city. Their apprentices soon spread the florists' flowers farther afield to Dunfermline, Glasgow and Paisley, where a florists' society was established by 1782. Huguenot traditions of growing and showing flowers merged with an older Scottish tradition of Gardeners' Lodges, such as Adam's Lodge in Aberdeen and Solomon's Lodge in Banff. These lodges were in part friendly societies, to help members in times of need, but 'mutual instruction' was their real *raison d'être*. There were secret signs and passwords and all the paraphernalia of the kind that Gaergoedt had explained to Wearmondt in the Dutch *Samenspraecken* (*see* page 163). The lodges staged competitive shows of flowers and, once a year, a great feast. An Adam's Lodge was set up in London on 4 June 1781, but in the main, the lodges were a Scottish tradition. By this time anyway, the

London Floral Feasts were already well established, the brainwave of the Fulham nurseryman and auricula buff, Thomas Wrench (c1630–1728).

The growth of florists' societies, including those devoted to the tulip, was the result of a new self-confidence in a new kind of British grower. In the seventeenth and early eighteenth centuries, the tulip had been mostly a rich man's plaything, a toy expensively acquired from The Netherlands or Flanders to be shown off as proof of the owner's good taste (and healthy bank balance). But as new fashions took over in the grand gardens, the tulip became *démodé*. Some sensible landowners, such as James Justice of Crichton, Midlothian, never lost faith with the flower, but the fabulous English florists' tulips developed through the late eighteenth and the whole of the nineteenth century were in the main bred, developed and shown by artisans such as the gunsmith, John Findlay, who swept the board with his tulips at the Paisley Florists' Society in 1796 and the shoemaking Gill family of Wakefield in Yorkshire. George Crabbe noted the trend in *The Parish Register* (1807), where in a florist's garden:

> The reed-fence rises round some favourite spot
> Where rich carnations, pinks with purple eyes,
> Proud hyacinths, the least some florists prize,
> Tulips tall-stemm'd, and pounced auriculas rise.

Rescuing the tulip from aristocratic scrap heaps, these amateur growers infused it with characteristics that had nothing to do with either French or Dutch influence. By the end of the nineteenth century, they had brought the flower to the peak of perfection. Then, unaccountably, they dumped it, adopting instead the dahlia and the chrysanthemum as their favourite show flowers. Of the hundreds of tulip societies that once flourished around Manchester, Bolton and other commercial centres of Yorkshire, Lancashire, Cheshire and Derbyshire, only the Wakefield and North of England Tulip Society now survives.

Up until this time, such breeding as took place was centred in France and Flanders. Dutch nurserymen to a great extent controlled the supply of bulbs, which were sold expensively to rich landowners. The English florists were not rich, but they had time and patience on their side. The way forward had been suggested by Philip Miller of the Chelsea Physic Garden. 'There are some curious persons who have lately obtained many valuable breeders from seeds sown in England' he wrote, 'and doubtless were we as industrious to sow the seeds of these flowers as

The tulip 'Double Oriflamme' from
John Hill's Exotic Botany 'illustrated in thirty-five figures of
curious and elegant plants: explaining the Sexual System; and
tending to give some new lights into the Vegetable Philosophy:
Printed at the expence of the author, 1759'

the people of France and Flanders, we might in a few years have as great a variety as is to be found in any part of Europe'.[5] Miller does not name these 'curious persons' but it is likely that they were amateurs rather than professionals and he was right in concluding that the key to establishing a separate identity for the English florists' tulip lay in initiating an independent source of supply.

The process began in the south where professional nurserymen, such as James Maddock the Elder (1718–1786), built up a thriving business supplying flowers to London florists. These were a different breed to the northern ones. They were amateur growers, not gentlemen, but certainly more comfortably situated than the typical members of a northern florists' society. Their gardens lay in suburbs such as Woolwich, Sydenham, Clapham, Lambeth, Pentonville and Camberwell. Maddock, a Quaker from Warrington in Lancashire, had his business at Walworth, south London and was said to be 'well known to the curious in flowers through-out the kingdom'. A record of the flowers sold at the nursery, published by Richard Weston in 1777, shows that at that time nearly all Maddock's stock (including 800 different tulips) was 'selected from the most esteemed and curious Dutch Florists'. But the fifty-two page *Catalogue of Flowers, Plants, Trees etc sold by Maddock & Son, Florists, at Walworth* published fifteen years later indicates a gradual shift to English stock. Maddock listed more than 700 tulips; of the 664 late-flowering florists' tulips, 103 now had English names. The most expensive tulips cost ten pounds each but they were not as costly as the most expensive hyacinth, a double red variety called 'Compte de la Coste'. Early-flowering tulips (the kind originally introduced in the sixteenth century) had by now gone completely out of fashion and were little grown. Only the beautiful red and white striped 'Viceroy', 'Duc van Thol' and 'Kongings-Kroon' were still used as early flowers in mid eighteenth-century gardens.

John Pearson (*fl.* 1780s–1825), who set up a nursery business at Chilwell in Nottinghamshire in 1782, was the kind of 'curious person' that Philip Miller had in mind. Pearson had started his working life as a stocking maker, while his wife ran a small dame school. He grew his florists' flowers in a small garden in front of his shop and gradually built up a lucrative business in polyanthus and tulips. The key to his success lay in controlling supply; he never released any of his seedlings until he had built up a good stock of the best kinds, such as his rosy Bybloemen 'Lady Stanhope'. Then he would let out perhaps a hundred bulbs at a time, charging ten shillings each for them. Once the bulbs were distributed, the price he could charge of course fell. In 1821, he sold eight beds of his seedlings, in full bloom, for five pounds a bed, which was how Nottingham florists first got their hands on the

Tulip finials from a wrought-iron gate
English, eighteenth century
Victoria and Albert Museum, London

209

famous tulips 'Magnum Bonum' and 'Royal Sovereign'. A local grower, Thomas Hewitt, bought one of the beds wholesale and it was from Hewitt that John Frederick Wood, editor of the influential magazine the *Midland Florist*, in turn had his tulips. The blood lines of flowers were understood and followed by florists as closely as aristocrats might study the antecedents of their racehorses.

Much tulip-breeding was carried out by amateur growers who could not afford to buy bulbs at nursery prices, but they could recoup some of their costs through the nurserymen by selling spare bulbs on to them. Nurserymen specialising in florists' flowers though were hard hit by the shift in taste and gardening style in the mid eighteenth century and the consequent falling off of rich customers who would pay fancy prices for rare tulips. Perhaps this is why James Maddock the Younger (1763–1825), son of the founder of the Walworth nursery, supported so enthusiastically the publication of James Sowerby's *The Florist's Delight*. Various florists, said Sowerby, had 'expressed a wish to see some of their best Fancy Flowers delineated' and perhaps it was Maddocks who suggested the tulip shown life size in Plate V, the ten-guinea 'The Rodney' described as a Bybloemen, raised in The Netherlands. Plate VI was the five-guinea Bizarre tulip, 'Peregrinus Apostolicus'; Plate XI another Bizarre, though cheaper, 'Castrum Doloris'. The penultimate plate is of a tulip simply labelled 'black and white'. The text gives every indication of a flower being 'talked up' by a dealer desperate to make back money laid out abroad. 'As diamonds are valuable when of the first water, or unique specimens to the naturalist, so this extraordinary tulip, from the many properties discovered by florists, is to them of the first consequence, and when compared with the original of its species, is almost a phenomenon; though it is very probable it may be more so this year than last: the present price of the root is 100gns. We will give the name in some future number; the present proprietor does not wish to have it made public at present.' The tulip could only have been 'Louis XVI', expensively sold to James Maddock by the Dutch collector and dealer, Schneevogt. It appeared in Maddock's 1800 catalogue at the more reasonable price of twenty guineas.[6]

Sowerby's lack of success did not deter Robert Thornton from beggaring himself with his own *Temple of Flora*, published between 1798 and 1807. A group of six tulips, painted by Philip Reinagle, was Thornton's choice for the first of the prints made for the work and although the flowers were set against a Dutch background, a significant shift of emphasis had taken place. Set alongside foreign tulips such as 'Louis XVI', 'La Majestieuse' and the famous Bizarre 'Gloria Mundi' are two English seedling tulips, one raised by Thomas Davey (c1758–1833) nurseryman and well-

Tulips from Robert Thornton's
Temple of Flora, *published between 1798 and 1807*

known tulip fancier of the King's Road, Chelsea, London, the other by John Mason (*fl.* 1780s–1810s), seedsman and florist who had a business at the Orange Tree, 152 Fleet Street, London. Thornton named the seedlings 'after two very distinguished patrons of this work, Her Grace the DUCHESS OF DEVONSHIRE, no less eminent for her fine sense and expressive beauty, than EARL SPENCER, for his memorable conduct of our navy, which has eclipsed, under his administration, even the glory of our ancestors, which was *previously* imagined to exceed almost the bounds of human credibility'.

Despite his distinguished patrons, Thornton's work was a financial disaster. He had to write an 'Apology' to his potential subscribers, attributing his problems to the fact that 'The once *moderately rich* very justly now complain that they are exhausted through *taxes* laid on them to pay armed men to diffuse *rapine, fire* and *murder*, over *civilised* EUROPE'. War had broken out against France in 1793 and peace was not finally established until after the Battle of Waterloo in 1815. The Paddington Green florist Thomas Hogg (1771–1841) noted 'the fresh spirit that has been infused into the cultivators of [tulips] since our return to peace and to peaceful pursuits'. Florists had been sufficiently encouraged to raise a fresh set of 'breeders', sowing seed saved from their finest flowers. 'The most gratifying and complete success' said Hogg, 'has attended the labours of Mr Carter of Foxgrove, Wilts, of a Mr Austen, a Mr Strong, a Mr Lawrence and a Mr Goldham who have raised from seed and matured and broke into colour perhaps some of the finest Tulips in the country. Mr Clarke of Croydon, a scientific and experienced florist, has the best breeders in the country, raised from the seed of "Louis", "Charbonnier", Davey's "Trafalgar" etc. with finely formed cups and clear bottoms; they are in very high repute among florists.'[7] With this, the shift was complete; an independent English strain of the florists' tulip had been forged. No longer content to accept a Flemish or a Dutch breeder's idea of beauty in a tulip, English growers could now impose their own.

Bursting, with all the shockingness of the new, onto the Augsburg stage in 1557, the tulip had remained a rare and stylish flower until at least 1720. Then it became the province of specialists: a hobby flower. At first, southern growers were preeminent, especially around London, and included trade growers as well as true amateurs. But the fancy soon became well established in the north and the two groups enjoyed a happy state of warfare until about 1860, when tulip societies began to die out in the south. Southern growers thought the form of the flower of paramount importance and looked for purity in the base and filaments. Growers in the north were prepared to overlook an unshapely petal provided the flower was correctly marked with its feathers and flames. The Bybloemen (deep purple markings on a white ground), the Rose (red or pink markings on a white ground) and the Bizarre (red or brownish-black markings on a yellow ground) were the hallowed triumvirate of the English florists' tulips and only flowers that conformed to one of these three types could be shown in competition. Feathered flowers had petals finely etched with contrasting colour round the edges. Flamed flowers had a broad beam of the darker colour running up the centre of each petal. The feathering had to be light, the flame up the centre of the petal symmetrical and steady. Good flamed flowers were reckoned to be easier to find than good feathered ones. Contrarily, tulip fanciers did not like double tulips, though double flowers were much prized by lovers of other florists' flowers such as hyacinths. In the long, narrow beds where florists grew their tulips, bulbs were planted in the strict grid arrangements recommended by the French designer, Dezallier-d'Argenville nearly 150 years earlier, the flowers with the longest stems in the centre and the shortest outermost. The width of the bed rarely varied as it was designed to accommodate seven tulips, planted in the same repeating pattern of Rose, Bybloemen and Bizarre. The length depended on the size of the collection, but when the tulips were in flower, the patterned planting gave the illusion that the beds were lengths of the finest silk brocade, the deep mustard yellows of the Bizarres contrasting sumptuously with the rich purple tones of the Bybloemens. Tulip fanciers never deviated from this mode of planting.

Hogg had wondered whether to include the tulip among the other florists' flowers in his 1820 *Treatise* as he felt they were generally out of fashion. That had perhaps been the case between 1780 and 1820, when poor Sowerby was trying to drum up support for *The Florists' Delight*. But by 1820, the tulip was being avidly cultivated again by florists who seized on the new race of English seedlings, bred first by the nurseryman Thomas Davey, then by William Clark (c1763–1831) of Dulwich, who raised many tulips from seed, including the famous 'Lawrence's La Joie'. He was an amateur, and, wrote his obituarist, 'never received money for flowers; but when he gave a seedling bulb away, he generally arranged to have one bulb of every flower that broke'.[8]

The yellow and red Bizarre tulip 'Marcellus' was another of Clark's seedlings, illustrated in fine style in the *Florist's Magazine* of 1836. The fact that so many common tulips were yellow made the Bizarres at first less highly valued than the red and white Roses or the purple and white Bybloemens, but from the 1820s

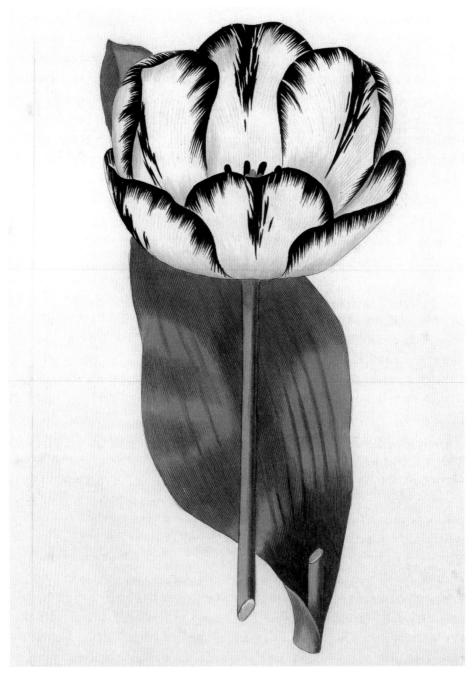

The Bybloemen tulip 'Daveyana' from the Florist's Guide *(1828)
'Broken' by M Dupree of Gothenburg and named after Thomas
Davey, nurseryman, of King's Rd, Chelsea. Mr Davey sold it for
£5 a bulb*

onwards, the Bizarres gained ground and became favourites, particularly among northern growers. 'Marcellus' was introduced *c*1826 but it did not increase easily and was always considered a 'delicate' flower. 'It has been sold at seven and eight guineas a root, which among florists is considered *moderate...*' said Frederick W Smith, correspondent of the *The Florist's Magazine*, in which 'Marcellus' was featured. Clark also raised the breeder from which 'Polyphemus', one of the most famous tulips of the early nineteenth century, was broken. It was the combination of very dark markings on the pale lemon ground that made it so highly valued. The Bybloemen 'Fanny Kemble' was another of his flowers, actors and actresses being then, as now, favourite sources of flower names. It was generally shown as a 'feathered' flower, the markings elegantly incised round the edges of the petals. Thomas Davey of the King's Road, Chelsea, London, gave William Clark £100 for his single bulb of 'Fanny Kemble'. Davey ranked high among florists, his spring exhibitions of auriculas, hyacinths, tulips and carnations always drawing huge and admiring crowds. At Davey's death, the 'Fanny Kemble' bulb with the two offsets it had produced passed to another fancier, John Goldham, who paid £72. 10s. for it. The tulip was a shy grower, slow at producing offsets, which was why it continued to command exorbitant prices.

When the English tulip breeders and florists began their work, there was already a broad understanding of the qualities of a perfect flower. Northern and southern growers enjoyed their skirmishes on points of detail, but there was general agreement that a fine tulip should rise to a height of at least three or four feet (approximately 1m. The height was a characteristic inherited from the sturdy Flemish Baguets). It should grow with perfect symmetry, the flower well supported on a firm and elastic stem. The cup of the flower should be perfectly adapted to the stalk, appearing neither too light nor too heavy for it. The flower itself should be regular, perfect in the margins of the petals, and of good texture. The colours had to be distinct, bright and glossy, the base of the flower bright and clear, and the petals of equal height, neither pointed, nor broken round the edges.

Agreed standards of excellence had to be set, once tulips began to be shown in competition. It was inevitable, too, that shows everywhere should offer the same six classes, allowing florists to exhibit feathered or flamed flowers in each of the three main groups – Roses, Bybloemens and Bizarres. What was surprising was the speed with which all this happened. When James Maddock of Walworth had first brought out his *Florist's Directory* in 1792, he was still using French terms such as Primo Baguets, Baguet Rigauts and Incomparable Verports to describe tulips. He

53

The Bizarre tulip 'Semplon' from the Florist's Guide *(1828)*
Drawn from a flower in the collection of W Strong, Esq

216

talks about the properties of 'fine *variegated* late tulips', rather than in terms of feathers or flames. He mentions Bybloemens and Bizarres, but not Roses, which were added later by Samuel Curtis in an 'improved' edition of 1810. Maddock, in the original edition, had been content to give credit to foreign tulip breeders.[9] Curtis had a different, more bullish slant on the matter. 'The perfection in which these flowers are now obtained is certainly owing to foreign cultivators; but so fond are the Dutch of their money, that they forego all English improvements, rather than become purchasers of our new varieties, many of which possess as much merit as any of theirs.'

This bullishness increased after Britain's victory over the French at the Battle of Waterloo. The growth of the florists' societies themselves was fuelled, too, by the cataclysmic changes which swept over Britain during the first quarter of the nineteenth century, when about half the world trade in manufactured goods was controlled by British ironmasters, owners of British cotton mills and other such entrepreneurs. Sir Robert Peel, father of the future Tory prime minister, alone employed 15,000 people in his calico mills. England's first railway, the Stockton and Darlington line, opened in 1825. Towns grew as the countryside emptied. Mill owners and other manufacturers were not slow to link the efficiency of their workers with the state of their health, so it was not entirely altruistic on their part to think of providing them with garden plots. These could be anything from a twelfth to a quarter of an acre in size, and were usually on outlying ground, separate from the typical tenements where the workers lived. Matthew Boulton (1728–1809), one of the inventors of the steam engine, created workers' gardens in Birmingham as early as 1761, buying a lease of ground around Handsworth Heath and turning it into dozens of small plots. Erasmus Darwin (a fellow member of Birmingham's famous Lunar Society) described Boulton's transformation of the barren heath as 'a monument to the effects of Trade on Population'. William Howitt described a typical plot at the Hunger Hill allotments in Nottingham, a florist's garden 'with his show of tulips, ranunculuses, hyacinths, carnations, or other choice flowers, that claim all his leisure moments, and are a source of a thousand cares and interests'.[10] It was in small plots such as these that the florists, always an urban phenomenon rather than a rural one, cultivated their flowers.

The florists' tulip shows followed a rigid pattern. First, a date had to be set that suited all the members of the local society. On 12 May 1803 Robert Carswell, D Smith and Thomas Robertson of Paisley were appointed surveyors 'to inspect the gardens of all those members which design to compete with Tulips…to determine the day appointed for the genus at competition but if they cannot with certainty give their decision upon next Thursday night they shall be allowed some more time to do it'. The surveyors must have come to a speedy decision because the following week, they fixed the show day for Friday 3 June, 'to make it agreeable to all parties both for late and early flowers'.[11] Seasons varied so wildly, dates for florists' competitions were never set far in advance.

Once the day was decided, shows were advertised in the local newspapers, the ground rules varying little from area to area. An Ipswich journal of 15 May 1776 sets the scene for a hundred similar events: 'The Tulip Shew will be at John Rycraft's in St Clement's Parish on Monday the 21st instant; when each Person who produces the two best Flowers (of his own Property three months) shall be intitled to two Pieces of Plate; and the third to five shillings: but no person will be admitted to shew any Flower there unless he is a Member of the Society. The Flowers to be at John Rycraft's by Twelve o'clock; Dinner at One; where the Company of Florists will be esteemed a Favour. Signed by Peter Burroughs, President and William Tayler and John Thorndike, Stewards.'

In Norwich, where the first florists' feasts had been held in 1631, the florists' tradition must have subsequently died out, perhaps when the original refugee Huguenots left East Anglia to set up their looms in Lancashire, but it blossomed again in the nineteenth century as part of a widespread cult of florists' flowers. The Society of Florists at Norwich was revived in 1828 'by the exertions of an artisan named Dover, who brought with him from the North and West of England, many choice roots. It consists of something over thirty members…men of very humble condition who devote their short minutes of leisure to such a pursuit'.[12] The 'artisan' was most probably George Dover (*fl.* 1820s–1850s), who had a nursery at Magdalen Street, Norwich. The society would have been good for business, as other nurserymen/florists like Thomas Davey had discovered. Davey had turned down an offer of £157. 10s. for his one bulb of 'La Joie de Davey'. The nurseryman Robert Holmes of 3 Mount Street, Westminster Road, Lambeth also raised and showed some fine seedling tulips, including 'Louis XVIII' which he later sold to John Goldham of Pentonville for £42. The prices that nurserymen charged for their best tulips outraged the Paddington Green florist, Thomas Hogg. 'A moderate collection of choice Tulips, of those beautiful, those exquisitely beautiful flowers, which are the pride and boast of every amateur who grows them, could not be purchased for a sum much less than one thousand pounds, at the usual catalogue prices, nor obtained and got together till after years of patient search and unwearied labour.

English Florists' tulips from William Pegg's sketchbook c1813

The high prices that have for many years been affixed to tulips in the printed catalogues of our Florists are so deterring and repulsive of the fancy, that persons with a taste and fondness for this flower are afraid to indulge and enter into it. Those prices are generally rated nearly one-half higher than they may be bought at ... This has a bad effect, and wears the appearance of imposition, and beyond doubt prevents a more extensive culture of them.'[13]

The *Account of Flower Shews held in Lancashire, Cheshire and Yorkshire etc*, published in Manchester every year during the 1820s, shows how quickly the fancy grew, gathering acolytes in all the major industrial centres of the north. Sixteen different tulip shows were listed in 1820, twenty-seven by 1826. In the potteries, workers translated their love of the flower onto the china they were painting. From the early nineteenth century onwards, tulips decorated many of the flower pots and stands, porcelain painted in enamel colours and gilt, made for instance by the Derby china factory.[14] Derby's star flower painter was William Pegg (1775–1851) whose father had been a gardener at Etwall Hall, near Derby, a hotbed of societies devoted to the English florists' tulip. By the age of ten, Pegg was already working in the potteries and after three years, became apprentice to a china painter, working fifteen hours a day in the factory. In 1796 he was offered a five-year contract at the Derby China Works, which was booming after taking over the illustrious Chelsea Pottery. But Pegg, who had heard John Wesley preach in Staffordshire in 1786, began to worry about the morality of decorating expensive porcelain with sinfully beautiful flowers for the tables of rich clients. In 1800 he became a Quaker and abandoned his paint box to start a new and spectacularly unsuccessful life as a stocking maker. Stockings may have satisfied the inner man but did little to sustain the outer one. Starving, Pegg was forced to return in 1813 to his former work at the Derby China Works, filling pages of a sketchbook with elegant florists' tulips which later found their way onto Derby's porcelain. After seven years, plagued once more by religious scruples, he left the Derby factory for good and died destitute in 1851.[15]

No such scruples haunted the publishers of periodicals; tulips starred in the magazines that, from the early nineteenth century onwards, catered to an increasingly discriminating audience. Samuel Curtis's magnificent *Botanical Magazine*, published from 1787 onwards, had a wider, more lofty purpose than to promote florists' flowers, but it featured its first plate of a florist's tulip in 1808, relatively early in its history. Florists' flowers though appeared exclusively in another Curtis publication, the *Beauties of Flora* which appeared from 1806–1820.[16] This never became as

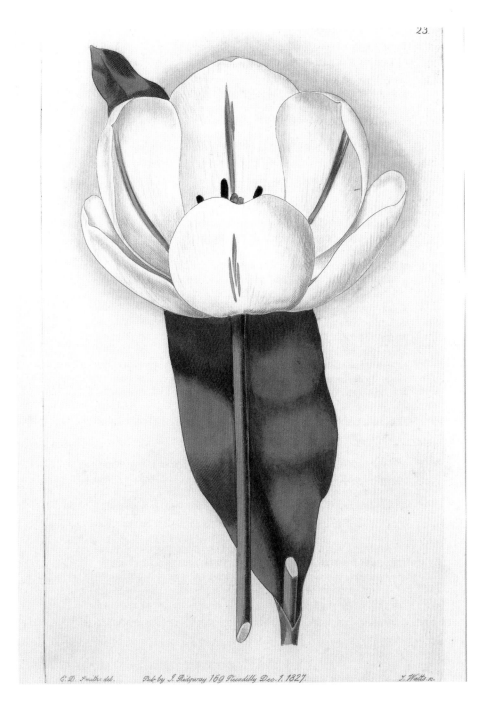

C.D. Smith. del.   Pub by J. Ridgway 169 Piccadilly Dec.1.1827.   J. Watts sc.

*The Bybloemen tulip 'Princess Charlotte's Cenotaph' from
the Florist's Guide (1828). Drawn from flowers in the collection of
Thomas Davey, nurseryman, of the King's Rd, Chelsea*

famous as Thornton's production, the *Temple of Flora*, although the plates were even bigger. Curtis's illustration of tulips was done by Thomas Baxter (1782–1821), one of the chief china painters at the Worcester and Swansea factories. Before the *Beauties of Flora* finished its run, Conrad Loddiges started to publish his *Botanical Cabinet* (1817–1833) which was followed six years later by the Chelsea nurseryman Robert Sweet's more parochial *British Flower Garden* (1823–1837). Gardeners were buried under a landslide of magazines: Benjamin Maund's *Botanic Garden*, launched in 1825, the *Gardeners' Magazine* (1826), founded and edited by the great polymath, John Claudius Loudon, another publication by Robert Sweet, the *Florist's Guide*, launched in 1827. During its five-year run, the *Guide* published more pictures of tulips than any other flower, sixty-one coloured plates with notes on the men who had raised them. It always *was* men. Women, prominent in the field of florists' pinks, seemed to have little to do with tulips. The Miss Dalton who, at the Lancaster Tulip Show on 22 May 1826, won first and second prizes with a black 'Baguet' and the popular feathered red and white tulip called 'Dolittle', was a rarity. Tulips even wandered into novels of the period; writing of Morgiana, one of his heroines, Thackeray said she was 'a tulip among women, and the tulip fanciers all came flocking round her'.[17]

For London florists, the competitive show was not the sole *raison-d'être* of the tulip year, as it was for growers in the north. Southern florists also paid ceremonial visits to celebrated tulip collections. Henry Groom (*fl.* 1820s–1850s), who had taken over after Curtis at the Maddocks' nursery at Walworth, hosted a number of such occasions, where 'connoisseurs assemble, compare, criticise, exchange and purchase, and afterwards dine together'.[18] Vast quantities of food and drink seemed an intrinsic part of tulip-growing. Groom had a tulip bed 130 feet long by 4 feet wide (45m x 1.2m), presenting, said a contemporary, 'a magnificent spectacle'. Mr Lawrence's tulip bed at Hampton, 'said to be one of the most select in the neighbourhood of London', was another regular place of pilgrimage. Lawrence had been the florist responsible for 'breaking' the elegant Bybloemen 'Lawrence's La Joie', a pure white variety, neatly edged with dark velvety purple. Mr Burnard, the *Gardening Magazine*'s correspondent, said he had found at Mr Lawrence's 'a number of connoisseurs, amateurs and men of leisure, among the last, the Duke of Clarence' inspecting and admiring the tulips, which included the yellow and black 'Polyphemus', the rarest and most valuable tulip in the bed.

The Groom and Lawrence tulip beds were perhaps the most famous of the time, but there were plenty of others round London in the 1820s: Mr Strong's at Brook Green, Mr Weltje's at Hammersmith, Mr Austin's at Upper Clapton, Mr Cheese's on Millbank. Islington was a hotbed of tulip fanciers. There was John Goldham who had bought the bulb of 'Louis XVIII' so expensively, Samuel Brookes who in 1819 had gone into partnership with Thomas Barr at the Northampton Nursery, Ball's Pond, Islington and Mr Franklin, a seedsman and florist of Cottage Place, City Road, Holloway. Rotherhithe, Bethnal Green and Lower Tooting also had their eminent tulip growers, and at Camberwell, Mr Bowler created a sensation with his red and yellow Bizarre tulip 'Everard'. Windsor had a clutch of tulip growers; so did Slough, where Charles Brown, nurseryman, was an *aficionado*. This was another marked difference between south and north. In the 1820s, many of the southern florists were also professional nurserymen, a fact which did nothing to endear them to the amateurs of the north.

The London florists had shows as well, the principal ones being held at Islington, Dulwich, Hammersmith and Chelsea. Thomas Hogg explained the rules of the Islington and Chelsea societies, where the subscription was one and a half guineas a year. Tulips were judged during the 'ordinary', generally served at 1pm, the flowers passed hand to hand between members seated at the dining table. After the meal and the judging, the flowers would go on general view. Hogg said there were other societies too, but the two he spoke of were 'not only the most numerous in point of numbers, but likewise the most respectable in regard to the members composing them'.[19] Some societies evidently still had a problem with their image.

From 1830 to 1850 the tulip fancy was at its zenith in Britain, prompting George Glenny to establish in 1832 the Metropolitan Society of Florists and Amateurs. The splenetic Glenny (1793–1874) trained in his youth as a watchmaker, but later became editor of the *Gardener's Gazette* and proprietor of the Dungannon Nursery, Fulham. As an editor Glenny was considered 'exacting and quarrelsome' but he had a great influence on the way the tulip developed in the early 1840s because of his set of 'properties', or rules, to which a good tulip should conform. Clearly understood standards made florists' flowers easier to judge in competition, so Glenny's 'properties' were eagerly seized on by florists of the time. It was a source of endless irritation to him that he was not always credited as the instigator of this great leap forward. Other florists, he wrote, carefully concealed the fact 'that their practice was built upon my foundation'.[20] This 'sense of neglect and injury had made him altogether uncontrollable' in the opinion of the *Gardener and Practical Florist*

48.

E. D. Smith del.   Pub. by J. Ridgway 169 Piccadilly June 1 1828   S. Watts sc.

The Bybloemen tulip 'Goldham's Maria' from the Florist's Guide
*(1828). Drawing taken from a flower in the collection of John
Goldham of White Cottage, White Conduitfields, London, who raised
it from seed*

224

magazine, but others praised him as an original and powerful force among florists, a man with a keen eye for a good flower. Glenny paid the huge sum of £140 for the entire stock (seven bulbs) of the 'Everard' tulip raised by Bowler of Camberwell.

But as the tulip bulb began to seem, once again, a valuable commodity, the problems that had afflicted Dutch growers in the early seventeenth century began to trouble British florists. In 1831 the *Hull Advertiser* reported a savage attack on 'Mr Marmaduke Carnaby's fine and valuable collection of auriculas and tulips' which took place in the Beverley Hills neighbourhood of Hull. John Slater of Albion Place, Lower Broughton, near Manchester complained that 'at a meeting where were exhibited some of the choicest blooms from the first beds in Lancashire, I won three firsts and two thirds; and a "Roi de Siam", which was unquestionably the finest flower I staged, was stolen, during dinner, before it was judged'.[21]

By the time Slater published his *Descriptive Catalogue of Tulips* in 1843, northern growers were beginning to eclipse those in the south. It was still possible in London, reported the *Gardeners' Chronicle* 'to see small beds of tulips in the back gardens of the houses abutting on the Walworth and Camberwell Roads with their protective canvas covering in May', but not as many as you could now see in Wakefield or Altrincham, Derby or Halifax. It rankled with northern growers that the southerners priced good new tulips so high. Slater, a Manchester man, noted that the catalogues of London growers contained bulbs at what they called moderate prices of £50 or £100 a bulb but grumbled at giving £3 to a country florist for a broken flower. The highest price known to have been offered in the north had been for 'Lady Crewe', a feathered pink and white tulip raised by Sherwood of Derby in the 1820s and that was only £5. London growers, said Slater, would do well 'to treat their country brethren with a little more liberality; if so, I do not doubt but Lancashire would soon excel London and its neighbourhood in Tulips, as it does in other florists' flowers'.[22]

But while George Glenny could still wield a pen, the southerners were not going to cede victory. Uncompromisingly, Glenny continued to trumpet the southern-raised tulip 'Polyphemus' as the best Bizarre in the land. Are the London, or the Lancaster florists the best judges of tulips asked a contributor to the *Floricultural Magazine* on 14 October 1841? He took the precaution of using a pseudonym – Jock Florum of Tulip Lodge, but Glenny had no such scruples. As far as he was concerned, northern growers were barbarians. How could they be anything else, when they set feather and flame before form? Glenny published his essay on the

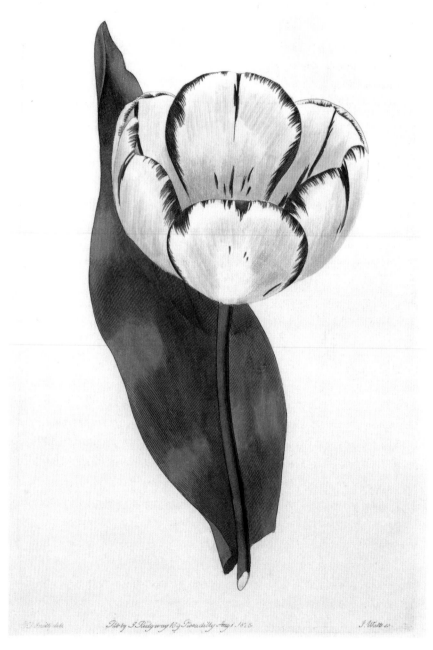

The rose tulip 'Juno' from the Florist's Guide *(1828)*
Drawn from a flower in the 'choice collection' of Mr Burnard of
Formosa Cottage, Holloway, north London

Properties of the Tulip in *The Gardener and Practical Florist* of 1843. Rule number one (of twelve) stated that the cup of a tulip 'should form when quite expanded from half to a third of a hollow ball'. Though he did not know it, Glenny had just fired the first shot in the Great Tulip War of the 1840s, the hostilities between north and south being brought to an uneasy truce with the formation of the National Tulip Society in 1849.

Glenny considered himself more than a match for Henry Groom, nurseryman and florist of Walworth (for whom perfection lay in the 'semi-oblate spheroid'), and of John Slater, author of *A Descriptive Catalogue of Tulips* (who championed 'one half and the sixteenth part' of a sphere. It mattered). But he had not reckoned with Dr W G Hardy (1801–1875). Hardy, born in Salford and schooled in Chesterfield and Stockport, had then been articled to a surgeon in Manchester. Obstetrics was his profession; the flute, the double bass and above all, the tulip, his passion. The dull slaty purple-coloured 'Talisman' was one of his tulips. When it 'broke', it produced a beautiful Bybloemen, the white ground elegantly marked with purplish-black. In 1847 Hardy published a seminal essay 'On Perfection of Form in the Tulip' in a new magazine, the *Midland Florist*, which was aimed particularly at growers in the Midlands and the north of the country. With a deadly pen, Hardy set out to demolish the arguments put forward by those who did not agree with him that the best, the only, form for a true florist's tulip was the half sphere.

Hardy took the semi-oblate spheroid form that Henry Groom had championed in the *Florist's Journal* of 1840 to mean a tulip that measured one-fifteenth part less than the simple half sphere. The unfortunate Groom had also dictated that 'the pole should be a little depressed' and that there should be 'a little swell outwards towards the lower part of the petal, which will give the flower a good shoulder'. Mercilessly, Hardy annihilated the thesis, invoking the image of a rainbow. If a rainbow had a dip in the middle and a bulge either side, would we regard this as an improvement, he asks? 'Such is the deformity Mr Groom would have us to regard as perfection in a tulip'.

Mr Slater, with his one half and the sixteenth part fared no better. The larger the petals, the greater the propensity for them to fold inwards, obscuring the centre, Hardy pointed out. If they reflexed outwards, this would be equally abhorrent to a lover of pure form in the tulip. But, he added magnaminously (Slater, after all, was a Manchester man), the quantity added by Mr Slater would be small enough not to matter had he not added other conditions with which no florist

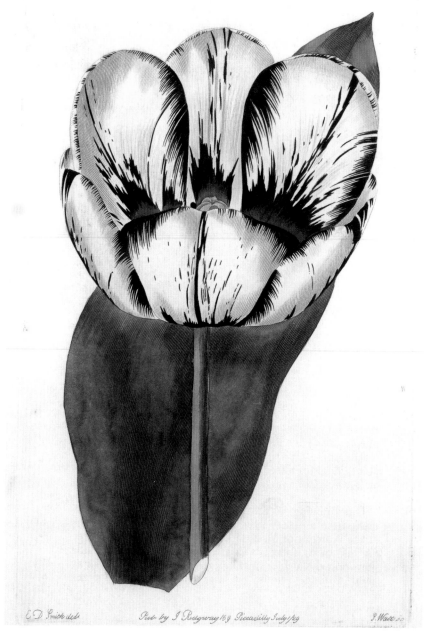

E.D. Smith del.   Pub. by J. Ridgway 169 Piccadilly July 1/29   G. Watt sc.

The Bybloemen tulip 'Lampson' from the Florist's Guide (1829)
Drawing made from a flower 'in the splendid collection of Tulips
at the Nursery of Messrs Brown at Slough, who succeed in growing
them stronger, and flowering them finer than any other Tulip grower'

could possibly comply. 'The cup of the flower', Slater had written, 'should be composed of six thick fleshy petals, which should run out from the centre at first a little horizontally, and then turn upwards, forming almost a perfect cup with a round bottom, rather wider at the top.' How could a cup be *round* in the bottom, and at the same time *horizontal* thundered Hardy, banishing Slater's theories, like Groom's, to outer darkness.

Glenny came off worst. He favoured one third of a hollow ball as the ideal shape to aim for, because 'all fanciers know that the beauty of a tulip depends on the entire inside surface... They know too that unless the entire inside surface can be seen at once, it must be seen under a disadvantage.' It was obvious to Glenny that the florist's tulip must be able to open up enough to show off its beauties, and that if the cup was larger than a third of a sphere, it would not be able to do this effectively. No, proclaimed Hardy. Mr Glenny's objection to the half-circle on account of its being too deep to reveal the internal complexities of the flower was 'altogether groundless'. Many of the best florists' tulips had markings of such complexity, the size of their petals was an important consideration. The half sphere produced a larger canvas for the painting of the feathers and flames. Hardy estimated that a tulip three and a half inches in diameter would, if conformed on the half-sphere principle, have petals nearly half an inch longer than one shaped as a one-third sphere. The advantages of the half sphere were so overwhelming, Hardy continued, that he had 'no hesitation in adopting it as the standard by which the form of every tulip ought to be tested'. Mr Gradgrind, Charles Dickens's Lancastrian manufacturer, would have approved. Bitser, Gradgrind's star pupil in *Hard Times,* could scarcely have done a better job in reducing the tulip, the sublime, reckless, irrepressible, wayward, unpredictable, strange, subtle, generous, elegant English Florists' tulip to a geometrical equation.

Unfortunately, tulips that fitted Hardy's tightly drawn specification were rarely to be found. Even such favourites as the feathered Bizarre 'Charles X', the fabulous feathered Bybloemen 'Bienfait', the old feathered Rose favourite 'Heroine' and Lawrence's flamed Rose 'Aglaia', if measured against his ideal, would be found to be too long in the cup. But, undeterred, Hardy returned to the attack in the next issue of the *Midland Florist*, when he considered the correct form for the rim or the margin of the flower and the most appropriate shape for the petals. Mr Groom and Mr Slater once more came in for criticism because when they talked of petals being 'well-rounded' they did not define what they meant by round. Should this roundness be half or any other designated portion of a circle? Mr Hardy thought he should be told. Mr Glenny is derided for preferring flat-topped tulips, which nature, as Hardy was at pains to point out, does not generally provide. Glenny, perched precariously on his high horse, retreated from the battlefield, saying he 'did not intend honouring the gentleman by any further notice'. Hardy also took violently against an illustration that had accompanied an article by his own editor, John Frederick Wood. The petals of Wood's tulip, he said, looked as though they had been chopped off with scissors. Florists, complained Hardy, subjected 'the operations of nature to laws as crude as their own imaginations, and regardless of the truthful lessons which she herself plainly teaches, vainly require the production of forms she was never designed to create'.

In the tulip, Hardy saw a 'manifest tendency to the production of graceful curves' and urged readers of the *Midland Florist* to examine a petal of the flower under a microscope or a powerful magnifying glass. By way of an elegiac appraisal of its underlying structure, he argued that in the tulip, function and form were indissolubly united. The curved margin was an intrinsic part of its make-up. Ever in search of finite parameters, Hardy concluded that the perfect curve was one that was equal in radius to half the diameter of the flower and added a magnificently complicated method by which judges could measure it.

At the end of his exhaustive treatise, Hardy proposed four rules which taken together would constitute perfection of form in the florists' tulip:

1. Every tulip, when in its greatest perfection, should be circular in its outline throughout; its depth being equal to half its width across from the top, or highest point, of one petal to the tip of the other immediately opposite.

2. It should be composed of six petals, three inner and three outer, which should all be of the same height, and have such a form as will enable them to preserve this circular outline; their edges being even, stiff and smooth; and their surfaces free from shoulder or inequality of every kind.

3. The breadth of the petals should be amply sufficient to prevent any interstices being seen between them, so long as the flower retains its freshness.

102

'Emperor of Austria' from the Florist's Guide *(1829)*
Sold in Thomas Davey's catalogue for £2 a bulb

4. There should be exact uniformity between the outline of the cup, and the outline of the upper margin of the petal, which should form an arc or curve, whose radius is equal to half the diameter, or whole depth of the flower.

Hardy was confident that his rules would stand the test of time and generally the 'Hardy protocol' was well received. Even up in Falkirk, where florists were a law unto themselves, the eminent tulip grower George Lightbody (1795–1872) took note. Lightbody had spent his early years in the navy, serving at the defence of Cadiz and in the war against the US. The medal he always wore commemorated his capture of a French vessel in the Mediterranean. The Hardy protocol, as he could see, was much needed. At a time of frenetic activity among breeders, when thousands of new seedling tulips were being released onto the market each season, some attempt to regularise the aims and objectives of the florist's ideal bloom had to be made. The form of a tulip was a more attainable objective for breeders than its markings. The volatile virus that provided the 'breaks' in a tulip and its consequent feathering and flaming, was not easily manipulated. Florists hoped too that the fixing of certain criteria would offset the irritating partiality shown by judges at tulip shows, both in the north and the south. The *Midland Florist* with a foot, geographically at least, in both camps, was perhaps the only possible arbiter between the northern growers, with their delight in markings, and the southern growers, with their insistence on form and purity.

Inevitably though, there was still friction between amateur growers of tulips and professional dealers, who used the burgeoning number of shows to unveil (and sell) their new seedlings. 'I think it would give far greater satisfaction, and even be more to their own interest' wrote a disgruntled amateur grower 'if the dealers, on such occasions, would come forward handsomely with their contributions, but leave the prizes to be contended for by amateurs only'.[23] He suggested the dealers should put up what we would now think of as a trade exhibit, 'ticketed with the name of the subscriber and his residence'. Amateur growers could then follow up with a visit to the dealer's plot and select bulbs for their own collections. Under the present system, continued the amateur, he felt disinclined to compete. But the line between the two was sometimes difficult to draw. James Haigh of Ashton-under-Lyne, killed in one of the cholera epidemics that raged

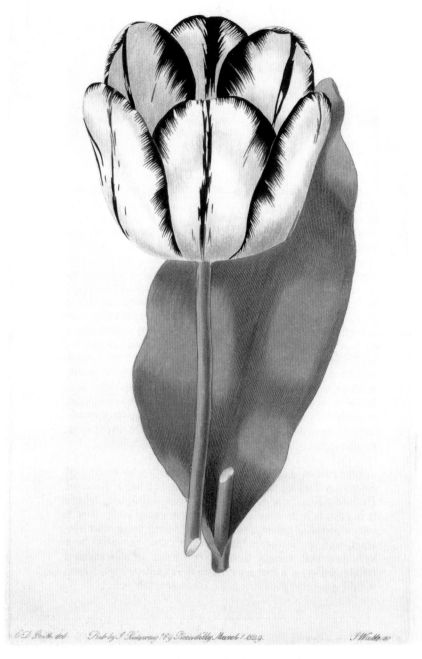

C.D.Smith del   Pub. by I. Ridgway 169 Piccadilly March 1 1829.   S.Watts sc.

The Rose tulip 'Daphne' from the Florist's Guide *(1829)*
Drawn from a flower in the 'choice collection' of Richard
Percival, Esq, of Highbury Park, Islington, north London

through Britain in the 1830s and 1840s, would generally have been regarded as an amateur florist. When he died in 1846, his valuable collection of tulips was put up for auction. That was standard practice. The proceeds of such sales provided necessary funds for the dead florist's family. But Haigh was also joint proprietor of the Buckler's Collection of seedling tulips, bought in partnership with his friend James Walker of Harper House, Ashton. The amateur begins to look more like a dealer.

Though the image of the noble artisan has dominated the iconography of the florists, the artisans needed richer, perhaps less skilled, less patient florists around them to buy their new seedling tulips. Florists such as Howitt described on the Hunger Hills allotments in Nottingham, depended for part of their income on collectors such as John Shelmerdine of Altrincham, who 'spared no expense' in building up his collection of tulips. The jewels of his tulip beds were seedlings raised from the old feathered black and white tulip 'Louis XVI'. Shelmerdine, typical of a type that might be classed as 'aldermen florists', died in the same cholera epidemic as James Haigh and a contemporary noted sadly that 'his place in the Altrincham Floral Society will perhaps never be supplied'. The Pickwickian turn of phrase is echoed in the poem written after the union of the Felton Florists' Society with the Floral and Horticultural. It was sung at the second exhibition of the Felton Union of Florists and Horticulturists on 23 June 1845 to the tune of the hymn 'Of a' the airs the wind can blow'.

> Hail, happy spring of forty-five!
> A union thou hast brought,
> Cementing interests all in one –
> Just what we all have sought:
> We'll show our beauties as before,
> While all will now declare
> That it is best for all to blend
> The useful with the rare.

After the introductory verse, the poem goes on to extol the virtues of parsnips, leeks and, finally, of tulips, which had been on show that day at the newly combined Felton Union show:

And while the tulip we extol,
We'll give the reason why;
'Tis not because their gaudy hues
Attract the vulgar eye, –
No! 'Tis because their varied charms,
As thus they brightly shine,
Remind us of the Almighty hand –
Omnipotence divine!

Pickwickian too is the report of the Open Tulip Show at Derby in 1847, when 'upwards of fifty gentlemen dined together at the Nag's Head. After the cloth had been removed and the usual loyal toasts responded to, Mr Sadler, who was in the chair, rose and in an able speech, which was repeatedly cheered in its delivery, dwelt upon the desirability of a Midland Horticultural Society.'

Competitive showing reached fever pitch in the late 1840s and early 1850s. At the King's Head, Barton, Lancashire, the feathered Bizarre 'Royal Sovereign', one of the key tulips of the age, triumphed at the show held on 24 May 1847. In Falkirk, a silver jug was the prize offered for the best pan of tulips, with one guinea going to the second-best. Richard Headley of Stapleford House, near Cambridge, swept the board at the rather smart tulip show held by the Cambridge Florists' Society in the concert room of the Lion Hotel on 18 May 1848. At Peter Eaton's tulip meeting, held at Bedford, near Leigh, Lancashire, the following day, the 'factory prize' (a kettle) was won by Thomas Belshaw with 'Rose Unique'. When purity came into fashion, northern growers found it very hard to abandon this old pink and white variety with its beautifully refined markings – but dirty bottom. It was perhaps inevitable that florists' feuds should erupt with such magnificent regularity. There were so many shows – at the Queen's Head Inn, Burslem, at the Woodman Inn, Gower Street, Leeds, at the Green Man Inn, Vindercliff near Bradford – to fuel their dissatisfaction. Only the bravest men took on the thankless task of judging. Mr Alexander of Lamb Farm, Kingsland in Islington, north London was generally reckoned to be 'an honest man' – no small compliment for a florist, but he was a southerner, so automatically suspect in the north, where the majority of the shows took place. John Frederick Wood, editor of the *Midland Florist*, was much in demand as a judge, as was John Slater (*c*1799–1883) of Cheetham Hill, Manchester. But Slater was also a breeder of tulips; his was the heavily feathered Rose tulip 'Julia Farnese' and the Bizarre seedling 'Adonis', raised

150.

A. Smith del.   *Pub. by J. Ridgway & Co. Piccadilly Augt. 1830*   *J. Watts sc.*

The Bybloemen tulip 'Louis XVI' from the Florist's Guide *(1830)*
A very variable tulip, shown here with light and heavy markings.
The former was more valuable. John Goldham, of White Cottage,
White Conduitfields, London, refused £100 for his one bulb of
this variety

236

from the famous 'Polyphemus'. Could his impartiality be relied on? Disinterested and competent judges were vital, if the fancy was to mature, but, as a disenchanted competitor wrote, finding them 'appears to be as great a difficulty as societies have to contend with'. There was uproar at the Wakefield Show of 1847 when one of the judges flung out a pan of tulips just because he had never heard of its name.

Competition (and the prizes it offered) inevitably encouraged skulduggery. It was impossible, wrote one competitor, who signed himself only as FAIRPLAY of Kirkstall, near Leeds, 'to make all *growers honest showers*...even a midnight prowl is not scrupled at, if an addition can be made to their own collection, at the expense of a poor man and a neighbour. I fear there are few, if any, societies whose lists are clear of these gentry. Of a similar class are those who, when unsuccessful, seek to vilify their more fortunate competitors.' Once again the open tulip show at Wakefield was the cause for complaint. An exhibitor from Leeds had taken the premier prize and a member of the home team got up a rumour that one of the prize-winning blooms had not been grown by the florist in question. Forty furious Leeds florists testified that the rumour was a calumny, but such occurrences became more and more common.

The idealists who set up the National Tulip Society in 1849 must have hoped that the National tag would paper over differences between north and south, as well as add dignity to their favourite flower. The northern growers were not to be so easily bought. The Great All England Tulip Show for 1851 was held at Derby, and Ephraim Dodwell, cigar merchant and tulip fancier, urged that organising committees be set up 'in every city and town, village and floral district, throughout the kingdom'. But this Olympian vision was unrealised and the All England turned out to be yet another local derby. E Y Ours (surely a pseudonym) could not hide his resentment. The show, he wrote 'went off much to the satisfaction of the great northern growers, and was especially pleasing to a class of dealers who cannot throw away foul tulips. Having secured three patrons of smudge-bottomed varieties for judges, and Mr Henry Goldham, from London, as a fourth, to give countenance to their proceedings, they did as they pleased. They would not disqualify foul-bottomed sorts, and the tulips which had prizes were a disgrace to the fancy. Mr Henry Goldham could not have carried his point against the lovers of foul flowers, but he could have retired, and upheld the dignity and taste of the South, which rejects as unworthy of notice, all varieties with dirty bases. He could have said "Gentlemen – As I am no use against three of you, and never will sanction a prize to a foul flower, I beg to retire, and leave you to the indulgence of a taste

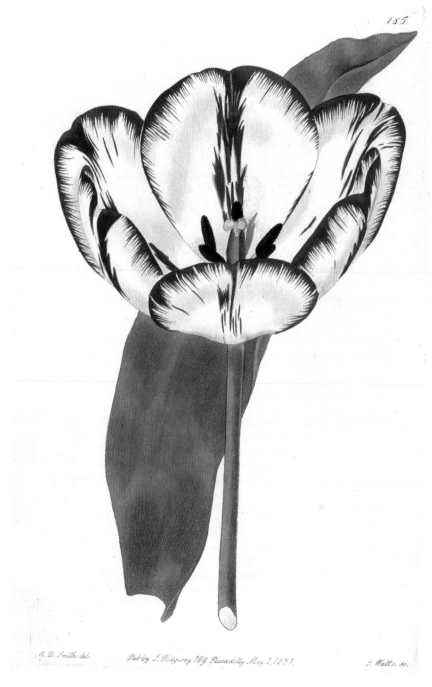

G. D. Smith, del.   *Pub. by J. Ridgway 169 Piccadilly May 1 1831.*   *J. Watts, sc.*

'Rose Bacchus' taken from tulips in the 'choice collection'
belonging to Mr Pile, Cambridge Rd, Mile End, London,
published in the Florists' Guide *1831*

which I hope will always be confined to the North." Mr Turner of Slough, the best professional, and Mr Edwards of Holloway, a spirited amateur, had to sit down quietly under the disgrace of being beaten with tulips that the poorest grower in the metropolis would not disgrace his stand with'.[24]

Despite the skirmishes, the belligerence, the slandering of judges and growers alike, expertise in the actual growing of the tulip was at a peak. This reflected a general trend in horticulture, which during the second half of the nineteenth century became a serious science, seriously assimilated. Growing techniques, in all fields, were endlessly refined. During the growing season, a man would have to spend every waking hour on his tulip bed, if he was to follow all the advice handed out by pundits in the *Floricultural Cabinet*, the *Gardeners' Chronicle*, the *Florist*, the *Cottage Gardener*, *Gossip for the Garden* and other such magazines which now appeared faster than buds in May. First, bulbs had to be planted in beds the regulation four feet wide. The earth may need liming. The beds may need earthing up to provide better drainage. Newcomers to the fancy may even have to make a bed, a complex sandwich of rubble, muck and carefully sifted compost, prepared as carefully as a bed for an emperor's state visit.

In spring there was the problem of water settling in the angle between leaf and stem and possibly injuring the embryo bloom. No better way to deal with it than crawl round the bed on all fours and blow the water out, advised one grower. Nets had to be set up on hoops over the emerging tulips, to protect them from hail, heavier covers to guard against frost. Jute canvas was thought to do the best job. John Cunningham, a Scottish grower, kept the winter rain off his beds with tents of yellow oilskin. Each tulip, as it grew, had to be carefully supported with a stake in case wind should snap the stem. Sometimes, lines of twine (painted green) were stretched from one end of the bed to the other, about two feet (0.6m) off the ground and the stems of the tulips tied to these with strips of green worsted.

Canker, every florist's nightmare, might strike the bed and the tell-tale withered foliage had to be removed before the disease reached the precious bulb itself. Awnings were rigged up to shade the tulip beds, because growers knew that the separate colours of broken tulips tended to 'run' in bright sunlight. Calico, lighter than jute, made the best summer covers, though growers in the Midlands often used Nottingham lace. Florists' plots with their mats, canvas, nets and attendant supports, said one observer, were more like the back yards of warehouses than gardens. Tulips of less than perfect shape were fitted with corsets; bands of the soft, fleecy thread known to the cotton spinners as 'rovings', were tied round the unopened cup and left in place until the last minute before judging on the show bench. Curls of wood shaving were used in the opposite way to keep the incurving cup of a flower open. Sometimes this was to coax the shape of a tulip closer to the Hardy standard, sometimes to allow the sun to bleach the base of a tulip from an unclean cream to the approved level of purity.

Slices of raw potato and turnip were laid over the tulip beds to lure the small black underground slugs, known as leatherbacks, away from the tulip bulbs. One grower reported he had enjoyed the 'melancholy satisfaction' of catching thousands of slugs in this way. When the tulips had died down, growers had to attend to the rigmarole of lifting them, in strict order, so that none of the named varieties got mixed up. The bulbs had to be dried off and then stored somewhere, not too hot, not too cold, not too dry, not too damp, until planting time came round again. Mice would have their own, destructive agenda.

Instructions for viewing the flowers were as particular as those for growing them. James Maddock, the founder of the Walworth nursery in London and author of the influential *Florist's Directory*, suggested that the paths by tulip beds ought to be lowered by several inches to bring the flowers nearer to the eye. For safety, a wooden frame two feet high should be built up round the bed 'to prevent the garments of spectators from rubbing against, or breaking off the flowers'. The flowers at least had the advantage of lasting longer than other florists' flowers; tulip lovers could expect a display for more than three weeks in season. Maddock also described a curious contraption, rather like a mole trap, which could be sunk into the bed to draw out any tulip which had failed to bloom, or which for any other reason was spoiling the display. The same cylindrical tool (illustrated in his *Directory*) could be used to slide a new bulb in full flower into the gap. Florists had another trick for keeping their beds of tulips in full, unblemished perfection. They cut flowers from spare bulbs, grown in a separate back-up area, put them in small pots or phials of water and then sank the pots underground, so that the flowers appeared to be growing out of the earth. The Turks had done exactly the same thing, 150 years earlier.

Instructions for cross-breeding tulips to obtain new strains, were so complex they needed whole books to themselves. It had taken some time for early tulip growers to realise that the best broken tulips did not come from seed of the best broken tulips. They had to breed from the best plain-coloured tulips, and then wait for the resulting seedlings to break into the longed-for feathers and flames. June

The Bizarre tulip 'Strong's King' drawn from a flower
in the collection of W. Strong, of Albion Cottage,
Brook Green, London, possibly broken from the breeder
tulip 'Hector'. From the Florist's Guide (1828)

241

was the key month for tulip breeders, who, armed with their camel-hair brushes, carefully transferred the pollen from the stamens of one flower to the stigma of the other. John Slater, the Manchester florist, recommended that growers should then cover the whole with a cap made of Nottingham net. With or without the cap, the seed pod had to be covered with a glass to keep it dry.

If this part of the operation was successful and the breeder got his seedpod safely through to fruition, he then had to negotiate the laborious seven years that it took for the seeds to grow into flowering-size bulbs. The length of time compared badly with the speed at which other florists' flowers could be bred, but, as one tulip lover observed philosophically, 'although life is at best uncertain, it is nevertheless quite certain that raising seedlings will do nothing to shorten it'. The best dates for sowing tulip seed were earnestly discussed. The preference for autumn sowing gradually dissipated in the face of evidence that an early-spring sowing gave better results. At all stages of growing, drainage was the key to success. Oystershell – oysters were then food for the poor rather than the rich – was often used to line the bottom of the seed tray. Old raisin boxes were converted into the trays themselves. Canvas sails became awnings.

The instructions handed out to tulip growers show the tremendous care, the attention to detail and the observant eye of the typical florist. Patience was important too. After the seven years of breeding, growers might wait ten or twenty years for a tulip to break and still have nothing to show for their labours. Although it was so central to the success or failure of the florists' efforts, it was still a mystery to them that some tulips 'broke' while others did not. As late as 1848, the *Midland Florist,* in response to an anguished reader's letter, was still quoting the plaster/dung hill recipe recommended more than a hundred years earlier by John Cowell in *The Curious and Profitable Gardener*. Cowell had also included water from jakes. In the acutely sensitive ambience of the mid nineteenth century, the *Midland Florist* thought it best to miss that bit out. Switching bulbs from place to place often brought about the desired effect. Other growers advised baking the dried-off bulbs under the hot sun in the summer. This was a thoughtful piece of reasoning, given the tulip's natural habitat, but it was not the right one. Some thought that a poor, dry soil gave the best results. Others advocated lashings of muck. But whereas early eighteenth-century growers had invoked alchemy and spells to get their tulips to break, nineteenth-century tulip fanciers sought more rational explanations. Ironically, the answer came only when the tulip fancy itself was almost extinct.

The 1855 auction of all the tulips, some 30,000 bulbs, by Groom's nursery, which had moved from Walworth to nearby Clapham Rise in the suburbs of London, marked the virtual extinction of trade growers in the south, following a falling-off of interest among amateurs. Only the previous year, Groom had still been advertising his new show tulips at ridiculous prices: 100 guineas for the tall feathered Rose tulip 'Duchess of Cambridge', 100 guineas for 'Miss Eliza Seymour'. In the hands of James Maddock, who established it in the 1770s, the Walworth nursery had become a tulip lover's nirvana. Its reputation continued unblemished under his son-in-law, Samuel Curtis, who had passed it on to Henry Groom in 1825. Now the tulip beds were emptied. The grand open days when Groom's prize tulips were exhibited in a bed fifty yards (45m) long were a thing of the past. Only a few years previously, the Rev. Richard Creswell (1815–1882) had described one such open day, with Groom's show bed standing proudly 'in the centre of a vast marquee, covered over at the top with linen cloth, and clothed at the sides and ends with coarse canvas. Both top and side cloths can be rolled up, so that sun or shade to any part of the bed can be commanded. By this method also the air is freely admitted, and the inside of the marquee, or awning, is cool and refreshing, and most beneficial to the flowers. Mr Groom, who is a gentlemanly and polite florist, introduced me without ceremony within the vail, and I, in a moment, was ushered into the company of kings and queens, dukes, lords, ladies and commoners. The sight was most dazzling and magnificent: the sun was shining, and each lovely flower was beautifully expanded'.[25] Groom's tulips were bought at auction for a startlingly low price by the Manchester grower, John Slater, the northern florists' revenge for the fortunes Groom had charged in the thirty years he had owned the nursery.

The first champions of the English Florists' tulip, mostly nurserymen such as James Maddock himself, Thomas Davey of the King's Road, London, Luke Pope of Handsworth, Birmingham, were already dead, Pope in 1825, Davey in 1833. Now many of the second phase of growers, the 'aldermen' florists, were fading away too. John Shelmerdine had gone. Charles Baron of Saffron Walden, a florist as well known for his hollyhocks as he was for his tulips, died in 1848, followed to his grave by the whole of the corporation, of which he was a prominent member. Mr Gibbons, whose race of tulips, the Chellaston seedlings, had caused such a sensation when they were first launched in the 1840s, had lapsed into obscurity, though John Spencer of Thulston, Derbyshire, who in 1847 had triumphed at Derby's Open Tulip Show with 'Magnum Bonum', a fine yellow tulip marked with a rich reddish-brown, was still going strong.

Tulip
George Hayward (Lawrence)
Plate 89.

Jⁿᵈ Andrews Zinco·   Printed by C Chabot

The Bizarre tulip 'George Hayward' from the Florist *(1856)*
Raised by R J Lawrence of Hampton by crossing a 'Polyphemus'
breeder with 'Pompre Funebre'

The founding fathers had been southerners, but it was northern growers, such as William Lea of Bedford Leigh, Lancashire, who raised the Rose tulip 'Industry', the handloom silk weaver David Jackson of Middleton, Lancashire and the fine group of growers based around Wakefield in Yorkshire who were now chiefly responsible for saving the superb, refined English Florists' tulips from extinction. The Wakefield growers included an extraordinary number of shoemakers, such as the brothers Tom and George Gill and William Mellor of Nettle Lane. In the same lane, bloomed the tens of thousands of English Florists' tulips cultivated by Tom Spurr, a treat for the crowds who made an annual pilgrimage there on the Sunday prior to the Wakefield show. Tommy Parker, another Wakefield grower, 'who would stay out half the night if he could chat with anyone interested in tulips', lives on in a street in Wakefield still called Parker's Fold. Sheffield was another safe haven for the breed. Here, Ben Simonite (1834–1909), a cutler like many of his fellow Sheffield florists, found time to breed pigeons, rabbits and greyhounds as well as tulips.

Up in Scotland the Paisley florists continued the long tradition of growing tulips that had been established in the area by the Huguenot weavers who originally settled there. On 9 July 1853, members of the Paisley society gathered to hear a letter from Mathew Perry, a former member of the society who had emigrated to America. Perry was hoping to buy a hundred tulip roots, ranunculus and other seeds to continue the florists' traditions in the new country. A committee of three, John Waterston, John Robertson and William McAlpine, was appointed to compose an answer. 'Out of respect to Mr Perry, he being lately a member of this club', the committee decided to send him free of charge a hundred tulip roots of different sorts and the other seeds mentioned in his letter. All that is, except the ranunculus. Flowering had been sparse and there was scarcely any seed to be had.

Despite these pockets of dedicated growers, found especially in Derbyshire, Lancashire and Nottinghamshire, the tulip was in decline as a florists' flower. It was not an easy thing to bring in a perfect state to the show bench and, increasingly, those florists for whom the arrival rather than the journey mattered, turned their attention to less-demanding subjects such as leeks and chrysanthemums. The tribalism that had fuelled so many enjoyable spats among the tulip growers could now be displayed, though in a more passive way, by identifying with a football team. Association Football's first cup final was played out in 1871 and, from the 1870s onwards, most towns of note had their own clubs. The rapidly changing face of towns and cities contributed to the decline too, the effect felt by all florists, not just

REV. F. D. HORNER.

The Rev. Francis Horner (1838–1912)
Florist of Kirkby Malzeard, Yorkshire

the tulip growers. The 1851 census had revealed that, for the first time in British history, more people lived in urban areas than in the country. An economic boom fuelled the growth of industrial centres such as Manchester, Nottingham and Derby, but increasingly, people worked in factories rather than at home, as the florist-weavers with their handlooms had done. The cost of the industrial boom was the loss of many of the small plots where generations of florists had grown their flowers; the passing of the Smallholdings and Allotments Act of 1906 came too late to save them. 'Many of our busy towns,' wrote the late-nineteenth-century florist, Rev. Francis Horner, 'which in the boyhood of men now middle-aged had outskirt gardens, the familiar haunts of old florists, have spread their unlovely over-growths of brick and mortar far beyond. It used to be a clear mile outside the town where in the earliest years of my florist life I grew Auriculas and Tulips; now, however, a raw and dreary street of monotonous tenements, and with an unmeaning name overlies the old green spot.'[26] In a dismal mood, Horner called in on the new occupants of Number 4, which he calculated had been built exactly over his tulip beds of twenty years ago. He was met with blank and uncomprehending stares.

A huge body of knowledge disappeared with the deaths of tulip growers such as George Lightbody of Falkirk (in 1872) and Richard Headley of Cambridge (in 1876). Their lives had spanned the whole of the century in which the English Florists' tulip had been the cynosure of beauty and the pinnacle of the florist's craft. For connoisseurs of tulips, the annual invitation to visit Headley's home, Stapleford House, during the flower's blooming in May was one that was never turned down. The month after his death, *The Garden* magazine advertised the sale (on 23 May 1876) of Headley's bulbs, which included many of his own breeding: the Bybloemen 'John Linton' and the crimson and white feathered 'Sarah Headley', which he had named after his wife. George Glenny, the horticultural journalist who crossed swords so spectacularly with Dr Hardy in the Battle of the Tulip, had died at Norwood in Middlesex in 1874 and was followed only a year later by his opponent. Dr George Wilmot Hardy, scourge of tulip judges, fount of thunderous prose, staunch member of the Liberal Party and Alderman of the Borough of Warrington, was buried in Warrington Cemetery after a service at St Paul's Church. The shutters of the shops were closed and the blinds of the houses drawn down as his funeral cortège passed by. His name lives on in the tulip raised by Tom Storer of Derby and 'broken' as a long-unsurpassed red Bizarre by Thomas Haynes in 1862. 'Dr Hardy' still wins prizes at the annual shows of the Wakefield and North of England Tulip Society.[27]

In earlier times, the death of one eminent tulip grower would have been sub-sumed by the advent of another, equally skilled. Now, only Samuel Barlow Esq of the Stakehill Bleach Works, Castleton rose to fill the gap left by the death of these four men, whose names, for an entire generation of growers, had been synonymous with the tulip. Barlow (1825–1893), who in 1871 had bought the bulk of Hardy's tulip collection, was a hero in the Arnold Bennett mould: a self-made man, an ener-getic county magistrate, Mayor of Middleton, a council member of the Manchester Botanical and Horticultural Society, President of the Manchester Arts Club, direc-tor of the Winterbottom Book Cloth Company Ltd – and sometime president of the National (now Royal National) Tulip Society. While contributing in no small measure to the problems of 'a district where the atmosphere is so fully charged with elements injurious to vegetable life that the surrounding country is almost denuded of trees', Barlow was a passionate horticulturist. The dichotomy seemed a positive virtue to one correspondent who wrote roundly that 'Mr Ruskin, and some of his followers, who waste time and energy by preaching up a perfectly Utopian crusade against "devil-driven machinery" as the enemy of natural beauty and truth, should go to Stakehill to learn how the two apparently hostile interests can, by patience, perseverance, and skill, be made to live peaceably together'.[28] Sixty factory chimneys, similar to Stakehill's own, could be counted from the Stakehill grounds.

A Lancashire man, Barlow was born in Medlock Vale, the son of 'one of that band of earnest and enthusiastic working-men botanists who have done so much to create a love of beauty and sweetness in the too frequently unlovely life of the Lancashire manufacturing districts'. Barlow followed his father, first into the bleach works of Messrs Otto Hulme and Sons at Medlock Vale and then later at Stakehill. From an early age he grew lupins and poppies, fancy primroses and auric-ulas; tulips were a latter passion, but he was already showing them by 1848. When his father died, Barlow, aged thirty, was made manager of the Stakehill bleach works. Just six years later, he became the owner. In its day, Stakehill was regarded as a perfect example of the way in which 'high culture and exquisite taste can be associated in the closest manner with the requirements of manufacturing industry'. Paintings by artists of the Manchester School covered the walls of Barlow's house. He was also one of the first people in this country to buy paintings by the French Impressionists, such as Camille Pissaro. Display cabinets overflowed with 'ceramic curiosities'. Outside, waggon loads of soil were brought by railway from a plot Sam Barlow owned at Great Orme's Head, Llandudno, to replace the poisoned earth of the neighbourhood. There were vineries, orchid houses, stove plants, choice bego-

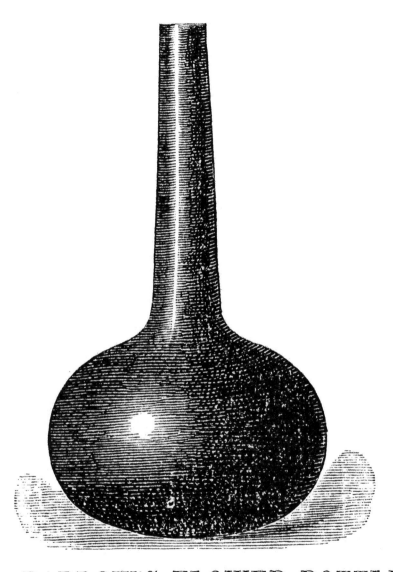

MR. BARLOW'S FLOWER BOTTLE.

Samuel Barlow's flower bottle
designed to be used at the
Royal National Tulip Society Exhibition 1882

nias, pelargoniums, rhododendrons, lilies. And English Florists' tulips, of which Barlow built up the biggest collection that anyone had ever owned.

Barlow, who was very much an 'alderman' florist, spared no expense on his hobby, and artisan florists such as David Jackson, the silk weaver of Middleton, benefited. Barlow had set his heart on acquiring 'Mrs Jackson', bred by Jackson around 1865. It was a strikingly fine Bybloemen with petals of good substance, heavily feathered with glossy black on a white ground. Its base (always an important criterion) was as white as snow. He wanted, of course, the whole stock of the variety, so that nobody else could say they had it, and offered Jackson, twenty years his senior, the weight of the bulbs in gold. He ended up paying even more, but as the Scottish florist James Douglas said at the time, 'they are weak in the head about Manchester'.

On his four show tulip beds, each containing 140 rows of seven flowers, he grew the shy flowering 'Bessie', a Bybloemen feathered with dark purple on a white ground, raised by the Halifax grower John Hepworth. He grew the feathered Bizarre 'George Hayward', marked with dark crimson maroon on a pure golden ground. First 'broken' in 1853, this was a famous tulip, which featured prominently in the *Florist* magazine the following year. Though it could be astounding, it was an uncertain flower, the feathers sometimes running wildly out of control. It had been raised by Lawrence of Hampton, a southern grower belonging to the previous generation of florists. Barlow also grew the perfect 'Annie McGregor', flamed with rosy-scarlet on a pure white ground, which had been bred by the Lancashire weaver John Martin. Its arrival marked one of those great leaps forward in breeding that occasionally occurred in the English Florist's tulip and, for decades, 'Annie McGregor' remained unsurpassed.

Mindful of his position as president of the Royal National Tulip Society, Barlow turned his attention to the show bench too. The English Florists' tulip had to a great extent been nurtured in the public houses of the north, and by tradition, tulips were staged at shows in nothing fancier than beer bottles of dark brown glass. Barlow designed a flower bottle, five and a half inches high, three inches in diameter, to be made in black glass, which he hoped might give 'a tone of order and regularity' to shows, especially those staged by the Royal National Tulip Society. But on 28 May 1893, Samuel Barlow, the man who 'created a floral paradise amid a forest of chimney shafts' died, after falling down the stairs of his Manchester warehouse. Fittingly, he too is commemorated by a tulip, raised, like 'Dr Hardy', by the railwayman and florist, Tom Storer, who grew his tulips along the embankments of Derby's railways. Indeed,

Tulip and Trellis *(1870)*
Tile designed by William Morris and made by William de Morgan
Victoria and Albert Museum, London

251

in the Bizarre tulip 'Sam Barlow' the two great tulip growers were united, for Storer had bred it by crossing 'Dr Hardy' with another superb Bizarre 'Sir Joseph Paxton'. The skill of generations of florists, the heartbreaking devotion of the tulip lovers who, for hundreds of years, had kept the blood of the English Florists' tulip running pure in the veins of their flowers, shone out in the flames of Sam Barlow's gold and scarlet flower. But that blood was now very thin.

CHAPTER VII

THE LAST HUNDRED YEARS

B Y THE END of the nineteenth century, the tulip, in its long and charismatic history, had already re-invented itself many times. It had been a rare novelty, a botanist's marvel. It had been a jewel flower, a snob flower grown by all the richest and most fashionable gardeners of Europe. When they got tired of it, it became a hobby flower, adored and brilliantly cultivated by groups of florists in France, Flanders, England and Scotland. They brought the flower to the peak of perfection before they too mostly abandoned it. The void was quickly occupied by the clever Dutch, who recreated the tulip as a flower for bedding out *en masse* and developed a highly lucrative trade in tulips as cut flowers. The process had been anticipated in the United States, where florists such as the late eighteenth-century clockmaker and silversmith William Faris had cultivated exquisite feathered and flamed tulips in his Chesapeake garden. Gradually men of his kind disappeared along with their flowers and mass displays became the norm. Six hundred different sorts of tulip were bedded out in the Linnaean Botanic Garden, Long Island in the spring of 1845, while in Britain and France, tulips were still the specialised darlings of the florist gardeners. E H Krelage created one of the first bedding-out displays seen in Paris, when in 1889 he filled the ground round the Trocadero Palace with massed plantings of his new Darwin tulips, carefully placed to catch the eye of visitors to the Great Exhibition of the Work of Industry of All

Nations (the Eiffel Tower was a more lasting memento of the occasion). At Kew, as a gardening correspondent of the time noted, tulips crammed the beds in front of the Palm House. 'It is the species and hybrids that now give colour to the elaborate arrangement, and we are pleased to see that such types, practically unknown a few years ago, are thus massed together in a conspicuous position in the Royal Gardens.'[1] 'Couleur Cardinal' with its rich dusky plum-red flowers filled the beds either side of the Broad Walk.[2] By 1896, Baylor Hartland, who raised many fine tulips at his Ard Cairn nursery, near Cork, was offering 'Tulips for Extensive Park Planting. Special Quotations to Superintendents' and tulips began to appear *en masse* in London's royal parks. The old Double Early 'Tournesol', red with a yellow margin, was bedded out at Grosvenor Gate, together with the white 'Joost van den Vondel', the tulips undercarpeted with auriculas, *Primula sieboldii* and yellow doronicum. Regent's Park glowed with beds of the brilliant red Double Early tulip 'Grand Maître'. Subtler combinations prevailed in Gunnersbury Park where the beautiful old Parrot tulip 'Markgraaf' with brown flowers veined and speckled with yellow was interplanted with another brown and red Parrot tulip, 'Café Brun'.[3] The same thing was happening in the public parks and botanic gardens of the great manufacturing centres of the north. In 1912, 30,000 tulips were bedded out at Sheffield Botanic Garden. The purity of the Single Early tulip 'White Hawk' was particularly noted, though this may have had more to do with the coal strike and the consequent reduction in smoke and dust than with the inherent qualities of the flower itself. On a former building site in Bradford, a miniature bulb field sprang up, 'a source of considerable speculation among tramway passengers and pedestrians passing along Morley St and Easby Rd'.[4] Fred Terry, a Bradford auctioneer, was the man behind the venture. Impressed by what he had seen in the bulb fields of The Netherlands, he took up an agency for the Dutch firm of Wagenaar and planted 10,000 tulips of seventy different varieties on the Bradford building site, the whole 'field' insured for £100. By the 1920s, 200 different kinds of tulips were being grown in the London parks alone, the bulbs all supplied by British growers and the cost jointly borne by the Empire Marketing Board (who wanted to promote home-grown goods) and the Office of Works.[5]

Gertrude Jekyll, the ultimate arbiter of taste in the Edwardian garden, had rather more subtle ways of using tulips than the keepers of Regent's Park. Everything depended on combining tulips of the right colours, she told readers of *The Garden*, which she edited from 1899 onwards. She used the blackish-purple tulip 'Faust' with 'Grande Monarque' which was lighter and redder. She paired the low-toned yellow of 'Bronze King' with 'Louis XIV' a much deeper bronze, heavily shaded with purple. She did not shy away from bright colours, but they were carefully chosen to complement each other. Her flame-coloured 'Orange King' tulips were interplanted with 'Panorama' which was in the same spectrum, but just a shade redder.[6] The Rev. Joseph Jacob, who contributed to the same magazine, noted that in 1911, the year of George V's coronation, visitors to his own garden in Whitwell, Flintshire, showed a marked preference for the red tulips among the 500 or so varieties that he grew. Jacob, a whimsical writer, wondered 'if it is the great event that suggests it, and so we unconsciously adopt it'. But several writers pointed out a practical problem associated with massing tulips in beds: they got in the way of the summer bedding – zonal pelargoniums, fuchsias, annuals – generally set out at the end of May. The tulips could not be allowed to die down naturally before they had to be chivvied out of the way. Sometimes they were dug up and thrown away as soon as they had finished flowering, a practice which suited the bulbmen of The Netherlands very well.

Not everyone was a convert to the new style. There was a xenophobic element that took against the new beefy bedding Darwins for no better reason than that they were foreign. Some finely tuned gardeners felt they were 'crude in the extreme like "Rule Britannia with Variations" to a musically educated man'. Others were even blunter: 'It is impossible to deny that the blending of foreign blood has seriously impaired the value of the true strains. Many of the continental sorts lack cleanliness and when they crop up amongst their purer sisters their appearance at once betrays them'.[7] Though, even in Edwardian times, tourists visited the Haarlem bulb fields to marvel at the tulips, some Englishmen felt that in their own gardens they 'did not want the bang in the eye which they give us'. Underplanting helped soften the effect and low-growing forget-me-nots, double arabis, limnanthes, silene, alyssum, aubrieta, primroses, polyanthus and London pride were often recommended as companions, to give tulips a more natural setting in the garden.[8]

Parallel with the craze for bedding out was a strong movement towards so-called wild gardening; the plants were no less primped and pruned but the general effect was supposed to mirror the effects of nature. The style was vociferously championed by the Irish gardener, William Robinson, whose book *The Wild Garden* had been published in 1870. At the fine garden he made at Gravetye, near East Grinstead, Sussex, Robinson put his principles into practice and his message was heard even across the Atlantic. 'Beautiful and permanent effects may be obtained by planting hardy bulbs in groups and masses on the lawn, in shady nooks, where

The Fine old Double Late tulip 'Blue Flag', known to French tulip-lovers as 'Bleu Celeste'.
Known since 1750, it is still in cultivation

they find a congenial and permanent home, flowering abundantly in their season, and requiring little or no care after being planted,' promised an American catalogue of the early twentieth century. 'This mode of planting is termed "naturalizing", and is now generally followed in Europe', it went on, recommending crocus and colchicums, as well as tulips, for the purpose. The tulip had come full circle. After all its reincarnations, here it was again as a wild flower, just as it had started out. But who knows how many millions of bulbs withered away in the New World before gardeners discovered that tulips are oddly fussy about where they will 'naturalise'? Nature had tethered them to the latitude of 40 degrees north. They needed some persuading that the virgin territory of 40 degrees south was as good. No tulips had existed in the New World before man took them there.

In the *Journal of Horticulture, Cottage Gardener* of 1895, more was written about tomatoes than about tulips; the fruit had only lately been introduced from the New World and was a great curiosity. But how the tulip had fallen! When on 25 May 1894, members of the Butley Tulip Society met at the Orange Tree Inn for their sixty-ninth annual show, how many of them could have predicted that within a few years, the society would be defunct? A silver cup was presented by Mrs Samuel Barlow, in memory of her late husband, and was won by Charles Needham of Hale, Cheshire. Only seven names were to be inscribed on that cup, for the society's 1901 show was the last ever held in a public house in the traditional way. The Rev. Francis Horner, a dinosaur among the dwindling band of florists, lamented the fact that the tulip collections of forty men were now amassed under one roof. The flowers staggered on – just – but those who knew how to grow them were dying and few replaced them. Only in Wakefield did they keep the faith. Tommy Parker, who had raised feathered tulips of a marvellous constancy in his plot under the town's gasworks, had gone, but the Mellors and Gills, the Calverts and Hardwicks were still represented, some of them third-generation tulip growers. William Mellor carried off the premier prizes for both flamed and feathered flowers at the Wakefield Society's 1893 show, held at the Brunswick Hotel, Borough Market. But thirty years on, even the Wakefield Society was tottering. 'Help us to keep the names of Sharpley, Mellor, Moorhouse, Schofield, Hepworth, Gill, Hardwick and many other tulip raisers of old to the fore,' begged the secretary in the society's 1928 Annual Report. 'Let us continue to keep the Wakefield and district evergreen to our noble flower – the English Florists' Tulip.'

The Royal National Tulip Society fared no better. Founded, with high hopes, in 1849, it never quite achieved its objectives: to unite the tulip growers of north and south and to overcome the northern florists' suspicion of those tulip fanciers whose only crime was the misfortune of having been born south of Watford. The 1890 show took place at the Botanical Gardens, Manchester, and the winners were nearly all northern growers – Wood of Manchester, Kitchen of Stockport, Knowles of Stalybridge. In 1894 the RNTS show was at York and afterwards, members of the Ancient Society of York Florists entertained their tulip brothers to lunch at the White Swan Hotel, Goodramgate. But that year, the shakily spliced society splintered into two sections, a Northern and a Southern. The fine gardener Ellen Willmott (1858–1934), who used shoals of tulips in her gardens at Warley Place, Essex and on the French Riviera, was a celebrated member of the society's Southern Section, which in 1895 held its own show at The Temple, London. The prizes went to Manchester, just the same. The northern growers had their own show three weeks later, at the Free Library, Middleton. Charles Needham and Samuel Barlow's nephew, James Bentley (1859–1924), both prizewinners at the show, led the celebrations afterwards at the Boar's Head. George Glenny's combative ghost was invoked against the judges officiating at the RNTS's 1896 show, held again at the Free Library. 'They will pardon us,' said a southern commentator icily, 'if we remind them that purity is the great essential quality in the Tulip...'[9] In the end, the northerners prevailed, as anyone might have guessed. In 1936 Sir Daniel Hall, the south-based president of the Royal National Tulip Society wrote to the Wakefield and North of England Tulip Society, the sole remaining society devoted to tulips in the country, saying that with Needham's death, the National was left with only two members, himself and the nurseryman, Peter Barr. He suggested that the balance of the National society's funds should be used to create a Needham Cup class at the annual Wakefield Show and sent, as well, all the silver trophies that had formerly been awarded at RNTS shows. The Wakefield Society's Minute Book solemnly records the gifts: 'one large cup, one small cup and one piece of plate. These were greatly admired by the Committee.'

The success had by the Dutch nurseryman E H Krelage in launching his new Darwins was jealously noted by professional English growers. As the tradition of tulip-growing gradually died out in Flanders, Krelage had bought one of the last great florist's collections and, selecting out the best varieties (at that stage all pinks and purples – no yellows) rechristened them with the permission of Charles Darwin's son, Francis. Krelage, a consummate marketer, lost no opportunity to promote his new brand. Meanwhile, Peter Barr (c1862–1944), the Covent Garden nurseryman, made a similar move. Barr's father, another Peter (1826–1909), had been born near Govan in Lanarkshire, but came south, first to a nursery in Worcester and then to establish a famous business at Covent Garden, London. With his bushy wild beard and his black beret, he looked more like a painter of the Impressionist school than a bulb grower but he was a well-known authority on daffodils and tulips. The Barr offensive was spirited and he was loyally supported in the press, who showed a distinct partiality in their treatment of the subject. 'During the last few days a large and interesting collection of English Florists' tulips has been in bloom in the Long Ditton Nurseries of Messrs Barr & Son. Several beds have been planted with them and it is safe to say that in no nursery in the British Isles has a more complete representation of this splendid type of tulip been seen together.'[10] By buying up collections such as Lloyd's of Petersfield, Peter Barr amassed more than 20,000 English Florists' tulips at his nursery, concentrating, like Krelage, on the plain-coloured 'breeders' rather than the feathered and flamed varieties. It was a moot point whether he was responding to demand or trying to create it.

Barr's purpose was to release the English florists' tulip from its exhibition straightjacket, as Krelage had done with the Flemish Baguet tulips. 'The Tulip of whatever class is essentially a garden flower and the florist's type is as precious as the gaudy Dutch kinds…' continued the faithful correspondent of *The Garden*. The 'gaudy' betrayed a deep prejudice against the Dutch flowers but, in truth, the English florists' tulip did not have a strong enough constitution to jostle its way through the mixed planting of an English herbaceous border. It was an aristocrat. It hated bad weather. It was used to being cosseted, covered, protected from harm. And slugs adored it.

Krelage, to his great credit, did not rise to the bait. Tenaciously, he took every opportunity to refute the English claim that their tulips were the only ones worth growing. When *The Garden* published a glowing account of the Parrot tulips to be seen in James Walker's Ham Nurseries, Krelage sent the magazine's editor some fine Dutch Parrot tulips, along with some examples of his best Darwins. The editor then was the splenetic William Robinson, of Gravetye, and he was not to be so easily bought. 'We confess,' he replied magisterially, 'to a greater partiality to the breeder forms of our English tulips amongst which are some great beauties, especially among the roses and bybloemens, with great moon-like, pure white centres and the most exquisite forms and often brilliant and delicately soft colours.'[11] But Krelage was right. The Darwin tulips were better adapted to the new vogue for mass

*Tulips massed in the borders of
the painter Alfred Parsons' Edwardian garden at
Luggers Hill, Broadway in the Cotswolds*

bedding than the English Florists' tulip. The Darwins had long, strong stems that pushed the flowers high, so that they could be enjoyed from the outside rather than the inside. This was essential for a flower that was used in the mass rather than as an individual. The beauty of the English Florists' tulips lay in the quality of the inner flower – the combined charms of the pure base, the anthers, the stamens and the feathered or flamed markings, which always showed more strongly on the inner surface of the petal than the outer.

Like Krelage, Peter Barr picked up many old tulips at the bulb auctions that, by tradition, followed the death of a florist of the old school. But he had a nose like a bloodhound for a good flower and gathered together old varieties from gardens all over Britain and Ireland. Gardens in the south and east of Ireland had long been happy hunting grounds for lovers of old-fashioned tulips, some of them descendants of the bulbs that early Huguenots had brought with them after the Battle of the Boyne. The fine old Lily-flowered tulip 'Mrs Moon', yellow and sweetly scented, first bobbed up in a bed of the Single Early tulip 'Ophir d'Or', planted in her Irish garden by a Mrs Butler. She sold surplus bulbs of 'Mrs Moon' at a few shillings a hundred, so must have been mortified to find, only a few years later, Irish nurserymen offering it at the vastly inflated price of two shillings and six-pence or three shillings a bulb. Tulips grew well in Ireland, as the nurserymen Hogg and Robertson discovered when they established their bulb farm on fifteen acres of flat and sandy plain at Rush outside Dublin. (They also had land at Boston, Lincolnshire and at Wisbech, Cambridgeshire.) But the most unlikely locales could provide treasures. Fred Burbridge (1847–1905), Curator of the Trinity College garden in Dublin, described a visit he made with Peter Barr to the Isle of Wight, where, in a small garden under the shadow of Carisbrooke Castle they found masses of old May tulips. 'Selfs, striped, flaked, splashed, and the sturdy old self purples shot with chocolate and some pure browns with yellow edges which I have heard called "Treacle Tulips" by village dames, and all were good to see. So Barr and I leaned over the low palings and admired until their owner came out in a frilled sun bonnet and invited us to take a closer view. She fetched a spade and said she would give us "some roots" but we explained that we were on a journey and could not well take them with us.'[12]

Other nurserymen joined Barr in the battle against Dutch domination. Robert Wallace (1867–1955) grew 50,000 tulips on his fields at Colchester, Essex. Sutton's staged 200 vases of tulips (2,000 blooms in all) at the Royal Horticultural Society's Westminster show on 30 April 1912. The tulips, all grown on the nursery's Reading bulb fields, won a silver-gilt Flora medal for the firm. Other bulb growers also brought tulips to the RHS shows: Robert Wallace of Colchester, George Massey & Sons, Hogg & Robertson ('Holland in Ireland' was their slogan), Alex Dickson, now better known for his roses than his tulips, R H Bath, James Box, nurseryman and cattle dealer of Haywards Heath, Sussex. Occasionally a rogue correspondent broke ranks and defiantly trumpeted the superior qualities of the Dutch article. The cerise-coloured 'Pride of Haarlem' bred by E H Krelage in 1894, was the best tulip to be seen in the whole of Barr's collection said the *Journal of Horticulture*.[13] Barr, though, continued the hard sell of his May-flowering tulips, retrieved from old cottage gardens where they had been blooming undisturbed for more than fifty years. But heart could not entirely rule head, and although Barr remained true to the English Florists' tulip (Wallace and Barr continued to offer them until the firm closed down in the 1950s), he had to accept that there was a demand for the sturdy, weatherproof Darwins and other Dutch tulips. If he did not supply them, they would. In 1907, Barr introduced the fine purple and white Parrot tulip 'Sensation' which had arisen in The Netherlands as a sport of 'Reine d'Espagne'. The name was apt, for this was the first purple and white Parrot tulip that anyone had ever seen. Although the type had been known since the mid seventeenth century, until 'Sensation' arrived, all Parrot tulips had been red and yellow Bizarres.

Infiltration of foreign markets by Dutch growers and nurserymen was not a new phenomenon. They had been exporting bulbs since the middle of the seventeenth century, with Voorhelm's business in the Kleine Houtweg, Haarlem well known to gardeners all over Europe. But at the beginning, the market was very different. Customers were well-to-do, princes and aristocrats, who bought a huge number of different kinds of tulips, but in tiny quantities at vast prices. As trade became more democratic, sales depots were established, fuelled by Dutch imports. Instead of selling to individual customers, Dutch tulip growers sent bulk consignments of bulbs to nurserymen in foreign countries, who sold the bulbs on at a profit. The golden age for Dutch growers started around 1860 as they began to establish a stranglehold on the tulip trade. There was a huge boom in tulip-breeding, fuelled by an increasing demand for the flowers, especially in the United States. But the demand could not have been met without extra land to grow bulbs and that meant radically improving drainage in parts of The Netherlands that had not previously been used for tulips. Cultivation, historically centred in the sandy silts round Haarlem, spread out into other areas, round Lisse and Limmen.

Nobody denied the commitment of the Dutch bulb growers. They were hard-working; they were not bedevilled by the us-and-them attitude that permeated so much of British industry. Dutch nursery owners worked as hard as anyone they employed. Dutch bulb growers also took the trouble to visit the countries which imported their bulbs so that they could better understand the markets they were supplying. Dutch bulb lists were routinely translated into English, German and French with prices listed in foreign currencies. 'How many English firms, even of the first rank, issue a simple foreign catalogue or even a short list?' asked *The Horticultural Advertiser*.[14]

The United States was an important market for the Dutch, and by the mid nineteenth century, American nurserymen were already looking for reliable suppliers abroad. Henry Dreer of Philadelphia put his trust in the Haarlem firm of E H Krelage, established in 1811: 'Having frequently noticed your name attached to catalogues of bulbs, sold in this country at auctions, and upon trial generally found them superior to others sold here, I am induced to address you with the view of importing directly from you yearly an invoice of bulbs suited to my sale. I am in this city in the seed and plant business, and wish to import every season from a house that I may always depend on receiving them in time and true to name and description.'[15] He pinpointed two crucial problems of the bulb trade, one of which still bedevils it. While cargoes of bulbs still crossed the Atlantic under sail, delivery dates were necessarily uncertain. There was no excuse for sending out bulbs wrongly named, but this same problem plagues customers even today.

The importance of the American market to Dutch growers was not lost on the Hillegom nurseryman van der Schoot, who in 1849 sent the first *bollenreiziger* or travelling bulb salesman to the States. He travelled from New York to Philadelphia, Baltimore, Washington, Boston, Albany and Buffalo. 'He has been to all the gardeners and gentlemen having fine gardens, and offered to sell very cheap. He has obtained a great many orders', reported Henry Dreer to Krelage.[16] Van der Schoot had tried to tempt Dreer away from Krelage by offering lower prices, but Dreer remained faithful. The fact that Krelage was generous in extending terms of payment may have had something to do with his loyalty. Van der Schoot flooded the market, which had a disastrous effect on prices. Another American nurseryman, John Milton Earle of Worcester, Massachusetts, said that huge quantities of bulbs, mostly van der Schoot's, had been sold at auction at Boston, for ridiculously low prices.

By the first decade of the twentieth century, the United States was importing a million dollars' worth of bulbs a year from The Netherlands and Dutch

Tulips in a Staffordshire Jug
by Dora Carrington (1893–1932)

growers were able to bring pressure on the US government to reduce import duty on the bulbs. The *quid pro quo* was that The Netherlands would continue to import American flour.[17] Some subversives muttered that there was no reason that US nurserymen should not grow their own tulip bulbs, but few truthfully thought that they could be produced as efficiently and economically there as they were in The Netherlands. And Holland was an important market for American corn, which was exported to few other European countries apart from Britain.

Tulips were always the most popular bulbs imported into the country, selling at least three times better than hyacinths or daffodils. In 1920, the US imported 54 million tulips, in 1925 106 million, in 1930 153 million. In the early days (1800–1850), just three firms, including Roozen and Sons at Hillegom and de Graff at Lisse, exported tulips to the States. At least seven firms joined the trade between 1850 and 1880, and in the boom years between 1880 and 1914, twenty-two Dutch nurserymen, including van Zanten at Hillegom and Grullemans at Lisse, sent tulips to American nurserymen and growers. Such fragmentation was characteristic of the Dutch bulb industry as most nurseries had only small holdings of land. Rijnveld and Son (raisers of the fabulous raspberry-ripple Parrot tulip 'Estelle Rijnveld') were unusual in having forty-five hectares planted with bulbs at Hillegom. Most nurseries were run on a much smaller scale. J Mooy had just one and a half hectares at Haarlem, the Roozens had thirteen hectares at Hillegom, Gerritt Segers only nine hectares at Lisse. But the bigger growers, such as Nelis and Sons at Heemstede, could support a number of export markets. They sent bulbs not just to the United States and Canada, but to Britain, Ireland, Germany, Austria, Hungary, Czechoslovakia, France, Belgium, Luxembourg, Switzerland, Italy, Spain, Portugal, Romania, Yugoslavia, Bulgaria, Greece, Turkey, Russia, Poland, Sweden, Norway, Denmark, Finland, Africa, South America, even to Australia and New Zealand. It was an impressive achievement.

As *The Horticultural Advertiser* had pointed out, the Dutch deserved their success. They took trouble with their catalogues.[18] They lost no opportunity to put their flowers in front of the public, donating millions of bulbs for mass plantings in the public parks of the Bronx in New York, at the Golden Gate Park in San Francisco, in the St Louis Botanic Garden. In Europe, the Dutch made sure their tulips were to the fore in the Tuileries gardens in Paris, in the Tiergarten at Berlin, at Sanssouci in Potsdam, in the public parks of Stuttgart and Budapest, Copenhagen and Warsaw. If there was an international exhibition anywhere in the world with flowers as the theme, they were there, helpful, dependable, generous with their gifts. In 1927 they were at the Paris extravaganza organised by the Société Nationale d'Horticulture de France. The following year they were in Gent. In 1932 they made a big splash at the show organised by New York's Horticultural Club. The next year they made an equally memorable impact at the Philadelphia Flower Show. Twenty thousand Dutch tulips of forty different kinds were displayed at the National Flower Show organised by the Society of American Florists at Houston, Texas between 17 and 19 February 1939. There was a cost of course, absorbed by the Centraal Bloembollencomite, which levied a charge on all Dutch bulb growers. In 1925, it cost them more than 3,000 florins to plant up the Bronx park in New York. In 1930, they sent tulips worth nearly 8,000 florins for the Tuileries gardens in Paris. But in marketing terms, the money was well spent.

Dutch entrepreneurs also organised trips to the bulb fields, which were fast becoming a tourist attraction. Whistlestop tours of the if-this-is-Thursday-it-must-be-Amsterdam kind are not a late-twentieth-century invention. More than a hundred years ago, a visitor reported that tulip tours were 'well planned, well carried out, affording the greatest amount of pleasure and interest, with the least amount of confusion and fatigue within five hours – museums, luncheon, speech of welcome by burgomaster, drive through the wood and bulb fields and back to *table d'hôte* Amsterdam'.[19] There were other ways of capturing potential customers too: gifts to American garden clubs, to Women's Institutes in Britain, to schoolchildren in Sweden, to horticultural societies in Bucharest. Nobody could match the Dutch in their tireless search for new markets to absorb the vast numbers of bulbs they produced.

In England and the United States the taste for late-flowering tulips gradually overtook interest in the early-flowering ones, so that by 1937, the US was importing 88 million late-flowering tulips, but only 21 million early ones. In Germany and Scandinavia, the market was reversed, with twice as many early-flowering tulips being sold as late ones. For a long time, the most popular early varieties had been old favourites such as the orange-scarlet scented tulip 'Prince of Austria', raised about 1860, and the fabulous scarlet-plum 'Couleur Cardinal', raised in 1845. The orange scented Single Early 'Fred Moore', raised about 1908, was another popular variety. But just before the outbreak of the Second World War, when the export of Dutch bulbs to Great Britain topped the billion mark, early-flowering tulips were being supplanted by newer cultivars of late-flowering tulips. By the post-war period, the transformation was complete. The cherry-red Darwin hybrid

'Apeldoorn', the purplish-violet 'Attila', the elegant Lily-flowered 'Aladdin', pink and white 'Blenda', brownish-red 'Cassini' and the elegant Triumph tulip 'Don Quichotte' dominated the markets. All were raised in the 1940s or early 1950s. At the end of the twentieth century, Lily-flowered tulips such as the elegant 'White Triumphator' (raised in 1942) and 'China Pink' (raised in 1944) still remain firm favourites with British gardeners.

For growers primarily interested in the cut-flower market, early-flowering tulips remained important because the highest prices were fetched by flowers that could be coaxed into bloom months before they appeared in the garden. The sweet-smelling yellow Double Early tulip 'Monte Carlo' remains unsurpassed as a cut flower more than forty years after it was introduced. So does the rich pink 'Christmas Marvel', first grown in 1954. Ivory white 'Inzell' with its fine, pale foliage is a more recent addition to the list of best-selling cut flowers, as is the rich purple 'Negrita', with anthers of a strange greenish yellow shining out in the centre of flowers as lustrous as a doge's cloak.

No tulips appeared in the price lists of cut flowers on sale at Covent Garden market during the 1880s, but they were being grown for sale in bunches by Walter Ware (c1855–1917) by 1893. Ware, the son of Thomas Ware of the Hale Farm Nurseries, Tottenham, was one of the most successful English growers of the age. From his nursery at Inglescombe near Bath, he introduced tulips such as the stunning 'Inglescombe Yellow', probably the nearest any British breeder ever got to matching the qualities of Krelage's Darwins. His most popular cut flower though was the Lily-flowered tulip 'Picotee', white-bordered with a pale pink that darkened to rose at the very edges of the petals.[20] Ware grew thousands of blooms for market, and the prices quoted for cut flowers in the first couple of decades of the twentieth century show that this must have been a lucrative trade. On 29 April 1911, tulips priced at sixteen shillings a dozen bundles were the most expensive flowers sold at the Covent Garden market in London. Most tulips were cheaper than that, but even at an average price, only cattleya orchids cost more.[21] But as the season progressed, prices dropped. By 20 May of that year, both Spanish iris and lily-of-the-valley were fetching better prices than tulips, though the best tulips could still command a shilling a bunch. Just before England's General Strike of 1926, tulips were delivering even better returns to growers. Prices of eighteen to thirty shillings a dozen bunches were quoted for the twelve different kinds of tulip on sale that spring.[22] Now more than a million tulips are sold every day during the season, but the more available they become, the less value they command. Dumped in buckets in petrol-station forecourts, tulips are now among the cheapest cut flowers you can buy.

The mass market that developed from the late nineteenth century onwards, tempted others besides the Dutch to invest in tulips. Bulb fields sprang up in the eastern counties of England, especially around Spalding in Lincolnshire. The drained, silty soils of the fens provided growing conditions that were at least as good as Haarlem's and by the 1920s flower production was an important part of the local economy. At the outbreak of World War II, a veto was imposed on home sales and instead The Bulb Export Company sent four million tulip bulbs (including 'Clara Butt', 'Bartigon' and 'William Pitt') to the US in exchange for arms. As trading opportunities opened up at the end of the nineteenth century, the tulip was introduced into Japan too. Japanese gardeners, who found even the rose a deeply unrefined flower, were unlikely to develop a taste for tulips in their own exquisitely rarified gardens, but they recognised a commercial opportunity and a bulb-growing industry rapidly developed during the 1920s in the temperate areas of Japan's west coast. Japan now produces more than 120 million bulbs every year, the flowers fitting into the cycle of the farmers' rice harvests. Tulip fields flourish in the Skagit Valley, Washington State and among the Dandenong mountains of Australia. They are grown commercially in Tasmania and in the south island of New Zealand, where they were introduced around 1908. They are bred in southern Chile and on the high table lands of South Africa. You will find them still in Ireland and in Denmark, where growing conditions resemble quite closely those of The Netherlands.

But despite the way the tulip industry has spread over the temperate areas of the world, the Dutch still remain identified with the flower in a way that nobody else has ever quite managed – even the Turkish. The Netherlands exports at least two billion tulip bulbs a year, two thirds of their total production. Almost half of the country's 34,000 sq km is covered in bulb fields and the area is increasing all the time with an export trade worth around £1,330 million. Breeders are constantly looking for new tulips that will bulk up quickly for the bulb trade, or that can be forced for the cut-flower industry. At the Dutch Centre for Plant Breeding and Reproduction Research (CPRO-DLO) scientists have found that very early on in a new seedling's growth cycle, they can detect one or other characteristic. Bulbs of some cultivars swell at a much faster rate than others. Some bulbs, such as those of the yellow and red Kaufmanniana tulip 'Stresa' develop offsets at a greater rate than others, as the early florists had found to their despair. Some of the most prized antique tulips such as the dark purple and white 'Louis XIV' were heart-breakingly slow to reproduce themselves. This very unwillingness increased the flower's value as far as the old florists were concerned, but in the new mass markets, breeders are impatient with such aristocratic delicacy. They want tulips that will bulk up as fast as rabbits. Usefully, breeders discovered that the tulips that produced most offsets, or 'daughter' bulbs, were also those that flowered most quickly from seed, giving growers a double advantage.

Forcing tulips for the cut-flower trade is now a more lucrative business than providing bulbs and half the bulb fields in The Netherlands are planted with the same twenty cultivars, all of which are used to provide forced, cut flowers. In fact half the cut-flower market in tulips is dominated by just ten cultivars, a hideous *reductio ad absurdum* for a flower that nature equipped with more than a thousand tricks. But breeders were quick to exploit early-flowering tendencies in seedlings when choosing new cultivars for the cut-flower market. The length of the tulip's stem, the firmness of the leaves, the way the leaves sit on the stem, the proportion of leaf to flower were other important considerations. Of course, it is also important that a flower should last as long as possible in a vase and fortunately, breeders discovered (as you might expect) that the tulips that lasted longest outside in the bulb fields were also those that lasted longest in water. The rich cherry-red tulip 'Debutante' with plum-purple anthers is one of the seedling tulips selected for the cut-flower market by CPRO-DLO scientists. The primrose-yellow 'Silver Dollar' is another. Breeders have also tinkered with the rate at which tulips mature. Left to itself, a tulip will generally take seven years to develop from seed to flowering bulb (*T. sprengeri* is quicker), but scientists persuaded some cultivars to mature in four years. By experimenting with light levels and storage temperatures, they also managed to coax the tulip to flower three times in two years, reducing the growth cycle from a year to eight months. The commercial advantages, even given the extra handling costs, are obvious.

But surmounting everything else is the beauty of the flower itself. No matter how long and strong the stem, no matter how symmetrically spaced the leaves, no matter whether the tulip has been chivvied into doing its work in two thirds of the time that nature intended, in the end we buy tulips because they are beautiful. On a grey, sunless day, when a northeasterly wind is whipping the skin off the backs of your knuckles, nothing cheers the heart more than a bunch of tulips, weaving and bending in their vase like a flock of inquisitive birds. Even the scientists recognised this and set out to analyse exactly how colour works in tulips, how

Tulips staged in the Needham Memorial Cup class
at the Wakefield and North of England Tulip Society's
annual show

the various overlays which give the petals such extraordinary silkiness of texture arrive at a colour which we call pink, or purple or orange or yellow. In their hands, beauty is reduced to chemistry. A blaze of yellow tulips becomes so much carotenoid. Red flowers are just particles of cyanidin. Orange tulips are merely melanges of carotenoids and cyanidins. But red flowers usually include another pigment called pelargonidin, a different shade of red, which combines with bluish delphinidin to produce purple tulips. Pink tulips are the most complex of all in their mix of ingredients, though the pigments are laid on with a lighter hand. But the bizarre and magical character of the tulip prevailed even in the laboratory. Flowers that, to the scientist's eye, seemed to be the same colour were found, when analysed, to be made up of completely different mixes of pigments. Conversely, flowers that in chemical terms at least, had the same pigments mixed in the same proportions looked completely different. Some seedling flowers were coloured with pigments that did not appear in the flowers of either of the parents. A yellow tulip containing only carotenoids when crossed with another yellow tulip with the same single pigment, may produce seedlings dominated by red cyanidins. Researchers concluded that the red colour must be a recessive trait in yellow hybrids, not always expressed, but lurking there, ready at unexpected moments to bob up and remind breeders of the tulip's wild forebears.

Flower shape has proved as difficult to pin down as flower colour. Over the years, breeders have tried making crosses from Lily-flowered tulips, double tulips and tulips edged with contrasting colours to try and 'fix' certain characteristics in cultivars. But when they crossed the bright red Lily-flowered tulip 'Dyanito' with a tulip that was not Lily-flowered, they found that none of the resulting seedlings had 'Dyanito's' characteristic waisted shape. Fortunately, crosses with the doubtful species *T. acuminata*, which has a long, thin, elegantly-waisted flower, produced many new and useful Lily-flowered seedlings – 'Novired' (bred 1990) and the sulphur-yellow 'Talbion' (bred in 1982). Seedlings bred from the Double Early red and yellow tulip 'Abodement' remained resolutely single, though the old Double Early 'Murillo' sports more easily than any other known tulip; since it was introduced in 1860, 139 different sports have been registered. Crosses with 'edged' tulips were more satisfactory; at least half of the resulting seedlings were 'edged' too.

The sports that 'Murillo' produced were natural mutations, not the result of breeders' crosses. The first Parrot tulips, the 'Monstreuses' noted by French and English growers of the seventeenth century, were also natural mutants. In 1975 a genetic Parrot was produced, the fuchsia-purple 'Amethyst', bred by 'selfing' the

Single Late carmine and white tulip 'Cordell Hull'. Now that the Parrot gene has been to some extent tamed, breeders have a better chance of producing other flowers with the Parrot's characteristic, mad, fringed petals. The tulip's natural ability to change its clothes, to produce flowers that are double rather than single, with petals that may be fringed or cut as well as smooth, flowers that are edged as well as plain, has been its chief fascination. Some cultivars, such as 'Murillo', have exceptionally slippery genes, but other tulips such as the red Single Late 'Bartigon', the lavender-coloured Single Late cultivar 'William Copland' and the cherry-red Darwin Hybrid 'Apeldoorn' are equally prone to sudden bright ideas about the way they should look. Scientists have found that to some extent, this tendency to mutate can be artificially stimulated by bombarding bulbs with X-rays. There are problems though. If the radiation treatment is given early (in August) many tulips emerge deformed the following spring. If the bulbs are irradiated late in the season (November), they seem normal in the first spring after planting, but may refuse to flower the following season. The score is still 'Nature 2, Man 1', though artificial radiation has produced the purplish-red mutants 'Santina' and 'Yvonne' from the deep-red Triumph tulip 'Lustige Witwe'.

There is another trap for breeders too. Most tulips are diploids with two sets of twelve chromosomes (2n=2x=24). Darwin Hybrids are triploid and there are just a few tetraploid tulips (2n=4x=48). The species tulips *T. clusiana*, *T. orphanidea* and *T. sylvestris* are all tetraploid. So is the strong, tall Single Late tulip 'Mrs John T Scheepers' with robust yellow flowers and the carmine and white Triumph tulip 'Judith Leyster'. Breeders like tetrapoloids because they are markedly more robust than diploids. But the catch is that they are all late-flowering and consequently of no use in the cut-flower business. Breeders tried crossing tetraploid tulips with diploid ones, to increase the range of triploids, but there was a catch here too. Most of the seedlings from these crosses turned out to be sterile, so could not be used in further breeding.[23]

In principle, the huge range of wild species should provide tulip breeders with a palette of characteristics unequalled in the flower world. Imagine the breeder, standing like a perfumier, surrounded by ranks of the tulip's wild cousins. What would he reach for to introduce into his perfect tulip? It would depend for whom he was creating this paragon. Growers for the cut-flower market prize early flow- ering above almost anything else, so here *T. pulchella*, which often produces its rounded purple flowers by the end of February, would seem to be a crucial ingre- dient. But *T. pulchella* has refused to cooperate in shotgun marriages arranged by tulip breeders and will not cross-breed with any garden tulip that has been introduced as a possible partner. Then imagine the breeder reaching for *T. turkestanica*, which has anything up to seven flowers on a stem. How useful it would be (again for those in the cut-flower business) to be able to offer customers a wider range of multi-flowered tulips. But once more, the tulip spurns the pimp. *T. turkestanica*, along with other tulips of the Eriostemenes group (*T. tarda*, *T. bakeri*, *T. dasystemon*, *T. saxatiles*), will not cross with garden tulips. Commercial growers would be interested too in finding strains of tulip that were immune to the virus that causes the flowers to break into feathers and flames. (Gardeners on the other hand would kill to get hold of some of those old, broken cultivars.) Here, the species were prepared to help. Absolute resistance to the tulip-breaking virus (TBV) is found in *T. fosteriana* and this resistance has been passed on to several *T. fosteriana* cultivars such as 'Cantata' and the *T. fosteriana* clone 'Princeps'. 'Cantata' has *T. fosteriana*'s fine foliage too. Not many tulips are noted for their leaves, but *T. fosteriana* has bright green foliage, as glossy as an arum's. The famous grower Dirk Lefeber of Lisse (1894–1979) pinpointed a typical irony facing the tulip breeder: when he had raised a seedling of the utmost perfection in terms of form, colour, markings and petal shape, a paragon fit to inspire even the fussiest *lalezari* of the Turkish court, it would always turn out to be a poor, weak grower. Lefeber also pointed out how extraordinarily random the business of breeding was: identical crossings of the same two tulips, carried out within a few hours of each other, could result in two entirely different batches of seedlings. But occasionally, breeders hit on a combination that produced such extraordinary results, everybody else was spurred on with new hope. From a single cross between *T. fosteriana* 'Madame Lefeber' and a Darwin tulip, Lefeber raised 364 seedlings, including the famous tulips 'Apeldoorn' and 'Gudoschnik', all of which were better than existing cultivars. For a tulipman, this was nirvana.

Breeders recognise that tulips can be coaxed, but not bullied. They understand that, hidden in even the most docile-looking flower, an anarchic streak persists. You see it in the little dashes of green that break through the clear red petals of the Triumph tulip 'Hollandia'. You see it in the sinuous mad curl of a petal of 'Mary Belle', a Triumph tulip introduced only two years ago, but evidently still wondering whether it should shock its creators by turning itself into a Parrot instead. You see it in the dagger points of the egg-yolk-yellow tulip 'Yokohama', as needle-sharp as the tulips that seventeenth-century Iznik potters painted on their tiles. You see

273

A florist and his flowers: Albert Tear selecting blooms for the
Wakefield and North of England Tulip Society Show

it in the little sparks of red fire lighting up the double flowers of 'Monte Carlo', which had always supposed that it was yellow. You see it in the surprising sky-blue base of the lustrous dark tulip 'Black Swan', another thoroughbred from the Rijnveld stable. That clear blue bottom was pursued through hundreds of years of breeding by the patient tulip lovers of Flanders, who endowed the flower with so many of its best characteristics.

What is there left to do? I put the question to Geert Hageman of Triflor as we wandered out into the bulb fields surrounding this experimental breeding station at Oude Niedorp in The Netherlands. The land stretched away flat to the horizon, blocked into rectangles of colour like a vast painting by Mondrian. Long black lines of ditches separated the blocks, draining water away to the sea penned up miles away behind the country's coastal barricades. Mr Hageman walked slowly between his rows of flowers, explaining the virtues of one tulip, the problems of another. Only one in a thousand of his tulip seedlings is likely to have a serious future and it would take twenty years to bring that one seedling successfully into the market. Fashion was too ephemeral a creature to follow, he explained. By the time he had created some new cultivar to cater to the present passion for dark-saturated tulips such as 'Queen of the Night' or 'Black Parrot', the stylemongers would have moved on to some new fad. He had to keep his gaze fixed on less transitory goals: re-establishing the tulip's natural elegance of form, its resistance to disease, exploiting its extraordinary capacity for diversity. And which of these thousands and thousands of seedlings so patiently bred, so rigorously assessed, did he dream of at night, I wondered? He walked over to a tiny block of flowers, almost invisible among the vast spreads of red and yellow around us. He bent down, picked a tulip and held it up in front of me. It was a dark striped Bybloemen, not the seventeenth-century 'Viceroy' that had caused so much havoc during the Dutch tulipomania, but a twentieth-century mirror image. Feathers and flames of the deepest purple crept over petals which were the colour and texture of the finest damask; the tulip's base was as pure as snow; in the centre, the stamens held themselves with the dark poise of butterflies' antennae. I had seen the future and it was ravishing.

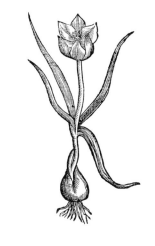

PART II

CHAPTER VIII

TULIPS: THE SPECIES

TULIPS ARE Old World rather than New World plants with the heart-land of the species lying in Central Asia, around the regions of the Tien Shan and the Pamir-Alai. Almost half of the 120 or so species currently recognised grow within a thousand-kilometre radius of this area. All tulips belong to the big family of Liliaceae and grow from bulbs, each of which is covered with a dark brown or black skin, called the tunic. The presence or absence of hairs inside the tunic is one of the ways that botanists identify different species. The flowers are carried on sturdy upright stems which have several leaves, alternate rather than opposite. The number of leaves varies. Sometimes there are only two, but usually there are more and they vary widely in width, length and colour. The single leaf formed by a bulb that is not going to flower (early tulip growers called them 'widows') is usually wider than the norm. Some species have leaves, described as 'undulate', which have waved and crinkled edges.

The flowers are usually borne singly, though some species such as *T. turkestanica* and *T. biflora* carry several flowers on each stem. The shape of the flower and of the petals or perianth segments varies widely. Some flowers make rounded bowl shapes, others splay open into stars. Some have long narrow petals, others, such as *T. maximoviczii* and *T. fosteriana*, native in the Samarkand area of Central Asia, have the broad, generous petals that made them, later, such useful building blocks in the breeding of garden varieties of tulip.

Tulipa suaveolens

T. suaveolens *(T. schrenkii)*
from which Dutch growers bred the Duc van Thol race of early-
flowering tulips

The species tulips generally have six petals, each one separately attached at the base. *T. sylvestris*, however, frequently produces flowers with seven or eight petals. In many species there is a noticeable blotch at the base of the petal, usually more distinct on the inner surface than the outer. Sometimes the blotch is no more than a smudge. Sometimes it makes a distinct star as in some forms of *T. julia* whose red petals have large bold black bases, each outlined with a narrow rim of yellow. There are six stamens and the colour of the pollen varies widely from species to species. In *T. hageri* the pollen is olive-coloured, in *T. bakeri* orange, in *T. clusiana* deep purple. Filaments and anthers also vary in colour. The seedpod develops as an oblong capsule at the top of the stem. Seed sets freely but in an English climate, few species except *T. sprengeri* increase by this means. *T. sprengeri* will flower from seed in about four years. Other tulip species take longer, often up to seven years.

Until recently, botanists divided tulips into two sections, the Eriostemones and the Leiostemones. The Eriostemones had funnel-shaped flowers, tapering to a narrow base. Such flowers are often pinched in at the waist, with filaments hairy at the base. The more diffuse Leiostemones were distinguished by their cup-shaped flowers, which usually had a rounded base. The petals of the tulips formerly placed in this group do not curve in to make a waist above the base, and the filaments of the flowers are smooth (glabrous is the term usually used) where they join the petals.

Traditionally, botanists have used five basic criteria to separate one species from another. They looked at the bulb tunic, to establish if it was hairy inside or smooth. *T. montana* for instance, a native of the Tabriz region of northern Iran, has an exceptionally woolly coat inside its tunic. They looked at the filaments to see if they had hairs at their base, as do *T. saxatilis* and *T. biflora*. They looked at the colour of the flower and the presence or absence of a basal blotch. They looked at the overall shape of the flower and finally at the number and colour of the leaves. In wild populations of tulips there is considerable variation within the same species. Sometimes, for instance, flowers of *T. armena* seem more different from each other than they are from a similar species such as *T. julia*. There have been many revisions of this superbly capricious genus: the latest comes from LWD van Raamsdonk and T de Vries who have proposed two different groups for tulips, the Eriostemones group (with three sub-sections) and the Tulipa group (with five sub-sections)[1].

They use thirty-five different criteria to distinguish between species. Some, such as date of flowering, a variable, dependent on seasonal temperature and rainfall, but, early or late, the researchers found that the species they studied always

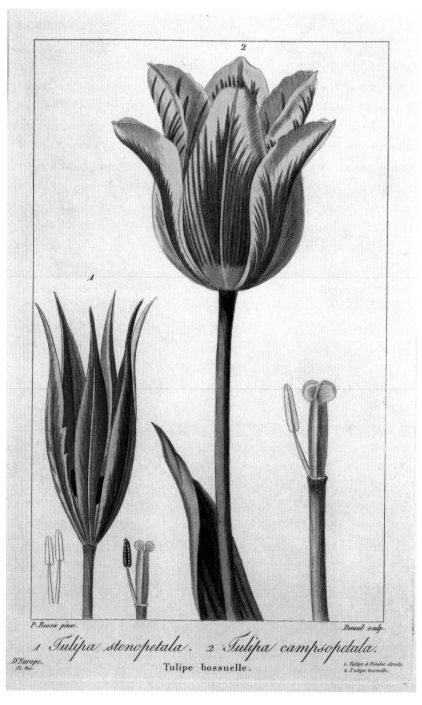

A typical example of the muddle over naming tulip species: T. stenopetala
(most probably T. acuminata *from Bessa's* L'Herbier Générale *(1819)*

282

flowered in the same order. They noted, too, the influence of geography on taxonomy. Tulips of the Eriostemones group migrated west into Europe from the primary gene centre around the Tien Shan and from a secondary centre in the Caucasus. Among the Eriostemones, tulips of the sub-section Australes crop up in Europe, around the Aegean Sea and Asia Minor. Species of the sub-section Saxatiles grow in the Near East and Crete. Tulips gathered in the sub-section Biflores range all the way from Eastern Europe to Central Asia.

So, in the two major groups, tulips which share certain characteristics are now assigned to particular sub-sections. In the Eriostemones group are the Australes (*T. australis, T. biebersteiniana, T. hageri, T. orphanidea, T. primulina, T. sylvestris* and *T. whittallii*), the Biflores (*T. biflora, T. dasystemon, T. neustruevae, T. polychroma, T. sogdiana, T. tarda* and the ancestral grandaddy of the group, *T. turkestanica*) and the Saxatiles (*T. aucheriana, T. bakeri, T. humilis, T. pulchella* and *T. saxatilis*). In the Tulipa group are the Clusianae, found south of the Pamir-Alai and the Himalayas (*T. clusiana, T. linifolia* and *T. montana*), the Eichleres, found in the Pamir-Alai, the Kyzyl-Kum and the Tien Shan (*T. albertii, T. dubia, T. eichleri, T. fosteriana, T. greigii, T. ingens, T. kaufmanniana, T. lanata, T. praestans, T. sosnovskyi, T. subpraestans, T. tschimganica, T. tubergeniana*), the Kolpakowskianae, found predominantly in the mountain ranges of the Tien Shan (*T. altaica, T. lehmanniana, T. tetraphylla*), the Tulipa, closely related to the cultivated tulip and found both in Europe and the Middle East (*T. armena, T. didieri, T. gesneriana, T. hungarica* and *T. suaveolens*) and the Tulipanum, found in Central Europe, Asia Minor, Lebanon, Syria, Iran, Iraq and Afghanistan (*T. agenensis, T. aleppensis, T. julia, T. kuschkensis, T. praecox* and *T. systola*). The number of species 'allowed' in the family depends on who is doing the counting. The *Classified List and International Register of Tulip Names* published in 1996 by the Koninklijke Algemeene Vereeniging voor Bloembollencultuur contains about 120 species. For ease of reference, the following list follows the *Classified List* in continuing to distinguish questionable species such as *T. bakeri* and *T. batalinii*. Some taxonomists for instance now list *T. bakeri* under *T. saxatilis* Bakeri Group and *T. batalinii* as *T. linifolia* Batalinii Group.

Not until the beginning of the nineteenth century was the wealth of species tulips from Central Asia made available to growers in Europe. This had a great deal to do with Dr Eduard Regel (1815–1892), who, after working in the botanic gardens of Gotha, Göttingen, Bonn, Berlin and Zürich, became in 1855 the director of the Imperial Botanic Garden, St Petersburg. Many plants, including previously unknown species of tulip, were brought to him as a result of military expeditions into west and central Asia. Some plants came to Regel from his son, Albert, who was a physician stationed at Kildja in east Turkestan (now Ining in China). Eduard Regel first described many of these new species of tulip in the German magazine, *Gartenflora*, which was one of the most influential horticultural magazines of the time. Scientists and collectors such as Bunge, Fedtschenko, Przewalskii (better known for his horses than his flowers) and Sewerzow followed in the wake of the army in Central Asia, finding yet more fine wild tulips[2]. By the 1870s, Dutch bulb firms such as Van Tubergen recognised the commercial potential of these new beauties and began increasingly to employ their own collectors. The bulbs they brought back were quickly bulked up in the Haarlem bulb fields by growers who were now unparalleled in their expertise and marketing skills. By this time, the use of cultivated tulips was generally in decline in English gardens, but the Central Asian species attracted a great deal of attention. Their dazzling panache (and the current vogue for rock gardens) corresponded with a prevailing snobbery, which set species above cultivars. Species were snob plants, cultivars were not, so the showier species had an assured place in many gardens in Europe.

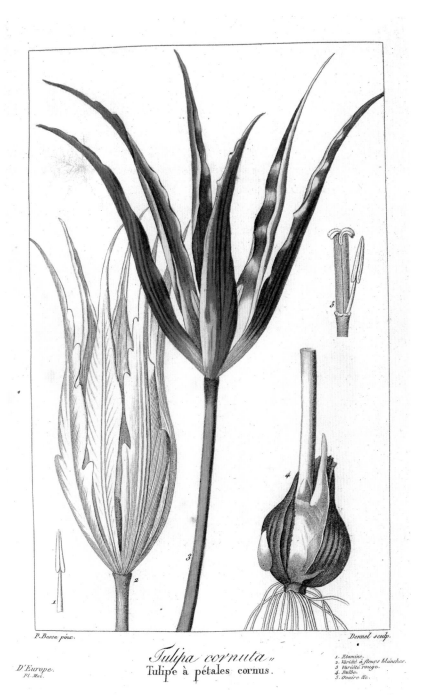

P.Bessa pinx.

Dennel sculp.

Tulipa cornuta »
Tulipe à pétales cornus.

D'Europe.
Pl. Mai.

1. Etamine.
2. Variété à fleurs blanches.
3. Variété rouge.
4. Bulbe.
5. Ovaire &c.

T. acuminata (*formerly* T. cornuta)
from Bessa L'Herbier Générale *(1819)*

285

T. ACUMINATA (VAHL EX HORNEM.)

Height 50 cm. Leaves (3) tall, broad, slightly undulating, glaucous. Crazy, very tall, thin bud opening to creamy flowers, sometimes streaked and flecked with red. Petals long, stringy and very pointed, giving the tulip its species name. They tend to twist in growth. The effect is spidery and mad. Filaments yellow or white, anthers reddish-brown. It is known only in cultivation; with its strange petals never more than half-inch across, it may have been the forerunner of the elegant dagger-petalled tulips detailed in Ottoman manuscripts such as *The Book of Tulips* (c1725).

This was one of several newly introduced species that the Rev. Henry Harpur Crewe had growing in his garden at Drayton Beauchamp Rectory, Tring, Herts, where he was Rector from 1860–1883. Writing in *The Garden* on 20 May 1876, he described *T. acuminata* as 'so quaint and curious that no one who has once grown it likes to be without it'. It flowers from the beginning of April.

T. AGENENSIS (DC.)

Height 20 cm. Leaves (3–5) lance-shaped, smooth, glaucous. Flowers large, bright red, sometimes overlaid with yellow on the outside, with black basal blotch, edged in yellow, which covers from half to a third of the length of the petal. The petals are about three times as long as they are wide, the outer ones more pointed than the inner. Filaments black or blue-black, anthers black. Described

1804. Found as a weed of cultivation in S and W Turkey, NW Iran, also naturalised in the Languedoc, Tarn and Garonne areas of France, and around Bologna and Florence in Italy. It flowers in April.

T. AITCHISONII (HALL)

Height 15 cm. Leaves (3–5) short, very narrow, slightly glaucous. Brilliant red, low-growing flowers open out to a flat star in the sun. Occasionally white flowers are found, with a crimson flush on the reverse of the petals. Very small basal blotch of purplish-black. The filaments and the anthers are the same colour. Flowers April. Found in Afghanistan, Chitral and Kashmir and described in 1938. Considered by some authorities to be a form of *T. clusiana*.

T. ALBERTII (REGEL)

Height 30 cm. Leaves (3–4) close set, broadly lance-shaped, glaucous blue. Flowers glossy vermilion red, orange or yellow, sometimes tinged on the outside with purple. Basal blotch black or dark purple, heart-shaped and bordered with yellow. The petals are long and strappy, the three inner petals forming a cup while the three pointed outer ones curl back on themselves. Filaments yellowish-orange, anthers usually dark purple, sometimes yellow. In the national collection of species tulips at the Cambridge Botanic Garden it grows with an unusually thick stem and long leaves which are crinkled on one edge only. The red petals have a purple streak up the midrib. It is

E.D.Smith del.   Pub by J.Ridgway, 169 Piccadilly July 1831.   Weddell sc.

Tulipa oculis-solis (*T. agenensis*)
from Robert Street's *The Ornamental Flower Garden*
published 1831

6439

H.T.D. del J.N.Fitch Lith

L.Reeve & C.º London

Vincent.Brooks Day & Son Imp

T. albertii
from Curtis's Botanical Magazine *(1879)*

found in Central Asia round the Tien Shan. It was first described in 1877 and is named after Albert Regel, who was a physician stationed at Kildja in east Turkestan.

T. ALEPPENSIS (BOISS. EX REGEL)

Height 45 cm. Leaves (4) thin, glaucous, slightly hairy. Flowers crimson, cup-shaped, the basal blotch black, sometimes narrowly margined with yellow, some-times absent altogether. The outer petals are inclined to reflex in sunshine; the inner ones are slightly shorter and more rounded. Filaments black, anthers black. In flower from March–May. Found in cultivated land in SE Turkey, around Beirut and in Syria. Hall described it from bulbs sent to him by a teacher at the École Française d'Ingénieurs at Beirut, where it grew on land that had been ter-raced to grow mulberry trees. He noted the close alliance between this species and *T. praecox*, though he thought *T. aleppensis* had the better, brighter flower. Hall grew it in a cool greenhouse and remarked on its habit of 'wandering by stolons'. These crept some way from the place where the original bulb was planted and lodged bulbs into crevices of the greenhouse wall.

T. ALTAICA (PALL. EX SPRENG.)

Height 30 cm. Leaves (3) set closely on the stem, pointed, slightly glaucous, erect. Flower opening like a pale lemon-yellow sunburst, no basal blotch, the outsides of the petals washed over with red and green. Filaments yellow, anthers yellow.

Introduced into cultivation by Dr Eduard Regel of St Petersburg Botanic Garden, who first described it in the influential magazine *Gartenflora*. Possibly the species that represents the most northerly limits of the genus, it is found in Central Asia from the Altai Mountains to W Siberia, where it grows at between 1,000 and 6,000 m. It flowers in April.

T. ANISOPHYLLA (VVED.)

Height 30 cm. Leaves (3–4) broad, mid green. Flowers yellow, the outer petals washed over with violet. Anthers yellow. Found in the Pamir-Alai region of Central Asia and first described in 1935.

T. ARMENA (BOISS.)

Height 15 cm. Leaves (3–4) broad, scimi-tar-shaped, very glaucous, often undulat-ing with fine hairs at the margins. They curve up and out in a graceful, though stiff line and have a distinct overlay of red. Flowers very variable, some cup-, some bowl-shaped, crimson, vermilion, yellow, or mixtures of all three. Basal blotch black, navy or yellowish-green, sometimes fan-shaped, sometimes bor-dered with yellow. Yellow flowers may be without a blotch. Filaments blackish-purple, anthers deep purple, occasionally yellow. Flowers from April–June. Found on rocky slopes and screes between 1,000–2,750 m in southern Turkey, NW Iran, Iraq, Transcaucasia. On the Marmaris Peninsula, it grows at much lower altitudes.

T. AUCHERIANA (BAKER)

Height 10–15 cm. Leaves (3–4) narrow, linear, glaucous, glossy, channelled, tinged with pink at the ends. They overpower the tiny flowers, which are low-growing, star-shaped, and vary from pale to deep rose-pink, the outer petals narrower than the inner. They appear in tiny bunches at the base of the seemingly enormous leaves. The shape is similar to that of a crocus. The mauve-pink drifts to a much paler colour at the base on the inside. Filaments yellow, anthers orange. Described 1883. Flowers from April to June. Once found around Teheran, Isfahan in W Iran and in Afghanistan, but now better known in cultivation than in the wild. Considered by some authorities as a form of *T. humilis* with smaller, more star-shaped flowers. It is a tulip of minimal pretension, but adapts well to gardens when grown in well-drained soil in a sunny position, where it will not need lifting and drying off in summer.

T. AUSTRALIS (LINK)

Height 25 cm. Leaves (3–5) long, narrow and folded down the middle. They are closely set on the stem, starting a little above the surface of the ground, slightly glaucous on the upper surface, shiny underneath. Stem narrow, slender with a purplish flush where it meets the flower. Sometimes two stems arise from the same bulb. Flowers yellow, scented, opening from an urn shape into a star. The outer petals are narrower and slightly shorter than the inner ones, the backs flushed with green and pink, most attractive when the flower is in bud. A greenish ridge runs up the centre of the back of the inner petals. The inside surface of both outer and inner petals is bright, clear yellow, no blotch. Filaments yellow, anthers yellow. It flowers in April.

Hall considered this species truly wild in uncultivated hill land along the northern Mediterranean, for example in the Apennines, the Cevennes and the sierras of southern Spain, Morocco and Algeria. He unequivocally identifies one of the yellow tulips shown in Lobelius's (M de l'Obel) text *Plantarum seu Stirpium Historia* published in Antwerp in 1576 as *T. australis* (the other he names as *T. sylvestris*). Other authorities however believe that no tulips are truly native to Europe, though some species have become naturalised, particularly in the area around the Mediterranean, where growing conditions suit them. Tulips of the *australis* type often have a pendulous bud, which straightens up as the flower prepares to open, but this is not a constant characteristic. Hall noted that the same bulb could bear pendulous buds one year and erect ones the next. The species is scarcely distinct from the similar *T. sylvestris* though *T. sylvestris* is generally larger in all its parts and is less eager to set seed. Some authors regard *T. australis* as a subspecies of *T. sylvestris*, but the cytologist William Newton presumed that *T. australis* was the diploid from which the triploid *T. sylvestris* had arisen. The variability of the species delighted the 'splitters' in the world of

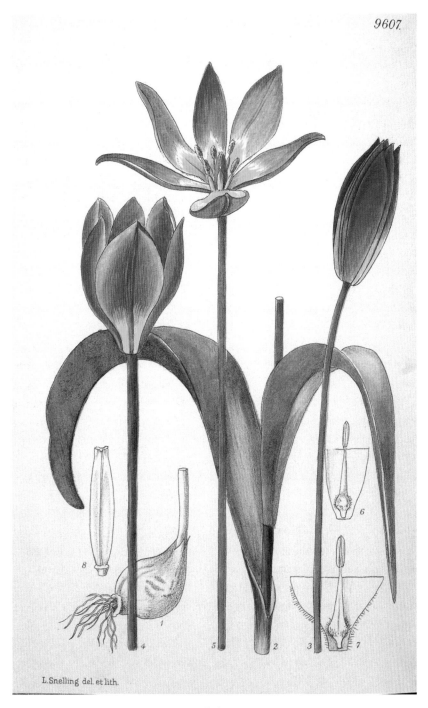

L. Snelling del. et lith.

T. bakeri
from Curtis's Botanical Magazine *(1940)*

291

taxonomy and twenty-seven *australis* lookalikes were given distinct species status. The busy pair Zoz and Klokow alone were responsible in the 1930s for naming ten different species with scarcely distinguishable characteristics. Fortunately the 'clumpers' have prevailed.

T. australis gives its name to one of the main sub-groups of the Eriostemones, which are either yellow selfs, like *T. australis,* or have a purplish anthocyanin superimposed on the yellow ground to give a brownish effect as in *T. orphanidea*. The group's distribution ranges from Central Asia through to Portugal, crossing over into Morocco and Algeria.

T. BAKERI (HALL)

Height 10 cm. Leaves (2–4) bright green and slightly shiny. Slender stem carrying a single erect mauve-purple flower (very occasionally two flowers), which is bell-shaped, the petals long, incurved and spoon-shaped. The backs of the outer petals are stained green while the inner petals have a well-defined green rib up their backs. The purple of the inside is met by a pronounced yellow basal blotch which covers at least a third of the length of the petals. The blotch is usually circled by a ring of muddy white. Filaments orange, anthers orange. Flowers early March. Found around Asomatos in Crete and named after G P Baker who exhibited it at the Royal Horticultural Society in 1895. The bulb is markedly stoloniferous. Some authorities consider *T. bakeri* a cultivar arising from the very similar *T. saxatilis*.

T. BATALINII (REGEL)

Height 8–10 cm. Leaves (5–7) narrow, pointed, edged with red when young. Flower palest lemon-yellow with outer petals slightly longer than the inner. The basal blotch is dull olive. Filaments yellow, anthers creamy-yellow. A charming, ethereal tulip which flowers in late March and April. Found in central Asia. W R Dykes raised hybrid forms by crossing *T. batalinii* with *T. maximoviczii* and the cross gave a series of related tulips in shades of apricot and bronze. Hall disapproved. 'Charming as are these hybrids', he wrote, 'I doubt if they are really wanted in the presence of two such good parental types.' Posterity has proved him wrong. 'Apricot Jewel' has flowers of apricot-orange with a yellow interior. 'Bright Gem' has flowers of sulphur-yellow, flushed with orange. 'Bronze Charm' has sulphur flowers feathered with apricot-bronze, 'Red Gem' has long-lasting flowers of bright red. 'Yellow Jewel' has pale lemon flowers tinged with pink. The species is named after Dr Batalin, a director of the Botanic Gardens at St Petersburg. He sent it to Kew, where it flowered in 1888. It was brought into commerce by P L Graeber, who collected for the Dutch bulb firm Van Tubergen and sent this particular type from Bokhara. *T. batalinii* only differs from the scarlet *T. linifolia* in colour and is treated by some authorities as a cultivar of *T. linifolia* rather than a species in its own right. Rix calls it a pale yellow form of *T. maximoviczii*. Hall set it within the Clusiana group, which also contains

M.S.del. J.N.Fitch.lith   Vincent Brooks Day & Son.Lt.Imp

T. batalinii
from Curtis's Botanical Magazine *(1904)*

293

T. linifolia, T. maximowiczii and *T. clusiana* itself and pointed out that none of this group would cross with tulips of other groups.

T. BIEBERSTEINIANA (SCHULT. F.)

Height 20 cm. Leaves (2–4) bluish-green, widely spaced, strap-shaped. Flowers bright yellow, washed over on the backs of the petals with a dull brownish-green. Scented. This species is found in the Crimea, around Lake Balkhash, in the Caucasus and the Aralo-Caspian region. Flowers early April. Regarded by some authorities as synonymous with *T. sylvestris*.

T. BIFLORA (PALL.)

Height 10–15 cm. Leaves (2) widely spaced on the stem, glaucous, strap-shaped, arching, slightly folded, showing some crimson on edges and backs. Stem carries up to four frail, tiny flowers, urn-shaped in bud. The fragrant flower opens flat and starry, white with a yellow base extending about halfway up the petal. The backs of the outer segments are flushed with green and a greyish-violet. This appears as a wash, which deepens to purplish-pink as the flower ages. The back of each inner petal is marked with a greyish-green midrib. Filaments yellow, hairy below, anthers yellow with purple tip. 'So small' said the Edwardian plantsman E A Bowles, 'that one does not feel they are really Tulips. They were Ornithogalums in their last life perhaps and are slowly working upward.' One of the earliest species to flower, starting early March. Native of SE Russia, the Crimea, Southern Yugoslavia, the Caucasus, E Turkey and N Iran to Afghanistan, extending into Siberia. Grows on steppes, screes, stony and rocky hillsides, where it may flower into April and May. Easy to grow in well-drained stony soil, kept dry in summer. A Victorian fan, writing in the RHS's journal *The Garden* in 1887 called it 'the most persistent flowering tulip in cultivation'. Very similar to the tetraploid *T. turkestanica*, which is larger in all its parts.

Writing in *The Garden* on 22 January 1876 H J Elwes (1846–1922) noted that this 'pretty and peculiar looking' species 'which has been lost or unheard of for many years' had been reintroduced by Haage and Schmidt of Erfurt.

T. BIFLORIFORMIS (VVED.)

Height 15 cm. Leaves (2) widely spaced, the margins often reddish. The creamy-white flowers smell faintly of honey. The backs of the petals are washed over with dull violet. The base is creamy-yellow. Anthers generally violet, sometimes yellow. The species is found in the Tien Shan region of Central Asia, growing on slopes of clay and stone at about 1,900m. It flowers in March.

T. BORSZCZOWII (REGEL)

Height 20 cm. Leaves (3) widely spaced on the stem, glaucous, reflexed, undulate, the margins thinly edged with white. Flowers yellow, orange or vermilion, with a pointed black basal blotch. Inner petals slightly longer than outer. Filaments and

a.2
a.1
a
b
b.1

A.B. del J.N. Fitch. Lith.

Vincent.Brooks Day & Son. Imp.

L. Reeve & Cº London.

T. biflora *and* T. iliensis
from Curtis's Botanical Magazine *(1880)*

anthers blackish-purple. Flowers April. Found in Central Asia and Iran. Similar to *T. armena*. Named after the botanist who gathered this species in the 1860s on the Kara-kum steppe of Turkmenistan, south of the Aral Sea. Later James Aitchison, botanist with the Afghan Delimitation Commission (1884–1885), found it near Herat and wrote 'In early spring the plains between Chasma-salz and Tirphul are coloured with this species, which varies from every shade of red to pure yellow, the base of the perianth always deep purple. The natives collect and eat the bulbs, which are rather nice in flavour.' Aitchison (1836–1898) was a distinguished nineteenth-century field collector who had served with the Bengal Medical Service and with the Kurram Field Force of 1879–1880.

T. BUTKOVII (BOTSCHANTZ.)

Height 15 cm. Leaves (3–4) closely set, broad, reflexed, glaucous, the margins faintly hairy. The solitary red flowers vary from ox-blood to jasper, the outer petals with an oblong basal blotch of maroon. The blotch on the inner petals is smaller. Filaments red, anthers yellow or brown. Flowers towards the end of April. Found in the western Tien Shan, Central Asia, where it grows on shingly slopes at about 1,800–2,000m. Similar to *T. armena*.

T. CARINATA (VVED.)

Height 30 cm. Leaves (3–4) broadly lanceolate, blue-green, the upper part often twisted around the keel. Crimson flowers large, solitary and graceful, the petals arranged in two pronounced whorls. Petals pointed, the crimson flushed on the outside with pink, tapering to a long, downy tip. Basal blotch small, yellow, or black bordered with yellow. Filaments black, anthers black tinged with red. Flowers towards the end of April. Found in Central Asia in the Pamir-Alai, Chulbair and Khodzka-gurgur-ata, where it grows on stony slopes. Similar to *T. ingens*.

T. CELSIANA (DC.)

Height 15 cm. Leaves (3–5) long and narrow, folded in the middle, sometimes edged with reddish tinge, though this colour seems to depend on growing conditions. The leaves are often prostrate, lying twisted along the ground. The stem may carry two or three flowers, drooping in bud, on short pedicels. The scented flower opens to a flat star of clear yellow. The backs of the outer petals, shorter than the inner ones, are flushed with red. Filaments yellow, anthers yellow. Flowers in May two or three weeks after *T. sylvestris* and *T. australis*. Found in the southern range of *T. sylvestris*'s habitat, in southern Spain, Morocco and the Atlas Mountains. Similar to *T. sylvestris* and *T. australis* but smaller and later-flowering than either. It has a distinctly stoloniferous habit. According to Curtis's *Botanical Magazine*, introduced to Kew (as *T. breyniana*) by Francis Masson in 1787. Named by de Candolle in Redoute's *Liliacées* published in 1803 and possibly introduced into cultivation by Dutch florists.

N.º 717

Syd. Edwards del.   Pub. by T. Curtis, St Geo: Crescent Feb. 1. 1804.   F. Sansom sculp.

T. celsiana
from a drawing made at the Botanic Garden, Brompton
Published in Curtis's Botanical Magazine *(1804) as* T. breyniana

Its name celebrates one of them, C Cels. 'Cette plante est cultivée, depuis quelques annees,' wrote de Candolle, 'dans le riche jardin du C. Cels... On ignore le pays natal de cette espèce de tulipe. Le C. Cels l'a reçue de Harlem, sous le nom de Tulipe de Perse ... J'ai donné à cette nouvelle tulipe le nom du Cultivateur-Botaniste.' Hall considered this a good tulip for the rock garden, increasing freely and blooming regularly. It opens widely in the sun and is slightly scented.

T. CHRYSANTHA see T. clusiana var. *chrysantha*

T. CLUSIANA (DC.) LADY TULIP

Height 30–45 cm. Leaves (3–5) long, narrow, upright, and palely glaucous. They are channelled and faintly marked with red. Neatly furled buds open to white flowers, tall and thin, rarely widening to make a star. They are usually single, occasionally two to a stem, the stem itself reddish where it joins the flower. The flower sits bolt upright on its stem. Petals are narrow, tapering, and the backs of the outer segments are washed with crimson, leaving a clear white edge around the margin of the petals. The great beauty of the flowers lies inside, the white set off against a basal blotch of deep purple. Filaments purple-black, anthers purple-black. Flowers in April. Found in Iran, near Shiraz, eastwards to the Himalayas and Tibet, also naturalised in southern Europe, where it grows in damp fields. Wanders freely by underground stolons.

Clusius, after whom this tulip is named, reported in *Curae posteriores* published in Antwerp in 1611 that this tulip had been sent to Florence from Constantinople in 1606. He himself got it from a Florentine called Matthaeus Caccini and flowered it in April 1607. It was even then called 'The Lady Tulip'. Parkinson knew it only as the early Persian tulip and wrote of it as 'this rare Tulipa, wherewith we have been but lately acquainted', but gives an accurate description. 'The root hereof is small, covered with a thicke, hard blackish shell or skinne, with a yellowish woollinesse both at the toppe and under the shell... bearing one flower...and is wholly white, both inside and outside of all the leaves [petals], except the three outermost, which have on the backe of them, from the middle towards the edges, a shew of a brownish blush or pale red colour, yet deeper in the midst, and the edges remaining wholly white: the bottoms of all these leaves are of a darke or a dun tawnie colour and the chives [stamens] and tippes of a darking purple or tawnie also. This doth beare seed but seldom in our countrie.' It is now naturalised in various locations in southern Europe and for a while in the 1920s and 1930s was cultivated as a cut flower along the Riviera.

Described in Curtis's *Botanical Magazine* in July 1811. 'We are indebted to Mr Anderson of Tooley Street for several specimens of this rare species' wrote the editor, 'the bulbs of which were imported by him from Sicily and

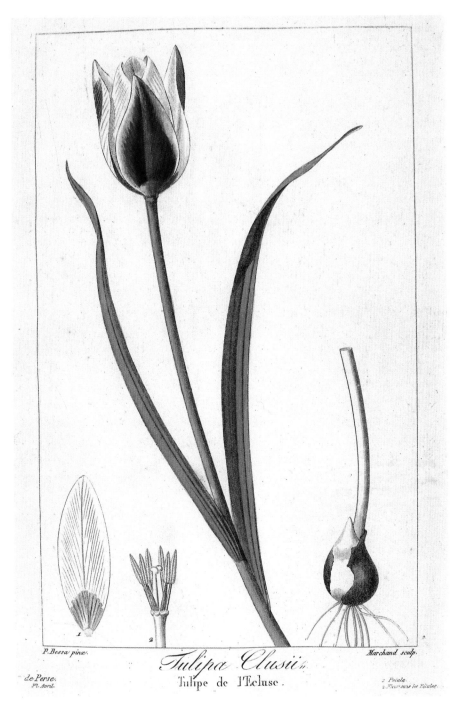

T. clusiana
from Bessa's L'Herbier Générale *(1819)*

flowered in April. It has been known in our gardens as far back as the days of Parkinson and Gerard, by whom it was esteemed tenderer and more difficult to preserve than others of its congeners. Found wild in the vicinities of Florence and Madrid and probably also in Sicily and Portugal.'

The Foreign Secretary Austen Chamberlain, a keen rock gardener, noted it in the 1920s, just emerging in early spring in the garden of Henri Correvon, the leading Continental authority on alpine plants. 'There is a Minister of Foreign Affairs in every country,' said Correvon approvingly afterwards, 'but there is only one who can identify *T. clusiana* by its leaves.'

A delicate and attractive tulip, but shy-flowering. Plant deeply in a warm, sheltered corner. For a while it may produce only leaves and spread, because of its habit of forming new bulbs at the end of long stolons. After a warm summer it may decide to flower.

Several cultivars were raised by Van Tubergen in 1959 including 'Cynthia', which has creamy-yellow flowers, the outsides of the petals flushed red with a green edge. 'Tubergen's Gem' (1969) has yellow flowers with the same red flushed petals.

T. clusiana var. *chrysantha* has golden-yellow flowers, the outside of the petals stained red or purple-brown. There is no basal blotch and the stamens are yellow. The foliage is greener than the type species. Hall noted that var. *chrysantha* had a more southerly distribution, appearing in Afghanistan, Kashmir, and on the slopes of the Himalayas into Tibet. James Aitchison of the Afghan Delimitation Commission thought that this was a high altitude form: 'the higher the plant goes the more yellow and dwarf it becomes,' he wrote.

T. clusiana var. *stellata* grows on a tall, wiry stem. The outer segments are backed with a very pale pink, and the flower does not have the dark basal blotch that characterises *T. stellata*. The stamens are cream.

The 'splitters', those botanists with tidy minds who liked species to conform to recognisable patterns, had a field day with the variable *T. clusiana*, showering around species names (*T. aitchisonii*, *T. aitchisonii cashmeriana*, *T. stellata*, *T. stellata chrysantha*, *T. chitralensis*) as liberally as confetti. Only *T. aitchisonii* is now recognised by some authorities as a separate species. There are however several distinct forms (as noted above). An illustration in W R Dykes's *Notes on Tulip Species* shows a dwarf *T. clusiana* captioned 'from Thibet' growing on a stem only about 6cm high. Dykes passed this bulb on to W C R Newton who worked with Hall at the John Innes Institute. Hall surmised that it was from Little Thibet, a district of northern Kashmir, from where he himself had received bulbs collected from the Rumbur Valley. When grown, these displayed exactly the same dwarf characteristics as Dykes's bulbs. This was the tulip that Hall called *T. aitchisonii*.

T. CRETICA (BOISS. & HELDR.)

Height 20 cm. Leaves (2–3) lance-shaped, shining green. Flowers up to three on a single stem, white, flushed with pink, giving an overall effect of the palest pink, shading to an indistinctly marked yellow base. The outer petals are spreading, the inner ones erect. The backs of the outer petals are tinged with pink and green. All petals have a prominent central vein which is almost transparent. Filaments yellow, anthers yellow. Flowers in early April. Found in the mountains of Crete, around Kisamos, Lapsili, Mt Ida, Cape Malacca, Sitra, Akrotiri, especially in the hedgehog scrub zone. Increases greatly by stolons. Grow in a bulb frame or very sunny place outside in stony soil, kept dry in summer.

T. CUSPIDATA *see T. montana*

T. CYPRIA (STAPF)

Height 20–35 cm. Leaves (3–5) lance-shaped, smooth and glaucous, the two basal leaves set on a short leg, the upper leaves narrow and pointed. Flowers deep crimson, the outside of the petals flushed green at the base. Basal blotch navy-blue, usually edged with yellow. Filaments deep purple, anthers deep purple. Flowers in April. Found in Cyprus, around Myrtou, Panteleimon, Nicosia. The discerning plantsman and nursery-man Claridge Druce had already noted the fine qualities of this species before it was named by Otto Stapf (1857–1933), a British botanist of Austrian origin. For the last eleven years of his life, Stapf edited the influential Curtis's *Botanical Magazine.* He described the species from bulbs sent to England from Cyprus by M T Dawe. It is related to *T. agenensis.*

Not easy to cultivate in England as it starts very early into growth, generally in December, and suffers in the subsequent cold weather. Even under glass the tips of the petals do not colour up properly and the plant is apt to die out.

T. DASYSTEMON (REGEL)

Height 10 cm. Leaves (2) strap-like, narrow, blue-green, very smooth. Flowers (3–5) bright yellow, the outside petals with a strong brownish-purple flush on their backs. The inner petals have a narrower, greener strip along the back of the midrib. No basal blotch. Opens to glossy, star-shaped flower. Filaments yellow, anthers yellow. Native of Central Asia, especially the Pamir-Alai and the Tien Shan mountains above Frunze (Bishkek) in Kirghizia, where it grows in stony places and sub-alpine meadows above 2,000m. It flowers in May and June.

The tulip described by W R Dykes in *Notes on Tulip Species* seems to be *T. tarda* rather than *T. dasystemon.* There was confusion over the two names for some time as the bulbs being distributed commercially as *T. dasystemon* were in fact *T. tarda.*

T. DIDIERI (JORD.)

Height 40–50 cm. Leaves (3–4), upright, lance-shaped, glaucous, the upper stem leaves more narrow and pointed than the lower. Flowers usually deep pinkish-red,

301

though white and yellow forms have been noted. The long, pointed petals may be slightly reflexed. Basal blotch black with a broad, creamy margin. Filaments yellow at the base, black for most of their length and then yellow again at the tips. Anthers purplish-black. A very elegant tulip, opening from narrow, pointed buds. It is found in southern Europe where it flowers in May.

Hall considered this species a stray from cultivation, one of the most common and typical forms of the neo-tulipae. It was first given species status in 1846, described as a native of the region around St Jean de Maurienne in Savoy and also of northern Italy.

John Baker, the Keeper of the Herbarium at Kew at the turn of the century, noted the variability of this species in a description written in 1890. 'Came last year from wild Italian stock in Upper Savoy' he wrote. 'Flowered the first year – was pure yellow. This year the flowers took on a reddish tinge.' Could the variability have anything to do with the age of the bulb? Perhaps its first-season flowering is yellow, settling then to the more usual red.

The *Gardener's Chronicle* of 1899 reported a white form, *T. didieri* 'Alba' flowering in Baylor Hartland's nursery at Ard Cairn, Cork. In the bud state it looked like a 'Niphetos' rose but it smelt of sweet peas.

T. DUBIA (VVED.)

Height 25 cm. Leaves (2–4) broad, glaucous and distinctly wavy along the edges. Flowers yellow, the outer petals covered over almost the whole of their backs with a bluish-pink flush. Basal blotch orange, fading indistinctly into the yellow of the upper part. Filaments orange, anthers yellow. Found in the western Tien Shan, Central Asia, especially around the area of the Chimgan valley, northeast of Tashkent, where it grows on slopes of earth and stone above 1,800m. It flowers in May and June. Similar to *T. kaufmanniana*.

T. EDULIS (BAKER)

Height 15 cm. Leaves (2–6) long, channelled, usually lying on the ground. The bracts carried on the pedicel about 2 cm under the flower are a marked characteristic of the species, so marked that some authorities assign this flower to a different genus, *Amana*. Flowers (1–2) are ivory, the outsides of the petals veined and feathered in dark reddish purple or mauve. Basal blotch green, flaring into a dominant yellow flame. Filaments pale green at base, almost white above, anthers yellow-brown. Found in NE China (round Kiangsi, Chekiang, Hupeh, Shantung), Korea and S Japan (Kyushu, Honshu, Shikoku) at the extreme eastern limit of the distribution of the genus, growing in meadows along rivers at low altitudes. Flowers from late winter to spring. There is a type *latifolia* which has leaves that are both shorter and broader.

Hall argued for the separation of this tetraploid into an entirely different genus, *Amana*, because of particular morphological oddities regarding its ovaries and bracts. The ovary of the flower is drawn out almost into a style, and just below the flower, the stem bears two, sometimes up to four, long thin bracts, about 2–3cm long. Although some species have short stem leaves, no other tulip has bracts similar to these. The stem proper is underground, the flowers borne on slender, drooping pedicels about 6cm long.

Siebold, who first gave this tulip its specific name, said that the Chinese and Japanese extracted starch from the bulbs of this species. They also roasted them and ate them like chestnuts.

Although this tulip adapts easily to garden conditions, it has little garden value. It is markedly stoloniferous and seems keener to make these underground stolons than to flower. The flowers, when they arrive, are small and insignificant, the most miniature of any tulip.

T. EICHLERI (REGEL)

Height 30cm. Leaves (4–5) broad, pointed, glaucous, the lowest and biggest at ground level, the upper ones shorter and narrower. Enormous, showy flowers opening out to a wide-mouthed bell, all the petals slightly recurved, giving the flower a definite waist. The tips of the petals have tufts of short white hairs. Colour: a clear bright crimson-scarlet, with a brilliant sheen on the inner surface of the petals. The outer surfaces are buff, especially those of the three outer petals, so the brilliant colour does not show in bud. There is a large round basal blotch on the outer petals, black

with a yellow margin. This does not show on the backs of the petals. The blotch is wedge-shaped on the inner petals and shows on the back. Filaments purplish-black, anthers purplish-black. This is a Central Asiatic tulip, found in SE Transcaucasia and NW Iran, where it grows on dry slopes and in cornfields, flowering in April and May. Hall considered this one of the best species for garden use. It grows easily in a sunny place outside, kept dry in summer, and increases rapidly from offsets. Some authorities deny this species separate status, considering it a form of *T. undulatifolia*. It is named after Herr Eichler who first discovered it near Baku.

Although grown at Kew in the late 1870s and 1880s, this tulip did not generally come into commerce until the turn of the century, when the bulb company Van Tubergen employed an explorer called A Kronenburg to find flowers with market potential. Kronenburg, who had spent much of his working life in Asia Minor collecting insects for museums, travelled for Van Tubergen from 1899–1909 along the frontier between Russia and Turkey. He also sent material back from northern Iran, Bokhara and Pamir up to the border with Tibet.

It was described at the beginning of 1876 in *The Garden* (p47) as 'A very showy species, native of Georgia…introduced by Mr Elwes, and first flowered in the spring of this year'. Henry Elwes, an eminent gardener living at Colesborne in Gloucestershire, modestly put the record

6177

W.Fitch. del et Lith.

Vincent Brooks Day & Son Imp.

T. eichleri *(formerly* T. baetica*)*
from Curtis's Botanical Magazine *(1875)*

straight in the following issue of the magazine. Writing in *The Garden* on 22 January 1876 he said, 'This is not quite the case, as though I do believe I was the first to flower it in England, I had nothing to do with its introduction. My bulbs came from Dr Regel of St Petersburg, and from my friend Herr Leichtlin of Carlsruhe. I rather fancy that the plant was introduced by Messrs Haage and Schmidt of Erfurt, under the name of *Tulipa julia*, but am not sure of this.'

T. FERGANICA (VVED.)

Height 25cm. Leaves (3–5) closely set, can be broad or narrow, but lance-shaped, reflexed, glaucous, the margins distinctly wavy. Flowers (1–2) are star-shaped, yellow, with the backs of the petals washed over with a pale milk-chocolate colour. No basal blotch. The petals are downy at their tips. Filaments orange-yellow, anthers orange. Found in Central Asia, especially in the Alai, Ferganskiy and Chatkal mountain ranges where it grows on stony slopes at about 1,800m. It flowers in April and May. Closely related to *T. altaica* and *T. dubia* and named after one of its habitats, the Ferganskiy mountain range in the Tien Shan region.

T. FOSTERIANA (HOOG EX W IRVING)

Height 15–50cm. Leaves (3–5) widely spaced on a stem that is pink-tinted. They are sometimes almost as broad as they are long and a bright, glossy green. This is the largest and most brilliant of the Central Asiatic tulips, with petals that can be 15cm long. Vivid red flowers with petals that are bluntly rounded rather than pointed, open out wide in the sun. Basal blotch black, sometimes making two or three peaks on each petal, the blotch boldly edged with yellow. Filaments black, anthers blackish-violet. Found in Central Asia, especially in the mountains south of Samarkand, where it grows in deep soil among limestone rocks at *c*1,700m, flowering in April. Faintly scented. It is easily grown in a sunny place in well-drained soil, kept dry or lifted in summer.

The species was introduced into commerce by Joseph Haberhauer, one of Van Tubergen's collectors. J M C Hoog of Van Tubergen remembered that 'he lived in Samarkand and was the man to whom we owe the magnificent tulip which to honour Sir Michael Foster I called *T. fosteriana*. He collected these in 1904 in the mountains near Samarkand, and I twice got important quantities. It is curious that the splendid variety which I called "Red Emperor" only appeared in the first importation, not afterwards. In 1914 he penetrated deep into Bokhara and collected a large quantity of exquisite things. Alas the cases containing these had arrived at the Russo-Austrian frontier when the war broke out. Needless to say they stopped there and were lost. This loss cost me several hundred pounds, and what is more serious, how and when can we get again the good things which then got lost?'

There seem to be at least two distinct forms. One has large, broad leaves with a

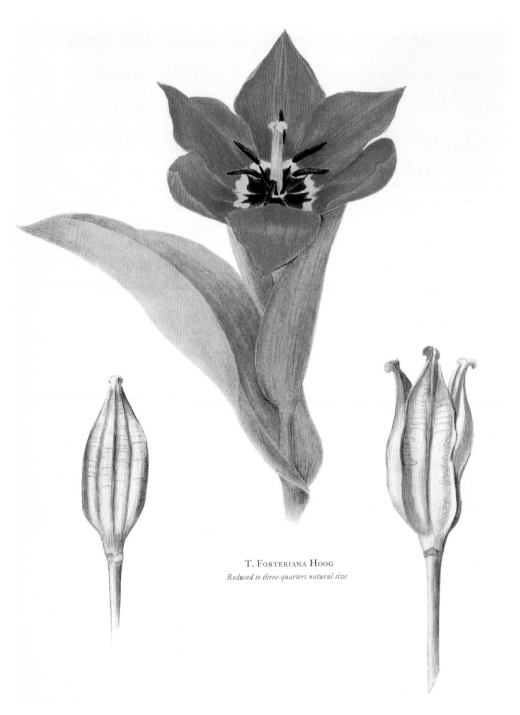

T. Fosteriana Hoog
Reduced to three-quarters natural size

The brilliant T. fosteriana *from* Notes on Tulip Species
by WR Dykes

distinct purple-red line along the edge and is at least 30 cm tall. The blotch at the base of the petals is variable. It may be all yellow or it may be absent altogether. When the blotch is present, the filaments and anthers are black with purple pollen, as described above. When there is no blotch, the filaments and anthers are yellow.

The second form is dwarf (see 'Princeps' below) with spreading foliage that can be up to 10 cm wide, the leaves telescoped into a rosette. The stem is usually no more than 15 cm high. The flower shows the same variations as the taller forms. It seems to miss its summer baking more than the tall form and so does not always flower or increase as well in the garden.

Crossed with *T. greigii* and *T. kaufmanniana*, *T. fosteriana* produced a race of useful Fosteriana hybrids. 'Princeps' has a very broad leaf at least 11 cm wide and flowers on a short stem, no more than 20 cm high. The flower appears almost from between the leaves, and is large but formless. Pointed basal blotch, black edged with yellow. 'Red Emperor' (syn. 'Madame Lefeber') is much larger, bolder. This variety was crossed with Darwin tulips to produce an important race of Darwin hybrids.

T. GALATICA (FREYN)
Height 20 cm. Leaves (4) broad, erect and very glaucous, distinctly hairy on the edges, which are crinkled. The two stem leaves are narrower than the basal ones. The reflexed petals are broad and bluntly

pointed, pale yellow inside, the outsides smoked with a greenish-brown. The basal blotch is yellowish-grey or olive-green. Filaments yellow, anthers yellow. Supposed to be a Turkish native. Flowers in May. Smaller and less telling than other yellow tulips, most probably a yellow form of *T. armena*, collected near Amasya.

T. GESNERIANA (LINNAEUS)
The collective name that Linnaeus gave in 1753 to a miscellaneous group of old cultivars.

T. GOULIMYI (SEALY ET TURRILL)
Height 25 cm. Leaves (3–5) closely set, may be broad or narrow, reflexed and glaucous, the margins often undulating. Flowers (1–2) orange or brick-red with no basal blotch. Filaments orange-yellow, anthers orange. Found on the island of Kythira in southern Greece.

T. GREIGII (REGEL)
Height 45 cm. Leaves (3–5) quite closely set and reflexed on the pink or brown-tinged stem. This is a most distinct species, with dark purple markings in the form of long stripes on the glaucous foliage. The leaves are long and pointed, but get shorter and narrower as they climb the stem. The large flower has a squared-off base, and the outer, blunted petals reflex considerably at the tip, giving a waisted effect. The inner petals are broad and rounded and remain erect. The colour varies widely from brilliant orange-scarlet, clear and shining, to

orange, yellow or cream. Some flowers are multi-coloured. The colour is slightly less bright on the reverse of the petals. The blotch may extend over a quarter of the petals, dark purple or black on red forms, red on yellow forms. The filaments may be black or yellow, the anthers purple-black. It is a native of Central Asia, especially in the valleys of the Tien Shan and the Syr-Dar'ya, where it grows on earthy slopes, and flowers in April. Although it rarely makes offsets, it is easily grown in well-drained rich soil in full sun, either kept dry in summer or dug up and ripened under cover. There are several cultivars, including 'Red Riding Hood' raised in 1953.

'I believe that P L Graeber, a German who lived in Tashkent, was the first to send large quantities of *T. greigii* bulbs to Europe', wrote J M C Hoog of Van Tubergen's. 'When I became acquainted with him, there was already since five or six years, large quantities of *T. greigii* bulbs on the European market, which were distributed by a horticultural establishment in Riga. It is certain that these came from Graeber. The idea then occurred to me that a man so fully equipped to collect bulbs in the steppes, might also be useful to bring into cultivation the numerous tulips described by Albert Regel. He then arranged with me that for a given sum, he would travel up to the eastern frontier of Turkistan and collect for me. At the same time others of his men, assisted by his wife, continued to collect *T. greigii*.'

The species, one of the first to be introduced commercially from the wild, flowered in cultivation in 1871, having been sent to St Petersburg by Albert Regel. It was named after the president of the Russian Horticultural Association by Regel's father, Eduard. The collector wrote: 'It inhabits the hilly steppes of the Sir Darja region, bulbs growing among natural vegetation, grasses, *Rosa berberidifolia*, ixioliron, corydalis, eremurus etc. No rain for five months in the summer. Bulbs a foot deep in heavy clay soil.'

By 1876 it was being grown by Rev. Henry Harpur Crewe in his garden at Drayton Beauchamp Rectory, Tring, Hertfordshire where he was rector from 1860–1883. Writing in *The Garden* 20 May 1876, he commended it as 'by far the best Tulip which I have seen for many a day... For some weeks past its handsome brown-spotted leaves have been a conspicuous ornament to the garden... It appears to be a very hardy and healthy species and comes up freely from seed.' In a later issue of *The Garden* (1900) F W Burbridge noted that the species had seeded freely in Italy and that some fine forms were being sold by Messrs Damman & Co. of San Teduccio. Unsuccessful attempts to hybridise the species were made at this time at the Paris Botanical Garden.

T. greigii 'Aurea' makes a floppy, formless flower of brilliant orange-scarlet. The wide leaves are marked with long dashes of purple, like a printed-out morse code. There is a purplish flush up the centre of the outer petals, which are very broad. The outer petals have a black blotch, the inner ones a yellow blotch. The stamens are big, spade-like, creamy yellow. A tulip of massive substance.

T. GRENGIOLENSIS (THOMMEN)

Height 25–40 cm. Leaves (3–4) pointed, glaucous, slightly wavy. Flowers cup-shaped, opening to form a star. Petals pale yellow, edged or striped with crimson. There are also red forms and pale yellow forms without the crimson edge. Blotch dark olive-green. Filaments black, anthers black. Found in Switzerland, the country's only endemic tulip, it takes its name from its home at Grengiols in the Haut-Valais, northeast of Brigue, where it grows at 900m. The species was described in 1946 by an amateur botanist, Édouard Thommen (1880–1961), who after a career in the Bureau International du Travail devoted himself to a study of the wildflowers of the Tessin and Valais regions. Because of changing agricultural practices, it is now extinct in its native region, but bulbs were collected in the 1960s by a French botanist from Grenoble University and sent to Holland, where they were bulked up by a Dutch firm. The species was first exhibited at the Chelsea Flower Show in 1975. It flowers in May.

T. HAGERI (HELDR.)

Height 20 cm. Leaves (2–7) longer than the flower stems, strap-shaped, faintly undulate, the green sometimes heightened by a dark purplish-red rim. They hug the ground to make a straggling star. Flowers (1–4) globe-shaped, dull coppery-red, a green or buff overlay showing substantially on the backs of the petals. The flower gets redder as it ages. Basal blotch dark olive-green, sometimes almost black, sometimes finely edged with yellow. Filaments brown or olive, anthers brown or olive. Found in the Eastern Mediterranean around Parnassus in Greece, Gallipoli, Smyrna, where it flowers towards the end of April. There is a variety 'Splendens' in which the flowers are bronze, tinted with red. The outside of the petals of this variety are dark red. Considered by some authorities to be a variant of T. orphanidea, and in the national collection of tulip species at Cambridge Botanic Garden, shown as T. orphanidea 'Hageri'. Sir Daniel Hall, however, maintained that T. hageri was the older and more stable of the two and that T. orphanidea had originated from T. hageri possibly by hybridising with T. australis. It is named after Friedrich Hager of Hanover who was with the botanist Theodor Heldreich (1822–1902) when he first found the flower around the ruins of Deceleia on Parnassus. This is a very good garden tulip which grows easily in a warm, well-drained situation.

T. HETEROPHYLLA ([REGEL] BAKER)

Height 10–15 cm. Leaves (2–4) stand sharply upright and are deeply channelled with wavy margins. When the buds first appear, they droop on the stem, but the flowers open to an upright cup shape. The insides of the petals are yellow, the outsides deeply stained with purple or green. There is no basal blotch.

T. Hageri Heldr.

T. hageri *from* Notes on Tulip Species
by WR Dykes

Filaments yellow, anthers yellow. It has the same elongated style as *T. edulis*. Found in Central Asia, especially the Tien Shan, where it grows on stony slopes and in alpine meadows above 2,500m. It flowers in June and July.

T. HOOGIANA (FEDTSCH.)

Height 45–50cm. Leaves (3–5) widely spaced on a dark, reddish-brown stem. The foliage is broad and relatively horizontal in growth. The leaves are sharply folded, strongly reflexed and a pale greyish-green. This species has the unusual habit of forming small bulbils in the axils of its leaves. The flower is ludicrously outsized for its height, the brilliant red petals slightly feathered, and not so strident (less orange) than *T. tubergeniana*. The tall, looped blotches form an inner flower of black. This tulip is slightly fragrant when it first comes out, but floppy. Filaments black, anthers dark wine-coloured, pink, beige or black. Found in Central Asia in the mountains of Turkmenistan, especially the Kopet Dag, where it grows on stony slopes, flowering in April and May. This tulip was named after J M C Hoog, head of the bulb firm van Tubergen. It was one of the many tulip species collected for van Tubergen's by P L Graeber.

This is a magnificently showy tulip, though because its petals are relatively narrow in relation to their length, the flower does not make a good shape. Like all tulips, it does best in a warm, sheltered spot. Hall noted that 'the bulbs have a habit of descending (as deep as two feet in the light Merton soil) and may easily be overlooked in lifting'.

T. HUMILIS (HERB.)

Height 10cm. Leaves (2–5) long, thin, channelled, slightly glaucous. The flowers are cup-shaped, but open to a star in sun, varying from pale pink, through crimson to purple. The inner petals are longer and wider than the outer ones. The basal blotch is yellow (very occasionally blue or purple) and covers at least a third of the petals. Filaments yellow, anthers yellow or purple. Found in southeastern Turkey, north and west Iran, northern Iraq and Azerbeidjan, where it grows on rocky slopes or thin alpine turf just below the snow line at 1,000–3,500m. It flowers between April and June.

T. humilis is a very variable species and it is possible that species such as *T. aucheriana* are actually variants of *T. humilis*. *T. humilis* was first described by the botanist William Herbert, who based his description on a bulb sent from Iran in 1838. Edmond Boissier then described and separately named *T. violacea*, also from Iran, in 1860, followed by Fenzl, who named *T. pulchella* from a bulb sent from the Cilician Taurus. In cultivation these species seemed distinct, but the distinctions muddied in 1930 when G Egger, collecting for van Tubergen's, sent back a number of bulbs all collected in the same locality, south of Tabriz near Lake Urmia in northwest Iran. When they flowered, the group variously showed the typical characteristics of all three different 'species' and every kind of mutation in between. Tulips laugh at taxonomy.

'It is reasonable to regard this group as no more than a single species,' wrote Hall, 'though in particular localities segregates have established themselves which, by reason of their uniformity and power of breeding relatively true, may be worthy of subspecific rank. The determination of a species must, however, always remain a matter of opinion and judgment, into which the geographical distribution and the extent of variation in the field should carry weight.'

J E T Aitchison, the botanist travelling with the Afghan Delimitation Commission, wrote in 1880 of this species in Badghis and the Har-Rud valley. 'This small tulip very like an anemone was common everywhere in the moist, clayey soil especially where there had once been cultivation. Usually one flower, not infrequently two or even three.'

The first bulbs of this species to be cultivated were sent to England in 1838 by the Austrian explorer Theodor Kotschy (1813–1866), who gathered them above Derwend in the Elbur Mountains north of Teheran. Between 1838 and 1843 he was collecting plants in Iran, from where he sent bulbs of *T. humilis* to the Reverend William Herbert (1778–1847), a botanising parson. Herbert, who gardened at Spofforth, nr Harrogate, Yorkshire, was responsible for popularising many of the bulbous plants then being introduced from the near East, and

T. humilis flowered in his garden in April 1844.

The species was reintroduced by Henry John Elwes in 1880, and popularised by the firm of van Tubergen, whose bulb collector, A Kronenburg, sent them from Salmas, a mountainous district to the north of Lake Urumia in Azerbeidjan.

This is an easily grown tulip, excellent for pans and rockeries, though the buds will not develop if the bulbs are starved of moisture in spring.

'Eastern Star' has rose flowers with a yellow base, the outsides of the petals flamed with bronze-green.

'Magenta Queen' has lilac flowers with a yellow centre, the outsides of the petals licked with green flames.

'Odalisque' has light-purple flowers with a yellow base.

'Persian Pearl' has flowers of a bright cyclamen-purple, each with a yellow base. The outsides of the petals are washed over with pale grey.

T. HUNGARICA (BORBÁS)

Height 15cm. Leaves (2–3) broad and bluntly pointed, usually arranged with two at the base and the third up the stem. The clear-yellow flower opens widely, the outer petals bluntly pointed, the inner ones rounded. There is a dark stain at the base. Filaments yellow, anthers purple, pollen yellow or olive-coloured. This is a strongly scented tulip, first described in 1882 after its discovery high among limestone rocks at Kazan in the Danube gorge, Hungary.

T. ILIENSIS (REGEL)

Height 20 cm. Leaves (2–4) upright, deeply channelled, glaucous with slightly hairy edges. Flowers (1–5) yellow, the outsides of the petals stained crimson or dull green. No basal blotch. Filaments yellow, anthers yellow. Found in Central Asia, especially Turkistan around the Pamir-Alai, where it flowers in May. Very close to *T. kolpakowskiana* but smaller in all its parts and flowering at least a fortnight earlier.

T. INGENS (HOOG)

Height 45 cm. Leaves (3–6) closely spaced on the reddish-coloured stem, broad, pale in colour. A pretty flower, wide and cup-shaped, the petals with a slight twist. A tiny pointed peak at the ends of the petals is whitish in colour. The backs of the outer segments are buff, but the inner surfaces are brilliant scarlet. Large black basal blotch, spoon-shaped, extending over a quarter of each petal. There is no yellow margin. Filaments black, occasionally dull yellow, anthers black, dark brown or wine-coloured. Not a good doer in the garden. This is a relatively recent introduction from Turkestan, one of the tulips collected by Graeber in the area around Bokhara. It flowers towards the end of April.

T. JULIA (K KOCH)

Height 30 cm. Leaves (3–4) lance-shaped, slightly glaucous, channelled, often reflexed on a brown-tinged stem. The flower opens to a wide cup, the colour ranging from dull crimson to orange-red, the outsides of the petals flushed with a white bloom giving a pink effect, or with yellow, which turns the outsides orange. The short basal blotch is greenish-black, sometimes thinly edged with yellow. Filaments black, yellow at base, anthers yellow or purple. Found in the southern Transcaucasus, northwest Iran and eastern Turkey, especially around Agri and Erzerum where it grows on dry, stony hillsides between 1,600 and 2,400m. It flowers in May.

The species was named by Karl Heinrich Emil Koch, a German botanist and director of the Royal Botanic Garden, Berlin. From 1836 to 1838 and 1843 to 1844 Koch travelled widely in northeastern Anatolia, journeying by way of Trabzon, Ispir, Hopa, Erzerum, Mus, Malazgirt, Kagizman and Kars. He described seven different species of bulbs from NE Anatolia.

The species is very similar to *T. armena* though *T. armena* is generally larger. The chief difference lies in the bulb tunics of the two species. *T. julia* has a thick, felt-like layer of hairs around the bulb.

T. KAUFMANNIANA (REGEL)

Height 20 cm. Leaves (2–5) closely set on the stem, which is often red-tinged. Foliage broad, slightly undulating, grey-green with darker veining. The bud is elongated and coloured from the beginning. The flowers (1–5) have a characteristic shape, quite unlike other tulips. The long, bluntly pointed petals reflex widely about a third of the way up from the base, which gives it its common name, the Water-Lily tulip. It opens to a wide, flat star. The colour varies widely from white and cream through yellow to a brickish kind of red. A typical flower is creamy-white inside, deepening near the base to yellow, with a band across each petal of indistinct red next to the yellow. The backs of the outer petals are slightly stained with red and purple. The flower is slightly fragrant. Basal blotch fan-shaped and bright yellow, covering almost half the petal and, at its end, fading indistinctly into the background colour. Filaments yellow, anthers yellow. Found in Central Asia, in Turkestan, especially the western Tien Shan, east of Tashkent, where it grows on stony slopes in the mountains, flowering in April and May. In gardens it tends to be much earlier in its flowering (sometimes the first week in March) which can be a problem. It is a good doer and in the right situation increases freely. This is one of the easiest of the species to grow. Plant bulbs deep in a dry and sheltered spot. It tends to form 'droppers', which often go a foot deep and sideways from the parent bulb.

The species has been much crossed with *T. greigii* and *T. fosteriana* to produce an excellent race of garden tulips. In the wild it seems to hybridise with *T. greigii*, *T. dubia* and *T. tschimganica*.

It was introduced into commerce by Graeber, who collected in Tashkent and Bokhara. 'It was he,' wrote J M C Hoog of van Tubergen, 'who first sent the colour varieties of *T. kaufmanniana* that I named "Aurea", "Brilliant" and others, which served to build up the exceedingly beauti-

ful colour varieties of *T. kaufmanniana* we now have.' The species got an FCC (First Class Certificate) from the RHS in 1897 and was exhibited by Wallace and Barr in 1900.

T. kaufmanniana was immediately recognised as an excellent garden plant, not least by the great plantsman and gardener E A Bowles of Myddleton House, Enfield. Writing to Bowles in a letter dated 1902, Hoog said 'One or two per cent of the collected bulbs are bright yellow and a still smaller percentage is a concolorous bright scarlet. As in a wild state *T. greigii* and *T. kaufmanniana* grow alongside, intermediate forms occur, but strange to say, the influence of *T. greigii* only seems to come in the foliage.'

T. KOLPAKOWSKIANA (REGEL)

Height 20 cm. Leaves (2–4) generally narrow, upright, deeply channelled, glaucous with wavy margins, but very variable. Often has several stems, or elongated pedicels, each carrying a flower. The buds at first are nodding, straightening as they open into first cup-shaped, then starry flowers. The petals are long and pointed, bright yellow inside, the backs of the petals washed over with a purplish-red. No basal blotch. Filaments yellow, anthers yellow. This is a variable species, a native of Central Asia, especially the northern Tien Shan and the southern Ala Tau, where it grows on rocky slopes and in scrub to 2,000m, flowering in April and May. It is easily grown in well-drained soil in a sunny position.

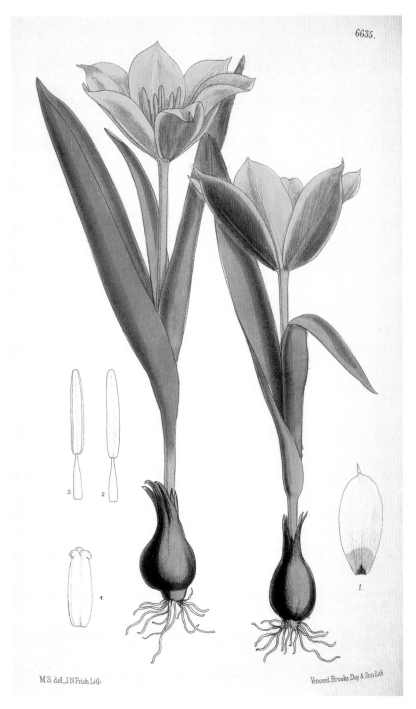

6635.

M.S. del. J.N Fitch Lith.

Vincent Brooks Day & Son Lith

T. kolpakowskiana
from Curtis's Botanical Magazine *(1882)*

T. KURDICA (WENDELBO)

Height 15 cm. Leaves (2–7) long and thin, usually longer than the stem, with dark wine-coloured margins. Globe-shaped flowers of a bright, rich brownish-red, the outsides of the petals often buff overlaid with green or purple. There is a greenish-black blotch at the base of the flower. Filaments brown or olive, anthers brown or olive. Found in northeastern Iraq where it grows on stony slopes by melting snow at 2,400–3,000m. It flowers in May and June.

T. KUSCHKENSIS (SEALY)

Height 30 cm. Leaves (3–5) narrow, upright, lance-shaped, widely spaced on the glaucous stem, which is usually shorter than the leaves. Flowers brilliant scarlet, cup-shaped, the outer petals rolling back on themselves. The basal blotch is black and extends halfway up the petal. Filaments black, anthers black. A thick coat of wool like a sheep's fleece lies under the bulb tunic. A native of Central Asia, especially in the loamy soil near the border between Turkestan and Afghanistan, where it flowers in April and May. This is a difficult species to establish in the garden.

T. LANATA (REGEL)

Height 40 cm. Leaves (4) may be broad or narrow, glaucous, reflexed, with red margins. They are pinched in at the top. The large, elegant, showy flowers are oblong in bud, brilliant vermilion-scarlet but not glossy. The petals are pointed and tip out very slightly at the top.

There is a bloom on the backs of the petals, cream, buff and very pale pink. Very neat, rounded basal blotch, olive-black, thinly bordered with yellow. Filaments black, anthers deep purple. A superb tulip. It comes from Baldschuan, Bokhara and the Pamir-Alai but also occurs in Kashmir, where it is an introduction and grows on the roofs of temples and mosques, especially around Srinagar. It flowers in April and lasts longer in flower than most other species. Its name comes from the inside of the bulb tunic, which is densely covered with soft wool.

It was introduced into commerce by a German, George Egger, who collected for van Tubergen's. 'He used to live in Tabriz, northwestern Iran' wrote J M C Hoog of van Tubergen, 'and he sent me from 1929–1933 a good quantity of the magnificent *T. lanata*.'

'One of the very finest and most brilliant tulips' wrote Hall in *The Genus Tulipa*. 'Hardy and successful in cultivation. It is difficult to exaggerate the elegance and brilliance of a group of it when open in sunshine in the garden.'

T. LEHMANNIANA (MERCKL.)

Height 20–25 cm. Leaves (2–4) long, thin, very glaucous, undulating. Nodding buds open to flowers which may be yellow or rich crimson, flushed scarlet or reddish-brown on the backs of the petals. Basal blotch black, dark olive-green, or purple. Filaments black, anthers yellow. Found in Central Asia, Afghanistan and NE Iran, where it flowers in April.

L.Snelling del et lith

9370

T. kuschkensis *from* Curtis's Botanical Magazine *(1934)*
Drawn from a bulb at the John Innes Institute, sent, via van
Tubergen's, from Professor Fedtschenko at Leningrad who had found
it on the border between USSR and Afghanistan

317

T. LINIFOLIA (REGEL)

Height 10 cm. Leaves (3–7), short and thin, are closely set on the stem. They sometimes have a faint pink line around their rims. The flowers are star-shaped, an exceptionally glossy soft red inside, slightly duller outside. Small black basal blotch, often edged with a pale cream-yellow. Filaments yellow or black, anthers greyish-yellow or black. Found in Central Asia, particularly along the banks of the Vakhsh river in Tajikistan, northern Iran and Afghanistan, where it flowers in May.

This tulip is scarcely distinguishable from *T. maximoviczii*. Its specific name comes from the numerous narrow leaves which clothe the stem or spring from the base of the plant.

It was described in *The Garden* (13 May 1893) as 'a delightful species...not much known as yet, but [it] will assuredly become popular, as it is a very hardy, free-growing kind, not showing the same uncertain character as *T. greigii*'.

Hall in *The Genus Tulipa* considered it 'one of the most beautiful species in cultivation, not large but graceful and brilliant. It should have a deep pocket in a warm place in the rock garden, exposed to the sun but sheltered from the wind, when in the sunshine it will form a patch of colour of unrivalled intensity.'

T. MARJOLETTII (E P PERRIER & SONGEON)

Height 40 cm. Leaves (3–4) greyish, upright and quite broad, similar in proportion to a garden tulip, though made on a smaller scale. The flowers are pale yellow or cream, edged delicately with pink. The outsides of the petals are flushed with a rosy mauve, especially along the midribs. The flush may appear as feathering mostly towards the bottom on either side of the petal. The inside petals have a green flash up the centre. No basal blotch. Filaments black, anthers pale yellow. A native of SE France, especially Aime in the Savoy, where it flowers in the first half of May. Introduced in 1894.

T. MAURITIANA (JORD.)

Height 45 cm. Leaves (3–4) long, wide, very slightly glaucous and undulate. The bell-shaped flowers are rich red, the three outer petals tending to break away from the inner ones. The outsides of the outer petals have a greyish cast which contrasts with the piercing clarity of the red on the inside of the flower. The basal blotch may be yellow, or black edged with yellow. Filaments yellow, anthers purple. Found in SE France, especially Savoy at St Jean-de-Maurienne. This area, together with Florence and Bologna, is one of the chief centres of the European tulip. Described in 1858. It flowers in late May.

T. MAXIMOVICZII (REGEL)

Height 10 cm. Leaves (4–5) are long and glaucous, sometimes waved, usually edged with red. The outer petals of this dwarf tulip reflex and are yellowish-red on the backs. Inside, the flower is brilliant, shining scarlet. A dark basal blotch extends roughly one sixth of the way up

M.S.del.J.N.Fitch.lith.

Vincent Brooks,Day & Son Ltd Imp

L. Reeve & Co London.

T. linifolia
from Curtis's Botanical Magazine *(1905)*

each petal. Filaments black, fading to white at the apex, anthers mauve or yellow. It is a native of Central Asia, especially the Pamir Alps, where it grows on rocky hillsides and flowers from April to June. It is very close to *T. linifolia* and is easy to grow in a sunny place in well-drained soil, kept dry or lifted in summer. In the garden it flowers during the first week of May.

T. MICHELIANA (HOOG)

Height 35 cm. Leaves (3–5) widely spaced on the stem, long, thin, greyish-green with fine wine-coloured stripes. Flowers scarlet or dark crimson with slightly waved petals, very glossy. The basal blotch, which is purplish-black, often thinly edged with pale yellow, covers almost half the length of the petals. It shows through strongly on the backs of the inner petals. Occasionally the blotch on the inner petals is fringed. Filaments black, anthers violet or yellow. Found in northeastern Iran, the Pamir-Alai and Central Asia, where it flowers in April. This tulip was introduced into commerce by P. Sintenis (1847–1907), a Silesian botanist, entomologist and a collector for van Tubergen's. He brought it back from an expedition into Transcaspia together with the beautiful *Allium albopilosum*. Admiral Paul Furse noted, 'It is curious that when we collect them the flowers almost always have black blotches without any yellow edging, yet when they flower at home they often have a yellow edge.' He was lucky to get them to flower. This is not an easy tulip to grow.

T. MONTANA (LINDL.)

Height 10–15 cm. Leaves (3–6) very narrow, lance-shaped, channelled, very undulate, glaucous and held on a pinkish stem. The leaves are finely outlined in red. Strangely large, cup-shaped flower of brilliant dark red, opening to make a flat circle in the sun. The flower almost sits in its cup of leaves, the petals as broad as they are long. The small basal blotch is dark green or purplish-black. Filaments black shading to wine-coloured, anthers creamy-yellow. A native of northwest Iran, especially around Tabriz in the Elburz and the Kopet Dag, and of Central Asia, particularly Turkmenia, near Aslikhabad, where it grows on stony hillsides up to 3,000m. It flowers from late April to June.

The species was first described by John Lindley (1799–1865) from a tulip which flowered in the Horticultural Society's garden in Chiswick in 1827. It had been sent to the Society by Sir Henry Willock, who collected it in the mountains of northwest Iran.

T. NEUSTRUEVAE (POBED.)

Height 20–30 cm. Leaves (2) widely spaced on the stem, linear, with reddish margins. Flowers (1–3) golden yellow, open into a star shape. They smell of honey. The backs of the petals are marked along the midrib with a brownish-violet. Anthers yellow. Like *T. ferganica* and *T. dasystemon*, this species grows in the Ferganskiy range of mountains in the Tien Shan, Central Asia, but at a lower level than the others. It flowers mid March.

T. Orphanidea Boiss. No. 702

T. orphanidea *from* Notes on Tulip Species
by WR Dykes

T. ORPHANIDEA (BOISS. EX HELDR.)
Height 20 cm. Leaves (2–7) long and straggly. Flowers (1–4) globe-shaped, but without the purity of form that characterises the closely related *T. whittallii* (below). The shape, when the flower is fully open is wide and generous, with no gaps between the petals. The colour is a dull brickish-red, orange-red or orange-yellow, the outsides of the petals darkly stained with green or purple. The green colour tends to fade as the flower ages and the background colour becomes more dominant. Basal blotch clear yellow. Filaments brown or olive, anthers brown or olive. Found in the eastern Mediterranean, especially Greece, Crete, Bulgaria and western Turkey where it grows among stands of *Pinus nigra*, in cornfields and stony places up to 2,000m. It hybridises naturally with *T. sylvestris*. It flowers in April.

This is a variable species and the type is much less showy than *T. whittalli*, which is treated by some botanists as a cultivar of *T. orphanidea*. 'Flava' has yellow flowers, the backs of the petals flushed with red. It is almost indistinguishable from *T. sylvestris*, but yellow forms of *T. orphanidea* have brownish anthers rather than the yellow of *T. sylvestris*.

T. OSTROWSKIANA (REGEL)
Height 15 cm. Leaves (2–4) very crinkled, lying low, almost horizontal along the ground, glaucous. Red, goblet-shaped flower opening from an oval bud. The colour is variable and may be orange, yellow, or a combination of all three. The petals are pointed and there is a slight purplish sheen on the outer ones. The blotch is small, scarcely more than a smudge of dark olive-black, margined in yellow. Filaments yellowish-olive, anthers purple. This species is later and larger than *T. kolpakowskiana*, but otherwise resembles it closely. It is found in Central Asia and around Teheran in Iran and was first described in 1884. It flowers in late April. This is an easy tulip if planted in the right place.

T. PASSERINIANA (LEVIER)
Height 20 cm. Leaves thin and widely spaced. Crimson flowers have dramatic black blotches, thinly margined with yellow. Known since 1884, but found only in Italy where it flowers in April.

T. PLATYSTIGMA (JORD.)
Height 40–55 cm. Leaves (3–4) tall, lance-shaped, slightly waved. Tightly wrapped buds with a twist of petals at the top open to fragrant flowers of purplish-rose. Basal blotch blue, edged with orange. Filaments violet, anthers violet. Found in SE France, especially around Guillestre in the Dauphiné region, where it flowers in late April and May. Described in 1855. Prone to virus, which produces flowers feathered and flamed in contrasting colours. Possibly one of the forerunners of the French and English Florists' tulip.

T. POLYCHROMA (STAPF)
Height 10 cm. Leaves (1–2), as long as or longer than the stem, markedly upright,

7920

M.S del. J.N.Fitch lith.

Vincent Brooks Day & Son Lᵗᵈ Imp

L Reeve & Cᵒ London

T. praestans
from Curtis's Botanical Magazine *(1903)*

deeply channelled. The bud is coloured as soon as it emerges and opens to a spreading, cup-shaped flower (1–2), dead white, rather than ivory. The outsides of the petals are green veined with red or greyish-lavender. There is a faint line running up the middle of the backs of the inside petals. The basal blotch is yellow and extends about a third of the way up each of the petals. Filaments yellow, anthers yellow. It is a native of Iran and Afghanistan, where it grows on high plateaux or on stony hillsides at about 3,000m. Very similar to *T. biflora* and considered by some authorities to be a variant of that species. It flowers very early in February, usually at the same time as *T. turkestanica*.

T. PRAECOX (TEN.)

Height 55 cm. Leaves (3–5) big, broad and glaucous, tapering to a sharp tip. The flowers, borne on a thick, stout stem, are like those of a garden tulip: big, orange-red, the pointed outer petals longer and broader than the rounded inner ones and streaked with green. As the flower ages, they curl back. The inner petals are flared with yellow up the midrib. The petals generally are broad in relation to their length. The small basal blotch is conical, dark greenish-brown edged with yellow. Filaments black or dark green, anthers black or dark green. Its heartland is probably the Middle East, though it has become naturalised in southern Europe, especially Provence, Languedoc and the Rhône valley and in western Turkey, where it grows on rocky slopes

and in cultivated land. It is familiar enough in Turkey to have a common name, *kaba lale*. It flowers at the end of March and the beginning of April.

This species is hardy, vigorous and, being stoloniferous, increases freely, but Hall, the tulip supremo, did not consider it a good garden flower. 'The colour is dull except in good seasons and warm soils; the flower is somewhat ungainly in shape and the stem seems too coarse and thick for the size of the flower.'

T. PRAESTANS (HOOG)

Height 35 cm. Leaves (3–6) widely spaced, broad, pale greyish-green and characterised by the sharply raised thick midrib on the under surface. The leaves are occasionally waved at the edges. The stem, which is sometimes hairy, carries 2–4 flowers, which are large, with petals that are sometimes pointed, sometimes broad and rounded. Some plants have a markedly stocky habit, the flowers appearing almost within the sheaf of leaves. The flowers open flat, the colour a clear, plain orange-red, drifting into yellow at the base. The yellow shows on the outside but not on the inside of the petals. Some forms have no blotch, or only a smoky patch at the base of the petals. Others have a black blotch. It is a variable species; the filaments may be red or dark purple, the anthers yellow, violet or dark reddish-purple. This large-flowered species only became known during the latter part of the nineteenth century when Russian travellers began to explore the regions of Central Asia. It is

6786.

.S.del. J.N.Fitch lith.

Vincent.Brooks,Day&Son.Imp.

T. primulina
from Curtis's Botanical Magazine *(1884)*

a native of Central Asia, especially Tadzikstan in the southern Pamir-Alai, where it grows on steep earthy slopes and in light woodland at 2,000m and flowers in early April. Hall says it is 'difficult to keep in health and very slow of increase', but this has become a popular species, with several named varieties, all of which are easily grown in well-drained soil in a sunny place.

'Fusilier' is a good form with very glaucous, hairy leaves and up to four small flowers of a glowing orange-red.

'Regel's Variety' has foliage that is distinctly hairy, especially when seen against the light. It is generally taller than the species type. The red petals are pointed, strappy, but there are rarely more than two flowers on a stem. The filaments are black.

'Unicum' is a showy but unrefined cultivar with leaves that are broadly edged with cream. There may be up to five flowers on a stem, red merging to yellow at the base.

'Van Tubergen's Variety' has large orange-scarlet flowers. It is named after the bulb firm that introduced it. Writing to W R Dykes in 1914, van Tubergen said, 'The bulbs sent last year come from a more northerly district than the former which were collected in Bokhara. Those with red filaments are an early flowering dwarf strain which I offer as "Tubergen's Variety".'

'Zwanenburg' has particularly striking flowers of a rich, clear red, which open more widely than other varieties. The filaments are deep purple.

T. PRIMULINA (BAKER)

Height 15–20 cm. Leaves (4–5) set very closely on the stem, thin and grassy, grey-green and slightly channelled. Two or three scented flowers rise from a central point, each seemingly on a separate stem. The petals look thin and papery, the pointed outer ones are often stained on the back with green and lavender. The inner petals, which are longer than the outer ones, have a distinct green line down the midrib. The inside colour is creamy-white, flushing to yellow at the base. The tips of the petals are gently tinged with purple. Hall noted that 'young and vigorous flowers do not open until an hour or so after noon, though old and withering flowers may be seen open, having lost the power of closing'. Filaments pale greenish-yellow, anthers yellow. A native of Algeria, especially the Aurès Mountains, west of Batna, where it grows in cedar forests at 2,000m. This is a relatively easy species in the garden, multiplying rapidly and flowering freely in a warm situation, but as Hall pointed out, its drawback is 'its frailty and its reluctance to open, even in sunshine, before the afternoon'.

The species was discovered by the famous Victorian plantsman Henry Elwes, who lived in Colesborne, Gloucestershire and spent a large part of his happy life travelling in search of sport and plants. 'I have crossed the Himalayas and the Andes,' he wrote, 'explored Siberia and Formosa, shot and fished in Norway and, as I grow older, I find there is more companionship, consolation and

W.H.Fitch del et Lith.

Vincent Brooks Day & Son Imp

T. pulchella
from Curtis's Botanical Magazine *(1877)*

true pleasure in gardening and in plants than in anything I have tried.'

Writing in the *Gardener's Chronicle* of July 1882, Elwes said, 'This very pretty little tulip was found by me in the Aurès Mts three hours west of Batna in Eastern Algeria in May 1882. It grows on the ridges and open glades in the cedar forest at an elevation of about 8,000ft, though not very plentiful, and flowers in May. It is extremely sweet scented. I previously knew of the existence of such a plant from a drawing and specimen collected by Mr Hammond at El Kantara, which is about 30 miles farther in the interior than the place where I found it and beyond the range of cedars. It was the only good bulbous plant I found in the Aurès Mts, where neither orchids nor ferns and very few bulbs seemed to exist.'

T. PULCHELLA ([FENZL EX REGEL] BAKER)
Height 15–20 cm. Leaves (2–3) long, thin, channelled, somewhat glaucous and closely set on the stem. From a narrow, funnel-like base, the flowers (1–3) open out to a goblet, the petals slightly larger than the very similar *T. humilis* (q.v.). They are rich rose-mauve, the backs of the outer petals washed over with green or grey, the inner petals with dark veins down the midribs. The outer petals are much thinner than the inner ones. The basal blotch is navy edged with white. Filaments white or yellow at base, navy-blue at tip, anthers deep purple. This is a native of Turkey, particularly the Taurus mountains where it flowers in late

March, early April.

Var. *albocaerulea-occulata* has flowers that are much paler, and the basal blotch does not have a white edge. It flowers earlier than the species type.

'Violacea' has neat flowers with deep violet, sharply pointed petals opening to the shape of an urn, the rounded yellow base margined with dark blue or greenish-black.

T. SAXATILIS (SIEBER EX SPRENG.)
Height 20 cm. Leaves (2–4) are unusual, broad, shining, completely hairless and of a particular rich mid-green, different from other tulips. They are very finely edged (and as the leaves age, tipped) with red. The glossy foliage appears in early winter, long before the flowers, and the leaves curl back on themselves into the shapes of scimitars. The scented globe-shaped flowers (1–3) seem rather small compared with the foliage. They are borne on short stems, the colour pinkish-mauve. Unusually for a tulip, the colour and texture of the petals is much the same on the inside as on the outside. The outer petals are flushed up the centre with green, the inner segments, which are broader, show only a thin green rib. There is a clearly defined basal blotch of bright yellow edged with white, which covers almost a third of the area of the petals and is visible on the outsides, though more markedly on the ring of three inner petals than the outer ones. Filaments orange-yellow, anthers dark yellow or chocolate-brown. Flowers during April and May.

T. suaveolens (T. schrenkii)
from Curtis's Botanical Magazine *(1805)*
'We have been gratified with the sight of a large bed of this
species of Tulip, forming a carpet of scarlet and gold, which,
when illumined by the sun, pours forth such a blaze of
resplendent colouring as can hardly be conceived,'
wrote the editor

329

Though this species had disappeared from cultivation until Henry Elwes re-introduced it from Crete in the late nineteenth century, it had long been known to gardeners. It is mentioned in the letters exchanged between Clusius and Caccini in 1606. It is illustrated in Crispyn de Passe's *Hortus Floridus* of 1614, where it appears as *Tulipa Candia*. Passaeus and Parkinson also both describe it as the Tulip of Candie (Crete). Parkinson says he has 'Not yet heard that it hath very often flowered in our Countrey'. As always, he was observantly correct. It needs a summer baking to bring it into flower. It should be planted deeply in good soil in a very warm, sunny position, lifted after flowering and kept all summer on a shelf near glass in a greenhouse. After a warm summer it is more likely to flower in the succeeding spring. The species is markedly stoloniferous, the bulbs pushing out horizontal stolons for a foot or more at the end of which new bulbs form.

The excellent gardener Frederick Stern thought that it was the stoloniferous habit of this tulip that distracted it from flowering. He surrounded his colonies, as you might a fig, with slates sunk vertically into the ground and found in his chalk garden at Highdown, Sussex, that when the stolons had filled all the available space, the tulip began to flower.

It is a native of Crete where it grows in fields and rocky places, especially round Cape Malacca, flowering in April. Colonies have recently been discovered by the Turkish authority Professor Baytop, growing on the Marmaris peninsula in southwestern Turkey. Very similar to *T. bakeri*, which has slightly darker flowers.

T. SCHRENKII (REGEL)

Height 10–30 cm. Leaves (3–5): the lower ones reflexed, the higher ones widely spaced on the stem. A solitary cup-shaped flower opens from a narrow bud. This is one of the most variable species in terms of colour: claret-red, yellow, pink, white and multi-coloured forms have been found. Filaments yellow or black, anthers yellow. Found in the steppes and semi-deserts of the Crimea, the Lower Don, in the Caucasus and Kurdistan, where it flowers in mid April.

T. SHARONENSIS *see T. agenensis*

T. SOGDIANA (BUNGE)

Height 10–25 cm. Leaves (2–3) spreading, slightly twisted, smooth and linear. Flowers (1–2) white tinged with a pale rosy-violet, the petals about half as wide as they are high. Base yellow. Filaments and anthers yellow. Found in sandy, stony desert areas, typically between Bukhara and Kermin in Central Asia, where it flowers in March and April.

T. SPRENGERI (BAKER)

Height 40 cm. Leaves (5–6) long, thin and glossy green. The habit of this tulip is markedly upright, the flower appearing well above the leaves, opening from an oval bud to a starry flower with narrow pointed petals. The petals are particularly

PLATE XLVI

T. Sprengeri Baker
Reduced to three-quarters natural size

T. sprengeri *from* Notes on Tulip Species
by WR Dykes

331

narrow at the base, leaving holes in the cup of the flower. The colour is clear but not brilliant, reddish-orange to bright scarlet, the backs of the outer petals, which are thinner than the inner ones, are buff suffused with olive and green. There is no basal blotch. Filaments bright red, anthers yellow. It is found in the Pontic Mountains, near Amasya, Turkey and is the latest of the species to flower, usually at the end of May and beginning of June.

It is a very distinct species, not only in its time of flowering, which is well after all other tulips have died down, but also in its general aspect and in the make-up of its filaments, which are arranged alternately long and short, the long ones the same length as the ovary.

It is one of the few tulips that can be persuaded to naturalise in grass in Britain, provided the turf is not too coarse. It also increases from seed quite readily, sometimes flourishing in surprisingly shady positions under shrubs.

'An Armenian schoolmaster, J J Manissadjian, who lived in Merzifon, supplied me up to the war with *T. sprengeri*', wrote J M C Hoog of van Tubergen. 'Besides he supplied quantities of choice things such as *Iris gatesii* for which a special trip had to be made. Alas he had to leave Armenia as his life was in constant danger.'

It was first found in 1892 by a German botanist, Muhlendorff, who lived at Amasya. He sent bulbs to a nurseryman called C Sprenger, whose business Damman & Cie was based near Naples, and it was introduced into cultivation in 1894.

T. STAPFII (TURRILL)

Height 25 cm. Leaves (4) broad and glaucous, the larger pair lying on the ground, the stem leaves narrower and more pointed. The flower is very upright and makes a closed, incurving cup, the colour deep crimson-scarlet. The basal blotch is dark violet, sometimes edged with yellow. Filaments deep purple, anthers deep purple. It is found in western Iran and northern Iraq, where it flowers in April.

The description of the species is based on a specimen collected from Ruwandiz in northern Iraq by Lady Rockley. It was named after Otto Stapf (1857–1933), a British botanist of Austrian origin who made a lifelong study of the genus *Tulipa*.

T. SUAVEOLENS see T. schrenkii

T. SUBPRAESTANS (VVED.)

Height 40 cm. Leaves (3–4) widely spaced on the stem, reflexed and waved. Flowers (2–3) spring from the axils of the upper leaves, the petals narrow, pointed and a glossy orange-red. The reflexed flower opens wide in sunshine, showing a tinge of yellow at the base. Filaments red, fading to yellow at the base, anthers yellow. A native of Central Asia, especially the Pamir-Alai, Sebistak and Sarsaryak, where it flowers in April.

T. SYLVESTRIS (L.)

Height 30 cm. Leaves (2–4) widely spaced on the slender stem, which is sometimes

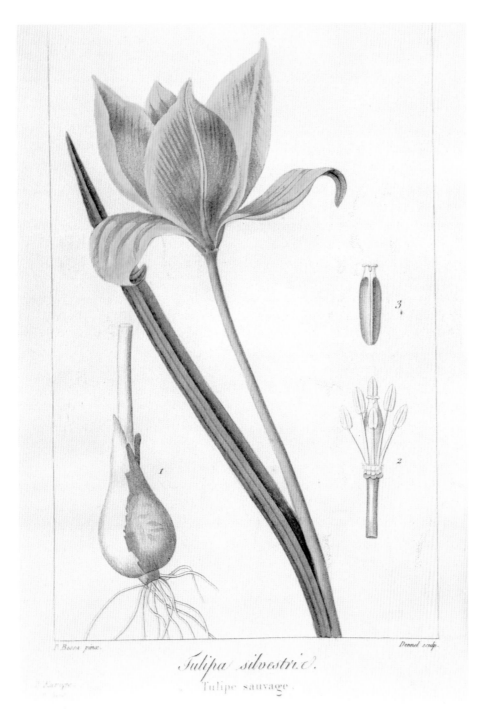

T. sylvestris
from Bessa's L'Herbier Générale *(1819)*

tinted red at its junction with the flower. A leafy species, the foliage is long, narrow, grey-green and vigorous, though the general habit of the plant is somewhat straggling. The elegant golden, scented flowers (1–2) open from slightly drooping buds. The outer petals are heavily netted with green, with a touch of maroon at each tip. They turn back on themselves at the tips, even when the flower is in bud. All the petals are long and narrow, very pointed and there is a pronounced green midrib up the outside of the inner segments. There is no basal blotch. Filaments yellow, anthers orange. The origin of this species is unknown, but it is naturalised in Europe, western Anatolia, north Africa, Central Asia and Siberia. It flowers at the beginning of April.

'Major' has larger flowers than the type, usually with eight petals rather than six. 'Tabriz' is taller, more upright than the type, the leaves erect rather than drooping, the large lemon-yellow flowers sweetly scented. Writing of it from Tabriz in 1927, B Gilliat-Smith said, 'It occurs here mainly if not exclusively in orchards. It is sold in the streets in April, towards the end of the month. When growing I have never known it open before 1 or 2 pm and it closes at sunset. I have not been able to find it in the desert hills near here like other bulbous plants found largely in orchards.'

T. sylvestris was known as a weed of cultivated land, especially vineyards, from very early times. It was described by Lobelius in his *Plantarum seu Stirpium*

Historia, published in Antwerp in 1576. He called it the yellow tulip of Bologna and saw clearly the difference between this type and another similar one, the tulip we now know as *T. australis*. But writing seven years later, Cesalpino said he knew *T. sylvestris* only at Barga in the Upper Serchio valley. Linnaeus described it in 1753, and a specimen is still in his herbarium in the Linnean Society. The first mention of it growing north of the Alps was made by Jeran Bauhin (1541–1612). In his *Historia Plantarum*, published in 1651, he mentions a tulip of this kind growing at Montbéliard. According to Solms-Laubach, the wine growers of the Colmar district in the Alsace looked on it as an indestructible weed, so abundant for instance in Niedermorschwhir that the vineyards were bright yellow with its flowers.

The distinction between the two species was made chiefly on the basis of their distribution. In Europe *T. sylvestris* is almost entirely a plant of cultivated land, found in Italy, the south of France and Spain, generally as a weed in vineyards. Having a strongly stoloniferous habit, it may have spread with the movement of vine stock. It has also been found in northern France, Germany, Switzerland, Belgium, Holland, Sweden and England, usually in places that suggest it has escaped from gardens. *T. australis* favours high, uncultivated land in the Apennines, Sicily, the south of France, Spain and Portugal. It has a smaller flower and a thinner stem than *T. sylvestris*. Experiments carried out by William

Newton (1895–1927) in 1927 suggested that *T. sylvestris* was tetraploid and *T. australis* diploid, the inference being that the latter was the true species of which the former was a variant.

The flower does not appear in the *Flora Anglica* of 1762 but was recorded in England in 1790 from a site in Norfolk. In the herbarium at Kew are specimens gathered from several localities in England, including Norwich, where it was found by Sir Joseph Hooker and James Leighton, and Bedfordshire where it was found by Septimus Warner. Claridge Druce remembered seeing it in the Thames valley, where it had become naturalised. 'It occurs in Christ Church meadows – I have seen a flower' he wrote, 'but it was doubtless originally planted. So, too, at Besilsleigh, where it flowered last year (1927) and there is a relic of Speaker Lenthall's garden. So, too, in a coppice at Charlbury where it is a relic of Lord Jenkinson's Pleasaunce and in Sarsdon where it is in Lord Dacre's park.'

Daniel Hall was sent it by a friend, H C Davidson, in whose garden, cut from a meadow at Silchester, it came up abundantly. Had it been brought over by the Romans with their vines? Hall suggested that it may persist in places where it is not noticed, for it rarely flowers in grass and the leaves are too thin and grassy themselves to cause much notice. In Britain, it is at the very edge of its preferred habitat.

Writing in the Alpine Garden Society Bulletin (December 1996) Phillip Cribb and Tom Cope noted that English colonies of *T. sylvestris* had benefited from the abnormally hot summer of 1995 and flowered brilliantly towards the end of April in the wood behind Haresfield Parish Church, Middlesex. 'This year' they wrote 'the Haresfield population sported about fifty flowers, including a staggering thirty in a single clump barely exceeding a metre square. It was a truly magnificent sight that will possibly not be repeated for a generation.'

Writing in *The Garden* 6 May 1893, a correspondent suggested that '*T. sylvestris* should be grown in broad patches in the woodland and wild garden. By its bounding stolons it soon makes wide masses, and it is otherwise vigorous and capable of holding its own. The spicy odour of this distinct species with scarlet-streaked deep yellow flowers renders it a most desirable kind. A dozen bulbs planted three years ago now form a patch 5ft across in light, rich soil. I do not think the progress would be so free in stiff land.' No, indeed.

Like *T. saxatilis* the tulip is best persuaded to flower if the stolons are contained in a subterranean cage of slates, sunk into the ground to a depth of 8 or 9 inches. It has a straggling habit but when sun tickles the scent buds and the flowers open wide, this tulip has a touching charm.

T. SYSTOLA (STAPF)

Height 25 cm. Leaves (3–5) very waxy and usually longer than the stem. The

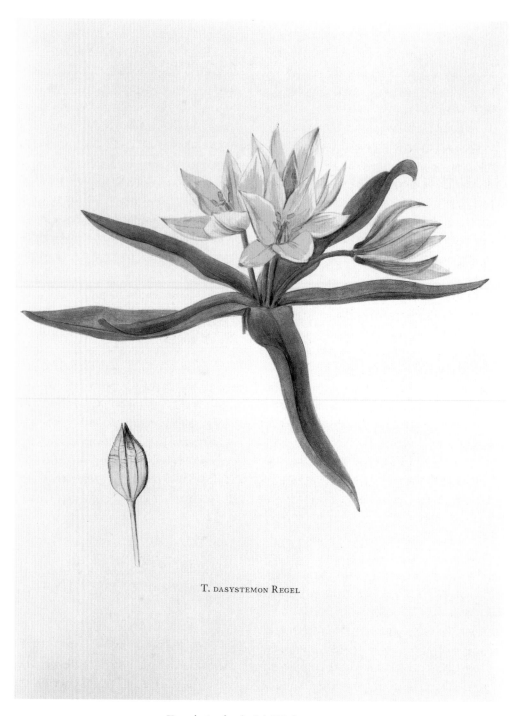

T. dasystemon Regel

T. tarda *(under the label* T. dasystemon,
from Notes on Tulip Species *by WR Dykes*

336

lower leaves are sometimes broad and wavy, but all the foliage is drawn out into long points. The flowers are deep tomato-red, loose and open, the broad petals streaked on the outside with grey. The pointed basal blotch is blackish-purple, sometimes margined with yellow. Filaments navy-blue, yellow at their tips. It is found in northern Iraq and western Iran, especially in the Bakhtieri mountains near Tabriz, where it grows in fields and rocky places up to 3,000m. It flowers in March and April.

In the Lindley Herbarium at Cambridge there is a specimen of this tulip, collected on General Chesney's expedition to the Euphrates, but Lindley has labelled it wrongly as *T. montana*.

Like other tulips which have their origins in Iran or Palestine, this is not an easy species to cultivate out of its native habitat. It starts into growth early and is not hardy.

T. TARDA (STAPF)

Height 10 cm. Leaves (3–7) closely set on the thin stem to make a straggly rosette, long, bright green with claret-coloured margins, often curving back on themselves. Flowers (4–5) are fragrant and broadly star-shaped. The inner petals are broader than the outer ones, opening to a yellow flower, tipped with white on the insides of the petals. The outer petals are flushed on their backs with a greyish-green. The inner petals have the white tip on the outside and a dark rib up the centre, three lines, the middle one green with purple either side. There is no basal blotch. Filaments yellow, anthers yellow. It is a native of Central Asia, especially the Tien Shan and eastern Turkestan, where it is found growing on stony and rocky slopes in the northern foothills of the Trans-Ilian Alatau. It flowers in late April and May, the flowers often lasting a month.

This species is markedly stoloniferous and increases rapidly if planted in the right place. It needs sun and, because it is so short, it is best in a rock pocket or low container.

T. TETRAPHYLLA (REGEL)

Height 35 cm. Leaves (3–7) thin, upright, closely spaced on the stem, the bottoms of the leaves often still in the ground when the flower comes out. The pale yellow flowers (1–4) open from drooping buds, the outer petals turning back on themselves and tinted with purple or lime-green along the midrib. They are waisted, but unlike the Lily-flowered tulips, the petals turn back in at the tops, to make an urn-shape. The inner petals are narrow and pointed. Basal blotch greenish-yellow. Filaments yellow-green, anthers yellow. Described in 1875. A native of Central Asia, especially the Tien Shan and the Dzungaria-Kashgar, where it flowers in April.

T. TSCHIMGANICA (BOTSCHANTZ.)

Height 20 cm. Leaves (3–4) greyish, very broad, large and long, closely set on the downy stem. The flowers open from conical buds into a star shape. The tall outer petals are yellow, mostly overlaid

T. TUBERGENIANA HOOG

T. tubergeniana
from Notes on Tulip Species *by WR Dykes*

with red on their backs, but leaving a neat yellow margin around the edges of the petals. The inside of the outer petals is yellow with a startling V-shaped red blotch which sometimes extends well up the petals. The inner petals are yellow, lightly flushed with red. Filaments yellow, anthers yellow or yellowish-brown. A native of Central Asia, especially the Tschimgan valley northeast of Tashkent, from which it gets its name. It grows in rocky places at 2,000m, flowering May.

This tulip grows in the same locality as *T. dubia* and *T. kaufmanniana* and may possibly be a hybrid between the two species.

T. TUBERGENIANA (HOOG)

Height 50 cm. Leaves (3–4) broad, upright, clasp the stem in early stages of growth and fold to form a V-shaped midrib at the back. The foliage is in proportion with the showy, well-shaped flowers and has a curious floury quality, as though moisture were condensing on the surface of the leaves. The stem is tinted reddish-pink where it meets the large flower. The broad petals reflex widely and show an inner surface of brilliant orange-scarlet, a little duller on the backs. All the petals have pronounced ogee points. The large black basal blotch is rounded on the outer petals, triangular on the inner ones. It may have a narrow yellow-orange margin. Both the blotch and the edge vary considerably. The filaments are black with an orange tip below the anthers, which are sometimes yellow,

sometimes deep purple. It is a native of Central Asia, particularly the Pamir-Alai, and flowers in April.

A bad doer, says Hall, but when it does flower 'it is very brilliant with that shining gloss characteristic of the Central Asiatic tulips'. This is a relatively young species, in terms of its being described and named. It was introduced from Bukhara in 1901 by the bulb firm van Tubergen and named by John Hoog in honour of C G van Tubergen, who was responsible for the costly and difficult expeditions made on the firm's behalf in Central Asia. It is a variable species, similar to *T. greigii* and *T. ingens*. Dykes considered that *T. tubergeniana* was a deeper colour, had more abundant foliage and flowered a little later than *T. ingens*.

T. TURKESTANICA (REGEL)

Height 20 cm. Leaves (2–4) longer than the flower stem, thin, widely spaced, the margins and tips rimmed with pink. Though the official description specifies thin leaves, the specimen in the National Collection at the Cambridge Botanic Garden has markedly broad leaves as does the *T. turkestanica* pictured in *Bulbs* (Phillips and Rix). Flowers (1–7) are small, opening to pointed stars. The petals are ivory-white, the backs of the outer ones heavily stained with greyish-purple. The inner petals are almost twice as broad as the outer ones and have a thin green line up the middle of their backs. The basal blotch is orange and covers about a third of the petal.

T. turkestanica regel

T. turkestanica
from Notes on Tulip Species *by WR Dykes*

340

Filaments orange, anthers purple or chocolate-brown. This species is larger and slightly later in flower than *T. biflora*, which it otherwise resembles very closely, though it has a horrible smell, whereas *T. biflora* is quite sweetly scented. It is a native of Central Asia, especially the Tien Shan and the Pamir-Alai and the Dzungaria region of NW China, where it grows on stony slopes, by streams and on rock ledges from 1,800–2,500m. It starts flowering early, at the beginning of March, but in the wild, depending on altitude, may continue until May.

T. UNDULATIFOLIA (BOISS.)

Height 20–30cm. Leaves (3–4) widely spaced on the stem, broad, reflexed, glaucous, very wavy. The two lowest leaves usually lie flat on the ground. The cup-shaped flowers are shiny crimson or dark red, with a pale creamy-green flare up the centre of the outside of the outer petals. They open wide and the outer petals curl right back on themselves as the flower ages. The neat basal blotch is black or purplish-black, often edged with yellow. Filaments black, anthers purplish. This is a native of Greece, Turkey, the Balkans and the south Caucasus, where it grows in cultivated land. It flowers in April and May.

T. URUMIENSIS (STAPF)

Height 10cm. Leaves (2–4) in a flat rosette, smooth and glaucous, almost twice as long as the stem. The scented flowers (1–2) open from nodding buds into solid yellow cups, which flatten into

stars in sunshine. The backs of the outer petals are flushed all over with greenish-purple. The inner ones have a purplish midrib. There is a purplish tip on the inside of the outer petals and the same on the outside of the inner petals. Filaments yellow, anthers yellow. Probably once a native of northwest Iran, although it is no longer known in the wild. It flowers in April.

This is one of the most dwarf of the species tulips and was introduced into commerce in 1928 by John Hoog of van Tubergen's from Salmas on the northern shore of Lake Urumiya in Azerbeidjan. It is relatively easy to maintain in the garden.

T. URUMOFFII (HAYEK)

Height 15–25cm. Leaves (3–5) glaucous, smooth, with fine hairs around the points. Flowers usually solitary, very occasionally two or three, are yellow to reddish-brown, with a strong rib up the centre of each petal and a greyish sheen on the exterior. The basal blotch may be black edged with yellow, but is variable, sometimes star-like, sometimes disappearing altogether. Filaments yellow, anthers buff or buff-green. Found around Belovo in southern Bulgaria, where it flowers in April.

T. VIOLACEA see T. pulchella 'Violacea'

T. VVEDENSKYI (BOTSCHANTZ.)

Height 25cm. Leaves (4–5) broad, glaucous, closely set on the stem. The showy cup-shaped flower is bright crimson-red,

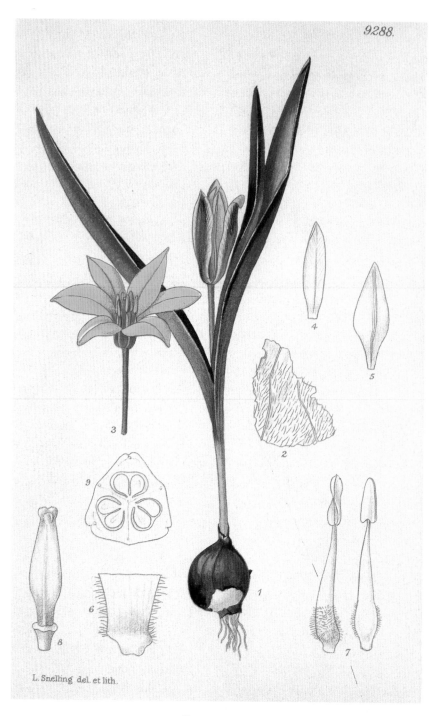

9288.

L. Snelling del. et lith.

T. urumiensis
from Curtis's Botanical Magazine *(1932)*

342

a bulky bloom with broad, pointed petals, all of which have a twist in them. The outer petals curl away from the centre and are flushed on their backs with purple. The backs of the inner petals are washed with yellow. There is an indeterminate plain yellow blotch at the base of the petals, which streaks up into the red, but it does not extend far. Filaments yellow or brown, anthers yellow or blackish-purple. It is a native of Central Asia, especially the valley of the River Angren in the western Tien Shan, southeast of Tashkent, where it flowers in late May and June. In cultivation, it is often in flower by late April. The species is named after the Russian botanist and taxonomist A I Vvedensky. 'Tangerine Beauty' is a form with flowers that are more orange than red.

T. WHITTALLII (HALL)

Height 30 cm. Leaves (3–4) long, but wider than those of the closely related species *T. orphanidea*. The margins are sometimes tipped with deep red. The stem is quite dark at the top, where it meets the flower. This is an outstanding tulip with neat, pointed petals. The colour is a burnt orange caramel, very distinct and unusual. The outer petals are smaller than the inner ones and are flushed with a pale creamy-buff on the reverse. A sharp, thin buff line is drawn, as with a ruler, up the midribs of the inner petals. The flower makes a perfect rounded bud with all the petals meeting at a sharp point in the middle. Smoky,

indeterminate basal blotch, greenish-black with a yellow halo, the dark colour drifting slightly up the veins of the petals, like water-colour paint on wet paper. Filaments dark green or olive, anthers almost black. Found in the eastern Mediterranean especially round Izmir (Smyrna) in western Turkey, where it flowers in April. Considered by some authorities to be a variant of *T. orphanidea* scarcely deserving species status.

This tulip was introduced by Edward Whittall (1851–1917), a descendant of an English family who settled in Izmir in 1809 and founded an export company, Whittall & Co. As a result of hunting trips, Whittall became interested in the flowers of western Anatolia and, eventually, horticulture became his main business. His own garden at Bornova near Izmir was filled with rare plants. Many of the local villagers collected plants and bulbs for him, some of which were exported to England and Holland. With the surplus, Whittall employed a team of men to plant the slopes of Nif Dag, a mountain near Izmir, and by 1893 he estimated that more than a million bulbs had been naturalised there.

Whittall sent bulbs of *T. whittalli* to Henry Elwes who worked up the stock in his Gloucestershire garden and distributed it. It was named in Edward Whittall's honour by A D Hall. Though small, this is an excellent garden tulip, growing well and increasing freely. The colour is rich and unusual.

343

9649.

S.Ross-Craig del. L.Snelling lith.

T. whittalli
from Curtis's Botanical Magazine *(1943)*

344

T. ZENAIDAE (VVED.)

Height 15 cm. Leaves (3) closely spaced at first but becoming further apart as the plant comes into flower, light green, veined with a brighter green, glaucous, the tips of the leaves often reddish. The flowers sometimes develop ragged petals similar to those of a Parrot tulip. They are elegantly waisted, the top third of the flower flipping outwards. The petals are yellow, overlaid with pink on their backs and a small, squarish black blotch at the base. Filaments and anthers yellow. There are forms with orange and red flowers and some without the black basal blotch. Found on stony slopes in the Tien Shan, Central Asia, where it flowers in the second half of April.

CHAPTER IX

TULIP CULTIVARS

TULIPS CAN reproduce themselves in two ways. The mother bulbs produce offsets, baby bulbs that grow alongside the parent bulb and take a few years to grow on to flowering size. The flower also sets seed, which can be grown on to produce a flowering size bulb in five to seven years. Offsets always show the same characteristics as the parent. Tulips raised from seed may not. So, by crossing certain tulips and sowing their seed, breeders could produce new tulips quite easily. But, as early tulip fanciers quickly discovered, not all species are equally malleable. Several interested growers have tried to trace the wild species in which the different garden tulips have their origin,[1] but as the species themselves are so wilfully variable, establishing clear links and breeding lines is a problem. Is, for instance, the variable species *T. schrenkii* (pointed red petals, bordered with yellow) closely related to the old, Single Early 'Duc van Thol' tulips? It seems likely. But did *T. schrenkii* also sink its genes into other Single Earlies such as 'Keizerskroon'? That is less clear.

From the first, gardeners appreciated the tulip's extraordinary ability to break from a plain colour into a brilliant melange of flamed and feathered colours, rose on white, dark brown on mustard-yellow, purple on red, each pattern, each petal as complex as a fingerprint. These selections, rather than the wild originals, were the tulips that were most prized in early oriental gardens. But in the early days of gardening, there was no scientific underpinning to the naming of plants. That happened thanks to the Swedish naturalist Carl Linnaeus (1707–1778), who worked out the first logical scheme for giving names to the different families and species of plants. In early pre-Linnaeus plant lists, such as that published by Caspar Bauhin (1560–1624) in 1623,[2] tulips were merely divided into early, mid-season and late-flowering kinds. The earliest of the tribe usually appear in March, the latest peak at the end of May. *T. sprengeri* rarely flowers before June. In the seventeenth century, cultivated tulips were often named after the people who had raised them, such as 'Tulipa Iacobi Bommii'.[3] Jacob Bom was a Haarlem grower, as was van Qaeckel, who gave his name to the 'Merveille van Qaeckel'. 'Admirael Pottebacker' was not an admiral at all. He was Hendrick Pottebacker, a tulip grower of Gouda. Other names celebrated the beauty of the flower: 'Schoone Helena', 'Bruyd van Enchuysen', 'Laprock', 'Non Pareille'.

Certain colour combinations, rose and white, mustard and yellow, were always highly prized, the Roses, Bizarres and Bybloemens that were later saved from extinction by the patient, discerning members of societies such as the Wakefield and North of England Tulip Society. The length and strength of the stalk, the size and shape of the flower, the colour of the stamens, all played a part in the final assessment of a particular tulip's virtues.

Feathered (short slanting stripes along the border of a petal) and flamed (a mark up the centre of the petal reaching all the way to the rim) are the two terms most commonly used now amongst tulip fanciers to describe the petals of two-tone tulips, but in the past the vocabulary was much wider. *Jaspis* tulips were spotted. Others were called jagged, striped or marbled. Sometimes they were described as winged, burnt, bruised and shredded.

The best information about the tulips that became a passion among rich gardeners of the seventeenth and early eighteenth centuries, comes from the tulip books and paintings of the period. But nobody then kept any control on tulip names or checked that so-called new varieties were not just the old ones masquerading under new names. The paintings show how the taste in tulips gradually changed during the seventeenth century. Eastern-style flowers with crisp outlines and pointed tops, or those with sharply defined waists, gave way to tulips that had larger, more rounded flowers in a wider range of colours. The subtlety of the markings became increasingly important. When tulips fell generally out of fashion in the later eighteenth and the nineteenth centuries, it was the finely marked tulips known as the English Florists' tulip that carried the genes of the first old cultivars through into the twentieth century.

By the end of the nineteenth century, when Dutch growers increasingly dominated the market, the names of garden tulips were in a great muddle. Identical tulips were being grown under half a dozen different names. In 1913, the Royal Horticultural Society set up a Tulip Nomenclature Committee and supervised trials of tulip cultivars at its Wisley garden. Gradually order was retrieved from chaos and a preliminary list of tulip cultivars was published in 1917. Thanks to the patient work of Arthur Simmonds, the Committee's Secretary, a fuller list (though still titled 'tentative') was published in 1929, with the cooperation of the Algemene Vereniging voor Bloembollencultuur (General Dutch Bulb Growers Society) of Haarlem. New lists have been published regularly since then, the Dutch organisation taking over sole responsibility for registration and nomenclature from 1958 onwards. The most recent list (1996) contains the names of more than 5,600 tulips, of which about 2,600 are in general cultivation. More than 600 of the tulips are historic cultivars, not commercially available, but maintained in collections such as the Hortus Bulborum at Limmen. New varieties are constantly being introduced, colour, size, form and stamina being the qualities that breeders strive to improve. Length and strength of stem is also important in garden varieties, as is immunity to disease. But many of the most beautiful of the 'broken' tulips are no longer available. Since it was discovered that the colour-breaking was caused by a virus, tulips such as the fabulous Rembrandts have been withdrawn by Dutch growers, who do not want the virus to spread to and infect their single-coloured stock. This is a great and important loss to gardeners.

After much re-ordering and re-arranging, as old classifications such as English Breeders and Mendel Tulips fell out of use, hybrids and cultivars are now listed under fifteen different divisions. The list starts logically with the earliest flowering types such as the Single Early (Division 1), continues by flowering time up to Division 11 (Double Late) and finishes with four divisions of tulips which have their immediate roots in species such as *T. kaufmanniana*.

Division 1 SINGLE EARLY: A relatively small group of tulips, which flower in late March and early April on short, sturdy stems, rarely reaching 40 cm, more commonly half that height. The important old 'Duc van Thol' tulips mentioned so often in early accounts of gardens of the seventeenth century were of this type and, in the 1939 Classified List, had their own Division at the head of the table.

Division 2 DOUBLE EARLY: These generally flower in early or mid-April. They are often taller (30–40 cm) than the Single Earlies. The flowers are wider than they are high, packed in a muddled way with petals. Most of the Double Early tulips (but not 'Scarlet Cardinal') originate from the mid-nineteenth-century tulip 'Murillo' and its sports. This gives the group an unusual homogeneity in terms of the height and flowering time of the flowers. 'The doubling of a flower is always a doubtful blessing', said Sir Daniel Hall, 'but to double a tulip is to destroy the finest and most distinctive qualities that it should possess. It may be argued that double tulips are more lasting, but it is no gain that a nightmare should ensure for two nights instead of one. Were permanence the great virtue, flowers might be made of pottery or enamelled iron... Under certain conditions of architectural garden design good use can be made of a row of double tulips – sturdy little martinets, with just that touch of the grotesque that appeals to lovers of the rococo.'[4] They are favourites for forcing in pots indoors. Outdoors, in bad weather, they suffer more visibly than singles.

Division 3 TRIUMPH: The name was invented in 1923 by a Dutch breeder, N Zandbergen of Rijnsburg, to distinguish a collection of seedling tulips which he had bought from the Haarlem firm of Zocher five years earlier. Other Dutch growers subsequently produced similar seedlings by crossing Single Early tulips with Dutch Breeder, Cottage and Darwin tulips. Height generally 45–50 cm, flowering time late April.

Division 4 DARWIN HYBRIDS: Introduced in 1943 by D W Lefeber of Lisse, who crossed Darwin tulips with species such as the brilliant *T. fosteriana* to produce a race of tulips which cover the yellow-orange-red spectrum. The single flowers are amongst the tallest of garden tulips (typically 60–70 cm) and flower during May. The group is an important commercial crop in The Netherlands, accounting for 15 per cent of all tulips grown. 'Apeldoorn' and its many sports is perhaps the most important of the cultivars.

Division 5 SINGLE LATE: This single division embraces Darwin and Cottage tulips, which were originally classified separately. But the two types were so intercrossed by Dutch breeders, it became impossible to maintain the difference between them. The original specification for Darwin tulips laid down that they were 'never yellow or brown' but already by 1929, breeders had made a nonsense of the ruling. From the beginning, the division of Cottage tulips acted as an *omnium gatherum*, collecting together all the old tulips that were worth preserving but

TULIPA.

Variegated Tulips.

W. Mallinson sculp.

Publish'd by Henry Fisher, Caxton, Liverpool. Aug. 1819.

A selection of feathered and flamed tulips, published in a copper engraving by Henry Fisher Caxton of Liverpool in 1819

which did not conform to the high standards of the English florists. This generally meant that they were long in the cup, with pointed petals and nipped-in waists. This characteristic was later seized on to produce the popular group of tulips known as Lily-flowered. Some are scented, most often those with a yellow ground colour. The original Cottage tulips were an older (and shorter) type of tulip than the Darwins, which were named and introduced by the Dutch firm of Krelage. These Darwins were selected from a race of old tulips, representing what the Flemish florists called Baguettes or Baquettes, all tall, strong-growing varieties. The tulips were first shown in 1886 in the grounds of Messrs E H Krelage & Son's nursery at the Kleine Houtweg, Haarlem. 'In a specimen tent two show beds of tulips are planted – containing the collection of Flemish late tulips (only violettes and roses) bought last year by Messrs Krelage from M Jules Lenglart of Lille (the last good collection there existing). Here are two beds – each containing 840 sorts.'[5] The report confirms that the Darwins were originally of French/Flemish origin, the progeny of tulips selected for many generations by growers around Lille.

The tulips were shown again the following year, and noted as 'an unrivalled collection of Flemish breeders, violets and roses, in the most striking and brilliant colours, which are of interest, not only as breeders, but also as bedding tulips'. Their usefulness as breeders (that is single-coloured tulips likely to break into one of the fancy kinds highly prized by English florists) was rated more highly than their value as tulips for bedding. In the 1880s, the craze for planting out tulips in huge blocks of a single colour had not yet taken hold and the trade in tulips as cut flowers had not yet started. No tulips appear in the price lists of cut flowers sold at Covent Garden during the 1880s.

A few years later Messrs Krelage began to distribute their stock, calling them Darwin tulips to distinguish them from the similar Cottage tulips. At that time they were a distinct race, characterised by their tall stems, their size and vigour. The petals of the true Darwins tended to be rounded at the top (unlike the Cottage tulips), very broad and fleshy. The flower opened into a short cup, square in shape.

This group is of most interest to those who love the tulips of Dutch flower paintings, for the Cottage tulips still have the blood of the old tulips running in their veins. This stretches in an unbroken line back to the garden tulips first cultivated in Eastern gardens. Of all types, they are the most prone to 'break' in the garden, producing flowers mottled and striped and flamed in contrasting shades. The Single Late tulips retain the vigour of the original Darwins, growing to 60–75cm and flowering in May.

Division 6 LILY-FLOWERED: The best were bred by Rengert Cornelis Segers (born 1899), who started work on this group in 1919, using an old Darwin called 'Bartigon' as one of the parents. By 1939 the Tulip Nomenclature Committee of the RHS was considering whether these tulips, at that time included with the Cottage tulips, ought not to command a division of their own. By 1958 this had happened and the group is now very popular, growing to 45–60 cm, flowering in May with long, waisted flowers, the petals pointed and sharply reflexed. The original Lily-flowered tulips possibly arose from a cross between a species *T. retroflexa* (now demoted to a cultivar) and a Darwin tulip. Many such crosses were made around 1914 by the famous firm of Krelage. Later the closely related Darwins were used in similar crosses. In style they are similar to the Ottoman tulips of the eighteenth century.

Division 7 FRINGED: A relatively modern grouping, first proposed in 1981. Early fringed flowers such as 'Sundew' (a sport of the Darwin 'Orion') were originally placed in the same division as Parrot tulips. The flowers have delicately fringed petals, the fringing sometimes of the same colour as the petals, as in yellow 'Maja', sometimes of a contrasting colour as in 'Burgundy Lace', where a white fringe edges claret-coloured petals. This is a fast-expanding division, the tulips growing to a height of 30–50 cm, flowering in May.

Division 8 VIRIDIFLORA: Not entirely green-flowered, as the name suggests, but a group of tulips with flowers that are streaked or mottled with green. Like the Cottage tulips, this is an ancient race, the tendency of the petals to retain green markings being noted by illustrators as early as 1613.[6] Flowers are generally 35–60 cm tall and appear in May. The division was introduced in 1981.

Division 9 REMBRANDT: A group of tulips much loved by gardeners but sadly banished by bulb growers some time after it was discovered that the virus causing the magnificent striped and feathered markings of the Rembrandts could be transmitted to other tulips which breeders wished to keep plain. These 'broken' tulips, derived from Darwins around the turn of the century and, named after the Dutch painter, bore a superficial resemblance to the superb English Florists' tulips, bred over several hundred years to a peak of perfection in the mid nineteenth century. Sir Daniel Hall, a passionate defender of the English Florists' tulip, was dismissive of Rembrandts. 'Very unsatisfactory to anyone with a florist's eye,' he wrote. 'They lack the brilliance and definiteness of the broken English tulip. The markings are irregular and coarse, with splashes of indeterminate breeder colour, and the white grounds are often dingy.[7] He singles out the breaks from the Single Late tulip 'Clara Butt' as worthy but spurns the rest. He was in a position to, surrounded by the elegant, highly refined blooms of his English Florists' flowers. Present-day gardeners would welcome the opportunity to be as picky. So few of the old 'broken' tulips can be got, each one seems a marvel. The gradual eradication of 'broken' tulips in favour of single-coloured (and sometimes harshly coloured) cultivars is the single greatest disaster of tulip breeding over the last twenty years. The coarse mixture occasionally offered now as 'Rembrandts' by tulip growers bears no relation to the original kinds available in shades of brown, mustard and smudgy purple. For a taste of what is missing, you need to make a pilgrimage to the annual show of the Wakefield and North of England Tulip Society. 'Cordell Hull' rose on white (Division 5) and 'Striped Bellona' red on yellow (Division 1) are pale reminders of the lost splendours of the old 'broken' tulips.

Division 10 PARROT: These arose as 'sports' or mutations from perfectly well-behaved tulips such as 'Clara Butt', which sported to produce the Parrot tulip 'Fantasy'. The soft rose of the original is crested and striped with green, and the petals, deeply slashed at the edges, curl and twist in all directions. The laciniated petals are the distinguishing feature of the Parrots. The name comes from the appearance of the flower in bud, which was thought to resemble a parrot's beak. In the Parrot class are some of the showiest and most daring of garden tulips, bred now with stems more capable of carrying their cargo than were the early cultivars of this class. The tulip's propensity to sport in this way was known from 1665 and Parrots appear in many early flower paintings. They were all 'Bizarres' (i.e. red and yellow colours) until in 1907 Barr & Son introduced the purple and white Parrot 'Sensation', a sport discovered in a bed of the Bybloemen breeder 'Reine d'Espagne'. The group contains many interesting cultivars, height 40–60 cm, flowering in May. Some, such as 'Orange Parrot', are scented.

Division 11 DOUBLE LATE: 'Better dead' said Hall, who sensibly never thought it worth disguising his prejudices. These tulips, sometimes called 'peony-flowered', have huge heads of flower, bursting in an untidy way with petals. Like the Single Lates, they do not stand up well to bad weather, but look wonderful in pots in cool conservatories, blooming mid to late May. They grow to 45–60 cm They are mentioned in the *Hortus Eystettensis,* published in 1613, but became fashionable only during the last quarter of the seventeenth century. Although tulip fanciers such as Hall considered them deeply unrefined, an old Double Late called 'Blue Flag' holds the record in my own garden for longevity of bloom, standing in good fettle for nearly a month.

Division 12 KAUFMANNIANA: The three groups of what are sometimes called 'botanical tulips' are based on the wild species from which the original selections were made. Now that so many cultivars are interbred from the three groups, the original distinctions are difficult to maintain. The Kaufmanniana tulips arise from the species *T. kaufmanniana,* called the water-lily tulip because of the way it opens flat in the sun. The petals tend to be long and thin, and the leaves are sometimes mottled with dark purplish-brown. The flowers are early (mid-March onwards) and generally short (from 15–25 cm).

Division 13 FOSTERIANA: *T. fosteriana* crossed with other species such as *T. greigii* and *T. kaufmanniana* produced this useful group of cultivars and hybrids. The splendid Fosteriana 'Red Emperor', selected by J M C Hoog of van Tubergen's from wild bulbs collected from the mountain region near Samarkand, was later crossed with Darwin tulips to produce the important race of Darwin Hybrid tulips. The foliage may be a clear glossy green as in the outstanding scarlet 'Cantata', or it may be grey-green. Fosterianas generally flower from early April onwards and are taller (20–45 cm) than the Kaufmannianas.

Division 14 GREIGII: The strongly mottled and striped, ground-hugging foliage of the species *T. greigii* is one of the outstanding characteristics of this group. The leaves often have wavy edges. The inner petals of the flowers tend to remain upright while the outer ones splay out extravagantly. D W Lefeber raised some of the most outstanding cultivars, such as 'Oriental Splendour' and 'Royal Splendour', by crossing *T. greigii* with Darwins to get extra large blooms on tall stems. First displayed in the Keukenhof gardens in Holland. Like the Kaufmanniana types, these are low-growing (20–30 cm) and generally flower in late March or early April.

Division 15 OTHER SPECIES: These are listed on pp 279–345. Some of the most useful for garden planting are *T. batalinii, T. pulchella* and *T. whittallii. T. sprengeri* is markedly late-flowering, appearing usually in June. In Britain, it is the only tulip that self-seeds with any success in gardens.

ABU HASSAN (Triumph)

Height 50 cm. Dark mahogany-red with edge of deep gold around the top half of petal. Outer segments have tendency to curl in on themselves. The flower never splays out, or opens up to show inside. Distinct yellow blotch at base of segments inside. Sulphurous yellow stigma, purple-black stamens and anthers. Flowers early May. Raised by J F van den Berg & Sons, C Roet & Sons in 1976.

AD REM (Darwin hybrid)

Height 60 cm. Scarlet, the edges of the petals touched with yellow, black base. Anthers yellow. Flowers in late April – May. Raised in 1960 by Konijnenburg & Mark.

ADDIS (Greigii)

Height 20 cm. Tall, thin, square-based bloom, sulphur-yellow inside, warm apricot-yellow outside, the tips of the petals stained with red which gradually spreads as the flower ages. Bronze base. Good foliage. Flowers in April. Raised in 1955 by A Overdevest.

AFRICAN QUEEN (Triumph)

Height 55 cm. Rich, glowing ruby-red, the base inside primrose-yellow edged with purple. Anthers purple. Raised in 1983 by J Ligthart.

ALADDIN (Lily-flowered)

Height 55 cm. Strongly reflexed flowers, scarlet edged with yellow. Yellow base. Flowers in mid May. Raised in 1942 by De Mol-Nieuwenhuis.

ALASKA (Lily-flowered)

Height 60 cm. Strongly reflexed yellow flower, now generally replaced by 'West Point'. Flowers in May. Raised in 1918 by E H Krelage and Son.

ALBINO (Triumph)

Height 45 cm. Pure white. Flowers in late April – early May. Raised in 1917 by E H Krelage and won many awards in its heyday.

ALEPPO (Fringed)

Height 50 cm. Outside dull red with a crystalline apricot-coloured fringe. The inside is apricot, flamed with purple. The base inside is bright yellow, but outside, the bottom of the petals is suffused with a bluish-grey. Anthers soft yellow. Raised by Segers in 1969.

ALFRED CORTOT (Kaufmanniana)

Award of Garden Merit (AGM)

Height 25 cm. Deep scarlet with a jet-black base, the outsides of the petals carmine-red. Heavily striped foliage. Flowers in March. Raised in 1942 by van Tubergen.

ALI BABA (Greigii)

Height 30 cm. The outsides of the petals are pale rose, the insides scarlet. Base yellow with red blotches. Mottled foliage. Flowers in March. Raised in 1955 by C V Hybrida.

ALICE LECLERCQ (Double Early)
Height 30 cm. Bright orange-red with a narrow yellow edge round the petals. Flowers mid to late April. Raised in 1952 by P Dames. Absolutely gorgeous.

ALL BRIGHT (Single Late)
Height 50 cm. Carmine-red with a lighter blood-red edge to the petals. Blue base. A sport of 'Bartigon', known since 1937. Flowers mid to late May.

ALLEGRETTO (Double Late)
Height 35 cm. Full double flowers, bright red edged with yellow. Flowers in May. Raised in 1963 by J F van den Berg & Sons.

AMULET (Triumph)
Height 45 cm. Exterior ivory-white, edged with buttercup-yellow. The insides of the petals ivory, tinged with yellow at the top. Anthers purple. Raised in 1965 by H Wiedijk, C J Wigchert.

ANCILLA (Kaufmanniana) AGM
Height 20 cm. The insides of the petals are pure white, with a distinctive red ring round the base. The outsides of the petals are flushed with soft pink and deep rose, yellow towards the base. Flowers mid – end March. Raised in 1955

by van Tubergen Ltd. Despite its AGM not a good-looking tulip.

ANGELIQUE (Double Late)
Height 45 cm. The small double pale pink flowers gradually darken as they age. The petals are edged and streaked with a lighter tone and the central ribs of the outer petals are flushed with green. Slightly scented. Flowers in mid May. A sport of 'Granda' raised in 1959 by D W Lefeber.

ANNE CLAIRE (Triumph)
Height 55 cm. Magenta-rose with a base of creamy-white. Flowers in early – mid May. Raised in 1958 by C Colijn & Sons.

ANNEKE (Triumph)
Height 50 cm. Exterior claret-rose, inside bright red with a buttercup-yellow base. Anthers purple. Raised in 1967 by H G Huyg.

ANTWERP (Triumph)
Height 60 cm. The insides of the petals are carmine, the outsides rosy-red. Sulphur-yellow base. Black stamens. Flowers late April – early May. Raised in 1962 by J F van den Berg & Sons.

APELDOORN (Darwin hybrid)
Height 55 cm. Exceptionally large, rounded orange-scarlet flowers with well-marked three-pronged base of yellow. Interior blotch black edged with yellow.

Stamens black. Flowers mid April. Raised in 1951 by D W Lefeber & Co.

APELDOORN'S ELITE (Darwin hybrid) AGM

Height 55 cm. Butter-yellow flowers, the outsides of the petals with a clean red central section, slightly larger than the yellow bands either side. Base yellowish-green. Flowers in late April – early May.

APRICOT BEAUTY (Single Early)

Height 45 cm. Triangular flat-based buds open to salmon-pink flowers faintly tinged with orange. Sport of 'Imperator'. Flowers early – mid April. Raised in 1953 by C van den Vlugt van Kimmenande.

APRICOT PARROT (Parrot) AGM

Height 50 cm. Pale apricot-yellow tinged creamy-white and rose. Purple stamens. A sport of 'Karel Doorman'. Flowers in mid May. Raised in 1961 by H G Huig. Slightly wishy-washy colour.

ARABIAN MYSTERY (Triumph)

Height 40 cm. A wonderful rich violet-purple, silvery-white at the edges of the petals. Flowers mid May. Raised in 1953 by P Hopman & Sons.

ARIE ALKEMADE'S MEMORY (Double Early)

Height 35 cm. Glowing vermilion-red. Flowers mid April. Raised in 1959 by C P Alkemade.

ARISTOCRAT (Single Late) AGM

Height 70 cm. Big egg-shaped flowers, clear magenta-pink with lighter edges around the petals. Flowers mid May. Raised in 1938 by Segers Bros when it was described as 'purplish-violet'.

ARLINGTON (Single Late)

Height 70 cm. Blood-red. Flowers early – mid May. Raised in 1942 by F Rijnveld & Sons.

ARMA (Fringed)

Height 35 cm. Cardinal-red, the edges of the petals frilled and fringed. Sport of 'Couleur Cardinal'. Flowers late April. Raised in 1962 by Knijn Bros.

ARTIST (Viridiflora)

Height 30 cm. Broad, stubby flower with pointed petals of subdued terracotta. There is a broad band of green flecked with purple up the centre of the outside of the petals. The insides are deep salmon-pink and green. Flowers in mid May. Raised in 1947 by Captein Bros.

ASTA NIELSEN (Single Late)

Height 70 cm. A large, long bloom, the insides of the petals bright yellow, the outsides sulphur. Flowers early – mid May. Raised in 1950 by Segers Bros.

ATHLEET (Triumph)

Height 45 cm. Large though not well-shaped flowers of pure white. A sport of

'Weber'. Flowers late April. Raised in 1942 by E Kooi.

ATTILA (Triumph)
Height 50 cm. Strong stems carry long-lasting magenta-pink flowers, rounded in form. Flowers early May. Raised in 1942 by G van der Mey.

AUREOLA (Single Late)
Height 60 cm. Bright red edged with golden-yellow. A sport of 'Elmus'. Flowers late April – early May. Raised in 1944 by N & J Roozen.

BALALAIKA (Single Late)
Height 70 cm. Bulky, glowing, clean turkey-red flower with a yellow base. The inside is beautifully marked with an arrow shape of yellow, dusted with black at the base. The base on the outer petals is the reverse shape and has more black, less yellow. Dark grey stamens. Flowers in early May. Raised in 1952 by Konijnenburg & Mark.

BALLADE (Lily-flowered) AGM
Height 55 cm. This has a broad profile for a Lily-flowered tulip, the long, sharply reflexed petals of the pink-mauve flower edged with white. The three outer petals curl back, but at first, the inner ones remain closed over centre. A faint creamy flush, very small, on the outside base of the petals. A rather surprising turquoise-green blotch on white ground on the inside base of the petals. The insides of all the petals are paler than the outsides. Stamens yellow-striped green. Flowers early – mid May. Raised in 1953 by Nieuwenhuis Bros.

BALLERINA (Lily-flowered) AGM
Height 55 cm. Outside flamed with blood-red on lemon-yellow ground with orange-yellow veined edge; inside feathered marigold-orange with bright red. Base a buttercup-yellow star with anthers of pale golden-yellow. Scented. Raised in 1980 by J F van den Berg & Sons.

BANDOENG (Triumph)
Height 40 cm. Mahogany-red flower flushed with orange. Flowers late April – early May. Raised by J F van den Berg.

BASTOGNE (Triumph)
Height 60 cm. Blood-red, the outsides of the petals flamed with cardinal-red. Flowers late April.

BEAUTY OF APELDOORN (Darwin hybrid)
Height 55 cm. The inside of the flower is golden-yellow with a black base, the outside is golden-yellow flushed with magenta. Black stamens. Sport of 'Apeldoorn'. Flowers in mid April. Raised in 1960 by Q M Bentvelsen.

BELCANTO (Single Late)
Height 50 cm. Exterior glowing cardinal-

red, feathered on a lemon-yellow edge. Inside blood-red, edged with lemon-yellow. Base yellow, anthers purple. Raised in 1965 by J F van den Berg & Sons.

BELLFLOWER (Fringed)

Height 60 cm. Clear rose-pink with a fine crystalline fringe, white base tinged with blue. Flowers in early – mid May. Raised in 1970 by Segers Bros.

BELLONA (Triumph)

Height 50 cm. A rounded, egg-shaped flower, deep golden-yellow, one of the best of this division. Scented. Flowers mid April and lasts longer in flower than the similar 'Candela'. Raised in 1944 by H de Graff & Sons.

BERLIOZ (Kaufmanniana)

Height 20 cm. Slightly pointed petals of lemon-yellow, the base on the inside a golden-yellow. The outside of the flower is flushed with reddish-brown. Foliage distinctly mottled with purplish-brown. Good in pots. Flowers mid March – early April. Raised in 1942 by van Tubergen Ltd.

BIG CHIEF (Darwin hybrid) AGM

Height 60 cm. Old rose flowers, the colour drifting to orange-red at the edges. The insides of the petals are flamed with cream. Indistinct base of canary-yellow which extends a good way up the inner petals. Flowers early May. Raised in 1960 by A Frylink & Sons.

BING CROSBY (Triumph)

Height 50 cm. Cup-shaped flowers of glowing scarlet, borne on strong stems. Flowers late April. Raised in 1947 by B P Heemskerk.

BIRD OF PARADISE (Parrot)

Height 40 cm. The inside of the flower is chrysanthemum-red, feathered with deeper red, the outside cardinal-red edged with golden-yellow. Base bright yellow. Anthers purple. Flowers mid May. Sport of 'Bandoeng'. Raised in 1962 by J de Goede.

BLACK PARROT (Parrot)

Height 50 cm. Glossy maroon-black, the inside dark purple, a most distinct variety. Flowers mid May. Sport of 'Philippe de Comines'. Raised in 1937 by C Keur & Sons.

BLACK SWAN (Single Late)

Height 70 cm. Fabulous dark, glossy, rounded flower, of deepest maroon. The base is pale blue, contrasting with deep maroon stamens. Lovely among wall-flowers or with bluebells. Raised in 1963 by Rijnveld & Sons.

BLENDA (Triumph)

Height 45 cm. Deep rose with a white base. Flowers late April. Raised in 1947 by L A Hoek.

The Double Late tulip 'Bonanza', raised in 1943

BLEU AIMABLE (Single Late)

Height 60 cm. A fine shade of lavender-mauve which improves as the flower ages. Base deeply stained. Hall condemned its 'ugly, spreading shape'. Flowers early May. Raised in 1916 by E H Krelage & Son.

BLUE HERON (Fringed)

Height 60 cm. A two-toned flower, the violet-purple petals lightening in colour towards the crystal fringed edges. Flowers early May. Raised in 1970 by Segers Bros.

BLUE PARROT (Parrot)

Height 55 cm. An enormous tulip with a strong stem, the flower a distinctive shade of bluish-purple, the outsides of the petals shaded with bronze. This is a subdued Parrot, the petals not as jaggedly outrageous as those of many others of its class. A sport of 'Bleu Aimable'. Flowers mid May. Raised in 1935 by Jan Dix Jnr.

BLUSHING LADY (Single Late)

Height 75 cm. Exterior yellow, the outside petals with a rosy flame. The inner petals have a gentle rose glow on the bottom halves. Base chartreuse-green on the outside, yellow on the inside. Anthers yellow. A sport of 'Temple of Beauty', raised in 1991 by D W Lefeber & Co.

BONANZA (Double Late)

Height 40 cm. Carmine-red edged with yellow. Flowers mid May. Raised in 1943.

BOULE DE NEIGE (Double Early)

Height 25 cm. Pure white. Flowers mid – late April. Raised in 1909.

BRAVISSIMO (Double Early)

Height 40 cm. Turkey-red with a deep yellow, brown-edged base. Flowers mid – late April. Raised in 1955 by P Nijssen & Sons.

BRILLIANT STAR (Single Early)

Height 30 cm. Dazzling vermilion-scarlet. Flowers early April. Good in pots. Raised in 1906.

BRUNO WALTER (Triumph)

Height 55 cm. Light orange. Flowers late April – early May. Raised in 1934 by E H Krelage & Son.

BURGUNDY (Lily-flowered)

Height 50 cm. Deep purplish-violet. Flowers mid May. Raised in 1957 by J J Grullemans & Sons.

BURGUNDY LACE (Fringed)

Height 70 cm. Wine-red flowers, each petal delicately fringed. Flowers mid May. Raised in 1961 by Segers Bros.

BURNS (Fringed)

Height 60 cm. The outside of the petals is phlox-pink, the inside rose, edged with violet. Base greyish-white. Flowers mid May. Raised by Segers Bros in 1968.

CABARET (Lily-flowered)

Height 55 cm. The inside of the petals is turkey-red, the outside cherry-red, with a clear yellow base. Flowers early – mid May. Raised in 1963 by Nieuwenhuis Bros.

CALAND (Parrot)

Height 55 cm. Purple with a deep blue base. A sport of 'Blue Parrot'. Flowers mid May. Raised in 1958 by Segers Bros.

CALYPSO (Greigii)

Height 30 cm. Outside tomato-red with a bright yellow margin, base blackish-brown, edged with lemon-yellow. Mottled leaves. Raised in 1992 by Jan van Bentem.

CANDELA (Fosteriana)

Height 35 cm. Large, oblong flowers of a uniform soft golden-yellow. Black anthers. Flowers early April. Raised in 1961 by K van Egmond & Sons.

CANTATA (Fosteriana)

Height 30 cm. Very thin pointed buds which open out to a well-shaped flower with pointed petals of bright vermilion-red. Foliage handsome and glossy. An outstanding tulip. Flowers early April. Raised in 1942 by van Tubergen.

CANTOR (Triumph)

Height 55 cm. Flowers of good substance in a pleasing shade of soft coral-pink. Flowers early May. Raised in 1960 by C Colijn & Sons.

CAPE COD (Greigii)

Height 30 cm. Yellow flowers have a broad indeterminate red stripe up the centre of the outsides of the petals. Base black edged with red. The grey-green foliage is marked with maroon stripes. Flowers late March – early April. Raised in 1955 by C V Hybrida.

CAPRI (Triumph) AGM

Height 40 cm. A brilliant cardinal red, deepening to claret inside. Purple base, edged with white. Raised in 1974 by Bik, Jac. Tol.

CAPRICE (Parrot)

Height 55 cm. Violet-rose flower. A sport of 'Blue Parrot'. Flowers mid May. Raised in 1951 by Segers Bros.

CAPTAIN FRYATT (Lily-flowered)

Height 50 cm. Garnet-red, gracefully reflexed. Flowers early – mid May. Raised in 1931 by van Tubergen.

CARLTON (Double Early)

Height 40 cm. Deep turkey-red. Flowers late April. Raised in 1950 by C P Alkemade.

CARNAVAL DE NICE (Double Late)

Height 50 cm. The stubby, full double flowers open to a wide, shallow bowl, sparkling white feathered with two tones of deep pink. A very showy garden tulip, with dark stamens set off against a pale cream base. Sport of 'Nizza'. The lance-shaped leaves are greyish-green, very finely outlined in white. Flowers in May. Raised in 1953 by van Tubergen.

CARRARA (Triumph)

Height 55 cm. Good late-flowering white selfs are rare as most lack vigour and constitution. This is a big, loose-petalled variety, with petals that reflex widely to make a flat bloom like a water-lily. The white is not brilliant, but white stamens contribute to the ethereal effect. The stem is rather weak for the size of flower. Flowers early May. Raised in 1912 by E H Krelage & Son.

CASHMIR (Single Late)

Height 70 cm. Light red. The base is yellow, thinly edged with green. Anthers yellow. A sport of 'Halcro' raised by Segers Bros in 1969.

CASSINI (Triumph)

Height 45 cm. Well-formed flower of deep velvety brownish-red. Flowers early May. Raised in 1944 by Segers Bros.

CESAR FRANCK (Kaufmanniana)

Height 20 cm. The outsides of the petals are carmine-red edged with lemon-yellow, the insides golden-yellow. Both colours are clean and clear but the combination is harsh. The three outer petals roll back on themselves. Good foliage, striped purple like snakeskin. Flowers mid March. Raised in 1940 by F Rijnveld & Sons.

CHARLES (Triumph)

Height 40 cm. A fine scarlet flower with a yellow base. Flowers mid April. Raised in 1954 by C P Alkemade.

CHARLES NEEDHAM (Single Late)

Height 60 cm. Scarlet flower with black base. Flowers early – mid May. Raised in 1931 by van Tubergen.

CHINA LADY (Greigii) AGM

Height 30 cm. A rose-coloured flower, edged with white. Base a curious bronze, streaked with red. Mottled foliage. Raised by Hybrida in 1953.

CHINA PINK (Lily-flowered)

Height 45 cm. An old, but supremely elegant tulip, the gently reflexed flowers opening from tightly furled, pointed buds. In sun, the flower makes a wide, flat star. The soft satin-pink petals fade to a white base, with a central ring of pale cream stamens. Long-lasting. Flowers in early May. Raised in 1944 by de Mol-Nieuwenhuis.

CHOPIN (Kaufmanniana)

Height 25 cm. The inside of the lemon-yellow flower has a dark blotch at the base. The grey-green foliage is mottled with brown. Flowers March. Raised in 1942 by van Tubergen.

CHRISTMAS DREAM (Single Early)

Height 35 cm. Outside fuchsia-red, inside

a paler rose. Large white base with indefinite yellow basal blotch, anthers greenish-yellow. A sport of 'Christmas Marvel', raised in 1973 by L J C Schoorl. Flowers late April.

CHRISTMAS GOLD (Single Early)

Height 45 cm. Long, narrow, pointed flower of bright clean canary-yellow. Pronounced ribbing up the centre of the petals, but no other colouring. Stamens orange, anthers yellow. Very like 'Candela' but with a longer, better-shaped head. It lasts well. Flowers mid March. Introduced in 1948 by P Nijssen & Sons.

CHRISTMAS MARVEL (Single Early)

Height 35 cm. Cherry-pink flower. Scented. Flowers late April. Raised in 1954 by L Schoorl.

CLARA BUTT (Single Late)

Height 55 cm. For a long time one of the most widely grown of all tulips, combining delicacy of colour with a graceful habit of growth. The petals are short but the flower makes a very good round cupped shape which opens well. The colour is soft, bright salmon-pink. The white base is stained with grey. Flowers early May. Raised in 1889 by E H Krelage & Son.

COMPLIMENT (Lily-flowered)

Height 40 cm. Rosy-purple outside, the inside closer to lilac. Large, prominent base of soft yellow. Raised in 1969 by Nieuwenhuis Bros.

CONCERTO (Fosteriana)

Height 30 cm. A sulphur-tinged white, the inside base of the flower black, ringed with yellow. Flowers April. Raised by C V Hybrida.

CORDELL HULL (Single Late)

Height 55 cm. Blood-red flooding over a white background makes this a showy garden tulip. The central disc is stained blue at the edges. Flowers mid May. A sport of 'Bartigon'. Known since 1933.

CORIOLAN (Triumph)

Height 40 cm. An orange-red flower edged with yellow. The inside of the petals is turkey-red. The base is yellow and green, the stamens violet. Flowers late April – early May. Raised in 1959 by Konijnenburg & Mark.

CORONA (Kaufmanniana)

Height 25 cm. Pale yellow flowers, the exterior flushed with red. Mottled foliage. Flowers March. Raised in 1948 by van Tubergen.

CORRIE KOK (Triumph)

Height 45 cm. Outside pinkish, inside red with a yellow base. Anthers purplish-blue. Raised in 1962 by van Zanten Bros.

CORSAGE (Greigii) AGM

Height 30 cm. The outside of the flowers is rose edged with yellow, the inside a richer shade of rose feathered with golden-yellow. Bronze base, yellow stamens. Mottled foliage. Flowers March. Raised in 1960 by C V Hybrida.

COULEUR CARDINAL (Triumph)

Height 35 cm. Among the latest of the early tulips. The flowers are large and form a good cup, of brilliant dark scarlet or cardinal-red with an attractive plum-coloured bloom on the outside of the petals. The colour is wonderfully lustrous, like the most expensive satin, dull on one side, rich on the other. Particularly resistant to bad weather. Flowers late April. Raised in 1845. 'Shines with the dusky splendour of old wine' said Walter Wright in 1911 when it was planted either side of the Broad Walk at Kew.

CRYSTAL BEAUTY (Fringed)

Height 55 cm. Exterior rose with a brightly coloured crystalline fringe, veering towards orange. Base black, edged with yellow. Raised in 1982 by P van Dijk & Sons.

DANCING SHOW (Viridiflora)

Height 45 cm. Canary-yellow, flamed with green on the outside of the petals. Anthers soft green. Raised in 1969 by Konijnenburg & Mark.

DAWNGLOW (Darwin hybrid)

Height 55 cm. Pale apricot flowers flushed with deep pink outside. Deep-yellow centre, purple anthers. Flowers mid – end April.

DAYDREAM (Darwin hybrid)

Height 55 cm. Lemon-yellow gradually turning to a soft apricot-orange. Flowers mid April. Raised in 1952 by van Tubergen.

DAYLIGHT (Kaufmanniana)

Height 25 cm. Brilliant scarlet with a black base striped with yellow. Mottled foliage. Flowers March. Raised in 1955 by M Thoolen.

DEMETER (Triumph)

Height 60 cm. Bright plum-purple. Flowers late April. Raised in 1932 by van Tubergen.

DIANA (Single Early)

Height 30 cm. Large, ivory-white, egg-shaped flowers are carried on strong stems. The petals are puckered in a marked way down the midrib. Good in pots. Flowers late April. Raised in 1909 by A van den Berg.

DIANTHA (Greigii)

Height 20 cm. Scarlet flower, slightly spotted on the insides of the petals with yellow. The base outside is greenish, inside bluish-black. Anthers yellow. Mottled foliage. Raised in 1982 by Uittenbogaard & Sons.

The Parrot tulip 'Doorman' raised in 1946

DILLENBURG (Single Late)

Height 60 cm. Neat, rounded, cup-shaped flowers, brick-orange edged with apricot. Flowers mid May. Raised in 1916 by van Tubergen.

DIX'S FAVOURITE (Triumph)

Height 50 cm. Glowing orange-red with a yellow base. Flowers early May. Raised in 1952 by J C Kavelaars.

DOCTOR JAMES PARKINSON (Triumph)

Height 60 cm. Glowing cardinal-red, with a small feathered white edge, the edge broader on the inside of the petals. White base with a small purple edge. Anthers pale yellow. Raised in 1981 by van der Wereld.

DOCTOR PLESMAN (Triumph)

Height 40 cm. A flower of good form and substance, vivid gleaming scarlet. Flowers early April. Fragrant. Raised in 1955 by van Graven Bros.

DOLL'S MINUET (Viridiflora)

Height 55 cm. Glowing purple with a wide deep-green streak down the outside of the petals. Small base of creamy-white. Flowers May.

DON QUICHOTTE (Triumph)

Height 50 cm. Unusually long-lasting, beautifully formed flowers of purplish-pink. Flowers mid May. Raised in 1952 by Konijnenburg & Mark.

DONNA BELLA (Greigii) AGM

Height 30 cm. The inside of the flower is creamy-yellow, the outside carmine edged with cream. The base is black with scarlet blotches. Handsome mottled foliage. Flowers March. Raised in 1955 by C V Hybrida.

DOORMAN (Parrot)

Height 50 cm. A stunning Parrot tulip, rich damask-red, twisted with yellow and green. Very large puckered petals. Yellow blotch stained black on inside of segments. Outside very little sign of base colour. Stigma cream, anthers and stamens blackish-yellow. Sport of 'Alberio'. Raised in 1946 by John B Meskers & Sons.

DOUGLAS BADER (Single Late)

Height 45 cm. A clear ivory-pink streaked with darker pink. Flowers April.

DOVER (Darwin hybrid) AGM

Height 55 cm. Enormous bloom of oriental scarlet, the outsides of the petals flushed with yellow at their base. The central blotch is purplish-black ringed round with yellow. Black stamens. Flowers late April. Raised in 1945 by D W Lefeber.

DREAMBOAT (Greigii)

Height 25 cm. Urn-shaped, long-petalled, amber-yellow flower, tinged with red. Base is greenish-bronze with red blotches. Grey-green leaves are striped with brown.

Flowers March. Raised in 1953 by C V Hybrida.

DREAMING MAID (Triumph)
Height 55 cm. Violet petals edged with white. This tulip is prone to 'breaking' and sometimes produces white flowers, wonderfully feathered and flamed with pinkish-purple. Flowers late April. Raised 1934 by J J Kerbert.

DREAMLAND (Single Late)
Height 60 cm. The egg-shaped red flower is flamed with cream. The inside is pinkish-red with a white base. Anthers yellow. Flowers early May. Raised in 1969 by H G Huyg.

DUKE OF WELLINGTON (Single Late)
Height 65 cm. White. Flowers early – mid May. Raised by J J Grullemans & Sons.

DUTCH GOLD (Triumph)
Height 40 cm. Bright buttercup-yellow. Flowers late April – early May. Raised in 1943 by de Mol-Nieuwenhuis.

DYANITO (Lily-flowered)
Height 55 cm. Glowing red with a deep yellow base. Flowers early May. Raised in 1949 by D van Buggenum.

EARLY HARVEST (Kaufmanniana) AGM
Height 25 cm. The outside of the flower is mandarin-red, finely edged with yellow, the inside yellow gently flushed

with carmine. Base deep yellow. Mottled foliage. Flowers March.

EARLY LIGHT (Single Early)
Height 35 cm. The inside of the flower is vermilion-orange, the outside red, edged with a slightly darker tone. Flowers mid – late April. Raised in 1961 by H G Huyg.

EASTER FIRE (Single Late)
Height 50 cm. Glowing cherry-red, the base buttercup-yellow. Anthers purple-black. Raised in 1965 by P Hermans.

EASTER PARADE (Fosteriana)
Height 40 cm. The inside of the flower is pure yellow with a complicated base, the outside yellow and red. Flowers April. Raised in 1954 by C V Hybrida.

EASTER SURPRISE (Greigii)
Height 40 cm. Rich lemon-yellow, the colour deepening to orange at the tops of the petals. Base bronze-green. Anthers deep purple. Mottled foliage. A sport of 'Tango', raised by Hybrida in 1965.

EL TOREADOR (Double Early)
Height 25 cm. Orange marked with a deeper orange. Flowers mid – late April. Sport of 'Tournesol'. Known since 1890.

ELECTRA (Single Late)
Height 25 cm. A flower of good form and substance, bright glistening cherry-

red. Sport of 'Murillo'. Flowers mid – late April. Known since 1905.

ELEGANT LADY (Lily-flowered)

Height 60 cm. Thin elegant bud opening to a creamy-yellow flower streaked with rose. Flowers mid May. Raised in 1953 by Nieuwenhuis Bros.

ELIZABETH ARDEN (Darwin hybrid)

Height 55 cm. A perfectly shaped flower of good substance, a beautiful rose-pink, gently flushed with violet. Small base of white and yellow. Flowers mid May. Raised in 1942 by de Mol-Nieuwenhuis.

ELMUS (Single Late)

Height 60 cm. Cherry-red edged with white. Flowers late April – early May. Raised in 1933 by J F van den Berg.

ENGADIN (Greigii) AGM

Height 35 cm. A rich red flower, edged with yellow on the outside, the yellow dominating inside. Mottled foliage. Raised in 1955 by C V Hybrida.

EROS (Double Late)

Height 55 cm. Enormous flower of rose-pink with broad cream-yellow flames up the centre of the outside of the petals. Strongly scented. Flowers May. Raised in 1937 by Zocher & Co.

ESPERANTO (Viridiflora)

Height 30 cm. Green and white flowers touched with raspberry-pink on the edges. Greenish-yellow base and greenish anthers. Variegated leaf, neatly edged with white. Flowers May. A sport of 'Hollywood', raised in 1968 by J Pranger.

ESTELLA RIJNVELD (Parrot)

Height 50 cm. Large flowers, one of the best of the Parrots, the petals deeply cut and waved, striped like raspberry-ripple ice cream with rich red on a white ground. Occasional flecks of green. Flowers mid May. Raised in 1954 by Dr de Mol of Segers Bros and named after his wife.

ESTHER (Single Late)

Height 50 cm. Fuchsia-pink flower with a lighter edge. Flowers mid May. Raised in 1967 by C J Keppel.

FAIR LADY (Kaufmanniana)

Height 25 cm. The inside of the flower is cream, striped with red, the outside carmine, edged with cream. Yellow base. Flowers March. Raised in 1939 by van Tubergen Ltd.

FANCY FRILLS (Fringed) AGM

Height 45 cm. Boudoir-pink flower with broad white base extending a third of the way up the petals, flaring up in lines to the tips. Inner petals have prominent midrib of white up the centre of the inside of the petal. The fringing goes off madly in all directions. There is a clean white centre on the inside base, pale

The Parrot tulip 'Flaming Parrot' raised in 1968 by P Heemskerk, C A Veerdegaal

370

creamy stigma, cream stamens, yellowish anthers. A pretty-pretty tulip, with its clean pale green stem. Flowers mid May. Raised in 1972 by Segers, W A M Pennings.

FANTASY (Parrot) AGM

Height 55 cm. A superb, huge, blowsy tulip which splays open in sunshine to show mad petals of soft rose, crested and striped with green. Wildly formless, but showy and fun, the petals having a rich, satiny sheen, paler on the outside than within. A sport of 'Clara Butt'. Flowers mid May. Known since 1910.

FASHION (Kaufmanniana)

Height 30 cm. Scarlet with a yellow base. Flowers March. Raised in 1962 by Hagen Bros.

FEU SUPERBE (Fosteriana)

Height 35 cm. Cardinal red, the black base edged with yellow. Flowers late April – early May. Raised in 1942 by van Tubergen Ltd.

FIDELIO (Triumph) AGM

Height 55 cm. A huge, longish, slightly formless but attractive flower, soft rich yellow, the outsides of the petals shaded with pale pink and green. Flowers early May. Raised in 1952 by G R Tromp.

FIREBIRD (Parrot)

Height 55 cm. Pale rose-coloured Parrot,

the petals feathered with green. A sport of 'Fantasy'. Flowers mid May. Known in 1939.

FIRST LADY (Triumph) AGM

Height 55 cm. A strong-stemmed tulip of reddish-violet, flushed with purple. Flowers late April. Raised in 1951 by C V Hybrida.

FLAIR (Single Early)

Height 35 cm. Buttercup-yellow, flamed and feathered on the outside with vermilion. The inside of the flower is a paler yellow. Good in pots. Flowers late April.

FLAMING PARROT (Parrot)

Height 70 cm. A beautiful Parrot, creamy-yellow, flamed and feathered with red. Primrose-yellow base. Flowers mid May.

FLORADALE (Darwin hybrid)

Height 60 cm. Exterior red, edged with a slightly paler red, the same colour as the insides of the petals. Base pale yellow on the outside, yellow and blue on the inside. Stamens black. Flowers mid – late April. Raised in 1954 by D W Lefeber & Co.

FLYING DUTCHMAN (Single Late)

Height 60 cm. Square bloom of vermilion-scarlet, the basal blotch light bluish-purple with a white edge. Flowers early – mid May. Raised in 1956 by Warnaar & Co.

The Fringed tulip 'Fringed Beauty' raised in 1931

FORMOSA (Viridiflora)

Height 30 cm. Golden-yellow tulip with a broad green stripe down the centre of the petals. Flowers May. Raised in 1926 by Polman Mooy.

FRANZ LEHAR (Kaufmanniana)

Height 30 cm. Sulphur-white inside, sulphur outside, blotched with red. Yellow base. Flowers March. Raised in 1955 by J C van der Meer.

FRASQUITA (Single Late)

Height 65 cm. Carmine edged with vermilion. Flowers early – mid May. Raised in 1953 by Konijnenburg & Mark Ltd.

FRESCO (Greigii)

Height 40 cm. The outside of the flower is rose, edged with cream, the inside signal-red. The base is black on yellow. Stamens black. Mottled foliage. Flowers March. Raised in 1959 by C V Hybrida.

FRINGED APELDOORN (Fringed)

Height 55 cm. Large flowers, the orange-scarlet petals topped with crystalline fringes. Flowers mid April.

FRINGED BEAUTY (Fringed)

Height 25 cm. Vermilion-red with fringed golden-yellow margins. Sport of 'Titian'. Flowers mid – late April. Known in 1931.

FRINGED ELEGANCE (Fringed)

Height 60 cm. Neatly fringed, primrose-yellow flowers, dotted on the outside with pink. Base bronze-green, anthers purple. Flowers early May. Sport of 'Jewel of Spring', raised in 1974 by Johan C van Reisen.

FRITZ KREISLER (Kaufmanniana)

Height 30 cm. Deep pink, the outside of the petals mauve, edged with sulphur-yellow. Base deep yellow with carmine-red blotches. Flowers March. Raised in 1942 by van Tubergen Ltd.

GAIETY (Kaufmanniana)

Height 20 cm. A flower like a water-lily, the inside creamy-white, the outside pinkish-violet, edged with cream. Orange base. Flowers March. Raised by van Tubergen Ltd.

GALA BEAUTY (Rembrandt)

Height 60 cm. Yellow streaked with crimson. Flowers May. Known since 1620 under the names 'Columbus' or 'French Crown'.

GALATA (Fosteriana)

Height 40 cm. Orange-red with a yellow base. Flowers April. Raised in 1942 by D W Lefeber & Co.

GANDER (Triumph)

Height 60 cm. Bright magenta. Flowers early May. Raised in 1952 by Segers Bros.

GANDER'S RHAPSODY (Triumph)

Height 60 cm. White ground, spotted and edged with cherry-red. Flowers mid May. Raised in 1970 by Jac. Tol.

GARANZA (Double Early)

Height 25 cm. Very large flower of rich peach-blossom pink. Sport of 'Murillo'. Flowers late April. Raised in 1944 by Segers Bros.

GARDEN PARTY (Triumph)

Height 40 cm. White ground with the outer petals very clearly marked in raspberry-ripple-red, making two straight lines meeting at the centre-top of the petals. Large flower, opening to a wide cup, the petals tipping slightly out at the tops. Inner petals mostly red with indeterminate white flushing at the base of the petals. The inner petals have arrow-shaped white flushes, the arrow head being the base. The insides of the outer petals are not so determinedly marked, but the whole makes a regular pattern. Base white, stigma pale creamy-green. Stamens white, anthers yellow. Flowers early May. Raised in 1944 by P Hopman & Sons Ltd.

GENERAAL DE WET (Single Early)

Height 40 cm. 'The most beautiful of all the early tulips' says A D Hall. A sport of 'Prince of Austria' with a bright yellow ground, finely netted over with deep orange or red-brown. Finely scented. In its best form, superb, but it has a tendency to drift into a less good type with rather dull splashes of light brown, instead of the fine grizzling of orange upon the yellow ground. Flowers mid April and beautiful with grape hyacinths, blue violets or forget-me-not. Known since 1904 and named after one of the commanders in the South African Boer War.

GENERAL EISENHOWER (Darwin hybrid)

Height 55 cm. A very vigorous tulip of brilliant scarlet. White base, edged with blue. Black stamens. Flowers mid April. Raised in 1951 by D W Lefeber & Co.

GEORGETTE (Single Late)

Height 50 cm. A multi-flowered tulip on a strong stem, producing up to four blooms of yellow, beautifully edged with red. Flowers mid May. Raised in 1952 by C V Hybrida.

GIUSEPPE VERDI (Kaufmanniana)

Height 30 cm. Tall, thin pointed flower, the outside carmine edged with yellow, the inside golden-yellow blotched with red. Mottled foliage. Flowers late March – early April. Raised in 1955 by J C van der Meer.

GLUCK (Kaufmanniana)

Height 20 cm. Sulphur-yellow, flushed on the outside with carmine red. Base golden-yellow. Mottled foliage. Flowers mid April. Raised in 1940 by van Tubergen.

GOLDEN AGE (Single Late)
Height 55 cm. Deep buttercup-yellow, the edges of the petals salmon. Flowers early – mid May. Raised in 1930 by van Tubergen.

GOLDEN APELDOORN (Darwin hybrid)
Height 55 cm. Wide-cupped, golden yellow flower with a star-shaped black base that shows bronze-green on the outside. Black stamens. Sport of 'Apeldoorn'. Flowers mid April. Raised 1960 by C Gorter Czn & A Overdevest Gz.

GOLDEN ARTIST (Viridiflora)
Height 30 cm. Bright golden-yellow, with a broad green flame up the back of each petal, the flame pushing the petal into a sharp point. Sport of 'Artist'. Flowers May. Raised in 1959 by Captein Bros.

GOLDEN EAGLE (Fosteriana)
Height 40 cm. Deep golden-yellow, the outsides of the petals apricot. The base is brownish-bronze with scarlet blotches. Flowers April. Raised in 1955 by C V Hybrida.

GOLDEN EDDY (Triumph)
Height 40 cm. Red edged with yellow. Sport of 'Edith Eddy'. Flowers late April

– early May. Raised in 1956 by N Zandbergen.

GOLDEN EMPEROR (Fosteriana)
Height 40 cm. Pure golden-yellow. Flowers early May. Raised in 1957 by C V Hybrida.

GOLDEN HARVEST (Single Late)
Height 60 cm. Lemon-yellow. Flowers early – mid May. Raised in 1928 by Nicolaas Dames.

GOLDEN MELODY (Triumph)
Height 55 cm. Buttercup-yellow, yellow stamens. Scented and lasts well. Flowers late April. Raised in 1961 by P Hermans.

GOLDEN OXFORD (Darwin hybrid)
Height 55 cm. Large solid flower of golden-yellow, carried on a strong stem. Yellow base, black stamens. Sport of 'Oxford'. Flowers late April. Raised in 1959 by A Overdevest.

GOLDEN PARADE (Darwin hybrid)
Height 60 cm. Yellow, the outside paler than the inside. Base greenish-black, stamens black. Sport of 'Parade'. Flowers mid – end April. Raised in 1963 by A Overdevest.

GOLDEN SHOW (Triumph)
Height 45 cm. Large bloom of deep yellow, sweetly scented. Flowers end April – early May. Raised in 1953 by Jac. Tol Jnr.

GOLDEN SPRINGTIME (Darwin hybrid)
Height 55 cm. Pure yellow with a yellow base. Sport of 'Springtime'. Flowers mid – end April. Raised in 1957 by D W Lefeber.

GOLDENES DEUTSCHLAND (Darwin hybrid)
Height 55 cm. Gold with a tiny red edge. The base green and anthers purple. A sport of 'Deutschland', raised in 1969 by D W Lefeber.

GORDON COOPER (Darwin hybrid)
Height 60 cm. Petals are deep pink outside, drifting to red at the edges. The inside is glowing signal-red with a black and yellow basal blotch. Black anthers. Flowers mid – late April. Raised in 1963 by Konijnenburg & Mark.

GOUDSTUK (Kaufmanniana)
Height 30 cm. The petals are deep golden-yellow inside, deep carmine edged with yellow on the outside. Flowers March. Raised in 1952 by van Tubergen.

GOYA (Double Early)
Height 25 cm. Orange-red with a yellow base. Sport of 'Oranje Nassau'. Flowers mid April. Raised in 1947 by P Bakker.

GRACEFUL (Greigii)
Height 35 cm. The outside is currant-red, edged with pale primrose, the inside scarlet. The base is buttercup-yellow blotched with bronzy-green. Flowers March. Raised in 1963 by Jac Uittenbogaard.

GRAND PRIX (Fosteriana)
Height 35 cm. The outside is scarlet edged with yellow, the inside golden-yellow with blood-red blotches. Flowers April. Raised in 1949 by van Tubergen.

GREEN EYES (Viridiflora)
Height 55 cm. Greenish-yellow, with deeper green stripes. Anthers yellow. Raised in 1968 by Konijnenburg & Mark.

GREEN SPOT (Viridiflora)
Height 55 cm. White with green stripes, the base dark blue. Anthers yellow. Raised in 1969 by Bik, Jac. Tol.

GREUZE (Single Late)
Height 55 cm. Generous cup-shaped flowers of violet-purple. Flowers mid May. Raised in 1905 by E H Krelage & Son.

GREVEL (Triumph)
Height 40 cm. Rose-pink edged with ivory-white. Flowers early May.

GROENLAND (Viridiflora)
Height 55 cm. One of the best of the Viridiflora tulips, a pale gentle pink, the flat-topped petals flared up the centre with a broad green stripe edged with cream. Flowers May. Raised in 1955 by J F van den Berg & Sons.

GUDOSHNIK (Darwin hybrid)

Height 60 cm. A huge pale yellow flower, spotted and flamed with red and rose. The colour is very variable, varying from an almost plain creamy-peach to a very heavily marked flower streaked overall with deep rose. Base bluish-black, stamens black. Flowers end April. Raised in 1952 by D W Lefeber & Co.

G W LEAK (Single Late)

Height 65 cm. Geranium-red. Flowers early – mid May. Raised in 1931 by van Tubergen Ltd.

HADLEY (Single Early)

Height 45 cm. Light salmon-pink flushed with orange. Flowers mid April. Raised in 1942 by Segers Bros.

HALCRO (Single Late) AGM

Height 70 cm. An oval-shaped bloom of immense size. Deep salmon-red. The base is yellow edged with green. Exceptionally long-lasting. Flowers mid May. Raised in 1949 by Segers Bros.

HAMILTON (Fringed)

Height 65 cm. Buttercup-yellow with a crystalline fringe of the same colour. Anthers yellow. Raised in 1974 by Segers Bros.

HAPPY FAMILY (Triumph)

Height 50 cm. Dusky-pink shading to a softer pink at the edges of the petals. Flowers early May.

HEART'S DELIGHT (Kaufmanniana)

Height 20 cm. Tall, thin flowers, the petals on the outside deep pinkish-red edged with a much paler pink, inside pale pink. Base is yellow with red blotches. Mottled foliage. Flowers March. Raised in 1952 by van Tubergen.

HENRY FORD (Single Late)

Height 60 cm. Carmine flower spotted with white and edged with raspberry-red. The base is purple edged with white, stamens purple. Flowers early – mid May. Raised in 1953 by J F van den Berg.

HIBERNIA (Triumph)

Height 45 cm. Large pure white bloom. Flowers early May. Raised in 1946 by Jac. Tol Jnr.

HIGH NOON (Triumph)

Height 45 cm. An outstanding variety, white with a broad carmine edge to the petals and a white centre. Flowers late April. Raised in 1953 by K Wiedijk.

HIGH SOCIETY (Triumph)

Height 45 cm. A strong, square bloom, salmon-orange, softening to orange yellow at the edges of the petals. Scented sport of 'Orange Wonder'. Flowers mid April. Raised in 1958 by Jac. Tol.

HIT PARADE (Fosteriana)

Height 40 cm. The outside petals yellow with a long scarlet flame and a broad yellow edge. Round blackish-brown base, edged with tomato-red. Anthers bright yellow. A sport of 'Easter Parade', raised in 1970 by W Lemmers Cz.

HOANGHO (Double Early)

Height 30 cm. Pure yellow scented bloom on a very strong stem. Flowers late April. Raised in 1940 by J F van den Berg.

HOLLAND'S GLORIE (Darwin hybrid) AGM

Height 60 cm. An immense flower carried on a very strong stem, the out-sides of the petals dazzling scarlet edged with poppy-red, drifting to yellow at the base. Inside mandarin-red with a green-ish-black base. Stamens black. Flowers end April. Raised in 1942 by D W Lefeber & Co.

HOLLYWOOD (Viridiflora)

Height 30 cm. Red flower tinged and streaked with green. Base yellow. Sport of 'Artist'. Flowers May. Raised in 1956 by Captein Bros.

HUMMING BIRD (Viridiflora)

Height 50 cm. A square-shaped flower on a strong stem, mimosa-yellow feathered with green. Flowers May. Raised in 1961 by D W Lefeber & Co.

HUMORESQUE (Fosteriana)

Height 45 cm. Cream-coloured bloom, the outside carmine-red edged with cream. Black base with blood-red blotches. Flowers April. Raised in 1952 by C V Hybrida.

HYTUNA (Double Late)

Height 40 cm. Buttercup-yellow, the inside lemon-yellow. Yellow stamens. Flowers mid – late April. Raised in 1959 by J F van den Berg & Sons.

IBIS (Single Early)

Height 30 cm. Deep rosy pink with a big arrow-shaped flame of white running up the outsides of the petals. Similar to, though not as well formed as 'Garden Party'. Sport of 'White Hawk'. Flowers mid April. Known by 1910.

ILE DE FRANCE (Triumph)

Height 50 cm. Stunning tulip with petals that are cardinal-red outside, blood-red inside. The base is dark bronze-green with a narrow yellow edge. Flowers May. Raised in 1968 by Blom & Padding.

INGLESCOMBE YELLOW (Single Late)

Height 45 cm. Yellow. One of a race of tulips including 'Inglescombe Pink' and 'Inglescombe Scarlet' raised by Walter Ware at Inglescombe, near Bath from 1902–1906.

INZELL (Triumph)

Height 45 cm. Ivory-white with yellow

The Lily-flowered tulip 'Jacqueline' raised in 1958

anthers. A sport of 'Blenda', raised in 1969 by N Koster & Sons.

IVORY FLORIDALE (Darwin hybrid)
Height 60 cm. The outsides of the petals are ivory-yellow, slightly spotted with carmine-red. The inside is creamy-yellow. Flowers late April.

JACK LAAN (Rembrandt)
Height 55 cm. The purple blooms are shaded with brown, the petals feathered with white and yellow. Flowers May. Raised in 1951 by C Colijn & Sons.

JACQUELINE (Lily-flowered)
Height 65 cm. A large elegant tulip of deep rose. Flowers mid May. Raised in 1958 by Segers Bros.

JAMES V FORRESTAL (Parrot)
Height 50 cm. Orange-red edged with yellow. Sport of 'Doorman'. Flowers mid May. Raised in 1955 by John B Meskers & Sons.

JAN VERMEER (Double Early)
Height 25 cm. Cardinal-red edged with yellow. Sport of 'Orange Nassau'. Flowers mid – late April. Raised in 1942 by P van Reisen & Sons.

JEANTINE (Kaufmanniana) AGM
Height 20 cm. Outside carmine edged with apricot, inside apricot-rose. Base golden-yellow. Flowers March. Raised in

1952 by van Tubergen.

JEWEL OF SPRING (Darwin hybrid) AGM
Height 60 cm. An enormous flower of sulphur-yellow, spotted with red. Base greenish-black, stamens black. Sport of 'Gudoshnik'. Flowers late April. Raised in 1956 by A Overdevest.

JIMMY (Triumph)
Height 35 cm. Inside jasper-red and orange, outside dull carmine-red edged with orange. Base lemon-yellow edged with green, stamens deep purple. Flowers early – mid May. Raised in 1962 by J van Hoorn & Co.

JOCKEY CAP (Greigii)
Height 25 cm. Outside deep carmine-rose edged with cream, inside signal-red. Base black edged with yellow, stamens purple-black. Mottled foliage. Flowers March. Raised in 1959 by C V Hybrida.

JOFFRE (Single Early)
Height 30 cm. Yellow. Sport of 'Brilliant Star'. Flowers mid April. Known by 1934.

JOHANN STRAUSS (Kaufmanniana)
Height 20 cm. A white bloom with a cream centre, the outside flushed with red. Brown striped foliage. Flowers March. Raised by van Tubergen.

JOHANNA (Triumph)
Height 45 cm. Salmon-rose with primrose

The Parrot tulip 'James V Forrestal' raised in 1955

base, black anthers. Flowers late April –
early May. Raised by Zocher & Co.

JUAN (Fosteriana)
Height 45 cm. A thin elegant tulip with
pointed buds opening into a long, square-
topped flower of brilliant orange overlaid
with scarlet. Base yellow, stamens yellow.
Very good foliage mottled with reddish-
brown. Flowers end March. Raised in
1961 by van Tubergen.

JUDITH LEYSTER (Triumph)
Height 55 cm. The red petals are flamed
with ivory and rose. Flowers mid May.
Raised in 1980 by IVT, G H van Went &
Sons.

KANSAS (Triumph)
Height 45 cm. A snow-white bloom of
good form and substance. Yellow base.
Flowers early May. Raised by Zocher &
Co before 1930.

KAREL DOORMAN *see* DOORMAN

KAREOL (Double Early)
Height 30 cm. Deep buttercup-yellow.
Flowers mid – late April. Raised in 1952
by C P Alkemade.

KEES NELIS (Triumph)
Height 45 cm. Blood-red edged with
orange-yellow. Base and anthers black.
Flowers early May. Raised in 1951 by H 't
Mannetje.

KEIZERSKROON (Single Early) AGM
Height 35 cm. One of the oldest of the
early tulips, a favourite since the eighteenth century. A tall, large tulip, each
petal making a bright scarlet flame with
a broad yellow edge. The outer petals are
much shorter than the inner ones.
Flowers April. Known since 1760 when it
was called 'Grand Duc'.

KINGSBLOOD (Single Late) AGM
Height 60 cm. Cherry-red edged with
scarlet. Flowers early May. Raised in 1952
by Konijnenburg & Mark.

K & M'S TRIUMPH (Triumph)
Height 40 cm. Glowing scarlet flower,
superbly flamed with cream on the
outside of the petals. Stubby flower, of
the shape favoured by the English
florists. Flowers late April – early May.
Raised 1952 by Konijnenburg & Mark.

KONINGIN WILHELMINA (Darwin
hybrid) AGM
Height 55 cm. Scarlet flower edged with
orange. Bright-yellow base. A scented
sport of 'Lefeber's Favourite'. Raised in
1965 by C Nieuwenhuis.

LA TULIPE NOIRE (Single Late)
Height 55 cm. Much recommended as
the darkest of all tulips. The colour is
brown-black rather than purple-black,
but the shape ragged and untidy. 'All
these dark tulips would be immensely

improved if they possessed the big white base of the English tulips' said A D Hall. Flowers early – mid May. Raised in 1891 by E H Krelage and Son.

LANDSEADEL'S SUPREME (Single Late) AGM
Height 60 cm. A glowing cherry-red bloom of great substance carried on a strong stem. Creamy-yellow base. Long-lasting. Flowers mid May. Raised in 1958 by D W Lefeber & Co.

LARGE COPPER (Greigii)
Height 30 cm. Glowing vermilion bloom flushed on the outside with violet. Brown base, lemon-yellow stamens. Flowers March. Raised in 1963 by L Stassen Jr.

LEEN VAN DER MARK (Triumph)
Height 45 cm. Exterior cardinal-red edged with white. The base ivory-white, spotted with pale yellow. Anthers greenish-yellow. Flowers mid April. Raised in 1968 by Konijnenburg & Mark.

LEFEBER'S FAVOURITE (Darwin hybrid)
Height 55 cm. An enormous, well-formed bloom of deep carmine edged with a glowing scarlet. Yellow base, black stamens. Flowers mid April. Raised in 1942 by D W Lefeber & Co.

LILAC TIME (Lily-flowered)
Height 45 cm. Intense violet-purple.

Yellow stamens. Flowers early May. Raised in 1943 by de Mol-Nieuwenhuis.

LONDON (Darwin hybrid)
Height 55 cm. A broad-petalled bloom of good texture, scarlet, flushed on the outside with blood-red. Black base edged with yellow, black stamens. Flowers late April. Raised in 1950 by D W Lefeber & Co.

LONGFELLOW (Greigii)
Height 50 cm. Signal-red, the outside of the petals vermilion, striped with a lighter red. Black base. Flowers March. Raised in 1960 by C V Hybrida.

LOS ANGELES (Triumph)
Height 45 cm. Signal-red, the petals edged on the outside with bright yellow. Base yellow, anthers black. Flowers late April.

LOVE SONG (Kaufmanniana)
Height 25 cm. Mandarin-red flower, flushed carmine on the outside, edged with yellow on the inside. Deep yellow base, mottled foliage. Flowers March.

LUCIFER (Single Late)
Height 50 cm. Orange-scarlet. Flowers early May. Known since 1907.

LUCKY STRIKE (Triumph)
Height 55 cm. Deep red edged with pale yellow. Flowers mid April. Raised in 1954 by P & J W Mantel.

LUSTIGE WITWE (Triumph)

Height 40 cm. Glowing deep red edged with white. Flowers early May. Raised in 1942 by G van der Mey's Sons.

MADAME LEFEBER (Fosteriana)

Height 40 cm. Generally considered one of the best early tulips. Long, thin buds open to very large, long-petalled flowers of brilliant oriental red. Neat basal blotch, black edged with yellow. Greyish foliage. Excellent, but not so stunning as 'Cantate'. Flowers late March – early April. Raised in 1931 by Dirk Lefeber of van Tubergen and named after his wife.

MADAME SPOOR (Triumph)

Height 50 cm. Mahogany-red edged with yellow. Flowers late April – early May. Raised in 1951 by N Zandbergen.

MADISON GARDEN (Fringed)

Height 50 cm. Exterior carmine, flamed red, with a pale yellow-pink crystalline fringe. The inside is carmine-pink, with a blue-tinted basal blotch on a creamy ground. Anthers dark grey. Raised in 1986 by W A M Pennings.

MAGIER (Single Late)

Height 60 cm. A glorious tulip, fine milky-white splashed with soft purple towards the edges of the petals. As the flower ages, the colour spreads over the whole petal. A most graceful and delicate bloom, with wide variations in the mark-

ings. Long-lasting. Flowers early May. Raised in 1951 by C V Hybrida.

MAJA (Fringed)

Height 65 cm. Cup-shaped flowers of pale yellow, the petals delicately fringed at the edges. Base bronze-yellow, anthers yellow. Flowers early May.

MAKASSAR (Triumph)

Height 45 cm. Dark canary-yellow. Flowers early May. Raised in 1942 by de Mol-Nieuwenhuis.

MAKE UP (Triumph)

Height 55 cm. Creamy-white flamed with cardinal-red towards the edges of the petals. Flowers mid May. Raised in 1969 by Bik, Jac. Tol.

MAMASA (Triumph)

Height 55 cm. Bright buttercup-yellow. Yellow anthers. Flowers early May. Raised in 1942 by de Mol-Nieuwenhuis.

MARCH OF TIME (Greigii)

Height 30 cm. Outside of the petals turkey-red, the insides deep orange. Base brownish-black, anthers yellow. Mottled foliage. Raised in 1970 by Captein Bros.

MARECHAL NIEL (Double Early)

Height 25 cm. Wide, stubby flower, the yellow pointed petals flushed with bright orange. Flowers late April. Sport of 'Murillo'. Known since 1930.

MARGOT FONTEYN (Triumph)

Height 40 cm. Bright red, edged with buttercup-yellow. Yellow base, black anthers. Flowers early – mid May. Raised in 1962 by H 't Mannetje.

MARIETTE (Lily-flowered)

Height 55 cm. A beautiful rose-pink bloom with very reflexed petals and a strong stem. Flowers mid May. Raised in 1942 by Segers.

MARILYN (Lily-flowered)

Height 55 cm. A boudoir flower, creamy-white with a broad blaze of strawberry-red at the tips of the petals and feathering of strawberry-red at the base. Flowers early May. Raised in 1976 by Verbruggen.

MARJOLEIN (lily-flowered) AGM

Height 55 cm. A sunset of a flower, orange, red and rose, a sport of 'Mariette'. Raised in 1962 by P Visser Cz.

MARQUETTE (Double Early)

Height 25 cm. Red edged with yellow. Sport of 'Murillo'. Flowers mid – late April. Known since 1914.

MARY ANN (Greigii)

Height 35 cm. The outsides of the petals are carmine-red edged with white, the insides pink on a white ground. Base bronze-green with scarlet blotches. Mottled foliage. Flowers March. Raised in 1955 by C V Hybrida.

MASKERADE (Single Late)

Height 55 cm. Yellow with narrow orange-red edges. Flowers early – mid May. Raised in 1942 by de Mol-Nieuwenhuis.

MAUREEN (Single Late) AGM

Height 70 cm. Long, oval bloom of great substance, white flushed with ivory. Strong stems. One of the best of the whites. Flowers mid May. Raised in 1950 by Segers Bros.

MAYTIME (Lily-flowered)

Height 50 cm. Purple-violet with a touch of white at the edges of the petals. Yellow base. Flowers early May. Raised in 1942 by de Mol-Nieuwenhuis.

MAYWONDER (Double Late)

Height 50 cm. A magnificent flower of old rose, very like a peony. Cream midribs up the backs of the petals. Flowers May. Raised in 1951 by C V Hybrida.

MEISSNER PORZELLAN (Triumph)

Height 55 cm. A variable tulip, rose and white, some all rose, others cream, edged very thinly with pink. Charming. Flowers late April. Raised in 1952 by Konijnenburg & Mark.

MENTON (Single Late)

Height 65 cm. Rose-pink petals are edged with pale orange. Base bright yellow and white, anthers yellow. A robust tulip, flowering in mid May. Raised in 1971 by W Dekker & Sons.

MERRY CHRISTMAS (Single Early)
Height 35 cm. Outside crimson edged with scarlet, the base of the petals blotched with white. Inside blood-red, the creamy-white base edged thinly with purple. Flowers late April. Raised in 1972 by Th. & W B Revs.

MERRY WIDOW *see* LUSTIGE WITWE

MICKEY MOUSE (Single Early)
Height 35 cm. Blood-red flamed on a yellow ground. Sport of 'Wintergold'. Flowers mid April. Raised in 1960 by E Kooi.

MINERVA (Triumph)
Height 45 cm. Outside of the petals cardinal-red, with a small white edge. The base soft yellow and the anthers black. Raised in 1969 by J F van den Berg & Sons.

MIRELLA (Triumph) AGM
Height 60 cm. A rich deep salmon-coloured flower, the colour running out at the edges of the petals. A sport of 'Advance', raised in 1953 by P Bijvoet & Co.

MIRJORAN (Triumph)
Height 45 cm. Carmine-red with a broad creamy-white edge. Flowers late April –

early May. Raised in 1944 by C V Hybrida.

MISS HOLLAND (Triumph)
Height 55 cm. Glowing blood-red flower, the base buttercup-yellow with a greenish margin. Anthers deep brown. Raised in 1973 by Bik, Jac. Tol.

MONA LISA (Lily-flowered)
Height 55 cm. Outsides of the petals primrose-yellow with a narrow red flame. Base slightly darker yellow. Anthers yellow. A sport of 'Marilyn', raised in 1988 by Verbruggen.

MONTE CARLO (Double Early) AGM
Height 30 cm. Double yellow, scented flowers, the colour paler on the outside, sparsely streaked with red. Flowers mid April. Raised in 1955 by Anton Nijssen & Sons.

MOST MILES (Triumph) AGM
Height 60 cm. Currant-red with a yellow base. Flowers early – mid May. Raised in 1944 by de Mol-Nieuwenhuis.

MOUNT TACOMA (Double Late)
Height 45 cm. Short stubby white flower that splays open wide to reveal a very full centre of short secondary petals. Untidy but generous. Stigma cream, anthers pale yellow. Very faint flush of yellow at base of petals and a rib of green up the outside of the outer petals.

Flowers May. Raised before 1924 by Polman Mooy.

MR VAN DER HOEF (Double Early)
Height 25 cm. Fine deep canary-yellow, but an untidy flower, thin for a double. Sport of 'Murillo'. Flowers mid April. Known since 1911.

MRS JOHN T SCHEEPERS (Single Late) AGM
Height 60 cm. Large refined egg-shaped flowers of canary-yellow with neat petals. An outstanding variety. Flowers mid May. Raised in 1930 by van Tubergen and subsequently used as a parent of many other Cottage tulips such as 'Halcro', 'Maureen' and 'Renown', all of which show features characteristic of the parent: long, oval-shaped heads, fairly tall stems and, above all, stamina.

MURILLO (Double Early)
Height 25 cm. White flushed with pink. Flowers mid April. Raised in 1860 by G Leembruggen. Fragrant. 'Its colour is such a delightful combination of rose flushed with white that ladies simply rave over it' wrote a correspondent in *The Garden* 1912, when it could be bought for 10d. a dozen. The origin of most other Double Earlies, with more than 130 sports to its name.

MURILLO MAXIMA (Double Early)
Height 30 cm. A larger and earlier-flowering sport of 'Murillo' with longer stems. Flowers early April. Raised in 1939 by P van Reisen & Sons.

MY LADY (Darwin Hybrid) AGM
Height 60 cm. Inside deep orange, outside salmon-orange. Base bronze-green. Sport of 'Holland's Glorie'. Flowers mid – end April. Raised in 1959 by John van Grieken.

NEGRITA (Triumph)
Height 45 cm. Purple, veined with darker seams of purple. Clear blue basal blotch, edged in cream. Anthers greenish-yellow. Raised in 1970 by Bik, Jac. Tol.

NEW DESIGN (Triumph)
Height 50 cm. Untidy, ragged-edged pale yellow petals fade to pinkish-white. The outsides are edged with red, the insides marked with apricot. Base buttercup-yellow, anthers brown. The leaves are neatly edged with pinkish-white. Flowers late April. Raised in 1974 by Jac. Tol.

OLAF (Triumph)
Height 40 cm. Bright scarlet with a deep yellow centre. Flowers late April. Raised in 1930 by J J Kerbert.

ORANGE BOUQUET (Triumph) AGM
Height 50 cm. A multi-headed tulip producing up to four flowers on a stem, bright scarlet with a pale yellow base. Flowers May. Raised in 1964 by Konijnenburg & Mark.

ORANGE CASSINI (Triumph)
Height 45 cm. Orange-red with a lemon-yellow base, edged with bronze-green. Anthers pale yellow. A sport of 'Cassini', raised in 1981 by J van der Burg.

ORANGE ELITE (Greigii)
Height 35 cm. The outsides of the petals are orange, edged with yellow, the insides apricot-rose edged with orange. Deep green base. Mottled foliage. Flowers March. Raised in 1952 by C V Hybrida.

ORANGE EMPEROR (Fosteriana)
Height 40 cm. A bright orange bloom with a buttercup-yellow base. Black stamens. Flowers late April. Raised in 1962 by Segers Bros.

ORANGE FAVOURITE (Parrot)
Height 50 cm. A superb Parrot, orange-scarlet tinged with old rose, faint featherings of apple-green on the outer petals. Yellow base. Sport of 'Orange King'. Very sweetly scented. Flowers mid May. Raised in 1934 by K C Vooren.

ORANGE GOBLET (Darwin hybrid)
Height 60 cm. A very large orange tulip with a yellow base. Flowers late April – early May. Raised in 1959 by A Frijlink & Sons.

ORANGE MONARCH (Triumph)
Height 45 cm. Exterior orange tinged with rose, interior apricot-orange. Orange-yellow base, purple stamens. Flowers early May. Raised in 1962 by G Lamboo.

ORANGE SUN (Darwin hybrid), *see* 'ORANJEZON'

ORANGE TORONTO (Greigii)
Height 35 cm. Marigold-orange edged with red. The insides of the petals are spotted with red. Base lemon-yellow. A sport of 'Toronto', raised in 1987 by W A M Pennings.

ORANGE TRIUMPH (Double Late)
Height 45 cm. Double soft orange-red flowers flushed with brown, the petals narrowly edged with yellow. Sport of 'Coxa'. Flowers May. Raised in 1944 by C Nieuwenhuis.

ORANGE WONDER (Triumph)
Height 45 cm. Bronze-orange shaded with scarlet, the petals slightly fluted. Small yellow base. Flowers late April. Raised in 1940 by A Sabelis.

ORANJE NASSAU (Double Early) AGM
Height 25 cm. Shaggy bloom of bright orange-scarlet, heavily suffused with orange, the outer petals shaded with cherry-red. Sport of 'Murillo'. Flowers mid April. Known by 1930.

ORANJEZON syn *ORANGE SUN* (Darwin hybrid)
Height 50 cm. Large, bright, pure orange

bloom with neatly arranged petals. Flowers mid April. Raised in 1947 by C V Hybrida.

ORATORIO (Greigii)
Height 30 cm. Large oblong bloom, rose-pink outside, apricot-pink inside. Base black. Grey-green leaves mottled with reddish-brown. Flowers March. Raised in 1952 by C V Hybrida.

ORIENTAL BEAUTY (Greigii)
Height 30 cm. Large bloom of carmine-red, edged with golden-yellow, the inside vermilion. Deep-brown base. Mottled foliage. Flowers March. Raised in 1952 by C V Hybrida.

ORIENTAL SPLENDOUR (Greigii) AGM
Height 50 cm. A big, long-lasting tulip, the outside yellow edged with red, the inside lemon-yellow. Black base. Flowers March. Raised in 1961 by D W Lefeber & Co.

ORNAMENT (Triumph)
Height 45 cm. Yellow, egg-shaped bloom. Flowers early – mid May. Raised in 1944 by L van Berkel.

OSSI OSWALDA (Single Late)
Height 55 cm. Pale creamy-yellow very finely edged with rose. An elegant tulip. Flowers early – mid May. Raised in 1939 by J J Grullemans & Sons.

OXFORD (Darwin hybrid) AGM
Height 55 cm. An extremely handsome flower, orange-scarlet flushed with purplish-red. Large sulphur-yellow base. Fragrant. Flowers mid April. Raised in 1945 by D W Lefeber & Co.

OXFORD'S ELITE (Darwin hybrid)
Height 55 cm. Cherry-red edged with orange-yellow, the insides of the petals feathered and spotted with red on an orange-yellow ground. Base lemon-yellow, anthers bluish-black. Scented. Raised in 1968 by G G Kol.

PAGE POLKA (Triumph)
Height 40 cm. Large, cup-shaped deep-red flowers striped with white. White base, yellow anthers. Flowers early May. Raised in 1969 by Konijnenburg & Mark.

PALESTRINA (Triumph)
Height 40 cm. A magnificent, large salmon-pink bloom flushed with green on the outside. Flowers mid May. Raised in 1944 by Captein Bros.

PANDOUR (Greigii)
Height 30 cm. Scarlet-rose with an under-tone of pale yellow. Mottled foliage. Flowers March. Raised in 1952 by C V Hybrida.

PARADE (Darwin hybrid) AGM
Height 60 cm. Signal-red flower with a showy black base, edged with yellow.

Black stamens. Flowers early May. Raised in 1951 by D W Lefeber & Co.

PARIS (Triumph)

Height 45 cm. Orange-red edged with yellow. Flowers early – mid May. Raised in 1947 by J F van den Berg.

PAUL CRAMPEL (Double Early)

Height 25 cm. Fine geranium-red with a centre of buttercup-yellow. Sport of 'Oranje Nassau'. Flowers mid April. Raised in 1937 by C J Zonneveld & Sons.

PAUL RICHTER (Triumph)

Height 50 cm. Geranium-red bloom. Flowers late April – early May. Raised in 1943 by F Rijnveld & Sons.

PAX (Triumph)

Height 45 cm. A solid-textured bloom of pure white. Flowers early May. Raised in 1942 by P van Kooten.

PEACH BLOSSOM (Double Early)

Height 25 cm. Double silvery-pink bloom flushed with deeper pink. Rather a strident, formless flower, generally squat and messy. There is nothing peachy about it. Sport of 'Murillo'. Flowers mid April. Known since 1913.

PEER GYNT (Triumph)

Height 50 cm. Cup-shaped flower, the fuchsia-pink petals edged with pale purple. White base, spotted with yellow,

purplish-grey anthers. Flowers late April. Raised by Konijnenburg & Mark in 1973.

PEERLESS PINK (Triumph)

Height 45 cm. A fine satin-pink. Flowers late April. Raised in 1930 by H Carlee.

PERLINA (Greigii)

Height 25 cm. Exterior porcelain-rose and lemon-yellow, interior glowing porcelain-rose. Base lemon-yellow, stamens purple. Heavily mottled foliage. 'One of the most lovely hybrids' said Walter Blom in the *Daffodil and Tulip Yearbook* (1968). Flowers mid April. Raised in 1960 by C V Hybrida.

PHILIPPE DE COMINES (Single Late)

Height 55 cm. Maroon black. Flowers early – mid May. Raised in 1905 by E H Krelage & Son.

PICTURE (Single Late)

Height 60 cm. Long-lasting bloom of lilac-rose, the petals slightly folded in on themselves and splayed to make a wide, low flower. Sport of 'Princess Elizabeth'. Flowers late April – early May. Raised in 1949 by G Baltus.

PIMPERNEL (Viridiflora)

Height 40 cm. Pointed, reflexed petals, rich crimson-purple feathered and striped with green. Flowers May. Raised in 1956 by D W Lefeber & Co.

PINK BEAUTY (Single Early)

Height 30 cm. One of the most attractive of the early tulips with a neat, well-shaped flower. Vivid electric-pink with a well-defined white edge to each petal. Flowers late April. Raised in 1889 by Baars & Dibbits.

PINK DIAMOND (Single Late)

Height 50 cm. Outside rose-purple, a paler tone around the edges of the petals, inside phlox-pink. Flowers May.

PINK IMPRESSION (Darwin hybrid)

Height 55 cm. Veined with rose on a pale rose ground, the edges of the petals feathered with a deeper shrimp-pink. Flowers end April.

PINK SUPREME (Single Late)

Height 50 cm. A very delicate but bright pink, paler around the edges of the petals. Sport of 'Utopia'. Flowers mid May. Raised in 1947 by Captein Bros.

PINK TROPHY (Single Early)

Height 45 cm. Pink flushed with rose. Flowers mid − late April. Raised in 1942 by B P Heemskerk.

PINKEEN (Fosteriana)

Height 40 cm. Vermilion-red with a greenish-yellow base. Flowers in April. Raised in 1945 by van Tubergen.

PINOCCHIO (Double Late)

Height 25 cm. Tall flowers with a pinched-in waist, the pointed outer petals flamed with scarlet, edged with ivory and blotched with green. Flowers March. Raised in 1952 by C V Hybrida.

PLAISIR (Greigii) AGM

Height 25 cm. Broadly urn-shaped bloom, the deep pinkish-red petals edged with pale yellow. The colour is rather too much like dressed-up raw steak to be pleasing, but the flower is very vigorous and of a good shape. Black and yellow base. Grey-green leaves mottled with reddish brown. Flowers March. Raised in 1953 by C V Hybrida.

POLO (Fosteriana)

Height 35 cm. Scarlet with a hint of yellow showing at the base of the petals on the outside. Inside, the basal blotch is black, thinly edged with buttercup-yellow. A sport of the fine 'Cantate' raised in 1982 by Jac. M van Dijk.

PRELUDIUM (Triumph)

Height 45 cm. Rose with a white base. Flowers early May. Raised in 1945 by P van Kooten.

PRESIDENT KENNEDY (Darwin hybrid) AGM

Height 60 cm. A large golden-yellow bloom overlaid with pinkish-red. Base deep bronze-green, stamens black. Long-lasting. Flowers late April. A sport of 'Apeldoorn', introduced in 1961 by P J de Groot.

PRINCE CARNAVAL see PRINS CAR-NAVAL

PRINCE CHARLES (Triumph)
Height 40 cm. Purple-violet. Flowers mid May. Raised in 1952 by P Hopman & Sons.

PRINCE KARL PHILIP (Triumph)
Height 50 cm. Glowing blood-red with a narrow yellow edge to the petals. Base lemon-yellow, anthers bluish-black. Raised in 1981 by J F van den Berg & Sons.

PRINCE OF AUSTRIA (Single Early)
Height 40 cm. One of the best all-round early tulips, brick-red, the colour made by a fine netting of red over yellow. Yellow base. Sweetly scented. Flowers mid April. Known since 1860.

PRINCEPS (Fosteriana)
Height 25 cm. A very large bloom of vermilion-scarlet. Bronze-green base. A showy variety for rockeries. A selected form of the Fosteriana species. Flowers April.

PRINCESS CHARMANTE (Greigii)
Height 45 cm. Orange flushed with carmine-red. Mottled foliage. Flowers March. Raised in 1965 by D W Lefeber & Co.

PRINCESS MARGARET ROSE (Single Late)
Height 55 cm. A magnificent tulip, deep yellow with a bright scarlet edge. Sport of 'Inglescombe Yellow'. Flowers late May. Raised in 1944 by J Bankert.

PRINCESS VICTORIA (Triumph)
Height 50 cm. Deep pinkish-red with a fine white edge along the tops of the petals. Flowers April. Raised in 1979 by J F van den Berg & Sons.

PRINS CARNAVAL (Single Early)
Height 40 cm. Yellow flamed with red. Scented. Sport of 'Prince of Austria'. Flowers mid April. Known since 1930.

PRINSES IRENE (Triumph) AGM
Height 35 cm. Soft orange flamed with purple and hints of green up the outside of outer petals. Much narrower flaming up the outside of the inner petals. The inside of the petals is orange with an indistinct yellow blotch at the base of the petals. Stigma pale green, stamens yellow, anthers very thin olive-green. A remarkable tulip. Sport of 'Couleur Cardinal', which is also a winner. Flowers late April. Raised in 1949 by P van Reisen & Sons.

PROFESSOR RÖNTGEN (Parrot)
Height 50 cm. The petals flamed with lemon-yellow on a scarlet feathered ground, the basal blotch green. A sport of

'Salmon Parrot', raised in 1978 by C A Verdegaal.

PROMINENCE (Triumph)

Height 40 cm. Dark red. Flowers late April – early May. Raised in 1943 by P van Kooten.

PURISSIMA (Fosteriana)

Height 45 cm. Very large milky-white flowers borne on strong stems, the leaves a light greyish-green. Sport of 'Madame Lefeber'. Scented. Flowers April. Raised in 1943 by van Tubergen.

PURPLE STAR (Triumph)

Height 45 cm. A large well-shaped bloom of deep purple. Flowers early May. Raised in 1952 by S J Zandvoort.

QUEEN (Darwin hybrid)

Height 60 cm. A vermilion flower, flamed with purple on the outsides of the petals. The base is lemon-yellow, blotched with dark green. Anthers black. Raised in 1968 by D W Lefeber & Co.

QUEEN INGRID (Greigii)

Height 35 cm. Outside carmine-red edged with yellow, inside lemon-yellow with red blotches. Black base. Mottled foliage. Flowers March. Raised in 1955 by C V Hybrida.

QUEEN OF BARTIGONS (Single Late)

Height 55 cm. Pure salmon-pink with yellow stamens. Sport of 'Bartigons'. Flowers mid May. Raised in 1944 by P Bakker.

QUEEN OF NIGHT (Single Late)

Height 60 cm. One of the darkest of all tulips, with long-lasting, egg-shaped, satiny maroon-black flowers on strong stems. Dark stamens. Flowers mid May. Raised in 1944 by J J Grullemans & Sons.

QUEEN OF SHEBA (Lily-flowered)

Height 60 cm. The brownish-red petals, only slightly reflexed, are edged with a broad margin of yellowish-orange. Very stiff stem and unusually long-lasting. Flowers early May. An outstanding tulip, raised in 1944 by de Mol-Nieuwenhuis.

QUEEN WILHELMINA (Darwin hybrid)

Height 55 cm. Oval bloom of brilliant flame-orange with a golden base. Flowers early May.

RECREADO (Single Late)

Height 50 cm. Rounded flowers of dark plum-purple, the edges of the petals gently puckered. Anthers plum-purple. Flowers mid April. Raised in 1979 by Visser Cz.

RED CHAMPION (Parrot)

Height 50 cm. Blood-red Parrot, a sport of 'Bartigon'. Flowers mid May. Raised in 1930 by H M Ruysenaars.

RED EMPEROR *see* MADAME LEFEBER

RED GEORGETTE (Single Late) AGM
Height 50 cm. Blood-red flower with a greenish-black feathered base on a primrose-yellow ground. Anthers dark violet. Bears more than one flower on the stem. A sport of 'Georgette', raised in 1983 by Visser Cz.

RED MATADOR (Darwin hybrid)
Height 65 cm. Intense bright fiery-scarlet, very brilliant. Yellow base shaded with black. Flowers late April. Raised in 1942 by van Tubergen.

RED PARROT (Parrot)
Height 70 cm. Large raspberry-red flowers on strong stems. Sport of 'Gloria Swanson'. Raised by J C Evers in 1940.

RED PRESENT (Triumph)
Height 35 cm. Blood-red flower with a bright yellow base, the basal blotch dark green. Anthers pale yellow. A sport of 'Yellow Present', raised in 1972 by J A Borst.

RED RIDING HOOD (Greigii) AGM
Height 30 cm. Beautifully formed urn-shaped flowers of vivid scarlet with jet-black bases. Dark spreading foliage is mottled with brownish-purple. Flowers late March. Raised in 1953 by C V Hybrida.

RED SENSATION (Parrot)
Height 45 cm. Glowing blood-red with a carmine flame on the outside of the petals, the base bronze-green on a yellow ground, the anthers plum-purple. A sport of 'Paul Richter', raised in 1975 by J G Kok.

RED SHINE (Lily-flowered) AGM
Height 55 cm. Vivid deep ruby-red. Flowers mid May. Raised in 1955 by C V Hybrida.

RED SURPRISE (Greigii) AGM
Height 30 cm. A brilliant scarlet tulip with a black base. Mottled foliage. Raised in 1953 by C V Hybrida.

RED WING (Fringed) AGM
Height 50 cm. Exterior glowing red, lighter towards the edges. The crystalline fringe is turkey-red. The inside of the flower is red with a tricorn-shaped black blotch, edged in yellow. Anthers bluish-black. It was raised in 1972 by Segers.

REFORMA (Triumph)
Height 50 cm. Sulphur-yellow, edged with golden-yellow. Flowers late April – early May. Raised in 1946.

RENOWN (Single Late)
Height 65 cm. Large oval flower, light carmine-red, slightly paler round the edges of the petals. Yellow base, edged with blue. Flowers mid May. Raised in 1949 by Segers Bros.

RETROFLEXA (Lily-flowered)

Height 50–60 cm. Leaves lance-shaped, glaucous. The flowers are golden-yellow, the upper half of the petals strongly reflexed. No basal blotch. Filaments yellow, anthers yellow. This is found, perhaps naturalised, in SE France. Hall considered this a seedling variety raised by V van der Winne, a Dutch florist, who sold all his stock in 1863. For a time it was considered a species in its own right and the flower was a vital parent in the breeding of the Lily-flowered race of tulips. All these arose from a cross between 'Retroflexa' and a Darwin tulip made in 1914 by J F Dix of the firm Krelage in Haarlem.

RHEINGOLD (Double Early)

Height 25 cm. Sulphur-yellow flower. Sport of 'Murillo'. Flowers mid April. Raised in 1942 by P van Reisen & Sons.

RIJNLAND (Triumph)

Height 50 cm. Crimson-red edged with yellow. Flowers late April. Raised by Zocher & Co.

ROCKERY BEAUTY (Fosteriana)

Height 20 cm. A particularly dwarf Fosteriana with pointed flowers of orange-scarlet. Black base edged with yellow. Excellent in rockeries and screes. Flowers early April. Raised in 1942 by Ant. Lefeber.

ROCKERY MASTER (Greigii)

Height 25 cm. Pale salmon-rose, the inside of the flower salmon-red. Base bronze-green. Foliage mottled. Flowers late March. Raised in 1952 by C V Hybrida.

ROCKERY WONDER (Greigii)

Height 30 cm. Orange flushed with bronze. Black base. Mottled foliage. Flowers in March. Raised in 1952 by C V Hybrida.

ROCOCO (Parrot)

Height 35 cm. Very rich velvety-red with green crinkling around the petals. Sport of 'Couleur Cardinal'. Flowers mid May. Raised in 1942 by H Slegtkamp & Co.

ROSARIO (Triumph)

Height 50 cm. Carmine-pink flower with a large white base. Raised in 1957 by P Nijssen & Sons.

ROSY WINGS (Triumph)

Height 60 cm. Long, elegant bloom, bright-pink with a pure white base. Flowers early May. Raised in 1944 by van Tubergen.

RUBY RED (Single Early)

Height 40 cm. A fine bloom of glowing scarlet. Flowers late April. Raised in 1944 by B P Heemskerk.

SAFARI (Greigii)

Height 35 cm. Fiery-red shining petals

with yellow rims. Blackish-brown base with a yellow rim. Anthers plum-purple. Raised in 1992 by Jan van Bentem.

SCARLET BABY (Kaufmanniana)
Height 20 cm. Tall, thin-petalled bloom, geranium-red with yellow base and anthers. Flowers March. Raised in 1962 by J C van der Meer.

SCARLET CARDINAL (Double Early)
Height 25 cm. One of the finest of the Double Earlies, vivid scarlet flushed with orange. Flowers mid April. One of the few Double Earlies that is not a sport of 'Murillo'. Raised in 1914 by J de Ruyter.

SCARLETT O'HARA (Single Late)
Height 60 cm. Geranium-red. Flowers early – mid May. Raised by F Rijnveld in 1943 from a cross with the Single Late tulip 'Charles Needham'.

SCHOONOORD (Double Early)
Height 25 cm. Large bloom of pure white. The best white double tulip, lovely with grape hyacinths. Sport of 'Murillo'. Flowers mid April. Known since 1909.

SCOTCH LASSIE (Single Late)
Height 60 cm. Deep lavender. Flowers early – mid May. Raised by J J Grullemans & Sons.

SHAKESPEARE (Kaufmanniana)
Height 25 cm. Deep red edged with

salmon outside, salmon flushed with red inside. Yellow base. Flowers March. Raised in 1942 by van Tubergen.

SHIRLEY (Triumph)
Height 50 cm. Ivory-white, the petals edged and lightly spotted with purplish-blue. Flowers mid May. Similar to but not as good as 'Magier' although 'Magier' does not have the beautiful sky-blue base of 'Shirley'. Raised in 1968 by Bik, Jac. Tol.

SHOW WINNER (Kaufmanniana) AGM
Height 25 cm. Cardinal-red outside, scarlet inside. Base buttercup-yellow edged with purplish-red. Mottled foliage. Flowers mid March. Raised in 1966 by Rijnveld & Sons.

SIGRID UNDSET (Single Late)
Height 60 cm. Creamy-white. Base yellow, flushed with bronze. Flowers in mid May. Raised in 1954 by H 't Mannetje.

SILENTIA (Triumph)
Height 50 cm. Ivory-white flower with a creamy midrib. Base and anthers yellow. Raised in 1977 by Jac. Tol, Th. van der Gulik.

SILVER DOLLAR (Triumph)
Height 55 cm. Ivory-white, flamed with primrose-yellow. The inside is a deeper shade of mimosa. Flowers mid May. Raised in 1984 by IVT, Van Darn.

The Viridiflora tulip 'Spring Green', raised in 1969

SINT MAARTEN (Single Early)

Height 30 cm. Orange, flamed with brick-red, a prominent star-shaped base of yellowish-green showing on the outsides of the petals. The same broad green star shows on the inside. Anthers greyish-blue. A sport of 'Brilliant Star Maxima', raised in 1983 by de Geus.

SMILING QUEEN (Single Late)

Height 60 cm. Rose edged with silvery pink. White base. Flowers mid May. Raised in 1938 by N L A Roozen.

SNOWFLAKE (Triumph)

Height 50 cm. Creamy-white flower, flamed with grey. Base brownish-yellow with yellow anthers. Raised in 1981 by Bito, Th. Bakker.

SNOWPEAK (Single Late)

Height 55 cm. Pure white. Flowers mid May. Raised in 1952 by Konijnenburg & Mark Ltd.

SORBET (Single Late) AGM

Height 60 cm. Rosy-white outside, white flamed with carmine-red inside. Creamy-white base. Yellow stamens. Sport of 'Smiling Queen'. Flowers mid May. Raised in 1959 by Jac. J van der Eyken.

SOTHIS (Fringed)

Height 40 cm. Blood-red. Sport of 'Sundew'. Flowers early May. Raised in 1942 by Segers Bros.

SPALDING (Triumph)

Height 45 cm. Rose. Flowers late April – early May. Raised in 1959 by P Nijssen & Sons Ltd.

SPARKLING FIRE (Greigii)

Height 30 cm. Vermilion-red with yellow base. Striped foliage. Flowers March. Raised in 1955 by C V Hybrida.

SPRING GREEN (Viridiflora) AGM

Height 50 cm. Creamy-white flowers with a broad green flame up the centre of each petal, the flame showing both on the back and the front. Extremely elegant, each petal with a slight sideways twist on it. Good planted in grass with cow parsley. Pale green anthers. Flowers May. Raised in 1969 by P Liefting.

SPRING PEARL (Fosteriana)

Height 40 cm. Pearl-grey edged with vermilion outside, vermilion inside. Base yellow. Flowers April. Raised in 1955 by F Rijnveld & Sons.

SPRING SONG (Darwin hybrid)

Height 55 cm. A bright red bloom flushed with salmon. White base. Flowers late April. Raised in 1946 by J H Veldhuizen van Zanten.

STOCKHOLM (Double Early) AGM

Height 30 cm. Scarlet with a yellow base. Flowers mid – late April. Raised in 1952 by Anton Nijssen & Son.

The Triumph tulip 'Striped Bellona', raised in 1973

STRESA (Kaufmanniana) AGM
Height 25 cm. A neatly pyramidal bloom, rich orange-red, with a deep-yellow band around the edges of the petals. Indian-yellow inside with blood-red blotches at the base. Flowers March. Foliage faintly striped. Raised in 1942 by van Tubergen.

STRIPED APELDOORN (Darwin hybrid)
Height 55 cm. Outside red striped and flamed on yellow, inside buttercup-yellow. Base bluish-black. Stamens black. Sport of 'Apeldoorn'. Flowers mid April. Raised by A Overdevest in 1963.

STRIPED BELLONA (Triumph)
Height 50 cm. Buttercup-yellow flamed with currant-red. Flowers mid April. Raised in 1973 by A. Berbee.

SUCCESS (Triumph)
Height 40 cm. Blood-red flamed with white. Flowers late April – early May. Raised in 1958 by P & J W Mantel.

SUMMIT (Fosteriana)
Height 40 cm. Outside mimosa-yellow, inside a slightly deeper shade of buttercup-yellow. Anthers purplish-black. Flowers mid April. Raised in 1962 by K van Egmond & Sons.

SUNDEW (Fringed)
Height 40 cm. Cardinal-red with a crystallised fringe. Sport of 'Orion'. Flowers early May. Raised in 1930.

SUNKIST (Single Late)
Height 55 cm. Deep yellow. Flowers early – mid May. Raised in 1933 by van Tubergen.

SUNRAY (Triumph)
Height 50 cm. Pale yellow edged with a darker band of yellow. Flowers late April – early May. Raised in 1959 by K van Kooten.

SUSAN OLIVER (Viridiflora)
Height 45 cm. Opal rose flamed with green up the outsides of the petals. The inside is claret-rose with a green stripe reaching from the base to the tip of each petal. Raised in 1971 by Konijnenburg & Mark.

SWAN WINGS (Fringed)
Height 55 cm. Pure white with delicately fringed petals. Black base and stamens. Flowers May. Raised in 1959 by Segers Bros.

SWEET HARMONY (Single Late) AGM
Height 55 cm. A distinct and unusual variety, lemon-yellow edged with ivory. Yellow base and stamens. Sport of 'Mrs Grullemans'. Flowers mid May. Raised in 1944 by Jac. B Roozen.

SWEET LADY (Greigii)
Height 30 cm. Peach-blossom-pink, the base greenish-bronze tinged with yellow. Mottled foliage. Flowers mid April. Raised in 1955 by J C van der Meer.

SWEETHEART (Fosteriana)

Height 40 cm. Outside ivory-white flamed with lemon-yellow, inside yellow with a paler yellow base. Anthers yellow. Flowers April. A sport of a white, unnamed Fosteriana tulip, which was mixed with 'Purissima', raised in 1976 by J C Nieuwenhuis.

TAMARA (Triumph)

Height 50 cm. Bright carmine-pink, flamed on the outside with ivory. A broad ivory base and yellow anthers. Raised in 1979 by Visser Czn.

TANGO (Greigii)

Height 40 cm. Orange-scarlet, the base black with yellow blotches. Mottled foliage. Flowers March. Raised in 1952 by C V Hybrida.

TEENAGER (Greigii)

Height 30 cm. Outside currant-red edged with ivory-white, inside red, the edges of the petals feathered with a lighter colour. Base ox-blood-red, stamens yellow. Flowers March. Raised in 1963 by Jac. Uittenbogaard & Sons.

TEHERAN (Triumph)

Height 50 cm. Apricot. Sport of 'Alberio'. Flowers late April – early May. Raised in 1945 by C Colijn & Sons.

TEMPLE OF BEAUTY (Single Late) AGM

Height 75 cm. A lily-shaped flower of salmon-rose. The leaves are slightly mottled. Raised in 1959 by D W Lefeber & Co.

TENDER BEAUTY (Darwin hybrid)

Height 50 cm. White with a wide edge of rosy-red. Base pure yellow. 'Unique richness of colour found in no other hybrid' wrote Walter Blom in the *Daffodil and Tulip Yearbook* (1968). Does not propagate easily. Flowers April. Raised in 1954 by C V Hybrida.

TEXAS FLAME (Parrot)

Height 45 cm. Bright buttercup-yellow flamed with carmine-red. Green base. Sport of 'Texas Gold'. Flowers mid May. Raised in 1958 by J J de Wit.

TEXAS GOLD (Parrot)

Height 45 cm. Clear yellow with a narrow red ribbon round the edges of the petals. Sport of 'Inglescombe Yellow'. Rather a strident Parrot, compared for instance with the intricate 'Orange Favourite'. Flowers mid May. Raised in 1944 by G van der Mey's Sons.

THE FIRST (Kaufmanniana)

Height 20 cm. Exceptionally early-flowering variety. Outside carmine-red edged with white, inside ivory-white with yellow base and stamens. Flowers March. Raised in 1940 by Frans Roozen.

THULE (Triumph)

Height 45 cm. Red edged with yellow. Flowers early May. Raised in 1954 by Anton Nijssen & Sons.

TOPSCORE (Triumph)

Height 45 cm. Geranium-lake-red with a yellow base. Black stamens. Flowers early May. Raised in 1944 by C V Hybrida.

TORONTO (Greigii) AGM

Height 35 cm. Multi-flowered tulip, bearing two or three long-lasting flowers on each stem. The broadly cup-shaped flowers have brilliant salmon-orange petals, slender and pointed. Base brownish-yellow, anthers bronze. Mottled foliage. Flowers early May. Raised in 1963 by Jac. Uittenbogaard & Sons.

TOULON (Fosteriana)

Height 40 cm. Outside deep orange tinged with geranium-lake, inside deep orange. Orange base, edged with yellow. Pale yellow stamens. Particularly good foliage, blotched and striped with reddish-brown. Flowers April. Raised in 1961 by van Tubergen.

TOWA (Greigii)

Height 30 cm. Scarlet flower with a star-shaped black base, the base narrowly edged with yellow. Mottled leaves. Raised in 1982 by Uittenbogaard & Sons.

TRANCE (Triumph)

Height 40 cm. Deep geranium-red with a yellow base. Flowers late April – early May. Raised in 1953 by C V Hybrida.

TRINKET (Greigii)

Height 25 cm. The inside of the flower is cream, the outside blood-red edged with white. Yellow base with brown markings, edged with scarlet. Yellow stamens. Flowers April. Raised in 1963 by Captein Bros.

TRIUMPHATOR (Double Early)

Height 25 cm. Rose-red. Sport of 'Murillo'. Flowers mid April. Known since 1919.

UNCLE TOM (Double Late)

Height 45 cm. Fat double peony-like flowers of glossy maroon-red. Flowers May. Raised in 1939 by Zocher & Co.

UNION JACK (Single Late)

Height 55 cm. Relatively shallow, cup-shaped flower, ivory-white, the petals flamed and feathered with rich raspberry-red. White base stained with blue. Sport of 'Cordell Hull'. Flowers mid May. Raised in 1958 by P Bakker.

VALENTINE (Triumph)

Height 45 cm. Violet-purple. Flowers early May. Raised by E H Krelage & Son.

VAN DER NEER (Single Early)

Height 25 cm. Deep, soft plum-purple.

Occasionally breaks to produce white feathering on the purple ground. Flowers mid April. Raised by G Leembruggen 1860.

VARINAS (Triumph)

Height 40 cm. Lilac-rose edged with silvery-white. Black stamens. Flowers early May. Raised in 1944 by G van Steyn & Sons.

VIKING (Double Early)

Height 30 cm. Enchanting stubby red flower, the outside of the petals flushed with yellow and green. The base is canary-yellow, the anthers purple. Spare petals occasionally spring from the stem below the base of the flower. Sport of 'Monte Carlo' and, like that flower, deliciously scented. Raised in 1984 by J W Reus.

VIVALDI (Kaufmanniana)

Height 25 cm. Outside carmine-rose edged with yellow, inside sulphur-yellow. Base golden-yellow flushed with bronze. Mottled foliage. Flowers March. Raised in 1942 by van Tubergen.

VIVEX (Darwin hybrid)

Height 60 cm. Outside deep carmine-rose edged with orange-yellow, inside mandarin-red. Base star-shaped, deep green on a yellow ground. Flowers late April. Raised in 1960 by Konijnenburg & Mark Ltd.

VLAMMENSPEL (Single Late)

Height 50 cm. Yellow flamed with blood-red. Sport of 'Inglescombe Yellow'. Flowers late April. Raised in 1941 by P Groot.

VUURBAAK (Double Early)

Height 30 cm. Bright orange-scarlet. Flowers mid-April. Raised in 1890 by C Alkemade Azn.

WALLFLOWER (Single Late)

Height 50 cm. Purple-brown with a yellow base. Flowers mid May. Raised by Nicolaas Dames.

WARBLER (Fringed)

Height 45 cm. An untidy tulip, very similar in colour to 'Fringed Elegance' but with wilder fringing. Huge flowers, clear yellow, no marking at base on outside or inside. Very long fringes, which is what makes it look so mad. Pale cream stigma, slightly darker stamens and anthers. Flowers May. Raised in 1987 by Segers Bros, W A M Pennings.

WEBER'S PARROT (Parrot)

Height 40 cm. Like a fop's handkerchief, the huge crinkled petals gently streaked with pale pink on a creamy-white ground. Formless, even for a Parrot, but fun. Sport of 'Weber', introduced in 1968 by van Graven Bros.

WEST POINT (Lily-flowered)

Height 50 cm. Bright yellow bloom with long, pointed petals, sharply recurved. Most elegant in its youth, but towards the end of its flowering resembles a crazed starfish. Flowers mid May. Raised in 1943 by de Mol-Nieuwenhuis.

WHITE DREAM (Triumph)

Height 50 cm. Ivory-white, cup-shaped blooms with canary-yellow anthers. Flowers late April. Raised in 1972 by J F van den Berg & Sons.

WHITE PARROT (Parrot)

Height 40 cm. A big ruffled bloom, the white petals flecked with green at the base. Sport of 'Albino'. Flowers mid May. Raised in 1943 by J Valkering & Sons.

WHITE SWALLOW (Triumph)

Height 50 cm. Ivory-white flower with a creamy flame. Anthers bright yellow. Raised in 1975 by Bik, Jac. Tol.

WHITE TRIUMPHATOR (Lily-flowered) AGM

Height 60 cm. Elegantly reflexed petals, white with a faint green flush. Flowers early May. Raised in 1942 by van Tubergen.

WHITE VIRGIN (Triumph)

Height 45 cm. White with a yellow base. Flowers early May. Raised in 1932 by E H Krelage & Son.

WILHELM KORDES (Double Early)

Height 25 cm. Orange-yellow flamed with red. Sport of 'Murillo'. Flowers mid April. Raised in 1943 by Segers Bros.

WILLEM VAN ORANJE (Double Early)

Height 25 cm. Orange flushed with coppery red. Sport of 'Peach Blossom'. Flowers mid April. Raised in 1933 by P Bakker.

WILLEMSOORD (Double Early)

Height 25 cm. Carmine-rose, edged with white. Sport of 'Electra'. Flowers mid April. Raised in 1930 by Paul Roozen.

WIM VAN EST (Single Late)

Height 60 cm. Rose-red. Flowers mid May. Raised in 1952 by Segers Bros.

YELLOW DAWN (Greigii)

Height 35 cm. The outside is old rose edged with yellow, the inside rich yellow. Base purplish-red with carmine blotches. Mottled foliage. Flowers March. Raised in 1953 by C V Hybrida.

YELLOW DOVER (Darwin hybrid)

Height 55 cm. Buttercup-yellow with black base and stamens. Sport of 'Dover'. Flowers late April. Raised in 1963 by D W Lefeber.

YELLOW EMPEROR (Single Late)

Height 40 cm. Golden-yellow. Flowers early May. Raised in 1930 by van Tubergen.

YELLOW EMPRESS (Fosteriana)

Height 40 cm. Golden-yellow with a deeper-yellow base and yellow stamens. Flowers early May. Raised in 1959 by C V Hybrida.

YELLOW PRESENT (Triumph)

Height 35 cm. Outside creamy-yellow, inside canary-yellow. Stamens yellow. Flowers April. Raised in 1953 by C V Hybrida.

YELLOW PURISSIMA (Fosteriana)

Height 45 cm. Bright yellow flower with greenish-yellow anthers. A sport of white 'Purissima', it was raised in 1980 by J N M van Eeden.

YOKOHAMA (Single Early)

Height 35 cm. Rich, golden-yellow bloom with pointed petals. Yellow stamens. Flowers mid April. Raised in 1961 by J F van den Berg & Sons.

ZAMPA (Greigii) AGM

Height 30 cm. Primrose-yellow with large carmine-red blotches on the outer petals. Base bronze and green. Mottled foliage. Flowers March. Raised in 1952 by C V Hybrida.

ZOMBIE (Fosteriana)

Height 35 cm. The outside carmine-rose edged with yellow, the inside yellow flushed with rose. Base black edged with red. Flowers early April. Raised in 1954 by C V Hybrida.

ZOMERSCHOON (Single Late)

Height 40 cm. Perhaps the oldest tulip in cultivation, cream streaked and feathered with salmon-pink. Flowers mid May. Known since 1620.

ZWANENBURG (Single Late)

Height 50 cm. Pure white with white base and plum-coloured stamens. Flowers mid May. Raised in 1912 by van Tubergen.

CHRONOLOGY OF TULIPS

1451	Tulip cultivated in the garden of Sultan Mehmed II (1451–1481)
1520	Under reign of Süleyman the Magnificent (1520–1566) tulip becomes an integral part of Ottoman culture
1545·	First botanic gardens in Europe established at Pisa and Padua
1546	The French explorer, Pierre Belon, begins his journey to Turkey and the Levant
1553	*Les Observations de Plusieurs Singularités*, by Pierre Belon, is published in Paris
1554	Ogier Ghiselin de Busbecq, Ferdinand I's ambassador to the Sultan's court, begins his journey to Turkey
1559	Conrad Gesner sees the first tulip to be described in Europe, growing in the garden of the Great Councillor Herwart at Augsburg
1561	Woodcut of tulip appears in *Annotationes in Pedacii* by Valerius Cordus
1561	Matthiolus brings out *Historia Plantarum* with another illustration of a tulip
1562	Tulips arrive in Antwerp from Constantinople
1565	The *Codex* by Leonhart Fuchs shows a tulip with eight petals

1565	*Commentarii in Sex Libros Pedacii Dioscoridis* by Pier Andrea Mattioli shows a tulip under the label of a narcissus
1568	First printed illustration of a tulip in Holland appears in *Florum et Coronarium* by Rembert Dodoens, the woodcut made by Pieter van der Borcht
1571	Forty-one kinds of tulip are described in herbal written by Matthias de l'Obel (Lobelius) of Lille
1572	Clusius meets Busbecq in Vienna and gets tulip seed and bulbs from him
1576	*Rariorum aliquot Stirpium…* by Carolus Clusius appears, with an important appendix that includes tulips
1576	*Plantarum seu Stirpium Historia* by Matthias de l'Obel
1577	Tulips are grown by James Garrett, apothecary, in his garden at London Wall. In his *Herball* (1597), Gerard says Garrett had been growing them 'these twenty years'
1581	Clusius records a double tulip 'a bad green'
1581	Publication of *Plantarum seu Stirpium Icones*, a collection of 2,173 woodcuts, mostly Plantin's, gathered together by Gobelius, physician to the Duke of Prussia
1590	Tulips noted growing in Leiden
1593	Clusius comes to Leiden as Professor of Botany and lays out a new botanic garden
1597	Publication of John Gerard's *Herball*
1598	Tulips noted growing at Montpellier
1600–1650	Tulip highly fashionable flower in European gardens
1600	Nurseries established by Dutch growers, along the Wagenweg and the Kleine Houtweg, south of Haarlem.
1601	Clusius describes different tulips including 'Cafe Lale' and 'Kavala Lale' in *Rariorum plantarum Historia*
1602	The Dutch East India Company is set up
1603	*T. gesneriana* (*T. suaveolens?*) is imported from the Crimea
1606	A *Florilegium* with tulips is published by Pierre Vallet in Paris
1610	Tulips appear as a motif on Dutch tiles
1611	Tulips flower in the Provençal garden of M Peiresc
1611	Tulips appear on a bill presented by the gardener John Tradescant to his employer, the Earl of Salisbury, at Hatfield

1612	Emmanuel Sweert publishes the first trade catalogue, the *Florilegium*
1613	Publication of the *Hortus Eystettensis*, showing highly developed tulips among the flowers growing in the garden of the Prince-Bishop of Eichstatt, Germany
1614	Fine engravings of tulips in the *Hortus Floridus* by Crispyn de Passe the Younger
1617	*Traité compendieux et abrégée des Tulippes* published in Paris
1618	John Tradescant's visit to Archangel, where he is told there are both 'tulipes and narsisus' – presumably wild species
1620	Parrot tulips are noted
1621	A botanic garden is established by the university at Oxford
1623	Wassenaer votes 'Semper Augustus' the tulip of the year and notes it sold for a thousand florins a bulb
1624	The first colonies are established in the New Netherlands by the Dutch West India Company
1629	John Parkinson's *Paradisus* mentions 140 varieties of tulip
1630	Sir Peter Syche sends 'Tulippe Caffa' to John Tradescant
1630	Publication of the list of tulips grown by Sultan Murad IV (1623–1640)
1631	The first Florists' Feast is held in Norwich
1634	The beginning of tulipomania
1636	The height of tulipomania which ended in 1637. Bulb traders earn the equivalent of £30,000 a month
1636	The inventory of the Margrave of Baden-Durlach's garden lists 4,796 different kinds of tulip
1636	*T. clusiana* known in England
1637	Publication of Adriaen Roman's satiric dialogues
1637	The Alkmaar tulip auction of 5 February
1640	Cornelius Johnson's painting of the Capel family
1651	The Austrian Ambassador, Schmid von Schwarzenhorn, brings forty tulips from Europe to Istanbul as a gift for the Emperor Mehmed IV
1651	The Paris nurseryman Pierre Morin publishes his first catalogue, which includes a vast array of tulips
1659	Sir Thomas Hanmer, tulip fanatic, completes his *Garden Book*
1660	Thomas Fuller's *Speech of Flowers* sneers at the 'Toolip, which hath engrated the love and affections of most people unto it'

1665	John Rea catalogues 184 tulips in *Flora; seu de Florum Cultura*
1670	The French grower Lombard sells the stock of seedlings which later become important 'breeders' for Flemish growers
1676	Three hundred tulips are named in 2nd edition of John Rea's *Flora; seu de Florum Cultura*
1678	Publication of *Remarques Nécessaires pour la Culture des Fleurs* by Pierre Morin
1680	'Keizerskroon' introduced – still available today
1684	Nurseryman Roger Looker of St Martins in the Fields, London, supplies the 1st Viscount Weymouth at Longleat with '100 best mixt tulips' for £5
1688	George Ricket's catalogue
1689	George Ricket's bill for tulips is sent to Levens Hall, Westmorland
1698	Tulips grow in John Tateham's Pennsylvania garden
1700	H. Van Oosten publishes *De Needer Landsen Bloemhof* in Leiden
1700 onwards	The tulip starts to be overtaken by the hyacinth
1703	Tulipomania in the Ottoman Empire under the reign of Sultan Ahmed III (1703–30)
1703	*The Dutch Gardener* by Henry van Oosten published in an English translation
1705	Nicholas Blundell plants 'Anemonyes, Pilianthes…and Tulops' in his knot garden at Little Crosby, Lancashire
1710	Steele's teasing piece in the *Tatler* 31 August
1726	*Defter-i Lalezale-i Istanbul* (*Notes of a Tulip Grower in Istanbul*) published by Ali Emiri Efendi Kutuphanesi
1728	The manuscripts of Sheik Mohammed who was 'lalizari' or tulip grower (1728–30) to the Grand Vizier Ibrahim Pasha show tulips in an advanced state of hybridisation. One manuscript lists 1,323 varieties
1729	Henry Woodman, nurseryman, sends tulips to Henry Ellison at Gateshead Park
1730	Nurseryman Samuel Smith advertises in the *York Courant*
1730	The Margrave of Baden-Durlach publishes a garden catalogue noting that he has bought bulbs from Dutch firms, 15 of them in Haarlem
1734	The Waermont and Gaergoedt dialogues are published again as a warning against speculation in hyacinths

1741	A list of the 2,400 tulips in the gardens of the Margrave of Baden-Durlach is published by G C Walthern
1742	Nurseryman James Maddock's catalogue lists 665 different tulips
1746	The Dublin Florists' Society is founded by Huguenot officers who fought for William of Orange at the Battle of the Boyne
1750	The beginning of a decline in the tulip's popularity
1750	Introduction of 'Keizerskroon', still cultivated on 2.3 hectares of land in Holland, the oldest tulip in production
1760	*Traité des Tulipes* by Le Père d'Ardène is published in Avignon
1760	*Traité des Fleurs a Oignons* by N van Kampen published in Haarlem
1760	Newspapers in Boston (US) advertise 50 different kinds of tulip for sale
1763	*Dutch Florist* by van Kampen translated into English
1768	Ancient Society of York Florists is founded
1775	Dr Tottie's tulip sale in Oxford
1776	The celebrated Bybloemen tulip 'Louis XVI' is raised, probably in Flanders
1777	James Maddock's catalogue lists 804 tulips
1780	Trade with Turkey opens up again
1786	First parts of Curtis's *Botanical Magazine* published
1789	'Louis XVI' is first offered for sale (at 250 guilders a bulb) by the Dutch florist and nurseryman M van Nieuwekerk
1796	James Maddock's catalogue lists 665 different tulips
1800	'Lousi XVI' appears in the Walworth Nursery catalogue, priced at 20gns a bulb
1815	Victory at Waterloo
1820	Dutch breeders expand towards Overveen and Bloemendaal
1825	Opening of Britain's first railway, the Stockton and Darlington line
1826	The great stud tulip 'Polyphemus' is raised by Mr Lawrence of Hampton
1827	A florist, Mr Goldham, is offered £100 for his 'Louis XVI' tulip
1830	English fancy at its height 1830–50
1835	The Wakefield and North of England Tulip Society is founded
1843	*A Descriptive Catalogue of Tulips* by John Slater
1845	'Couleur Cardinal' is introduced, still grown on 23 hectares in Holland
1845	Six hundred different kinds of tulip are bedded out in the Linnaean Botanic Garden, Long Island

1847	Launch of the *Midland Florist*
1849	Hendrick van der Schoot is the first travelling salesman ('*bollen-reisiger*') to go to the US
1849	The National Tulip Society is founded
1850 onwards	Dutch breeders expand towards Hillegom, Lisse and Noordwijk
1850	Beginning of the decline in the English fancy
1850	Pre-eminence of Tom Storer of Derby, engine driver and tulip maniac
1854	Catalogue of nurseryman Henry Groom of Walworth offers three varieties of tulip at 100gns each
1860	Single Early tulip 'Prince of Austria' and Double Early 'Murillo' are introduced
1871	Association Football's first cup final
1878	Albert Regel discovers *T. kaufmanniana* in Turkestan
1885	The sale of Jules Lenglart's collection brings to an end a 300-year-long tradition of tulip growing in Flanders
1886	Darwin tulips are introduced by the firm of E H Krelage
1897	The great Tulip Conference of the Royal National Tulip Society is held at the Royal Botanic Society's gardens, Regent's Park, London
1901	The last of the traditional 'public house' shows held by a florists' society (the Butley Tulip Society at the Orange Tree Inn, Butley)
1917	Report of the Tulip Nomenclature Committee
1928	Research by Dorothy Cayley of the John Innes Horticultural Institution, Merton, unravels the process of tulip 'breaks'
1929	The Royal General Bulbgrowers' Association publishes the first *International Register* of tulips
1936	Demise of the Royal National Tulip Society
1942	Survey of early tulip books published by E H Krelage
1943	Introduction of Darwin Hybrids by D W Lefeber
1975	Introduction of the first genetically manipulated Parrot tulip, the fuchsia-purple 'Amethyst'
1994	Dutch growers export 2 billion bulbs to eighty different countries

NOTES

Introduction

[1] There are twenty-one *azen* to the gram. The weight was important, for the larger the bulb, the more likely it was to flower and to produce a precious offset, or daughter bulb.

[2] Zbigniew Herbert, *Still Life with a Bridle*, London (1993).

[3] OED 'An infectious organism that is usually sub-microscopic, can multiply only inside living cells, in many cases causing diseases.'

[4] Adriaen van der Donck, *Beschryvinge van Niew Nederlant* (1655).

[5] The tunic is the technical term for the outermost coat of a tulip bulb. It is generally papery in texture and varies in colour from a pale ginger to a dark chocolate brown. The 'wool' is an accumulation of fine, silky hairs which, in some species lie directly beneath the tunic, surrounding the fleshy sheaths of the bulb. In *T. clusiana*, the hairs stick up in a tuft from the apex of the bulb. The presence or absence of hairs beneath the tunic can help in the identification of species tulips.

Chapter I A Flower of the East

[1] *Irshad az-zara'ah* c1515.

[2] *Babur-Nama* trans. A S Beveridge (1922).

[3] Istanbul University Library.

[4] Tile panel with tulips of the sixteenth century, Topkapi Palace Museum, Istanbul.

[5] D Yildiz, 'Tulips in Ottoman Turkish Culture and Art' in *The Tulip: a symbol of two nations*, M Roding, H Theunissen (eds), Utrecht/Istanbul (1993).

[6] George Sandys, *Travels*, London (1615).

[7] Mehmed Aski, *Takvimu'l-kibar fi Miyari'l-szhar* (1779) in Ali Emiri Efendi Library, Turkey.

[8] Ahmed Refik, *Esk: Instanbul*, Istanbul 1931.

[9] *Surname* in the Topkapi Palace Library.

[10] *Travels in Persia, 1627–1629*, London, (1928).

[11] In the Habibganj Collection, Aligarh Muslim University, India.

[12] Miniature in the V&A Museum, London.

[13] Miniature in the Fitzwilliam Museum, Cambridge.

[14] Seyh Mehmed Lalezari, *Mizanu'l ezhar* [The Habit of Flowers] (1703), in Ali Emiri Efendi Library, Turkey.

[15] Sir John Chardin *Travels in Persia* (1686).

[16] Translated by H F von Diez under title *Wage der Blumen*, Halle-Berlin (1815).

[17] Quoted in T Baker, Journal of the Royal Horticultural Society Vol. 56 (1931).

[18] Translated from the original quoted in Le Père d'Ardene, *Traité des Tulipes*, Avignon (1760).

[19] It was then bought by the bibliophile Robert de Belder, who built up an outstanding library of horticultural books (and an arboretum) at Kalmthout in Belgium. It came up for sale again at Christie's in London on 19 May 1998, when it was sold for £100,000 to a private collector.

[20] E H Ayverdi, *Onsekizinci Asirda Lale*, Istanbul (1950).

[21] Turhan Baytop, *Istanbul Lalesi*, Ankara (1992).

Chapter II The Tulip in Northern Europe

[1] Z R W von Martels, *Augerius Busbequius...*, Groningen (1989).

[2] *Les Observations de Plusieurs Singularités*, third book, p208.

[3] The letters were edited by F W T Hunger and published as *Charles de l'Ecluse: Nederlandsch Kruidkundige 1526–1609* (1927).

[4] Nicolas Wassenaer, *Historisch Verhaal* (1625).

[5] Wassenaer op. cit.

[6] *Caspari Collino Pharmocopoeo*, published in Strassburg in 1561 as an appendix to Valerius Cordus's *Annotationes in Pedacii* which Gesner edited.

[7] Described in the *Historia generalis plantarum*, Lyons (1587), based on the memoirs of Jacques Dalechamp, the French physician and botanist.

[8] Published in facsimile as the *Conradi Gesneri Historia Plantarum – Nachlass Van Conrad Gesnor (1516–1565) in der Universitatsbibliothek Erlangen*, edited by H Zoller and M Steinmann, Dietikon-Zurich (1987–1991).

[9] *Kreutterbuch* (1563), an album of watercolours by Kentmann in the Sachsischen Landesbibliothek, Dresden, contains a similar yellow tulip labelled *T. turcica*.

[10] *Florum et Coronarium Odoratarumque Nonnularum Herbarum Historia*, Antwerp (1568).

[11] M Lobelius, *Plantarum seu Stirpium Historia*, Antwerp (1576).

[12] S Gobelius *Plantarum seu Stirpium Icones*, Antwerp (1581).

[13] F. Stafleu and R. Cowan, *Taxonomic Literature*, Utrecht (1976).

[14] *Rariorum Plantarum Historia*, Antwerp (1601).

[15] *Mira calligraphiae monumenta* of 1561–1562, published in facsimile, Malibu (1992).

[16] In the Kunstinstitut, Frankfurt am Main.

[17] *Aigentliche Beschreibung der Raiss… in die Morgenlander*, Lauingen (1583).

[18] The *Theatrum Tuliparum* in the Staatsbibliothek, Berlin is a similar work showing the tulips which flowered in the Berlin Lustgarten in 1647–1648.

[19] Two volumes of Walther's work, bought in the eighteenth century by Lord Bute, a keen gardener, are now in the Victoria and Albert Museum, London.

[20] Bayerische Staatsgemaldesammlungen, Munich.

[21] Peter Thornton, *Seventeenth Century Interior Decoration in England, France and Holland*, New Haven, (1978).

[22] Purchased in 1888 by the Museum of the Jardin des Plantes.

[23] *Le Floriste François, traitant de l'Origine des Tulipes,* Caen (1654).

[24] English translation from Henry van Oosten, *The Dutch Gardener*, London (1711).

[25] Tulips were certainly known and valued in Portugal. The Victoria and Albert Museum in London has a superb silver salver made in Lisbon in the mid seventeenth century, decorated around the rim with tulips of characteristically waisted shape and pointed petals.

[26] *Connoissance et Culture Parfaite des Belles Fleurs: des Tulipes rares, des Anémones extraordinaires,* Paris (1696) published anonymously but probably written by de Valnay, Comptroller of the Royal Household.

[27] John Rea, *Flora, seu de Florum Cultura*, London, (1665).

[28] *Les Caractères* (1691).

[29] John Cowell, *The Curious and Profitable Gardener*, London (1730).

[30] *La Théorie et la Pratique du Jardinage*, Paris (1709) quoted in *Garden History* Vol. 21 (2), Mark Laird and John Harvey, 'The English Flower Border 1660–1735'.

[31] d'Ardène's 'theatre' is a reference to the practice of displaying pots of tulips, like auriculas, on the shelves of small, open-air cabinets.

Chapter III Early British Growers

[1] Thomas Fuller, *Antheologia*, London (1655).

[2] Published in 1578 as a translation of Rembert Dodoens's original *Cruijdeboeck*.

[3] John Gerard, *The Herball or Generall Historie of Plantes*, London (1597).

[4] R E G Kirk and E F Kirk eds *Returns of Aliens 1571–97* published by the Huguenot Society of London.

[5] Hatfield House, Bills 58/3. The date amended to the modern calendar would be 1612.

[6] National Portrait Gallery, London.

[7] First used in 1623 by Sir Henry Wotton: 'It hath given me acquaintance with some excellent Florists (as they are stiled)' OED.

[8] The *Hortus Siccus* was made from flowers grown in the Duchess of Beaufort's garden. Dried, pressed and beautifully arranged on the page, they provide a botanical record of this plantswoman's extraordinary collection.

[9] Ruth Duthie, *Florists' Flowers & Societies,* Haverfordwest (1988).

[10] Bodleian Library, Oxford.

[11] MS. of Strode's poems in Bodleian Library, Oxford.

[12] Matthew Stevenson, *Poems upon Severall Occasions* (1645), Bodleian Library, Oxford.

[13] Andrew Marvell, *Upon Appleton House. To My Lord Fairfax.*

[14] Gibson, *Description of Gardens near London in 1691*, preserved in *Archaeologia* (1794).

[15] *The Retir'd Gard'ner* (1706).

[16] *The Great Diurnal of Nicholas Blundell of Little Crosby, Lancashire* published by the Record Society of Lancashire and Cheshire (Crosby papers in the Lancashire and Cheshire Record Office, Preston, Lancs). I am indebted to David Tarver for bringing these papers to my attention.

[17] John Harvey, *Early Nurserymen*, London (1974).

[18] Minutes of the meetings can be seen at The Museum, Broad Street, Spalding.

[19] Ruth Duthie, *Garden History,* Vol. 10 (1). In the northeast of England, tulip shows were held during the 1740s at Newcastle, Bishop Wearmouth and Sunderland.

[20] John Cowell, *Curious and Profitable Gardener*, London, (1730).

[21] James Justice, *Scots Gardiners Director* (1754).

[22] Rev. Archibald Allen, *History of Channelkirk*, Edinburgh (1900).

[23] Saltoun papers SB90 1758 quoted in Priscilla Minay's article on James Justice in *Garden History* Vol. 4 (2) (1976).

Chapter IV The Dutch and Tulipomania

[1] Translated from Petrus Hondius's poem, *Of de Moufe-Schans*, Leiden (1621).

[2] Nicolas Wassenaer, *Historisch Verhaal* (1625).

[3] Ella Schaap, *Dutch Floral Tiles in the Golden Age*, Haarlem (1994).

[4] Tile panel (c1630–1640) in the Museum Boymans van Beuningen, Rotterdam.

[5] J Huizinga, quoted in *The Art of Botanical Illustration* by Wilfrid Blunt and William Stearn, London (1950).

[6] Paul Taylor, *Dutch Flower Painting 1600–1720*, London (1995).

[7] National Gallery, London.

[8] Museum Bredius, The Hague.

[9] Rijksmuseum, The Hague.

[10] Fitzwilliam Museum, Cambridge.

[11] National Museum, Stockholm.

[12] Frans Halsmuseum, Haarlem.

[13] Museum Boymans van Beuningen, Rotterdam.

[14] Private collection.

[15] Articor Collection, Geneva.

[16] Mauritshuis, The Hague.

[17] Fitzwilliam Museum, Cambridge.

[18] Private collection.

[19] Private collection.

[20] Prinsenhof, Delft.

[21] National Gallery, London.

[22] Museum of Fine Arts, Boston.

[23] *Cahier van de Verpandinghe* (Register of owners of houses and gardens) Anno 1628, Haarlem State Archive reproduced in A van Damme, *Aanteekeningen Betreffende de Geschiedenis der Bloembollen*, Leiden (1976).

[24] Outger Augerius Cluyt, *Memorie der vreemulen blom-bollen, wortelen etc etc*, Amsterdam (1631).

[25] Jacob Marrell's tulip book is in the Rijksprentenkabinet, Amsterdam.

[26] Museum Boymans van Beuningen, Rotterdam.

[27] Dr Sam Segal, *The Tulip, A Symbol of Two Nations*, Utrecht/Istanbul (1993).

[28] Lindley Library, London.

[29] *Samenspraecken*, Haarlem (1637).

[30] Documents in the Gemeente Municipal Archive, The Hague, from *Aanteekeningen Betreffende de Geschiedenis der Bloembollen*, by A van Damme, Leiden (1976).

[31] John Rea, *Flora; seu de Florum Cultura* (1665).

[32] Paul Taylor, op. cit.

[33] Record Office, Haarlem Solicitors' Acts No 165 fol. 271.

[34] Original documents in the Rijks Archief transcribed in A van Damme, op.cit.

[35] Record Office, Amsterdam Solicitors' Acts No 1269.

[36] Record Office, Haarlem Solicitors' Acts No 57 fol. 89.

[37] Dordrecht's Museum, The Netherlands.

[38] *Journal of Economic and Business History* Vol. 1 No. 3 May 1929.

[39] Zbigniew Herbert, *Still Life with a Bridle*, London (1993).

[40] Originally painted by Pieter Nolpe (1613/14–1652/3), later engraved by Cornelis Danckerts, Department of Prints and Drawings, British Museum (London).

[41] First painted by Hendrik Pot (1585–1651), then engraved by Crispyn de Passe the Younger.

[42] Frans Halsmuseum, Haarlem.

Chapter V Dutch Dominance

[1] Frans Halsmuseum, Haarlem.

[2] Fitzwilliam Museum, Cambridge.

[3] Narodni Gallery, Prague.

[4] Frans Halsmuseum, Haarlem.

[5] Museum Boymans van Beuningen, Rotterdam.

[6] Frans Halsmuseum, Haarlem.

[7] Frans Halsmuseum, Haarlem.

[8] See tapestries hanging at Doddington Hall, Lincolnshire.

[9] Ronald Brouwer, 'Turkish Tulips and Delft Flowerpots', in *The Tulip: A Symbol of Two Nations*, edited by Michiel Roding and Hans Theunissen, Utrecht/Istanbul, (1993).

[10] There is a fine example at the Fitzwilliam Museum, Cambridge.

[11] Fragments of Delft pottery retrieved during the restoration of Het Loo have been reconstructed to make four flower holders, dated to around 1680, which makes them amongst the earliest in The Netherlands.

[12] Gilbert's book had run into many editions. So did van Oosten's, being translated into English in 1703 with a second English edition appearing in 1711.

[13] E H Krelage, *Drie Eeuwen Bloembollenexport*, 's'Gravenhage (1946).

[14] *Haerlemse Courant* 14 May 1711.

[15] *Traité des Fleurs à Oignons contenant tout ce qui est nécessaire pour les bien Cultiver*, Haarlem 1760, translated into English as *The Dutch Florist*, London 1763. An Italian edition (*Trattato de' fiori*) was produced in 1773.

[16] The tulip was named after Dr Martinus van Thol who raised it and it was first listed in Dutch bulb catalogues in 1722.

[17] E H Krelage, op. cit.

[18] John Slater, *Descriptive Catalogue of Tulips*, London (1843).

[19] *Traité de la Culture des Tulipes*, Paris (1846).

Chapter VI The English Florists' Tulip

[1] *Ipswich Journal* 21 April 1750.

[2] *Journal* 16 April 1767.

[3] William Hanbury, *Whole Body of Planting and Gardening* (1770–1771).

[4] E D Burrowes, 'The Huguenot Colony at Portarlington Ulster', *Journal of Archaeology* 3 56–7.

[5] Philip Miller, *Gardener's Dictionary*, London (1747).

[6] *The Florist's Delight* was issued in three sets from 1790 onwards by James Sowerby (1757–1822). Each set contained six engravings of florists' flowers. Business cannot have been brisk, as the project foundered after Plate XVIII.

[7] Thomas Hogg, *A Concise and Practical Treatise*, Paddington Green (1820).

[8] Clark's obituary appeared in the *Gardener's Magazine* (1831).

[9] 'It is chiefly to the exertions of Dutch, French and Flemish florists, that we are indebted, for the perfection to which this flower is at present arrived.'

[10] William Howitt, *Rural Life in England*, London (1844).

[11] Minute Book of the Paisley Florists' Society.

[12] *Norwich Mercury* 11 July 1829.

[13] Thomas Hogg, op. cit.

[14] There are good examples in the V&A Museum, London.

[15] William Pegg's *Sketchbook* c1813 at the Royal Crown Derby pottery's museum.

[16] This was a boom time for magazines: 845 titles were launched in London alone during the 1840s.

[17] W M Thackeray, *Ravenswing*, London (1837).

[18] *Gardener's Magazine* Vol. 1 1826.

[19] Thomas Hogg, op. cit.

[20] George Glenny, *The Culture of Flowers* (1860).

[21] *Horticultural Cabinet*, May 1838.

[22] *Horticultural Cabinet*, April 1840.

[23] *Midland Florist* (1847).

[24] *Cottage Gardener* 12 June 1851.

[25] *Midland Florist* (1849).

[26] James Douglas, 'Introduction' to *Hardy Florists' Flowers*, London (1880).

[27] I am grateful to Mr Trevor Mills of the Wakefield and North of England Tulip Society for sharing his knowledge of Dr Hardy.

[28] *Gardeners' Chronicle* 28 April 1883.

Chapter VII The Last Hundred Years

[1] *The Garden* 6 May 1893.

[2] *Journal of Horticulture, Cottage Gardener* Vol. 62 1911 page 457.

[3] *The Garden* Vol. 59 1901.

[4] *Journal of Horticulture and Home Farmer* Vol. 58 1909.

[5] *Gardener's Chronicle* Vol. LXXXIV 3 November 1928.

[6] *The Garden* Vol. LXXV 10 June 1911.

[7] *Journal of Horticulture* 1894 page 4.

[8] *Gardener's Magazine* Vol. LIII 1910.

[9] *Journal of Horticulture, Cottage Gardener*, 4 June 1896.

[10] *The Garden* 20 May 1893.

[11] *The Garden* 27 May 1893.

[12] *Journal of Horticulture, Cottage Gardener* 1893 page 446.

[13] *Journal of Horticulture, Cottage Gardener* Vol. 62 1911 page 458.

[14] *Horticultural Advertiser*, 10 October 1934.

[15] 14 June 1844.

[16] 9 July 1849.

[17] *The Modern Miller* 19 June 1909.

[18] R W Adlam in the *Gardener's Chronicle* (23 January 1888) called Roozen's list 'a model of what a descriptive bulb list should be'.

[19] *Gardener's Chronicle* 21 April 1877.

[20] *Journal of Horticulture, Cottage Gardener* (1893).

[21] *Gardener's Magazine* Vol. LIV 1911.

22 *Gardener's Chronicle* 10 April 1926.
23 Dolf Straathof and Wim Eikelboom, 'Tulip Breeding at CPRO-DLO' in *Daffodil and Tulip Yearbook 1997–8*.

Chapter VIII Tulips: The Species

1 'Biosystemic studies in Tulipa sect. Eriostemones (Liliaceae)' in *Plant Systemics and Evolution* Vol. 179 pp27–41 and 'Species relationship and taxonomy in Tulipa subg. Tulipa (Liliaceae)' in *Plant Systemics and Evolution* Vol. 195 pp13–44.
2 Important work on the Central Asian species was published by Professor A Vvedensky in his monumental *Flora of the USSR* 1968.

Chapter IX Tulip Cultivars

1 Michael Hoog, 'On the Origin of Tulipa' from *Lilies and Other Liliaceae* (1973).
2 Caspar Bauhin, *Pinax Theatri Botanici* (1623).
3 Crispyn de Passe, *Hortus Floridus*, plate 46 (1614).
4 Sir Daniel Hall, *The Book of the Tulip* (1929).
5 *Gardener's Chronicle* 22 May 1886.
6 Basilius Besler, *Hortus Eystettensis* (1613).
7 Sir Daniel Hall, op. cit.

BIBLIOGRAPHY

(Note: Where more than one edition of a book exists, the edition listed is the edition
that has been used)

BOOKS

Amherst, Hon. Alicia *A History of Gardening in England* London 1895

Ardène, le Père d' *Traité des Tulipes* Avignon 1760

Baytop, Turhan *Istanbul Lalesi* Ankara 1992

Belon, Pierre *Les Observations de Plusieurs Singularités* Paris 1555

Bentley, J W *et al. The English Tulip and its History* (Messrs Barr & Sons 1897) reprinted by
   the Wakefield and North of England Tulip Society Wakefield 1973

Besler, B *Hortus Eystettensis* facsimile edition London 1994

Blunt, William *Tulipomania* Harmondsworth 1950

Blunt, Wilfred and Stearn, William *The Art of Botanical Illustration* London 1950

Botschantzeva, Z P (trs. H Q Varekamp) *Tulips* Rotterdam 1982

Brenninkmeijer-de Rooij, Beatrijs *Roots of Seventeenth-century Flower Painting* Leiden 1996

Chardin, Sir John *Travels into Persia* 1686

Clusius, Carolus *Rariorum aliquot Stirpium* Antwerp 1576

Clusius, Carolus *Rariorum plantarum Historia* Antwerp 1601

Coats, Alice *Flowers and their Histories* London 1968

Cordus, Valerius *Annotationes in Pedacii* Strasbourg 1561 bound with Conrad Gesner's
   Caspari Collino Pharmocopoeo

Cowell, John *The Curious and Profitable Gardener* London 1730

Damme, A van *Aanteekeningen betreffende de geschiedenis der bloembollen* Haarlem 1899–1903 reprinted Leiden 1976

Davis, Dr P H (ed) *Flora of Turkey* Edinburgh 1965–68

Desmond, Ray (ed) *Dictionary of British and Irish Botanists and Horticulturists* London 1994

Dodoens, Rembert *Florum et Coronarium Odoratumque Nonnularum* Antwerp 1568

Douglas, James *Hardy Florists' Flowers* London 1880

Duthie, Ruth *Florists' Flowers and Societies* Aylesbury 1988

Dykes, W R *Notes on Tulip Species* London 1930

Fisher, John *Mr Marshall's Flower Album* London 1985

Gerard, John *Herball* London 1597

Gesner, Conrad *Caspari Collino Pharmocopoeo* bound with Valerius Cordus's *Annotationes in Pedacii* Strasbourg 1561

Gilbert, Samuel *Florist's Vade mecum* London 1682

Gobelius, S *Plantarum seu Stirpium Icones* Antwerp 1581

Hall, A D *The Book of the Tulip* London 1929

Hall, A D *The Genus Tulipa* London 1940

Hanbury, Rev William *A Complete Body of Planting and Gardening* 1770

Hanmer, Sir Thomas *Garden Book* (edited by Eleanour Sinclair Rohde) London 1933

Hartland, Baylor *Original Little Book of Irish Grown Tulips* Cork 1896

Harvey, John *Early Nurserymen* London 1974

Hendrix, Lee and Vignau-Wilbert, Thea *Nature Illuminated* London 1997

Herbert, Zbigniew *Still Life with a Bridle* London 1993

Hogg, Thomas *A Concise and Practical Treatise on the Growth and Culture of the Carnation, Pink, Auricula, Polyanthus, Ranunculus, Tulip, Hyacinth, Rose and Other Flowers* Paddington Green, Middx 1820

Howitt, William *Rural Life in England* London 1844

Hulton, Paul *The Work of Jacques le Moyne de Morgues* London 1977

Jacob, Rev Joseph *Tulips* London 1912

Jardine, Lisa *Worldly Goods* London 1996

Jeffers, Robert H *The Friends of John Gerard* Falls Village, Connecticut 1967

Johnson, G W *A History of English Gardening* London 1829

Justice, James *The British Gardener's Director* Edinburgh 1764

Kampen, Nicholas van *The Dutch Gardener* London 1763

Komarov, V L (ed) *Flora of the USSR* translated from the Russian by the Israel Program for Scientific Translations Jerusalem 1968

Kouwenoorn, Pieter van *Verzameling van Bloemen* 47 folios containing *c*200 drawings *c*1630 Lindley Library, London

Krelage, E H *Bloemenspeculatie in Nederland* Amsterdam 1942

Krelage, E H *Drie Eeuwen Bloembollen Export* 's-Gravenhage 1946

Landos, David *The Wealth & Poverty of Nations* London 1998

Levier, E *Les Tulipes de l'Europe* Neuchâtel 1884

Lobelius, Matthias *Plantarum seu Stirpium Historia* Antwerp 1576

Loudon, John *Encyclopaedia of Gardening* London 1822

Maddock, James *The Florist's Directory* London 1792

Mathew, Brian *The Smaller Bulbs* London 1987

Mathew, Brian and Baytop, Turhan *The Bulbous Plants of Turkey* London 1984

Mattioli, Pier Andrea *Commentarii in sex libros Pedacii Dioscoridis* Venice 1565

Miller, Philip *The Gardener's Dictionary* (ed Martyn) London 1805

Monstereul, de la Chesnee *Le Floriste Français* Caen 1684

Morin, Pierre *Remarques Nécessaires pour la Culture des Fleurs* Paris 1678

Nelson, C and Brady A (eds) *Irish Gardening and Horticulture* Dublin 1979

Oosten, Henry van *The Dutch Gardener* London 1703

Parkinson, John *Paradisi in sole paradisus terrestris* London 1629

Pasinli, Alpay and Balaman, Saliha *Turkish Tiles and Ceramics* Istanbul 1991

Passe Crispyn de *Hortus Floridus* Utrecht 1614

Payne, C. Harman *The Florist's Bibliography* London 1908

Platt, Sir Hugh *The Garden of Eden* London 1655

Punch, Walter (ed) *Keeping Eden* Boston 1992

Rea, John *Flora, Ceres and Pomona* London 1665

Roding, Michiel and Theunissen, Hans (eds) *The Tulip: A Symbol of Two Nations* Utrecht/Istanbul 1993

Roman, A *Samenspraecken* Haarlem 1637

Sanders, John *The Select Florist* Derby 1829

Schaap, Ella B *Dutch Floral Tiles in the Golden Age* Haarlem 1994

Segal, Sam *Tulips Portrayed* Amsterdam 1992

Sievert *Hortus Florum Imaginum* (volume of paintings c1720 in the Lindley Library, London)

Slater, John *A Descriptive Catalogue of Tulips* London 1843

Slikke, C M van der *Tulpenteelt op Kleigrond* Berlikum 1929

Sowerby, James *The Florist's Delight* London 1790

Stafleu, Frans A and Cowan, Richard S *Taxonomic Literature* Utrecht 1976

Step, Edward and Watson, William *Favourite Flowers of Garden and Greenhouse* 1897

Stevenson, Rev Henry *The Gentleman Gardener's Director* 1769

Stork, A L *Tulipes Sauvages et Cultivées* Geneva 1984

Sweert, Emmanuel *Florilegium* Frankfurt 1612

Taylor, Paul *Dutch Flower Painting 1600–1720* London 1995

Thornton, Peter *Seventeenth Century Interior Decoration in England, France and Holland* New Haven 1978

Thornton, Robert *Temple of Flora* London 1807
Titley, Norah and Wood, Frances *Oriental Gardens* London 1991
Tournefort, J P de *The Compleat Herbal* 1719–30
Wakefield and North of England Tulip Society *The English Florists' Tulip*
Wassenaer, Nicolas *Historisch Verhaal* 1625
Weinmann, Johann Wilhelm *Phytanthoza-Iconographia* 1745 (Lindley Library, London)

PERIODICALS

Tatler 1710 (No. 218) essay by Sir Richard Steele
Curtis's *Botanical Magazine* 1787–1983
Beauties of Flora (ed. Samuel Curtis) 1806–1820
Botanical Cabinet (ed. Conrad Loddiges) 1817–1833
British Flower Garden (ed. R Sweet) 1823–1838
Botanic Garden (ed. B Maund) 1825–1850
Gardeners' Magazine 1826/1831/1907/1910/1911/1912
Florist's Guide (ed. R Sweet) 1827–1832
Horticultural Register and General Magazine 1831–1836
Floricultural Cabinet and Florist's Magazine 1833–1859
Floricultural Magazine 1839/1840/1841
Midland Florist 1847/1848/1849/1850/1855 (especially articles by Dr G W Hardy in 1847
   and 1855)
Florist (see also *Florist and Garden Miscellany*) 1848
Cottage Gardener (founded and edited by G W Johnson) 1848–1861
Florist and Garden Miscellany (see also *Florist, Fruitist etc*) 1849–1850
Florist, Fruitist and Garden Miscellany (see also *Florist and Pomologist*) 1851–1861
Gossip for the Garden conducted by E S Dodwell and John Edwards printed in London and
   Derby 1856
Botany 1874 Journal of the Linnaean Society (especially article by J G Baker 'Revision of
   the Genera and Species of Tulipa' Vol. IX 1874)
Journal of Horticulture, Cottage Gardener 1881/1890/1893/1894/1895/1897/1909/1911/1912
   (especially the list of tulips published by J W Bentley in 1894–5)
Florist and Pomologist 1877/1881/1883
The Garden 1872/1876/1893/1900/1901/1908/1911/1912/1926
Gardeners' Chronicle 1881/1883/1886/1893/1899/1911/1912/1926/1928 (especially 22 May
   1886 'Tulips in the nursery of E.H. Krelage & Son, Kleinen, Haarlem' and *Weizen und Tulpe*
   by von H Grafen zu Solms-Laubach, Professor at Strasburg University, translated in 1899)

Journal of the Royal Horticultural Society 1879/1892/1896/1909/1925/1931 (especially the articles published by H J Elwes in Vol. V 1879, F D Horner in Vol. XV 1892, J G Baker in Vol XX 1896, W S Murray in Vol. XXXV 1909, W R Dykes in Vol. L 1925 and A Baker in Vol. LVI 1931)

Gardeners' Magazine 1907

Journal of Botany 1899

Daffodil and Tulip Year Book 1913/1914/1915/1947/1960/1968/1969 (especially Walter Blom *'Tulips in our Gardens of Today'* 1968 and S Unver *'History of Tulips in Turkey'* 1969)

Lilies and Other Liliaceae Year Book 1973 (especially M Hoog 'On the Origin of Tulipa')

Garden History (especially Vol. 1, Vol. 2, Vol. 3, Vol. 4, Vol. 6, Vol. 10, Vol. 12, Vol. 15, Vol. 16, Vol. 18, Vol. 19, Vol. 21, Vol. 24)

Journal of Economic and Business History Vol. 1 No. 3 May 1929 (N W Posthumus)

Plant Systemics and Evolution Vol. 179 (pp 27–41), Vol. 195 (pp 13–44)

CATALOGUES

De Tulp published by the Museum voor de Bloembollenstreek, Limmen

Hortus Librorum Early Botanical Books at Dumbarton Oaks catalogued by Laura Ten Eyck Byers Washington 1983

The Anglo-Dutch Garden in the Age of William and Mary Journal of Garden History published as catalogue of exhibition at Het Loo, Apeldoorn 1988

Segal, Sam *Flowers and Nature: Netherlandish Flower Painting of Four Centuries* published as catalogue of exhibition at Osaka 1990

Taylor, Paul *Dutch Flower Painting 1600–1750* Catalogue of exhibition Dulwich Picture Gallery 1996

An Important Botanical Library catalogue (Parts I and II) of Christie's sale New York 5 June 1997

Tulip Mania catalogue of Sotheby's sale Amsterdam 16 June 1998

The Turkish Sale, Sotheby's London 16 October 1998

CLASSIFIED LISTS

Report of the Tulip Nomenclature Committee of the RHS 1917

A Classified List of Tulip Names RHS London 1939

A Classified List of Tulip Names RHS London and General Dutch Bulbgrowers Society, Haarlem 1948

Classified List and International Register of Tulip Names KAVB, Haarlem 1963

Classified List and Register of Tulip Names KAVB Hillegom 1996

ACKNOWLEDGEMENTS

Anyone writing about the tulip must acknowledge a great debt to Sir Daniel Hall, whose works *The Book of the Tulip* (1927) and *The Genus Tulipa* (1942) remain essential reading. Ruth Duthie's pioneering book *Florists' Flowers and Societies* (1988) is another crucial text for anyone interested in the English Florists' tulip.

Many people have given generous help while I have been working on my own book, but most outstanding is the debt I owe to the librarian and staff at the Royal Horticultural Society's Lindley Library in London. Over the past six years, Dr Brent Elliott, Jennifer Vine, Helen Ward and Elizabeth Gilbert have provided more support and encouragement than any researcher dares hope for.

I would also like to thank Professor Turhan Baytop of Istanbul University for help with tulip sites in eastern Turkey and for permission to quote from his book, *Istanbul Lalesi*; Deborah Cutler, who provided much valuable research material by way of prints and drawings; Alan Davey for information on the bulb-growing industry of the Fens; Werner Dukamp of Transtech for translations from Dutch and German documents; the Royal Dutch Bulbgrowers' Association (KAVB) for statistics relating to the tulip industry; Fergus Garrett for invaluable help as guide

425

and interpreter in eastern Turkey; Dr Oliver Impey of the Ashmolean Museum, Oxford for information on tulips in art; Anne Kindersley for historical references on the tulip in the Ottoman Empire; Geert Hageman of Triflor for information about tulip-breeding; Christopher Lloyd for teaching me how to look at plants; Brian Mathew, editor of *The Bulb Newsletter*, for detailed help on the ever-shifting taxonomy of tulips and for sharing information on sites of wild species; Karen Richards for transcribing original documents; Dr David Scrase, Keeper of Paintings, Drawings and Prints at the Fitzwilliam Museum, Cambridge for allowing me to study works not normally on show; Dr Paul Taylor for his helpful comments on Dutch flower-painting of the seventeenth century; William Tear for lending material relating to his career as a tulip-grower; and the Wakefield and North of England Tulip Society for making available papers relating to the society's early history.

Quotations for documents in the archive at Hatfield House, Hatfield, Hertfordshire are included by kind permission of the Marquess of Salisbury. Quotations from the Thynne Papers are included by permission of the Marquess of Bath, Longleat House, Warminster, Wiltshire.

Liz Calder has been an inspired and generous editor. My grateful thanks are due to her and to the rest of those at Bloomsbury who have worked so hard on the book. Meg Calvert tracked down the pictures.

ILLUSTRATIONS

Grateful acknowledgement is made to the following sources for permission to reproduce images: Bayerische Staatgemaldesammlungen, Munich, p. 83; British Museum, London, pp. 14, 174; Christie's Images, pp. 44, 47, 49, 52, 84, 202, 207; ET Archive, p. 144; Fitzwilliam Museum, University of Cambridge, pp. 12, 29, 42, 87, 89, 97, 123, 179; J. Paul Getty Museum, Los Angeles, pp. 3, 59, 74; Peter Goodchild, p. 133; Frans Halsmuseum, Haarlem, pp. 5, 170, 176; Het Loo, Apeldoorn, p. 183; Historisch Museum, Amsterdam, p. 154; International Flower Bulb Centre, pp. 360, 366, 370, 372, 379, 381, 397, 399; Lindley Library (Royal Horticultural Society), pp. i, 25, 72, 111, 156, 211, 277, 288, 291, 293, 295, 304, 315, 317, 319, 323, 325, 327, 342, 344, 440; Mauritshuis, The Hague, pp. 148, 150; Municipal Archives, Delft, p. 172; Museum Boijmans Van Beuningen, Rotterdam, pp. 146, 181; Museum Bredius, title page; National Trust Photo Library, p. 125; Natural History Museum, London, p. 71; Rijksmuseum, Amsterdam, pp. 10, 91, 94, 164, 196; Royal Doulton Ltd, p. 219 and endpapers; Sotheby's, pp. 116, 158, 162; William Tear, pp. 256, 270, 274; Teylers

Museum, Haarlem, pp. 185, 198; University Library, Erlangen, p. 66; Victoria & Albert Museum, London, pp. 40, 85, 100, 113, 120, 209, 251; Yale Center for British Art (Paul Mellon Collection), p. 108.

INDEX

A NOTE ON THE AUTHOR

Anna Pavord is the gardening correspondent for the *Independent*, and the author of widely praised gardening books including *The Flowering Year* and *Gardening Companion*. As well as writing for the *Observer* for twenty years, she has contributed to *Country Life*, *Country Living*, and *Elle Decoration*, and is an associate editor of *Gardens Illustrated*. She lives in Dorset, England, in an old rectory with a large garden that she has been developing for twenty years. Constantly experimenting with new combinations of flowers and foliage, she finds it a tremendous source of inspiration.